Emperor Charles V, Impresario of War

Campaign Strategy, International Finance, and Domestic Politics

Emperor Charles V (1500–1558) asserted his princely authority by deciding at times to lead his own armies to war, despite the misgivings of advisers. But because Europe's wars were fought with money borrowed against future revenues, even an emperor had to share power with his bankers and his parliaments. This book examines all three dimensions of European warfare. Charles's role as commander in chief is evaluated by measuring the strategic aims of his personal campaigns. The process by which bankers took control of the finances of the Habsburg lands becomes clear from an examination of where the money came from to pay for Charles's campaigns. Finally, a comparison of the realms that provided most of Charles's revenues – Castile, Naples, and three Low Countries provinces – shows how some parliamentary bodies, if not all, successfully pursued long-term local interests by exploiting the dynasty's need for money.

James D. Tracy has been a faculty member at the University of Minnesota since 1966. He was a professeur associé at the Université de Paris-IV for spring 2001 and has also been a visiting lecturer at the Rijksuniversiteit te Leiden. He is the editor of *City Walls: The Urban Enceinte in Global Perspective* (2000) and *The Political Economy of Merchant Empires: State Power and Global Trade, 1350–1750* (1991) and the author of *Europe's Reformations, 1450–1650* (1999) and *Erasmus of the Low Countries* (1996). He is also the editor of the *Journal of Early Modern History*.

Emperor Charles V, Impresario of War

Campaign Strategy, International Finance, and Domestic Politics

JAMES D. TRACY

University of Minnesota

CAMBRIDGE UNIVERSITY PRESS

PUBLISHED BY THE PRESS SYNDICATE OF THE UNIVERSITY OF CAMBRIDGE
The Pitt Building, Trumpington Street, Cambridge, United Kingdom

CAMBRIDGE UNIVERSITY PRESS
The Edinburgh Building, Cambridge CB2 2RU, UK
40 West 20th Street, New York, NY 10011-4211, USA
477 Williamstown Road, Port Melbourne, VIC 3207, Australia
Ruiz de Alarcón 13, 28014 Madrid, Spain
Dock House, The Waterfront, Cape Town 8001, South Africa

http://www.cambridge.org

First published 2002

Printed in the United Kingdom at the University Press, Cambridge

Typeface Bembo 11/12 pt.   *System* LATEX 2ε   [TB]

A catalog record for this book is available from the British Library.

Library of Congress Cataloging in Publication data

Tracy, James D.
    Emperor Charles V, impresario of war : campaign strategy, international finance, and
domestic politics / James D. Tracy.
        p.   cm.
    Includes bibliographical references and index.
    ISBN 0-521-81431-6
        1. Charles V, Holy Roman Emperor, 1500–1558.   2. Europe – Economic
conditions – 16th century.   3. Holy Roman Empire – Kings and rulers – Biography.
4. Holy Roman Empire – History – Charles V, 1505–1555.   5. Europe – History,
Military – 1492–1648.   6. Finance, Public – Holy Roman Empire – History – 16th
century.   I. Title.
D180.5 .T73   2002
943'.03'092 – dc21
[B]   2002023395

ISBN 0 521 81431 6 hardback

For David Kieft

Contents

Contents

Illustrations

Tables

Acknowledgments

Some years ago, a textbook publisher asked me for a new biography of Charles V that was to be done in time for the 500th anniversary of his birth (2000). In his own day Charles was a ruler of European scope, but in his own day it seems fair to say he was more feared than admired. Seeing Charles mainly as a man of war, I took it as my challenge to tell the story of his wars mainly from the emperor's point of view, but with some appreciation of how others saw him, and of the long-term impact of his campaigns. That the book did not appear in 2000, and is not a biography, will suggest that there have been some detours along the way. In its final form, *Emperor Charles V* owes a great deal to the careful criticisms of Cambridge University Press's three readers, whom I wish to thank, and to those of my Minnesota colleague, David Kieft, whose friendship and support of my work over the years I wish to recognize in a special way.

Abbreviations

AJ	Andries Jacobszoon, "Prothocolle van alle die reysen . . . bij mij Andries Jacops gedaen [1522–1538]," Gemeentearchief, Amsterdam.
Aud.	Algemeen Rijksarchief/Archives Généraux du Royaume, Brussels, "Papiers d'État et de l'Audience."
"Berichte"	"Berichte und Studien zur Geschichte Karls V," I–XIX, *Nachrichten von der Akademie der Wissenschaften zu Göttingen, Philologisch-Historische Klasse*, 1934–1941.
Busto	Otto Adalbert Graf von Looz-Corswaren, ed., *Bernabé de Busto, Geschichte des Schmalkaldischen Krieges* (Burg, 1938) = *Texte und Forschungen im Auftrage der Preussischen Akademie der Wissenschaften, herausgegeben von der Romanischen Kommission*, Band I.
Corpus Documental	Manuel Fernández Alvárez, ed., *Corpus Documental de Carlos V* (5 vols., Salamanca, 1973–1981).
Estado	Archivo de Simancas, Valladolid, Colecion Estado.
Familienkorrespondenz	*Die Korrespondenz Ferdinands I:* vol. I, Wilhelm Bauer, ed., *Familienkorrespondenz bis 1526* (Vienna, 1912); vol. II, Wilhelm Bauer and Robert Lacroix, eds., *Familienkorrespondenz 1527–1528* (Vienna, 1930); vol. III, Wilhelm Bauer and Robert

Lacroix, eds., *Familienkorrespondenz 1529 und 1530* (Vienna, 1938); vol. IV, Herwig Wolfram and Christiane Thomas, eds., *Familienkorrespondenz 1531 und 1532* (Vienna, 1973) = *Veröffentlichungen der Kommission für Neuere Geschichte Österreichs*, vols. 11, 30, 31, and 58, Lieferung 1.

GRK   Rijksarchief van Zuid-Holland, The Hague, "Graafelijkheids Rekenkamer."

HHSA-B   Haus- Hof- und Staatsarchiv, Vienna, "Belgien."

Lanz   Karl Lanz, ed., *Korrespondenz des Kaisers Karls V aus dem Königlichem Archiv und der Bibliothèque de Bourgogne zu Brüssel* (3 vols., Leipzig, 1844–1846).

Lille B   "Comptes des Receveurs Généraux de toutes les finances," Series B, Archives du Département du Nord, Lille. Film copy at Algemeen Rijksarchief/Archives Généraux du Royaume, Brussels.

RSH   *Resolutiën van de Staten van Holland, 1524–1795* (278 vols., Amsterdam, 1789–1814).

Staatspapiere Karl Lanz, ed., *Staatspapiere des Kaisers Karls V aus dem Königlichem Archiv und der Bibliothèque de Bourgogne zu Brüssel* (Stuttgart, 1848).

Introduction

This book uses Charles V's personal campaigns to give a rounded picture of war as an act of state. Hence the focus is on three main issues. First, from a strategic perspective, what were the emperor's objectives in going on campaign, and how far did he succeed or fail to achieve them? Second, in light of the ancient maxim that money is the sinews of war, how did the emperor find the ready cash to keep his soldiers – many of them mercenaries – marching under the imperial banner? Finally, because Charles's subjects sooner or later had to pay the bill, with interest, under what circumstances were the parliamentary assemblies of his various realms willing to approve the necessary increases in taxation?

To pose these questions for all the campaigns of all the wars of Charles's reign would be a gargantuan undertaking. Merely to list the titles by which Charles ruled in his many territories took a full page in the handwriting of contemporary scribes, sometimes two. No one has even attempted an enumeration of all the wars fought in the emperor's name, from North Africa to the plains of Hungary, and from the Low Countries to southern Italy's Adriatic shore. Finally, very little has been published of the pertinent documentation from archives all across Europe – the correspondence of the emperor and his collaborators, the fiscal accounts and parliamentary debates of multiple realms. Of necessity, I have narrowed the focus in each of these respects.

Three Realms: The Core Provinces of the Low Countries, Naples, and Castile

Charles was head of the House of Austria, or, as one would now say, the House of Habsburg. But Austria itself, ruled by his younger brother Ferdinand, will largely be left to one side. Charles was also Holy Roman Emperor, after his election by the empire's seven electoral princes in 1519. But the German lands of the empire – some three thousand separate

I

territories controlled neither by Charles as emperor nor by Ferdinand as King of the Romans (designated successor) – do not figure largely in this discussion either. Some of the lands that Charles ruled directly he inherited from his mother's parents, Isabella of Castile and Ferdinand of Aragón: Castile and Aragón in Spain, and, in Italy, the Kingdoms of Naples and Sicily. Others he inherited from his father's mother, Mary of Burgundy, who ruled most of what would now be called the Low Countries. In choosing which of these lands to focus on, one might well pick the realms that were most often ravaged by the wars of Charles's reign: in Spain, Aragón,[1] whose long Mediterranean coastline exposed it to constant raids from North African privateers; in Italy, the duchy of Milan, the chief prize of contention between France and the Habsburgs, which Charles decided to rule in his own name, as a fief of the empire, in 1535; and in the Low Countries, the French-speaking provinces bordering on France that were so often invaded – Artois, Hainaut, and Namur. Instead I have picked the realms that mattered most to Charles for reasons of strategic importance, family pride, and, not least, revenue: in the Low Countries, the provinces of Flanders, Brabant, and Holland; the Kingdom of Naples in Italy; and Castile in Spain.

With additions made during Charles's reign, the Habsburg Netherlands included seventeen provinces.[2] The task of negotiating with the separate states or parliaments representing these provinces[3] Charles entrusted first to his aunt, Margaret of Austria, regent from 1517 to 1530, and then to his sister, Mary of Hungary, regent from 1531 to 1556. But though he lived elsewhere most of his life, Charles was born in Ghent (Flanders) and his native language was the French spoken by the Low Countries aristocracy, even in Netherlandish-speaking provinces like Flanders.[4] Throughout the

---

[1] Famous for the fabled autonomy of its Cortes or parliament: Ralph Giese, *If Not, Not: The Legendary Oath of the Aragonese and the Laws of Sobrarbe* (Princeton, 1968). For a contemporary account, Raphael Martin de Viciana, *Chronyca de la Inclyta y Coronada Ciudad de Valencia y de su Reyno* (4 vols., Valencia, 1564).

[2] Flanders, Artois, Tournai and the Tournaisis, Hainaut, Namur, Luxemburg, Limburg, Brabant, Flanders, Zeeland, Holland, Utrecht and Overijssel (both added 1527), Friesland (added 1517), Groningen and Drenthe (added 1536), Cambrai and the Cambrésis (added 1543), and Gelderland (definitively added 1543).

[3] The States of Brabant, the States of Holland, the Four Members of Flanders, etc. There was also a States General, to which these assemblies sent deputies, but during Charles's reign it was a forum for hearing the government's requests, not a body that made decisions for the whole country. See Chapter 12.

[4] Since late Roman times there has been a linguistic frontier in what is now Belgium, originally following the Roman road that connected Cologne on the Rhine to Boulogne on the sea, dividing speakers of Romance dialects related to modern French from speakers of Netherlandish dialects related to modern Dutch. Holland and most of the Flanders and Brabant of Charles V's era lay to the north of this line.

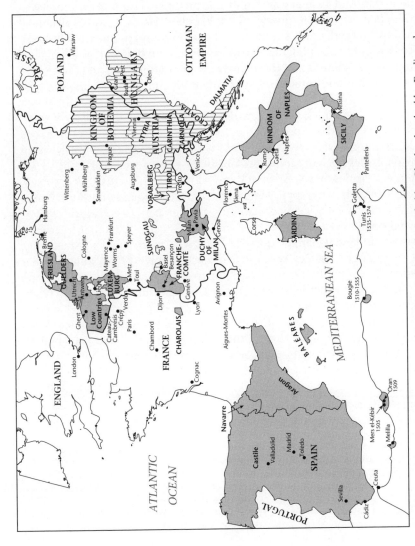

Map Int. 1. Habsburg dominions in Europe, 1555: shaded realms ruled by Charles, hatched by Ferdinand (based on Brandi, *Kaiser Karl V*)

3

reign, though less so as time went on, Charles's inner circle included men who had learned their politics and savoir-faire at the Habsburg-Burgundian court in Brussels. He could thus never be deaf to urgent appeals from Margaret or Mary on behalf of the safety of his native lands, the patrimony of their Burgundian ancestors. But some provinces counted for more than others. The three "core provinces" of Flanders, Brabant, and Holland, all or mainly Netherlandish-speaking,[5] where the country's trade and industry were concentrated, made up the most densely urbanized region in all of Europe (see Chapter 12). Not surprisingly, they also accounted for most of the subsidy income entered in government accounts – for example, 75.5% for 1531.[6]

In Naples, to which Charles made only one extended visit (1535–1536), he was represented by a series of viceroys, of whom the most important was Pedro Alvárez de Toledo (1532–1553). If controlling Milan was a constant goal in Charles's Italian campaigns, one of the main reasons for doing so was to protect Naples: never far from mind was the near disaster of 1527–1528, when a French army, bypassing Milan, roused a great rebellion in the kingdom and nearly toppled Habsburg rule in Italy (see Chapter 13). As Charles once explained to his brother, if it ever came to a choice between the two mainland Italian territories, Naples was "patrimony" for the family, Milan was not.[7] Naples was also the nerve center of Habsburg power in the peninsula. Owing to fiscal reforms introduced after 1535, Milan's revenues would eventually grow appreciably. But during Charles's reign, especially the early years, the duchy's disposable income was hardly enough to maintain the garrison of the citadel in the capital.[8] Hence, even though the revenues of the southern kingdom were not sufficient to cover the cost of defending and administering it,[9] Charles and his Genoese bankers still managed to extract large sums from Naples for garrisons in

[5] The term "Dutch" properly refers to the standardized literary language that developed in the northern provinces (centered on Holland) as they gained their independence from Spain during the Eighty Years' War (1568–1648).

[6] "Comptes des Receveurs Généraux de toutes les finances," Series B, Archives du Département du Nord, Lille, film copy as Algemeen Rijksarchief/Archives Généraux du Royaume, Brussels, (hereafter abbreviated as Lille B), no. 2363, account of the Receiver-General for all Finances for 1531. Totals for other years are similar. The term "core provinces" I borrow from Jonathan Israel, *History of the Dutch Republic: Its Rise, Development and Decline* (Oxford, 1995).

[7] Charles to Ferdinand, 27 November 1527, *Familienkorrespondenz*, Letter 130, II, 148–152: if both Milan and Naples are threatened by the French, Naples has priority, for unlike Milan it is "the patrimony of our predecessors."

[8] Antonio de Leyva to Charles, 14 July–4 August 1527, Lanz, Letter 100, I, 241–242. For Milan's finances, Giorgio Chittolini, "Cities, 'Territories' and Countryside in Lombardy under Charles V," in *The World of Charles the Fifth*, a collection of essays to be edited by W. P. Blockmans and M. E. H. N. Mout.

[9] Guido D'Agostino, *Parlamento e società nel regno di Napoli, Secoli XV e XVI* (Naples, 1979).

Lombardy, not to mention the emperor's own campaigns in Germany and elsewhere.

The emperor chose Castile as his adopted homeland, and he spent more of his reign in Valladolid (where his son Philip II was born) than in any other city.[10] After Charles abdicated from all his titles (December 1555–January 1556), he lived out his last few years at a monastery in Yuste, near Guadalajara. Castile was also the realm whose incomes were most coveted as assignations for their loans by the bankers who financed Charles's wars; this was especially true of certain kinds of revenue found only in Castile, including shipments of treasure from the New World (see Chapter 5). As may be expected, Castile's Council of State did its best to discourage Charles's ambitions outside of Spain, arguing for allocating resources to strengthening the kingdom's coastal defenses as well as the frontier against France.[11] To some degree, Charles had to respect this embryonic sense of Castile's national interests. Nonetheless, he was over time increasingly reckless in demanding of his ministers in Castile that they find somehow or other the money he needed (Chapters 9–11); in the latter part of the reign he also had better luck persuading the Cortes or parliament that his glorious victories abroad redounded to the glory of Castile (Chapter 14).[12]

Nine Campaigns: Charles V as an Impresario of War

In terms of military costs one can usefully distinguish between expenses routinely carried on the budgets of Charles's separate realms, and those specifically ordered by the emperor himself, as having priority over other needs. The Habsburg governments in Brussels, Valladolid, and Naples (among others) had regular expenditures during the cold months of the year for garrison wages and for the strengthening of fortifications.[13] During the warm months of the year – in other words, the fighting season – they found revenues to pay for field armies that could, as needed, defend against

---

[10] The most important archive for Charles's reign is still to be found at the Castle of Simancas, outside Valladolid, where Charles ordered that his archive be deposited in 1542.

[11] In this age of the "military revolution," key sites were strengthened by expensive new-style fortifications built to withstand artillery bombardment: Christopher Duffy, *Siege Warfare: The Fortress in the Early Modern World, 1494–1660* (London, 1979); Amelio Fara, *Il sistema e la città. Architettura fortificata dell'Europa moderna dai trattati alle realizzazione, 1464–1794* (Genoa, 1989).

[12] In 1557, when Philip II declared a kind of bankruptcy (forcibly converting Castile's short-term obligations into low-interest, long-term obligations), he was merely accepting the necessary consequence of his father's excessive borrowing: H. Keniston, *Francisco de los Cobos* (Pittsburgh, 1960), 264–265; M. J. Rodriguez-Salgado, *The Changing Face of Empire: Charles V, Philip II, and Habsburg Authority, 1551–1559* (Cambridge, 1988), 118–126.

[13] The best detailed study of the costs of fortification in the new Italian style is Simon Pepper and Nicholas Adams, *Firearms and Fortifications: Military Architecture and Siege Warfare in Sixteenth-Century Siena* (Chicago, 1986).

invaders or strike into enemy country. But Charles himself sometimes identified a conflict in a particular theater as of sufficient importance to require
support from realms other than those most closely affected. The Parma
campaign of 1550–1551 offers an example of what one might call an imperial war. When papal forces began a siege of Parma, held by Ottavio
Farnese, Charles decided that France's only major ally in Italy had to be
defeated at all costs. Hence the siege, though ultimately unsuccessful, was
supported not just by troops from nearby Milan but also by substantial
loans charged against Castile's revenues, and by a temporary appropriation
of savings Mary of Hungary had accumulated to pay off government debt
in the Low Countries.

In some cases, Charles not only made a particular campaign an imperial
priority but also decided that "honor and reputation" required him to take
the field in person. This meant increasing the size of the army, so as to
provide every assurance that the emperor would not be in peril, even if
one could not guarantee victory. Thus, if nearly a million Spanish ducats
were expended on imperial troops engaged in the futile, eleven-month
siege of Parma (1550–1551), Charles spent more than 3 million ducats for
the twelve-month campaign in which he either outlasted or defeated the
armies of Protestant Germany's Schmalkaldic League (1546–1547).[14]

To be sure, the emperor could involve himself in a campaign in different
ways. Charles was in the Low Countries in 1521 when war began, with
French-sponsored attacks on Luxemburg and Spanish Navarre, the latter
resulting in the capture of the important city of Fuenterrabía. The young
emperor determined to "regain reputation" by joining in a march against
"the famous city of Tournai," then held by France, taking with him "his
whole court and his household." In Spain a few years later (March 1524)
he insisted on joining the army that set out to reconquer Fuenterrabía,
even though the march lay through a Navarre still covered in snow. On
both occasions he remained at safe distances – at Valenciennes and at
Vitoria – while his commanders successfully completed their work.[15] In
these campaigns Charles merely added himself to an ongoing operation.
But in nine following campaigns he set the objectives and saw operations
through to the end.

In 1529–1530, it was he who decided to form an army in northern Italy,
and when the hoped-for invasion of Provence did not materialize, it was he
again who decided how his troops might best be employed. Just as Charles
arrived in Italy, Sultan Suleyman the Lawgiver (r. 1520–1566) was leading

[14] For a comparison of these two campaigns, see Chapters 10 and 11.
[15] Alonso de Santa Cruz, *Crónica del Emperador Carlos V*, vols. I–III, ed. Francisco de Laiglesia
y Auser (Madrid, 1920–1925); vols. IV–VI, ed. Antonio Blázquez y Augelera and Richardo Beltrán
y Rozpide (Madrid, 1928); see pt. I, chap. 59–61 (vol. I, 485–496), and pt. II, chap. 12 (vol. II,
76–81).

a huge Ottoman army to the very gates of Vienna; the city was able to hold out only because of the timely arrival of a relief force sent not by Charles but by the diet or parliament of the empire. Hence in 1532, when Suleyman came a second time against Austria in person, the emperor was obliged to put himself at the head of his contingent in a gigantic Christian war flotilla that sailed down the Danube, only to learn that the sultan had already withdrawn.

Advisers in Spain and Naples had talked for years of an all-out assault on Khair-ad-Din Barbarossa, chief among the corsairs of North Africa's Barbary Coast. But Charles determined to act only after Barbarossa had conducted a humiliating raid on Naples and then seized Tunis, dangerously near to Habsburg Sicily; he commanded the armada that conquered Tunis, perhaps his greatest victory (1535). Meanwhile, France's conquest of the duchy of Savoy, a Habsburg ally, provided an excuse for the invasion of Provence that had to be canceled some years earlier. Plans called for an army to march across the Alps from Lombardy, to be supported from a galley fleet that would seize one of Provence's harbors; but the defensive planning of France's Constable Anne de Montmorency – the fortification of key towns and river crossings, combined with a scorched-earth policy – proved far more effective (1536). Meanwhile, Barbarossa was causing as much havoc as before, from a new safe harbor in Algiers. After some false starts, Charles sailed at the head of a second great armada, only to suffer a terrible blow to his prestige as fierce autumn storms smashed many of his ships before the landing at Algiers could even be completed (1541). Heartened by his enemy's discomfiture, France's King Francis I (r. 1515–1547), with help from Sultan Suleyman and some of Germany's Protestant princes, members of the Schmalkaldic League, organized attacks on Habsburg lands from several directions at once. During 1542 Charles was preoccupied by a threat to Perpignan, on Aragón's Pyrenees frontier. But the next year he prepared and led a successful invasion of the lands of his most troublesome German foe, the duke of Cleves. This was only half of the emperor's "great plan." In the summer of 1544 he struck into northern France; though short of cash, he kept his men in the field long enough to force Francis I to accept a peace treaty, which (among other things) gave Charles the freedom to weigh the advisability of a frontal assault on the Schmalkaldic League.

Although his best and wisest councillors advised against it, Charles decided on a trial of force in Germany in 1546–1547. Backed by the credit-worthiness of Castile's revenues, he was able to outlast one of the Schmal-kaldic armies that faced him, then pursue and defeat the other. Thinking that his victory gave him the "reputation" to force real change, the emperor now tried to impose on Lutheran Germany a policy of conformity with Catholic religious ceremonies. But as he then tried to force his will on Ferdinand, with regard to the sensitive question of imperial succession, Charles failed to keep track of the comings and goings of supposed allies

among the empire's Protestant princes. Hence, when Duke Moritz of
Saxony marched on Innsbruck, Charles's had to make an ignominious flight
through Austria's Alpine valleys to the safety of Villach in Carinthia. From
Villach he ordered the mobilization of a huge army, big enough to punish
Moritz and his principal backer, King Henry II of France (r. 1547–1559).
But by the time his units were mobilized, Ferdinand, for reasons of his
own, had made a peace with Moritz that Charles could not break. His
best option, or so he thought, was to march against Metz, an imperial city
recently occupied by French troops. Yet it was by now almost November,
late in the year to begin a siege, and Charles and his commanders were
not able to counter the effective defense of Metz mounted by the duke
of Guise. Compelled to admit that all was in vain, Charles broke camp
(1 January 1553) and set off for Brussels, lamed by gout and broken in
spirit.

In the usage of the era, a campaign was an "enterprise," an *emprinse*
or *empresa*. For these nine "enterprises" Charles was the *impresario*,[16] a
grandmaster of the arts of war. With the advice of his councillors, but
not always guided by it, he determined the goals of the campaign, set
out guidelines for the recruitment of troops, decided how best to respond
to enemy maneuvers in the field, and stood by his men in the thick of
the action. Even after his defeat before Metz, despirited though he was,
he did not abandon the *métier* of war; indeed, he could hardly do so,
because France's Henry II (r. 1547–1559), capitalizing on his foe's loss of
prestige, organized major assaults on the Low Countries during the next
two years. In 1553 the town of Thérouanne in Artois opened its gates to
the French king. When the exiled Duke Philibert-Emmanuel of Savoy,
Charles's commander in chief, retook the city following a bombardment,
it was the emperor himself who ordered that Thérouanne be razed, an
act that still darkens his reputation. Fighting was more intense in 1554. As
Henry II entered Hainaut at the head of a large force, Mary of Hungary's
new-style fortress at Marienbourg opened its gates to him. Henry then
forced the surrender of Dinant on the Meuse, a town belonging to Charles's
ally, the prince-bishop of Liège. Marching east again through Hainaut, the
king laid waste to Binche, the town where Mary had built her summer
residence. Suffering from gout, Charles had himself carried on a litter
from Brussels to Namur, where Philibert-Emmanuel was marshaling his
forces. The imperial army caught up with the French in Artois, where
they were bombarding the town of Renty. In what turned out to be

---

[16] I use this term because "enterpriser" is preempted in the literature for military chieftains at a lower
level, the commander-entrepreneurs who organized and led the German mercenary regiments that
always played a key role in imperial armies: Otto Redlich, *The German Military Enterpriser and His
Work Force* (Wiesbaden, 1964).

the decisive engagement of the campaign, German heavy calvary under Günther von Schwartzburg stormed one of two hills dominating the area and drove off a counterattack by French cavalry. Even though French infantry subsequently retook the position, Henry II lifted the siege and retired to France. This was not so much the emperor's war as one in which he participated, as in 1521 and 1524. To be sure, the one account of the Renty campaign that has come to my attention eulogizes the invincible emperor, but its real point is to extol the derring-do of Schwartzburg, with whom the author served.[17] Things were different between 1529 and 1552, when Charles took personal charge of nine "enterprises" by which he hoped to effect some real change in the balance of forces confronting the House of Austria. These campaigns, not the others, are the subject of discussion here.

A Selection of Sources

Strategy

For Charles's views of the dynasty's objectives, the best source is his correspondence. I have mainly used published collections of the emperor's letters,[18] supplemented by reference to archives in Brussels,[19] Simancas,[20] and Vienna.[21] Charles needed help in managing his far-flung lands, and those he trusted most – those to whom he gave latitude to do the right

---

[17] Iacobus Basilicus Marchetus, Despota Sami, *De Morini quod Terouanam Vocant atque Hedini Expugnatione, deque Prelio apud Rentiacum, & Omnibus ad hunc usque diem Vario Eventu inter Caesarianos & Gallos Gestis, brevis et Vera Narratio* (Antwerp: Johannes Bellerus, 1555), bound with Bellerus's collection of accounts of Charles's Mediterranean campaigns, with a preface by Cornelis de Schepper, *Rerum a Carolo Augusto in Africa Bello Gestarum Commentarii* (copy in the James Ford Bell Library, University of Minnesota). For a judicious summary of contemporary accounts of these campaigns, Fray Prudencio de Sandoval, *Historia de la Vida y Hechos del Emperador Carlos V*, ed. Carlos Seco Serrando (3 vols., Madrid, 1955–1956) = *Biblioteca de Autores Españoles*, vols. 80–82, bk. XXXI, chaps. liv–lv, vol. 82, 436–437. Sandoval's *Historia* was first published in Valladolid, 1604–1606.

[18] There three most important collections are: (1) Manuel Fernández Alvárez, ed., *Corpus Documental de Carlos V* (5 vols., Salamanca, 1973–1981), hereafter abbreviated as *Corpus Documental;* (2) *Die Korrespondenz Ferdinands I:* vol. I, Wilhelm Bauer, ed., *Familienkorrespondenz bis 1526* (Vienna, 1912); vol. II, Wilhelm Bauer and Robert Lacroix, eds., *Familienkorrespondenz 1527–1528* (Vienna, 1930); vol. III, Wilhelm Bauer and Robert Lacroix, eds., *Familienkorrespondenz 1529 und 1530* (Vienna, 1938); vol. IV, Herwig Wolfram and Christiane Thomas, eds., *Familienkorrespondenz 1531 und 1532* (Vienna, 1973) = *Veröffentlichungen der Kommission für Neuere Geschichte Österreichs*, vols. 11, 30, 31, and 58, Lieferung 1, hereafter abbreviated as *Familienkorrespondenz;* and (3) Karl Lanz, ed., *Korrespondenz des Kaisers Karls V aus dem Königlichem Archiv und der Bibliothèque de Bourgogne zu Brüssel* (3 vols., Leipzig, 1844–1846), hereafter abbreviated as Lanz.

[19] Algemeen Rijksarchief/Archives Généraux du Royaume, Brussels, "Papiers d'État et de l'Audience," hereafter abbreviated as Aud.

[20] Archivo de Simancas. Valladolid, Colecion Estado, hereafter abbreviated as Estado.

[21] Haus- Hof- und Staatsarchiv, "Belgien," hereafter abbreviated as HHSA-B.

thing, even if it contravened the letter of his instructions[22] – functioned best if told not just what to do but what he hoped to accomplish by a particular directive. One should be cautious in claiming that any document gives access to the emperor's private thoughts, but Charles's letters to the family members who helped him govern the Habsburg lands do give, at the very least, a good sense of the reasoning he thought they would find plausible.

Ferdinand (1502–1564) was reared at the court of his namesake, Ferdinand of Aragón, and the Spanish advisers he brought with him on assuming control of the dynasty's Austrian lands (1519) did not win him friends in Germany. He complained repeatedly of a lack of respect among princes of the empire, and even after Charles had worked to secure Ferdinand's election (1530) as King of the Romans, the emperor's designated successor, the princes remained for some time unimpressed. Members of his personal entourage whom Charles periodically sent to Germany did not think highly of Ferdinand either; they believed he was easily led by venal advisers (be it noted that Ferdinand's advisers sent to Spain had equally grave doubts about Charles).[23] Much to Ferdinand's disappointment, Charles was reluctant to support campaigns against the Turks in Hungary, and he was also, for some time, inclined to temporize with the German Protestant princes whom Ferdinand found increasingly aggressive. But because the dynasty's enemies searched eagerly for any sign of disagreement between the brothers, Charles was determined to have it appear that he and the King of the Romans followed the same path.[24] Thus Ferdinand had to be convinced that Charles's path was the correct one, a task to which the

---

[22] E.g., Margaret to Ferdinand, 2 October 1526, *Familienkorrespondenz*, Letter 242, II, 471– 474: to respond to Ferdinand's desperate need for funds, in light of an anticipated Turkish invasion, Margaret hoped to divert the 100,000 ducats Charles had sent to a Spanish merchant in Antwerp, to be held for use in the expedition he planned to Italy, but the merchant, Hernando Bernuy, would not release the money without a direct order from Charles. Margaret presumed latitude to act as she thought circumstances required; Bernuy could not.

[23] Paula Sutter Fichtner, *Ferdinand I of Austria: The Politics of Dynasticism in the Age of Reformation* (New York, 1982). For complaints about Ferdinand and his advisers during the early years of Ferdinand's rule: Ferdinand to Charles, 18 December 1523, *Familienkorrespondenz*, Letter 51, II, 92; Hannart (a member of his inner circle) to Charles, 13 March 1524, *Lanz*, Letter 52, I, 106–107; Hannart to Charles, 4 April 1524, *Lanz*, Letter 55, I, 124–126; Ferdinand to Charles, 27 April 1524 (a complaint about Hannart), *Familienkorrespondenz*, Letter 66, I, 125–130; Ferdinand to Charles, 10 and 12 June 1524, *Familienkorrespondenz*, Letters 72, 75, I, 140, 146–147; and Ferdinand to Bredam, his envoy to Charles, 13 June 1524, *Familienkorrespondenz*, Letter 76, I, 175–176. For a sample of similar complaints in later years, Johann von Weeze, archbishop of Lund, to Charles, 15 September and 1 and 3 October 1534, *Lanz*, Letters 379, 382, II, 118, 129–130.

[24] For an early example, Charles to Ferdinand, 20 June 1523, *Familienkorrespondenz*, Letter 41, I, 68–70, requesting (for the fourth time, he says) that Ferdinand give Charles's envoys in Venice power to negotiate with the republic in his name as well, lest the two brothers "show the world how we disagree" (Ferdinand did not believe the treaty Charles's envoys had accepted dealt adequately with Austrian claims against Venice).

emperor devoted some of the longest of the autograph letters that were
meant to be particularly authoritative.[25]

In the Low Countries, neither Margaret of Austria (regent from 1519 to
her death in 1530) nor Mary of Hungary (regent from 1531 to 1555) allowed
herself to be cowed by the blustering egos of the great nobles who traditionally served on the Council of State. Indeed, as one recent scholar has
said, Mary in particular also found it "difficult to tolerate interference or resistance either from the area she governed or from her brother and nephew
[the future Philip II], whom she was bound to serve."[26] Perhaps because
these two women of the family were alumnae of the same "Burgundian"
school of politics in which the emperor himself and most of his early advisers had their training, Charles tolerated from Margaret and especially Mary
a level of frankness in criticizing his plans that Ferdinand seldom managed.
In fact, Charles's sense of dynastic priorities often clashed with the distinctive interests of the Low Countries, as both Margaret and Mary came to
understand and in some measure defend. Simply put, the vital international
trade of this region (especially the three core provinces) depended heavily
on land or sea connections that were imperiled by hostilities in virtually
any quarter. Thus, whenever Charles determined on war, he could count
on a long memorandum from Margaret or Mary explaining why a shaky
peace was preferable to a good war; once war was underway, he would be
told it was now all the more difficult to pry money loose from skeptical and
tight-fisted provincial parliaments.[27] Like Ferdinand, Margaret and Mary
had to be persuaded to put their authority behind Charles's plans.

During the years that were vouchsafed to her as Charles's helpmate
(1526–1539), Empress Isabella of Portugal never ventured to associate herself with complaints from the Council of State about how Castile's resources were being expended. But once young Felipe (the future Philip II,
born in 1527) was old enough to stand in for his absent father, beginning
with Charles's departure for Germany in 1543, filial deference did not prevent him from restating as his own objections to Charles's policy raised by
the council.[28] He too, like Mary and Ferdinand, had to be persuaded.

Troop Strength, Campaigns

Charles's letters are also a valuable source for plans as to the number
and kinds of troops to be raised, and for retrospective summaries of key

---

[25] E.g., Charles to Ferdinand, Brussels, 10 December 1548, a ten-page autograph dealing with the
religious and political settlement in Germany, HHSA-B, PA 5.

[26] Rodriguez-Salgado, *The Changing Face of Empire*, 5.

[27] E.g., Mary to Charles, 28 August 1542, HHSA-B, PA 33, Konvolut 1: despite an imminent French
invasion, the estates are "incredules du dangier ou ilz soient."

[28] See Chapters 10 and 11.

engagements. There are useful details also in the *Memoires* that Charles himself penned in 1550 but never allowed to be printed,[29] and in the published correspondence of Martín de Salinas, who represented Ferdinand at his brother's court from 1522 to 1539.[30] For a fuller picture, including estimates of the number and kinds of troops that actually showed up for the muster, one must turn to contemporary accounts. Unfortunately, scholars have yet to undertake the basic work of measuring these texts against one another – like the sixty-odd books and pamphlets dealing with Charles's Tunis campaign of 1535 – to determine which seem to be more or less trustworthy and on which points.[31] But the *Historiarum sui Temporis* of Paolo Giovio (1483–1552) seems a good place to start. Though present in person for only one of Charles's campaigns (the Danube war flotilla of 1532), Giovio had close contacts with the emperor's Italian commanders, especially Alfonso d'Avalos, the marquess of Vasto. His neutrality in the great-power conflicts of the era is also a mark in his favor: he was critical of Charles's ambitions for the House of Austria, and he turned down an invitation to be the emperor's official historian, either because the salary was not high enough, or because he feared compromising his independence as he carried out his plan to write the history of his times.[32]

Charles of course wanted an official historian to present his case to the reading public, as part of a broader effort to shape a favorable image of the emperor and of his position as Christendom's anointed leader in the struggle against Islamdom.[33] In Spain there were many scholars who at one time or another accepted an appointment as official historian, but

[29] The text survives only in a Portuguese translation: Alfred Morel-Fatio, *L'historiographie de Charles-Quint. I. Première partie, suivie de memoires de Charles-Quint. Texte portugais et traduction française* (Paris, 1913).

[30] Antonio Rodríguez Villa, *El Emperador Carlos V y su Corte según las cartas de Don Martín de Salinas, embajador del Infante Don Fernando (1522–1539)* (Madrid, 1903).

[31] For an example of the kind of work that needs to be done, see Heinz Duchhardt, "Das Tunisunternehmen Kaiser Karls V, 1535," *Mitteilungen des Österreichischen Staatsarchivs* 37 (1984): 35–72.

[32] *Pauli Iovii Opera* (9 vols. Rome, 1956–1987), including vol. III, Dante Visconti, ed., *Historiarum sui Temporis, tomus primus* (Rome, 1957); vol. IV, Dante Visconti, ed., *Historiarum sui Temporis, tomi secundi, pars prior* (Rome, 1971); and vol. V, Dante Visconti and T. C. Price Zimmerman, eds., *Historiarum sui Temporis, tomi secundi, pars altera* (Rome, 1985). On the man and his work, T. C. Price Zimmerman, *Paolo Giovio: The Historian and the Crisis of Sixteenth-Century Italy* (Princeton, 1995).

[33] The five-hundredth anniversary of Charles's birth has called forth a spate of public celebrations and scholarly conferences over the past two years. The published conference proceedings that have appeared to date are specially notable for detailed and lavishly illustrated examinations of various aspects of the vast propaganda campaign orchestrated by the emperor and his advisers. For the artistic dimension of this program, see the illustrations in Pedro Navascués Palacio, ed., *Carolus V Imperator* (Madrid, 1999), and Hugo Soly, ed., *Charles V, 1500–1558, and His Time* (Antwerp, 1999); for an overview, Peter Burke, "Presenting and Re-Presenting Charles V," in Soly, *Charles V*, 393–476.

only a few who produced what they promised.[34] The most interesting of these works (though little cited by scholars) is the voluminous *Crónica del Emperador Carlos V* of Alonso de Santa Cruz, not published until the twentieth century. Santa Cruz served also as the emperor's official geographer or *cosmografo mayor*.[35] His *Crónica* covers the entire reign, up through 1550. Though he seems never to have left Spain, his contacts at court lend credibility to the claim that the many documents he includes are copies of authentic texts to which he was given access by crown secretaries. Pedro de Mexia (1497–1551), an alderman of Seville, was a bit more inclined to flatter the subject of his work, and his *Historia* covers Charles's reign only to 1530, but he seems to have good information on the Italian campaigns.[36] Bernabé Busto, a doctor of theology and court chaplain, accompanied the emperor on his wars in Germany and France (1543–1544) and during the First Schmalkaldic War (1546–1547), where he was able to consult musterbooks found in a camp abandoned by the Protestant army. Busto's history of the 1543–1544 campaigns remains in manuscript, but his account of the Schmalkaldic War was published in Germany in 1938.[37] Luis de Ávila y Zuñiga, a veteran of many of the emperor's previous campaigns, offers a soldier's perspective on the First Schmalkaldic War.[38]

For each of Charles's maritime crusades, against Tunis (1535) and Algiers (1541), there are also good eyewitness accounts. The *Commentarium Expeditionis Tuniceae* of Antoine Perrenin, one of the emperor's secretaries,

---

34 Richard L. Kagan, "Las cronistas del emperador," in Navascués Palacio, *Carolus V Imperator*, 183–212.

35 This massive work is frequently cited in Manuel Fernández Alvárez, *Carlos V, el César y el hombre* (Madrid, 1999), but merits only a brief mention in the summary article by Kagan, "Las cronistas del emperador."

36 Juan de Mata Cariazo, ed., *Historia del Emperador Carlos V, por el magnifico caballero Pedro Mexia, veinticuatro de Sevilla* (Madrid, 1945); Kagan, "Las cronistas del Emperador," 202–203.

37 Otto Adalbert Graf van Looz-Corswaren, ed., *Bernabé de Busto, Geschichte des Schmalkldischen Krieges* (Burg, 1938) = *Texte und Forschungen im Auftrage der Preussischen Akademie der Wissenschaften, herausgegeben von der Romanischen Kommission*, Band I. Both parts of the work are described as unpublished by Morel-Fatio, *L'historiographie de Charles-Quint*, and (on this basis) by Kagan, "Las cronistas del emperador," and by Burke, "Presenting and Re-Presenting Charles V," 435.

38 I have used not the original Spanish text, published in Venice in 1548, but a Latin translation: *Commentariorum de Bello Germanico a Carolo V Caesare Maximo Augusto Libri II, translati per Gulielmum Malinaeum Brugensem, et iconibus illustrati* (Antwerp: Johan Streelsius, 1550), copy in Special Collections, University of Minnesota Libraries. On the connections between Malinaeus (Guillaume van Male, named a gentlemen of the emperor's chamber in 1550), Avila, and Lodewijk van Praet (one of the emperor's inner circle), to whom this translation is dedicated, see the preface in Baron be Reiffenberg, *Lettres sur la Vie Intérieure de l'Empereur Charles-Quint, Écrites par Guillaume van Male, Gentilhomme de sa Chambre* (Brussels, 1846). Burke, "Presenting and Re-Presenting Charles V," 435, points out that Avila flattered the emperor through implicit comparisons to Julius Caesar's conduct as a commander, as described in the Gallic Wars.

was published first in his native French and later in a Latin translation.[39] The
Knights of Rhodes, based from 1530 on Malta, were perennial foes of the
Barbary corsairs and always joined in the expeditions mounted by Charles's
naval commanders. Nicholas Durand de Villegagnon (1510–1571?), captain
of the French nation of the Knights, published his Latin narrative of the
Algiers campaign in Paris in 1542, perhaps as a vain warning against the
Habsburg-Valois war that was then about to break out, distracting Christendom once again from the struggle against Islam.[40] For Kheir-ad-Din
Barbarossa, the Ottoman naval commander who was Charles's great foe in
the Mediterranean, the *Crónica de los Barbarrojas* of the clergyman Francisco
López de Gómara seems to have been based on information scrupulously
gathered, unlike the work for which the author is best known – a flat-
tering account of the overseas exploits of his patron, Hernán Cortés, the
conqueror of Mexico.[41] None of these works can stand by itself. But taken
together, and in conjunction with Charles's correspondence, they offer a
plausible basis for reconstructing the emperor's career as an impresario of war.

State Finance, Bankers' Loans, and Parliamentary Subsidies
The general picture of Low Countries finance presented here depends on
summaries of income and expenditure prepared for discussions within the
Council of State.[42] For the early decades of the reign I have also used
annual summaries prepared by the receiver general for all finances,[43] and
for Flanders a monograph from 1978.[44] For references to the county of
Holland in particular, I rely on archival collections used in previous works
on Holland,[45] including the annual accounts of the receiver of subsidies;[46]

[39] Johannes Etrobius [Jean Bérot], *Commentarium seu potius Diarium Expeditionis Tuniceae a Carolo Imperatore Maximo Semper Augusto Susceptae* (Louvain, 1547), copy in the James Ford Bell Library, University of Minnesota.
[40] Villegagnon, *Expeditio Caroli V Imperatoris in Africam ad Argieram* (Paris, 1542), copy in the James Ford Bell Library, University of Minnesota.
[41] Gómara, *Crónica de los Barbarrojas*, in *Memorial Historical Español: Coleccion de Documentos, Opusculos, y Antigüedades que Publica la Real Academia de Historia* (Cuaderno 23, Madrid, 1853), 329–439; in a brief preface (329–330) the unnamed editor notes points of agreement between Gómara's work and contemporary Arabic chronicles available in French translations.
[42] Aud. 650, 867, 868, 873, 874, and 857.
[43] Lille B. For the reference, see note 6.
[44] N. Maddens, *De Beden in het Graafschap Vlaanderen tijdens de Regering van Karel V (1515–1550) = Standen en Landen/Aciens Pays et Assemblées d'État*, vol. 72 (Heule, 1978).
[45] Tracy, *A Financial Revolution in the Habsburg Netherlands: "Renten" and "Renteniers" in the County of Holland, 1515–1565* (Berkeley and Los Angeles, 1985); *Holland under Habsburg Rule, 1506–1566: The Formation of a Body Politic* (Berkeley and Los Angeles, 1990).
[46] The series "Graafelijkheids Rekenkamer," Rijksarchief van Zuid-Holland, The Hague, hereafter GRK.

the correspondence of the Council of Holland,[47] which represented the prince's authority in the province; the *Resolutiën*, or Resolutions of the States of Holland;[48] and the travel journals of men who regularly participated in meetings of the states.[49]

For Naples, a lengthy summary of the state of the kingdom's finances at the beginning of Charles's reign was prepared by Charles Leclerc, president of the Chamber of Accounts in the Low Countries, who was sent to Naples for this purpose in 1517.[50] For roughly the first half of the reign Giuseppe Coniglio has published an important collection of financial documents, including summaries of annual income and expenditure, and the questions raised about them by auditors in Spain.[51] For the Parlamento of 1536, the only one at which Charles addressed his Neapolitan subjects in person, there are useful details in the memoirs of Gregorio Rosso, who played an important role in the city of Naples and in the politics of the realm until he ran afoul of Charles's strong-willed viceroy, Pedro de Toledo (1532–1553).[52] Toledo's tenure in office, during which the Parlamento became a pliable instrument of the sovereign's will, is treated in a number of good and fairly recent studies.[53] Finally, for the Genoese bankers who were the kingdom's principal creditors – quite apart from the support of Charles's own campaigns – there is now the fine work of Arturo Pacini.[54]

For Castile, Ramón Carande Thobar's *Carlos V y sus banqueros*, after more than three decades, still has no peer among studies of the finances of Charles's reign.[55] Carande does not trace how the sums charged by Charles

---

[47] Especially the correspondence of Lord Gerrit van Assendelft, first councillor and acting president from 1528 through the end of Charles's reign, as found in Aud.

[48] *Resolutiën van de Staten van Holland, 1524–1795* (278 volumes, Amsterdam, 1789–1814), hereafter RSH. The first volume covers the years 1524–1543.

[49] The most important is Andries Jacobszoon, "Prothocolle van alle die reysen...bij mij Andries Jacops gedaen [1522–1538]," Gemeentearchief, Amsterdam, hereafter AJ.

[50] Leclerc, "Rapport et Recueil de tout le Royaulme de Naples," British Library, Egestorn Collection, no. 1905. I am grateful to Professor John Marino of the University of California at San Diego for making available to me his xerox copy of Leclerc's 192-folio report.

[51] Coniglio, ed., *Consulte e bilanci del Viceregno di Napoli dal 1507 al 1533* (Rome, 1983).

[52] Rosso, *Istoria delle Cose di Napoli*, in *Raccolta di Tutti i Piu Rinomati Scrittori dell'Istoria Generale del Regno di Napoli* (Naples: Giovanni Gravier, 1770).

[53] For Toledo's relations with the *Parlamento*, see D'Agostino, *Parlamento e società nel regno di Napoli*; for the coterie of supporters he built up among the great nobles, Carlos José Hernándo Sanchez, *Castilla y Napoles en el siglo XVI. El Virrey Pedro de Toledo. Linaje, estado y cultura (1532–1553)* (Junta de Castilla y Léon, 1994).

[54] Arturo Pacini, *La Genova dell'Andrea Doria nell'impero di Carlo V* (Florence, 1999).

[55] Volume I was first published in 1943, and revised by the author for the second edition of 1967. Volumes II and III were published in 1949 and 1967, respectively, and not subsequently revised. In the most recent edition (3 vols., Editorial Crítica, Barcelona, 2000), with a preface by the author's son, Víctor Bernardo Carande, the chapter titles and the pagination are the same as in the second edition of volume I, and in the first editions of volumes II and III.

against various incomes in Castile were spent, but his careful record of long-term loans contracted for by the emperor or his officials is indispensable, not only because of the preponderance of loans were charged to Castile but also because of Carande's fine sense for the workings of international finance in this period.[56] For the Cortes of Castile, I have used the published record of petitions to the crown from the *procuradores* of the eighteen towns with voting rights,[57] together with recent literature on the towns themselves.[58]

Part I, "Strategy and Finance" (Chapters 1–5), outlines the conditions under which Charles went to war, and the means he employed for raising the money to pay his troops. Part II, "Impresario of War: Charles's Campaigns, 1529–1552" (Chapters 6–11), discusses the nine "enterprises" on which the emperor took command of his troops, with estimates of how much the campaigns cost and where Charles got the money. Part III, "War Taxation: Parliaments of the core provinces of the Low Countries, Naples, and Castile" (Chapters 12–14), shows how the elites that spoke for Charles's subjects met his needs, but in their own way and for their own reasons.

Putting all theses dimensions of warfare in Charles's reign together makes for a broader picture of the subject than has hitherto been available. But in the study of history breadth and depth are always in a state of tension. No work can be better than the primary sources on which it is based, and readers familiar with pertinent archives will notice important omissions in the foregoing enumeration. Should scholars working (for example) in the fiscal records of Naples or Castile present findings that invalidate some of my conclusions, I will take it as an indication not that my work has missed the mark, but that it has been useful in the ongoing process of understanding the past. For the historian, it is ambition enough to earn a respected place in the roll of predecessors who have to be proved wrong.

---

[56] E.g., Götz Freiherr von Pölnitz, *Anton Fugger* (4 vols., Tübingen, 1958–1967), sometimes accepts the gossip of sixteenth-century financial markets without checking it against the accounts, as Carande does.

[57] Manuel Colmeiro, *Cortes de los Antiguos Reinos de Léon y Castilla* (4 vols., Madrid, 1883–1886).

[58] Charles David Hendricks, "Charles V and the Cortes of Castile," Ph.D. dissertation, Cornell University, 1976; José Ignacio Fortea Perez, *Fiscalidad in Córdoba. Fisco, economia y sociedad: Alcabalas, encabezamientos, en tierras de Córdoba* (Córdoba, 1986); Juan Sanchez Montes, *1539. Agobios carolinos y ciuades castellanas* (Granada, 1975).

PART ONE

Strategy and Finance

Before taking up the campaigns that are the central topic of this book, some general considerations about why Charles went to war and how he paid for his campaigns are in order. Chapter 1 considers whether Charles and his advisers had a "grand strategy" to guide them in decisions about when and where to go to war, and whether the emperor himself should take command. Chapter 2 highlights the struggle against France – the conflict to which Charles and his advisers attached the highest priority – and its principal theater, northern Italy. Chapters 3, 4, and 5 take up the financial dilemma that was peculiar to European states of the late medieval and early modern era. Together with the Ottoman Empire to the east, these Christian states were historical successors to ancient Rome and its Byzantine prolongation. Thus in military terms the great model from the past was the imperial army, regularly paid four times a year. There were some echoes of this practice in Christian Europe, notably in France, where standing cavalry units dating from the fifteenth century, the *compagnies d'ordonnance*, were paid four times a year – even if, in the sixteenth century, revenues set aside for this purpose were often diverted to the larger and more expensive mercenary companies of the king's army.[1] But from a broad view of the sixteenth century, one discerns an important contrast between the Ottoman state and the other "gunpowder empires"[2] of Islamdom and the states of Latin Christendom. In the former realms, as in the Ottoman Empire, the fiscal resources of the state were mobilized effectively for the support of a standing military organization. Not counting irregulars who served in the hope of booty, the regular forces of Sultan Suleyman I have been estimated for 1528 at 87,000 men, of whom 37,000 were holders of *timar* or military prebends (collecting taxes to support themselves and the men they raised), while the remaining 50,000, including

---

[1] Philippe Hamon, *L'argent du roi. Les finances sous François I* (Paris, 1994), 18.
[2] Safavid Iran and the Mughal Empire in India.

the famed Janissary infantry, received a salary paid four times a year.[3] Against this massive military establishment, the few standing military units to be found in Europe – like the *companies d'ordonnance* maintained by the dukes of Burgundy and their Habsburg successors – cut a very poor figure.[4] European garrisons and field armies were mostly made up of men who contracted for their services; these men obviously had to be paid, but, unlike the Roman or the Ottoman army, there were no revenues earmarked for their wages.

Hence, at least since the thirteenth century, bankers had played an essential role in European wars, by advancing sums for which they expected to be compensated from state revenues in subsequent years.[5] As in so many other aspects of finance, Italian bankers led the way in this development. For example, Florentine firms bankrolled efforts by the King of Naples to reconquer the rebel province of Sicily (1283), as well as the attempt by one of his sons to carve out a principality for himself in Morea (the Peloponnesus, 1322–1323); bankers in Pera, the Genoese suburb of Constantinople, helped fund the recapture of Gallipoli from the Turks by Count Amadeo VI of Savoy (1366).[6]

Unlike town governments in sixteenth-century Europe,[7] princely governments seldom kept their books in balance. Charles V was no different in this respect from his "cousins" who occupied royal and ducal thrones in other lands.[8] For 1534 Ramón Carande Thobar found a budget projection at the royal archives in Simancas (figures in ducats):[9]

---

[3] Halil İnalcik and Donald Quatert, eds., *An Economic and Social History of the Ottoman Empire*, vol. I, *1300–1600* (Cambridge, 1997), 88–99.

[4] Le Baron Guillaumne, *Histoire des Bandes d'Ordonnance des Pays-Bas = Mémoires de l'Académie Royale des Sciences, des Lettres et des Beaux-Arts de Belgique, Classe des Lettres*, 40 (Brussels, 1873).

[5] Martin Körner, "Public Credit," in Richard Bonney, ed., *Economic Systems and State Finance* (Oxford, 1995), 507–538.

[6] Kenneth Setton, *The Papacy and the Levant, 1204–1571* (4 vols., Philadelphia, 1976), I, 143, 159, 309.

[7] Towns balanced their books with the help of low-interest, long-term debt, created either by imposing forced loans on wealthy citizens, as was done in Venice and Florence, or, as in much of the rest of Europe, by issuing bonds funded by a particular city revenue, like the beer excise or the wine excise; in northern France and the Low Countries, where such bonds were common from the late thirteenth century, they were known as *rentes* (incomes) in French, and *renten* in Netherlandish. For an overview, James D. Tracy "Taxation and State Debt," in Thomas A. Brady Jr., Heiko A. Oberman, and James D. Tracy, eds., *Handbook of European History during the Late Middle Ages, Renaissance, and Reformation, 1400–1600* (2 vols., Leiden, 1994), I, 563–588.

[8] The polite form of address in correspondence between crowned heads was *mon cousin*.

[9] Carande Thobar, *Carlos V y sus banqueros*, II, 579–580. The difference between gross and net income is largely explained by the fact that *juros* (treasury bonds) were funded by the cluster of incomes known as *rentas ordinarias*; as more and more of these bonds were sold during Charles's reign, the cost of annual interest charges approached and eventually reached 100% of the revenue expected from the *rentas ordinarias*.

Gross income	1,372,925
Standing charges	838,743
Net income	544,182
Projected expenses	979,300
Deficit	435,118

It bears emphasizing that 1534 was a year of peace for all of the lands ruled by Charles. If there were deficits of more than 30% of gross income in time of peace, even in Castile, his richest and most populous realm, how could he possibly manage the cost of a war?

Rulers had three options. First, they had the accounts examined more closely, to find ways to reduce expenses, and to squeeze more from the so-called ordinary revenues that made up the realm's most familiar sources of income. Second, through the parliamentary assemblies that had grown up all over Latin Christendom since the thirteenth century, they called upon their subjects to approve new and larger subsidies. Third, they borrowed against future revenues of both kinds, principally through high-interest, short-term loan contracts with agents of the great banking houses. These three options were linked in various ways, and rulers often chose to pursue all three at once. Nonetheless, it will be convenient for present purposes to consider separately how each option was managed in the Habsburg realms. Hence, Chapter 3 considers attempts at fiscal reform; Chapter 4 takes up the troubled relations between Charles's governments and the parliaments of his realms during the initial years of his reign; and Chapter 5 looks at the bankers from whom the emperor borrowed, and the terms and conditions on which they were willing to lend.

Chapter 1

The Grand Strategy of Charles V

Military historians working on periods as far apart as the Roman Empire and the twentieth century have adopted the term "grand strategy" to denote the highest level of thinking about the interests of the state. To quote a recent definition,

> Strategy is the art of controlling and utilizing the resources of a nation – or a coalition of nations – including its armed forces, to the end that its vital interests shall be effectively promoted and secured against enemies, actual, potential, or merely presumed. The highest type of strategy – sometimes called grand strategy – is that which so integrates the policies and armaments of the nation that the resort to war is either rendered unnecessary or is undertaken with the maximum chance of victory.[1]

If one applies this definition strictly, especially the implication that the wealth of a nation is a "resource" to be enhanced by government policy, Charles V cannot be said to have had a grand strategy. His sister, Mary of Hungary, regent of the Low Countries (1531–1555), clearly grasped the importance of strengthening the commercial relations of the Netherlands; for example, she tried to discourage Charles from going to war to put his niece on the throne of Denmark, a scheme that had little chance of success, and threatened to disrupt altogether Holland's vital Baltic trade.[2] Similarly,

---

[1] A quotation from Edward Mead Earle, *The Makers of Modern Strategy* (Princeton, 1943), viii, in Paul Kennedy, "Grand Strategy in War and Peace: Toward a Broader Definition," in his *Grand Strategies in War and Peace* (New Haven, Conn., 1991), 2.

[2] Daniel Doyle, "The Heart and Stomach of a Man but the Body of a Woman: Mary of Hungary and The Exercise of Political Power in Early Modern Europe," Ph.D. dissertation, University of Minnesota, 1996, chap. 6. Charles's sister Isabella had married King Christian II who was driven from his throne in 1523. During the so-called Counts' War of 1533–1536, Charles ordered the mobilization of Low Countries shipping to carry to Denmark an army enrolled under the banner of Frederick of Wittelsbach, brother of the Count Palatine of the Rhine, and husband of Dorothea, daughter of Isabella and Christian II.

Francis I had ambitious plans for enriching the Mediterranean trade of his kingdom by making French-held Savona a rival to the busy port of Genoa.[3] But there is, to my knowledge, nothing in Charles's correspondence to suggest an awareness that the trade or agriculture of his realms was an asset to be nurtured and protected, for the future profit of the crown. He seems not to have seen beyond the fact that wealth of subjects could be called upon to support the great deeds of princes, as in a speech to the Council of Castile in 1529, explaining his decision to embark on a military campaign in Italy: "It is very pusillanimous for a prince to forgo undertaking a heroic course of action merely because money is wanting, for in matters of honor a prince must not only risk his own person but also pledge the revenues of his treasury."[4]

Geoffrey Parker has applied a more limited concept of the term to Charles's son Philip. As against critics of the idea of a "grand strategy" for Philip's reign, Parker acknowledges that neither Philip nor his councillors had a "comprehensive master-plan." But one can discern "a global strategic vision" in the initiatives of the king's government, as when he ordered simultaneous *visitas* or inspection tours of Spain's three Italian provinces, Milan, Naples, and Sicily (1559). Through his councils Philip had a systematic procedure for sifting and evaluating incoming reports about threats to Spain's interests in various parts of Europe and overseas. There was also a systematic collection of information that could be useful in the governance of his realms, as in the twenty sectional maps the king had made of Iberia,[5] which were "by far the largest European maps of their day to be based on a detailed ground survey." Unlike "more successful warlords," such as his great rival, King Henry IV of France (1589–1610), or his own father, Charles V, Philip did not appreciate the strategic importance of "seeing the situation in a theater [of war] for oneself," or of "building bonds of confidence and trust with theater commanders through regular personal meetings." But Philip did inherit from his father what Parker calls a "blueprint for empire" to guide his thinking and that of his ministers. This was the so-called political testament of 1548, written for Philip's instruction, "a highly perceptive survey of the prevailing international situation, and of the Grand Strategy best suited to preserve Philip's inheritance intact." Because Philip's possessions were physically separated from one another, and the object of widespread jealousy, he must take care to maintain friends and informants in all areas, so as to understand the actions of other states and anticipate danger.[6]

---

[3] See Chapter 6.

[4] Santa Cruz, *Crónica del Emperador Carlos V*, II, 456.

[5] From 1580, Philip was also king of Portugal.

[6] Geoffrey Parker, *The Grand Strategy of Philip* II (New Haven, Conn., 1998), 2–6, 9–10, 21–25, 40, 59–63, 77–79. For the text of Charles's testament of 18 January 1548, *Corpus Documental*, Letter

It makes sense to apply this qualified idea of a grand strategy to Charles's reign also, but only if a further adjustment is made. Although Philip's dominions were indeed scattered, the policy of the monarchy was governed by Spanish interests. This was not yet so in Charles's time, primarily because the crown he wore as Holy Roman Emperor was more prestigious than the crowns of Castile and Aragón, and implied responsibilities lying well beyond the zone of Spanish concerns. Hence one cannot say of Charles that his thinking about war and peace was undergirded by a sense of "national" interest. Moreover, although panegyrists compared him with the Caesars of Rome, his empire, unlike theirs, never made up a contiguous territory with common interests and common enemies.

The lands Charles ruled at least in name[7] were a motley collection making up nearly half of Europe.[8] In Spain he was (from 1516) king of Castile and Aragón by right of his maternal grandparents, the Catholic kings, Isabella of Castile and Ferdinand of Aragón. In the Low Countries, he ruled a fistful of provinces inherited from his paternal grandmother, Mary, the duchess of Burgundy, including Flanders, Brabant, and Holland. Across the French border, he claimed to be the rightful duke of Burgundy, even though the duchy was reincorporated into France in 1477. In Italy, he was king of Naples (including Sicily), thanks to the conquest of that realm by his Aragonese great-grandfather, King Alfonso V (d. 1458). Meanwhile, and with minimal attention on Charles's part,[9] his subjects added the great Aztec and Inca realms to Castile's overseas possessions. Finally, in the vast and ramshackle Holy Roman Empire, where each prince and city-state ruled more or less without interference from the emperor, Charles and his younger brother Ferdinand were heirs to Habsburg Austria, yet another collection of separate provinces. Upon the death of their grandfather, Emperor Maximilian I (1519), Charles was able to succeed him by vote of the empire's seven prince-electors, but only thanks to indecently large bribes advanced by Augsburg's great banking houses.

How does one understand the interests of a prince ruling so many lands, whose discernible interests were often in direct conflict with one another?

CCCLXXIX, II, 569–592; and for the place of this document in a series of such testaments, Karl Brandi, "Die politische Testamente Karls V," II (1930), 258–293, in "Berichte und Studien zur Geschiche Karls V," nos. I–XIX, *Nachrichten von der Akademie der Wissenschaften zu Göttingen, Philologisch-Historische Klasse,* 1930–1941, hereafter abbreviated as "Berichte."

[7] The order in which his titles were listed varied slightly with the secretary's home base; for a Spanish version, Rodriguez-Salgado, *The Changing Face of Empire,* 33.

[8] Wim Blockmans, "The Emperor's Subjects," in Soly, *Charles V,* 234: in a western and central Europe estimated to have had 70 million people in 1550, those who could be called subjects of Charles numbered about 28 million.

[9] For Charles's legislation on the Indies, Ciriaco Pérez Bustamente, "Actividad legislativa de Carlos V, en orden a las Indias," in *Charles-Quint et son temps* (Paris, 1959), 113–121.

Or what were Charles's interests as holder of an imperial crown to which no lands or revenues were attached, only a vague prestige that evoked the jealousy of other crowned heads? There were no precedents to fall back on, because no prince in living memory – indeed, no one since Alexander the Great, or Charlemagne[10] – had ever ruled such a large and heterogenous complex of territories. Nonetheless, Charles groped his way toward a settled understanding of his interests, and those of the "House of Austria," including a grasp of European affairs that in his mature years was indeed highly perceptive. To be sure, this was not a wisdom gained in a single campaign, or a single season of hearing ambassadors' reports read in council. The first time Charles wrote down his thoughts about the choices facing him (February–March 1525), he gave no evidence of ideas more complex than the traditional chivalric sense of honor that required him, as he thought, to undertake an expedition to Italy.[11] The young emperor had to learn from his councillors, especially Mercurino Gattinara, grand chancellor of the empire. It will thus be useful to look first at the advisers who surrounded Charles, before examining the elements of a grand strategy that he drew from their counsel and, in time, reformulated in his own terms.

Charles's Advisers

From an early age Charles took governing seriously. France's King Francis I (d. 1547) is said to have been happiest when "riding to the hounds, tilting in a joust or performing in a masque."[12] Charles, though not adverse to taking his pleasures, maintained throughout his life a daily routine that included meeting with one or another of his councils, hearing reports from abroad read aloud, dictating letters or dispatches, and, in special cases, writing out long missives. Even when afflicted with gout, he used his distinctive hand as a means of underlining his instructions; recipients knew at once they had been favored with such a letter and were meant to be impressed.[13]

---

[10] The example of Charlemagne's conquest and subjugation of the stubbornly pagan Saxons was evoked as a precedent for what Charles might have to do to stubborn Lutherans, concentrated in roughly the same part of Germany: Cardinal Lorenzo Campeggi to Charles, end of June 1530, *Staatspapiere*, Document 8, 41–50; cf. Ferdinand to Charles, 1 February 1531, *Familienkorrespondenz*, Letter 451, III, 17: "Y . . . la tierra de Saxonia ha sido en tiempos passados rreduzida dos vezes a la fe."

[11] For text and commentary, Karl Brandi, "Eigenhändige Aufzeichnungen Karls V aus dem Anfang des Jahres 1525," in "Berichte," IX, 1933, 220–260; see also Federico Chabod, *Lo stato e la vita religiosa a Milano nell' epoca di Carlo V* = *Opere* (5 vols., Turin, 1964–1985), III, 133–135.

[12] R. J. Knecht, *Renaissance Warrior and Patron: The Reign of Francis I* (Cambridge, 1994), 107.

[13] See, eg., the gratitude of Charles de Lannoy, viceroy of Naples (1522–1527), to have letters in the emperor's own hand: to Charles, 20 April 1525, Lanz, Letter 67, I, 160, and 25 May 1526,

His earliest mentors were men who had received their political and military education at the Habsburg-Burgundian court in Brussels. Gattinara, a Piedmontese, came to the Low Countries with Charles's aunt, Margaret of Austria, widowed duchess of Savoy, for her first term as regent (1506–1514). Upon Gattinara's death in 1530, Nicholas Perrenot, lord of Granvelle in Franche-Compté (d. 1550), succeeded him as the emperor's chief adviser for the affairs of France and the empire, though not as chancellor of the empire (this position was not filled again in Charles's reign). Other key advisers had been chamberlains to Charles in his boyhood, hunting with him in the Zoniënbos outside Brussels: Guillaume de Croy, lord of Chièvres in Hainaut, the grand chamberlain (d. 1521); Philibert of Châlons, prince of Orange (d. 1530); Orange's son-in-law and heir, Count Henry of Nassau (d. 1538), lord of the Low Countries lands of the German princely house from which he came; Charles de Lannoy, lord of Molembaix (d. 1527); Lodewijk van Vlaanderen, lord of Praet (d. 1551), representing an illegitimate branch of the old comital house of Flanders; Adrien de Croy, lord of Roeulx, the brother of Chièvres; Jean Hannart, lord of Likerke; and Charles de Poupet, lord of La Chaulx.[14]

Only slowly did these "Burgundians" give way in the inner circle to Castilians. There were first of all the ecclesiastics, who traditionally occupied high positions at the court in Valladolid, notably Alonso de Fonseca (d. 1534), archbishop of Toledo and president of the Consejo de Estado or Council of Castile. Juan Pardo de Tavera (d. 1545), archbishop of Santiago, was especially effective at building a clientele among servants of the crown at various levels.[15] He succeeded Fonseca both as primate of Spain (archbishop of Toledo) and president of the council. Though men from grandee families – the highest rank of the nobility – were excluded from the councils of state in the time of Ferdinand and Isabella, there were a few for whom Charles made exceptions, including three men from the House of Alba: Fadrique Alvárez de Toledo (d. 1531), the second duke of Alba; his younger son, Pedro Alvárez de Toledo (d. 1553), marquess of Villafranca; and Villafranca's nephew, Fernando Alvárez de Toledo (d. 1581), the third

---

Lanz, Letter 89, I, 210–211. Ferdinand's suggestion that Charles need not trouble writing in his own hand is taken by Wolfram as a hint that Ferdinand, following his election (1530) as King of the Romans and thus as designated successor in the empire, now had less need of direction from Charles: Ferdinand to Charles, *Familienkorrespondenz*, Letter 669, IV, 639.

[14] For biographical sketches, Michel Baelde, *De Collaterale Raden onder Karel V en Filips II, 1531–1578, Verhandelingen van de Koninklijke Vlaamse Akademie van Wetenschappen, Letteren en Schoone Kunsten van België, Klasse der Letteren*, XXVII (Brussels, 1965).

[15] On rivalry between different *bandas* or *partidos* within the councils of Castile, José Martínez Millán, ed., *Instituciones y elites de poder en la monarquía hispana durante el siglo XVI* (Madrid, 1992); see also his "La Corte de Carlos V: Corientes espirituales en la casa de Castilla del emperador," in Blockmans and Mout, *The World of Charles V*.

duke of Alba.[16] Some lesser nobles also rose to positions in the inner circle, like Juan de Silva, count of Cifuentes, as did officials of nonnoble birth like Lope de Soria, who began his career as a secretary to the Council of Aragón, and the adviser on whom Charles came to rely most, Francisco de los Cobos (d. 1547), initially a secretary to the Council of Castile. Cobos gained the emperor's confidence by his ability to find, within Castile's labyrinthine financial system, revenues that were not as yet pledged, thus permitting the flow of loans to continue. Like Tavera, he was adept at building a coterie of supporters, and the two informal groupings of courtiers and officials formed a single *banda* or faction in the eyes of outsiders.[17]

After he concluded an alliance with the emperor in 1528, Andrea Doria (d. 1560), the admiral from a family of Genoese bankers, was Charles's most trusted adviser on maritime affairs, but he seldom attended on the emperor in person, and was never quite accepted by those in the inner circle as one of their own.[18] The key ambassadorial posts were usually awarded to insiders, like Granvelle for France, Soria for Genoa, and Cifuentes for the papal court in Rome. When Ferdinand was required to send an envoy to the Sublime Porte in Istanbul, Charles prevailed upon his brother to appoint first Cornelis de Schepper (a protégé of Gattinara) and later Geraard Veltwijk (a protégé of Granvelle); both were humanist scholars who had risen through the ranks to become members of the Council of State in Brussels.[19] Finally, for managing his affairs in Italy, Charles depended on members of Aragonese noble families whose presence in the Kingdom of Naples dated from its conquest by Alfonso V (d. 1455): Antonio de Leyva, prince of Ascoli; Ferrante de Avalos, marquis of Pescara (d. 1525); and Pescara's nephew, Alfonso de Avalos, marquess of Vasto. Though repeatedly entrusted with commands in Italy and beyond, these men were never part of the inner circle. For the key post in Italy, the viceroy of Naples, Charles turned to Lannoy (1522–1527), Orange (1527–1530), and Pedro de Toledo (1532–1553) – never a Leyva, a Pescara, or a Vasto (see Chapter 13).

In practice it is sometimes difficult to separate the emperor's personal council – those who attended on him wherever he was – from the councils

---

[16] William S. Maltby, *Alba: A Biography of Fernando Alvarez de Toledo, Third Duke of Alba, 1507–1582* (Berkeley, 1983); Hernándo Sanchez, *Castilla y Napoles.*

[17] Keniston, *Francisco de los Cobos*; Granvelle to Cobos, 10 February 1540, Estado, 497.

[18] There is unfortunately no modern biography of Doria, but for an excellent study of Doria (with his kinsmen and rivals) in the context of Genoese politics and Genoese banking, see Pacini, *La Genova di Andrea Doria nell'impero di Carlo V.* See also his "Genoa and the Genoese in the Spanish Imperial System," in Blockmans and Mout, *The World of Charles V.*

[19] Robert Finlay, "Prophecy and Politics in Istanbul: Charles V, Sultan Suleyman, and the Habsburg Embassy of 1533–1534," *Journal of Early Modern History* 2 (1998): 249–272.

of state in his various realms.[20] Indeed, the same man, serving in the two capacities, could be pulled in different directions.[21] On the occasions when those giving their opinions on a particular matter are listed by name, one finds councillors of both types joining in with no apparent differentiation. For example, when Castile's Council of State voted (1528) on whether Charles should engage the king of France in single combat, those voting included four men who had recently come from the Netherlands in Charles's train: Granvelle, Nassau, Praet, and Poupet de la Chaulx. When the Council of State in Brussels gave its advice on whether Charles should seek a personal meeting with the warring kings of France and England (1545), the duke of Alba and Juan de Figueroa, president of Castile's Consejo de Estado, voted along with their Low Countries peers.[22] There was nonetheless an important difference between councillors of a realm, interpreting their loyalty to Charles in terms of local interests, and the traveling councillors who were expected to adopt a dynasty-wide perspective. This was probably the reason why Charles never named a Neapolitan as viceroy of Naples.[23]

Elements of a Grand Strategy

World Emperor, Leader of Christendom, or Head of the House of Austria?
From an early date, key members of Charles's entourage promoted the idea that their sovereign was marked out by God to be *imperator mundi*, emperor of the whole world. This was apparently why the sixteen–year-old archduke of Burgundy chose as his personal device the Pillars of Hercules (Straits of Gibraltar), an emblem symbolizing not merely the known limits of navigation but also the idea of a metaphorical "No Farther" (*Non Plus Ultra*) setting bounds to human pride. The motto affixed to his device, *Plus Ultra* ("Farther," that is, beyond the Straits of Gibraltar), could refer either to the lands across the sea newly discovered by Spain, or to the

---

[20] Santiago Fernández Conti, "El gobierno de los asuntos y la guerra en Castilla durante el reinado del Emperador Carlos V," in Martínez Millán, *Instituciones y elites de poder*, 73: on leaving Spain for Italy in 1529, Charles decreed that eight members of his council should accompany him, while four others remained behind to serve as Empress Isabella's council of state.

[21] Maltby, *Alba*, 41: "[Alba's] Castilianism and pride of caste would always be at war with his allegiance to an international and theoretically absolute monarchy."

[22] Charles's instructions for Willem van Montfoort, 8 October 1528, *Familienkorrespondenz*, Letter 232, II, 307–308; Alba to Cobos, 4 October 1545, *Corpus Documental*, Letter CCCXXXII, II, 426.

[23] The national prejudices of Charles's advisers were another reason: Pierre de Veyre to Charles, 30 September 1527, Lanz, Letter 101, I, 251–252, passing on the advice of a Castilian long in Spanish service in Naples, Don Hugo de Moncada, viceroy of Sicily, not to name a native to the post, "for all of them together have not the savoir faire of a good half viceroy."

idea that this was a prince who brooked no limits.[24] To many politically conscious Europeans, including some of his own subjects,[25] Charles seemed in fact the very incarnation of an overweening thirst for domination, an Alexander *redivivus*, not to be satisfied until he had brought the whole earth under his rule. Meanwhile, the struggle for power between Christendom and Islamdom was in the popular imagination projected onto a global stage. Both Christian and Islamic lands were rife with prophecies that a single ruler must come to be master of the whole world, either Charles himself, or his great Ottoman Turkish rival, Sultan Suleyman the Lawgiver (r. 1520–1566).[26]

Within the inner circle, the chief protagonist of the idea of world empire was Gattinara, Charles's tutor in foreign affairs. Gattinara sought to inculcate political sagacity in the young emperor through nuggetlike aphorisms, like those favored by educators of the day.[27] For example, if "Genoa and Milan are the gate and the key for keeping and controlling Italy," then "Italy well and truly subjected to your authority is the seat and scepter for dominating all the world."[28] In the language of the period, the Latin *regnum* meant kingship over a particular territory, while the Greek *monarchia* denoted a universal monarchy. Scholars have differing opinions about whether Charles himself embraced Gattinara's vision of *monarchia*,[29] but in his mature years he disclaimed such ambition. In a speech before the papal court (1536), apparently not vetted in advance

[24] Burke, "Presenting and Re-Presenting Charles, V," 422–425; Earl Rosenthal, "*Plus Ultra* and the Columnar Device of Emperor Charles V," *Journal of the Wartburg and Courtauld Institutes* 34 (1971): 204–228. The twin pillars of Charles's device became the twin-pillar emblem of Spain's gold reales, later transmuted into the dollar sign.

[25] See the opinions of Erasmus of Rotterdam, a typical Netherlander in his suspicions about the ambitions of Charles V and his government, as discussed in James D. Tracy, *Erasmus of the Low Countries* (Berkeley and Los Angeles, 1996), 171–174.

[26] Sanjay Subrahmanyam, "Du Tage au Gange au XVIe siècle: Vne. Conjuncture Millénariste à l'échelle Eurasiatique," *Annales* 56 (2001): 51–84. Finlay, "Prophecy and Politics in Istanbul." Cf. Erasmus to an Italian correspondent, dated Freiburg, 11 April 1531: "The rumor here – indeed, not a rumor, but public knowledge – is that the Turk will invade Germany with all his forces, to do battle for the great prize, whether Charles or the Turk be monarch [*monarcha*] of the entire globe, for the world cannot any longer bear to have two suns in the sky": P. S. Allen, *Opus Epistolarum Desiderii Erasmi Roterodami* (12 vols., Oxford, 1906–1958), IX, 254 (my translation).

[27] The best-known example would be Erasmus, *Adagiorum Chiliades* (Venice: Aldus Manutius, 1508, and Basel: Froben, 1515).

[28] Minute of a meeting of Charles's council (November–December 1523) at which Gattinara was present, in "Berichte," XIX, 1941, 165–257, Document 2, 211–213. Cf. Margaret of Austria's appeal to Charles to keep Milan for himself, rather than returning it to the control of Duke Francesco Sforza, because "it is the key to Italy, by which the Kingdom of Naples can be preserved."

[29] For a good summary of arguments pro and con, Alfred Kohler, *Karl V, 1500–1558. Eine Biographie* (Munich, 1999), 94–102.

by his advisers, Charles rejected the charge that he sought *monarchia*.[30] He was not the aggressor, but merely the defender of his inherited lands against attack by France and other enemies. He was also, as emperor, the paladin of Catholic Christendom, responsible to God for its defense against the machinations of Lutheran heretics, Turkish infidels, and perfidious Frenchmen. To refute the more specific charge that he was aiming at "tyranny" over Italy, he pointed to his willingness to entrust Milan to a friendly third party (this too had been part of Gattinara's teaching), rather than claiming it for himself, even though Milan was an imperial fief.[31] Yet if one makes allowances for ordinary political suspicions, the informal hegemony that Charles maintained in Italy, so long as he ruled in Naples and had disposition over Milan, was not very different from the tyranny that Italian states feared.[32] Similarly, when Charles presented himself as the chief defender of Christendom, refusing (for example) to share with France's Francis I the command of a proposed expedition against the Turks,[33] was he acting on behalf of Christendom, or on behalf of the House of Austria? This question, perhaps never answered clearly even in Charles's own mind, shadowed his reign as emperor from the first years until the end.

One may also put the question more concretely: was Charles the paladin of Christendom, faithfully defending the Catholic Church against all its enemies, despite the perfidy of some Catholic princes? Or were France's Valois monarchs, Francis I and Henry II, the defenders of Europe's liberty against the overweening ambition of an Alexander *redivivus*? The Habsburg-Valois rivalry, the key to many other strategic issues, is complicated enough to require a separate discussion (see Chapter 2).

[30] Charles's report of his speech: to Hannart, his ambassador to France, 17 April 1536, in Lanz, Letter 428, II, 226. See the comment by Fernández Alvárez, *Corpus Documental*, at Letter CXCVII, I, 490–491. Cf. Francis I's oblique characterization of Charles's motives, as reported by Granvelle: "Those who desire peace in Christendom can see that, for his [Francis's] part, he makes no claim to monarchie": Granvelle to Charles, 31 March 1528, Lanz, Letter 107, I, 265–270; and Charles's instructions for Montfoort on his mission to Ferdinand, 3 April 1529, referring to Suleyman's "insaciable apetito de hazerse monarca y senor universal," in *Familienkorrespondenz*, Letter 279, III, 386–396.

[31] See the minute of Charles's council (1523) cited in note 28; also Charles to Clement VII, 18 September 1526, Lanz, Letter 94, I, 219–221; Ferdinand (who wanted Milan for himself) to Charles, 31 May 1527, *Familienkorrespondenz*, Letter 69, II, 85–88; and Charles to Isabella, 18 April 1536, *Corpus Documental*, Letter CXCVII, I, 488–489.

[32] For a recent Italian overview of the Wars of Italy (1494–1559), Susanna Peyronel Rambaldi, "Milano nel tempo delle guerre d'Italia," in Franco Della Peruta, ed., *Storia illustrata di Milano* (7 vols., Milan, 1992–1997), IV, 981–1000.

[33] A point made by Mia Rodriguez-Salgado, "Obeying the Ten Commandments: Charles V and France in the 1520s," in Blockmans and Mout, *The World of Charles V.*

"*Conjuncture*"

In each of Charles's realms, subjects and councillors alike thought in terms of settled interests that changed little from one reign to the next, like fending off raids by North African corsairs along the Spanish and Neapolitan coasts, or, in the Low Countries, turning back incursions by Rhenish princes allied with France. By contrast, the discussions within Charles's inner circle were dominated by a keen sense of *conjuncture*, meaning an ephemeral constellation of circumstances favorable or adverse to particular interests of the dynasty. Thus in 1523 Charles hoped to time his planned departure for Italy to coincide with the announcement by the constable of Bourbon, a prince of the blood royal, that he was renouncing his allegiance to France; "con aquella bona conyuntura," Charles believed, one could hope for good results against the French in Italy. In 1528, just after a large French force attacking Naples had been defeated, Charles urged Ferdinand to take advantage of "les choses advenues en si bonne conjuncture" by attacking France from the east. In 1535, having just conquered Tunis, Charles and his advisers considered an immediate strike against Algiers, the new corsair base in North Africa, because "en esta conyuntura con la reputacion de la victoria" one could accomplish the objective "more easily than at other times." In 1545, sensing that the warring kings of France and England both desired peace, Charles wrote Mary that "la vraye conjuncture" had come for advancing Habsburg interests by mediating a truce between the two.[34] To judge from their correspondence, Charles and his entourage thought of the dynasty not so much as having settled interests but as being confronted with constantly shifting perils and opportunities. Thus, although incoming letters pleading for the abiding concerns of the various realms were always received courteously, the tacit understanding was that a problem could only be addressed when the time was ripe.

Going to War, and Building an Army

On military issues, the inner circle, representing in the aggregate an impressive experience of war and politics in various parts of Europe, tried to help Charles guess where the dynasty's resources might best be allocated. Was the king of France likely to go to war in the coming campaign season? And would the pope and other Italian princes of dubious loyalty support him if he did? When hostile armies were already mobilizing the questions were more pressing: were the troops massing in the south of

---

[34] Charles to Soria, 14 December 1523, *Corpus Documental*, Letter XIX, I, 88–89; Charles's instructions for Montfoort, 8 October 1528, *Familienkorrespondenz*, Letter 232, vol. II, 301–303; Charles to Soria, 16 August 1535, *Corpus Documental* CLXXXI, II, 441–444; Charles to Mary, 6 August 1543, HHSA-B, PA 42, Konvolutz; cf. Alba to Cobos, 4 October 1545, *Corpus Documental*, Letter CCCXXXII, II, 426.

France intended for a strike across the Alps, or across the Pyrenees; and would the great army the sultan was raising march this year against his foe to the east, the Shah of Iran, or against Habsburg Austria? Reports from Charles's ambassadors and from other sources[35] were read aloud and weighed against the experience of those present. It goes almost without saying that a decision to expect or initiate hostilities in one quarter always entailed a complementary decision to avoid war on other fronts. For example, when Charles anticipated a renewal of war with France, he would send instructions to Ferdinand to seek a truce with the Ottomans and, likewise, with Janos Zapolyai, the Transylvanian magnate who, backed by the Sublime Porte, contested Ferdinand's claim to the Hungarian crown.[36] When Charles planned a naval campaign against Tunis or Algiers, Mary of Hungary in Brussels would be instructed to bend over backward to avoid giving France any excuse to invade the Low Countries.

The likely theater of conflict being identified, it remained to determine what level of forces was required. As the reign advanced, so too did the size of the armies required. France's use of siege artillery in successive invasions of Italy (starting in 1494), battering down with little trouble the high curtain walls of medieval towns, had changed the character of warfare. In response, Italian military architects created a new system of fortification involving low, earth-backed walls, which could absorb the impact of shot, and triangular projections (bastions),which were used both for flanking fire along the walls and for the emplacement of cannon to keep besiegers at a distance. Owing to its great expense, the so-called *trace italienne* spread only slowly from northern Italy to the rest of Europe. But even if present only here and there, such fortifications meant that armies had to be much larger in order to reduce important towns. King Charles VIII of France had invaded Italy with 18,000 men in 1494, but Francis I led a force of 32,000 across the Alps in 1525, and Henry II had 40,000 under his command when he captured the imperial city of Metz in 1552.[37]

Deciding what kinds of troops to engage – especially the infantry – was at least as important as deciding how many men were needed. By twice

---

[35] E.g., Giovan Battista Lomellino, governor of the province of Bari and Otranto and marquis of Atripalda, who frequently collected and passed on directly to Charles information from his network of spies and informants about Ottoman provinces on the other side of the Adriatic: José Maria de Morial, *El Virrey de Napoles Don Pedro de Toledo y la guerra contro el Turco* (Madrid, 1966), 61–80.

[36] At the death of Louis Jagiello (battle of Mohaćs, 1526), Mary of Hungary's brother, Ferdinand, claimed the crowns of both Bohemia and Hungary, according to the terms of a Habsburg-Jagiello marriage treaty of 1515. In Bohemia his claim was not disputed. In Hungary he was able to establish his authority in some parts of the kingdom that had not fallen under Ottoman control after 1526. But Szapolyai's claim was backed by many among the nobility and supported by the Porte.

[37] Geoffrey Parker, *The Military Revolution* (Cambridge, 1988), chap. 1, "The Military Revolution Revisited." On the bastion trace, Faro, *Il sistema e la città*, and Duffy, *Siege Warfare*.

trouncing Charles's great-grandfather, Duke Charles the Bold of Burgundy (d. 1477), the Swiss opened a new age in European warfare, dominated by infantry. The men of the Swiss cantons, planting their fifteen-foot pikes, could stop any cavalry charge; massed in great phalanxes and trained to charge in unison, they could break any enemy line. Under the aegis of Ferdinand of Aragón, Charles's maternal grandfather, Spain's commanders developed improvements on Swiss tactics, especially during the war that resulted in the conquest of Granada, Iberia's last Muslim principality (1492). Instead of being massed in phalanxes, the infantry comprised smaller units or companies, each of which included a number of men – perhaps a sixth – armed with arquebuses. In battle, *arcabuceros* and field artillery were positioned between squares of pikemen, to have a clear field of fire. The efficacy of this formation was proven anew when Ferdinand's commander in Italy, Gonsalvo de Córdoba, ended the brief French occupation of Naples and claimed the kingdom for Ferdinand (1503). While French cavalry outnumbered the infantry two to one, as was common in medieval armies, Gonsalvo's infantry outnumbered his cavalry three to one. This was to be the pattern for Charles V's wars.[38]

During the first decade or so of Charles's reign, it became common to organize infantry companies of 300 to 500 men in groups of ten, under a senior captain with the title of *maestre de campo*. In a military ordinance issued following his failed campaign into Provence (Genoa, October 1536), Charles, in speaking of his Spanish infantry, refers for the first time to the *tercio* of Naples and Sicily, the *tercio* of Lombardy, and the *tercio* of Malaga (men recruited for the Tunis campaign who had fought also in Provence). According to René Quatrefages, it is not clear that in this text the term has anything more than its literal meaning, that is, the "third" of the infantry based in Naples and Sicily, the third based on Lombardy, and so on. Very soon, however, a *tercio* came to mean a regiment of ten companies under a *maestre de campo*. There were to be roughly 300 men per company, while two of the ten companies were now made up entirely of *arcabuceros*.[39]

To Charles's subjects, for whom foreign soldiers of any kind were a curse, Spaniards were no better than the rest. When he saw the havoc wreaked by a Spanish contingent near Krems in Austria (1532), Roeulx for once found peasant complaints about the passage of armies all too believable. Mary of Hungary would have preferred Germans to the Spaniards

---

[38] For the best account of these developments, see René Quatrefages, "L'organisation militaire de l'Espagne, 1492–1592," Thèse de doctorat, Université de Paris-IV, 1989; Luis A. Ribot Garcia, "Les types d'armée en Espagne au début des temps modernes," in Philippe Contamine, ed., *Guerre et concurrence entre les États européens du XIVe au XVIIIe siècle* (Paris, 1998), 52–53.

[39] Quatrefages, "L'organisation militaire de l'Espagne," 311–347; R. Trevor Davies, *The Golden Century of Spain* (New York, 1965), 22–24.

Charles sent for the defense of the Low Countries (1543), because they were easier to send home once the campaigning season was over. Towns in Naples sometimes rioted against their Spanish garrisons, and the kingdom's Parlamento demanded cancellation of the special tax that was levied in their support.[40] But Charles and his military advisers regarded the Spanish infantry to be without peer in battle conditions. Following the great victory at Pavia (1525; see Chapter 2), Lannoy said that despite not having been paid for three months, his Spaniards "did wonders, and in one charge they won the day." Five years later Charles hoped the 2,000 Spaniards he sent from his Italian garrisons might help Ferdinand reconquer the portions of Hungary now controlled by the Ottomans.[41] To be sure, the reputation of Spain's fighting men led to conflicting demands for their use. In 1543 the emperor wanted 2,000 men who had just returned from Spain's North African outposts sent on to Italy. But Philip, speaking for the Consejo de Estado, insisted that they were needed for the key Pyrenees border town of Perpignan, threatened by the French. Bowing to necessity, Charles countermanded his order because "the seas are not safe" for bringing men to Italy.[42]

Swiss pikemen would have been the best alternative. In France they commanded a better wage than the highly sought south German *Landsknechte*.[43] Charles carefully maintained the treaty of friendship the Austrian side of his family had concluded with the Swiss Confederation, but he could not match the pensions that kept leading men of various cantons loyal to France and assured Swiss regiments for any French force marching into Italy.[44] Instead, Charles's recruiters turned to the densely populated countryside of south Germany – High Germany, for contemporaries, as distinct

[40] Rouelx to Charles, 6 September 1532, Lanz, Letter 290, II, 5; Mary to Charles, 24 February 1543, Aud., 54, 22–25v (see also Charles to Mary, 25 July 1545, HHSA-B, PA 42, Konvolut 2, authorizing 15,000 Holland pounds for damages to civilian property done by these same Spaniards); Hernándo Sanchez, *Castilla y Napoles*, 389, and D'Agostino, *Parlamento e società, nel regno di Napoli*, 282, 296.

[41] Lannoy to Charles, 25 February 1525, Lanz, Letter 62, I, 153–154; Charles to Isabella, 8 July 1530, *Corpus Documental*, Letter LXXVI, I, 218.

[42] Philip to Charles, 7 August 1543, *Corpus Documental*, Letter CCLIX, II, 143; Charles to Phillip, 27 October 1543, *Corpus Documental*, Letter CCLXII, II, 167. According to I. A. A. Thompson, *War and Government in Habsburg Spain, 1560–1620* (London, 1976), 104, it was not until the 1570s that it became difficult to find new recruits for Spain's *tercios*.

[43] Hamon, *L'argent du roi*, 26: in 1523, Swiss mercenaries were paid seven livres tournois a month, south German *Landsknechte* six, and French *aventuriers* five.

[44] Charles to Ferdinand, 25 May 1524, *Familienkorrespondenz*, Letter 69, I, 131–133; Ferdinand to Charles, 4 May 1525, *Familienkorrespondenz*, Letter 139, I, 296; and Cornelis de Schepper to Charles, 17 December 1531, Lanz, Letter 256, I, 636–637. Hamon, *L'argent du roi*, 53, estimates pensions to private persons in Switzerland during the reign of Francis I at between 40,000 and 50,000 ecus per year.

from the Lowland plains of the north. The key for tapping into this pool of manpower was to keep "military enterprisers" on one's payroll.[45] Charles either had Ferdinand make arrangements for him or, as in 1534, instructed his special envoy to Germany to meet with the "supreme captains" or "colonels," each of whom was to have ten "captains" ready if needed to command a "banner" of (usually) 400 men. These commander-recruiters had the trust of men who had fought with them, and they also had sufficient credit to keep the men marching when money from the emperor's paymasters ceased to flow. One colonel, Franz von Thamise, complained of having to keep fifteen banners of men at his own expense for seven weeks.[46]

Even an army mainly composed of infantry still needed cavalry support. Charles could recruit heavy cavalry in Germany, in the same way he recruited *Landsknechte*, or he could call upon his *guardas* in Castille, or his *compagnies d'ordonnance* in the Low Countries. For light cavalry, needed for scouting and for mobility, he had *jinetes* from Spain or Italy, but his recruiting ranged far afield, sometimes extending to Poland or Albania. He also needed engineers to supervise field works and cannoneers for the siege guns, not to mention wagoneers to manage the artillery and supply trains, and "pioneers" to do the labor of entrenching that soldiers often scorned. Nonetheless, in this age of infantry, if his *tercios* were en route to the designated point of assembly, and his military enterprisers had the recruitment of *Landsknechte* well in hand, Charles knew he had the basic building blocks for a successful strike force – if, that is, that the men who had sworn fealty to him would be paid well enough to continue marching under the imperial standard.

"Putting My Own Person at Risk"
Though deemed more reliable than their Low German counterparts,[47] High German *Landsknechte* could cause a great deal of trouble if neither the emperor's paymasters nor their own commanders were able to pay their wages. In the terminology of the era, a "pay" (*paye* or *paga*) was a month's wages for one man – for example, 4 Rhine gulden (2.83 Spanish ducats)

---

[45] Redlich, *The German Military Enterpriser.*

[46] Roland von Hemste (brother of Franz von Hemste, also known as Thamise) to Charles, 7 April 1536, Lanz, Letter 423, II, 218–219.

[47] Praet to Charles, 24 September 1542, assessing the fighting qualities of various contingents raised by Mary, Lanz, Letter 498, II, 264–267: there are some good men among the Low Germans, but "some of them are very badly trained [*conditionez*] and disobedient"; Mary to Granvelle, 1 July 1545, HHSA-B, PA 41, Konvolut 1, attempting to dissuade Charles from the war against German Protestants he now contemplated: High German troops could not be trusted [presumably because of Lutheranism], but Low Germans (Anabaptists and Sacramentarians) would be worse – could one truly pursue a holy cause by employing such execrable men?

for a foot soldier.[48] Conscious of the demand for their services, mercenaries sometimes held their employers to ransom. In 1526 a force of High Germans at Cartagena refused to embark for Italy unless guaranteed 15,000 "pays" per month, instead of the 12,000 for which they had contracted. In 1528 the banner captains themselves threatened to lead a pillage of Buda, still loyal to Ferdinand, unless their arrears were satisfied. In 1529 men who had just helped withstand the Turkish siege of Vienna cried out "money or blood," demanding 5 pays at once, without subtracting (as was usual) for the food they had consumed and the rooms they had occupied. In 1543 the German troops holding Düren for Charles threatened to surrender the town to the duke of Cleves, the emperor's enemy, if they were not paid.[49]

Particularly embarrassing were the occasions when an army of *Landsknechte* jumped the traces altogether. The German force recruited by Ferdinand for the constable of Bourbon to lead into Italy on Charles's behalf in 1523 "broke up" of its own accord, either because Ferdinand was too far away to keep them in line (as Charles suggested), or because Bourbon had failed to provide the cavalry arm on which infantry depended for its safety. The same thing happened with troops sent to Italy under Duke Henry of Brunswick in 1528, either "because of the machinations of our enemies" (as Charles was told) or simply from want of pay.[50] The worst such incident occurred in 1527, when a large and poorly paid force in Lombardy refused orders to march to the aid of Naples, then besieged by the French. Instead, the mixed army of Germans and Spaniards and Italians, nominally under Bourbon's command, cut a swath of destruction through the Papal States, culminating in the frightful Sacco di Roma (see Chapter 2).[51]

---

[48] Charles to Ferdinand, 5 October 1531, *Familienkorrespondenz*, Letter 553, IV, 367–369: eight banners of High Germans, with 400 men each, were reckoned at 4,320 "pays," since for each banner one had to count 40 "lost pays" (320 in all) for the salaries of captains, flag bearers, sergeants, and provosts. Each man was to receive 4 Rhine gulden for a month calculated at thirty days. Spanish infantry on garrison duty in Naples at this time received 3.25 Spanish ducats per month: Morial, *El Virrey de Napoles y la guerra contro il Turco*, 111.

[49] Lannoy's instructions for J. Durant, 17 May 1527, Lanz, Letter 284, I, 692–694; Mary to Ferdinand, 23 August 1528, *Familienkorrespondenz*, Letter 216, II, 278–282; Ferdinand's instructions for Salinas, after 16 November 1529, *Corpus Documental*, Letter XLVII, I, 179–180; Mary to Charles, 4 January 1543, Aud. 54, 8–9v.

[50] Charles to Ferdinand, December 1523, *Familienkorrespondenz*, Letter 48, I, 78–79, and Hannart to Charles, 13 March 1524, Lanz, Letter 52, I, 108–109; Charles to Ferdinand, 9 October 1528, *Familienkorrespondenz*, Letter 234, II, 308–314, and Charles's instructions for Sanchez, 8 November 1528, *Familienkorrespondenz*, Letter 240, II, 328–329.

[51] Lannoy's instructions for Durant, 27 May 1527, Lanz, Letter 284, I, 702–705; De Veyre to Charles, 30 September 1527, Lanz, Letter 101, I, 249–251; Charles to Ferdinand, 27 November 1527, *Familienkorrespondenz*, Letter 130, II, 148–152. For the ensuing propaganda war, focusing on whether

Disasters like this will have given Charles occasion to ponder whether he might not have a better chance of holding troops together if he commanded them in person. But whether the emperor should "put my own person at risk" in this way was perhaps the most contentious of all the questions Charles and his advisers had to settle. The hazards were only too obvious. In 1529, when it became clear that Charles was resolved to lead a campaign in Italy, Margaret of Austria tried to warn him off by recalling recent history: in 1477 their ancestor, Duke Charles the Bold, brought shame and defeat on the House of Burgundy by leading his army against superior forces in a vain attempt to conquer Lorraine; in 1494 France's Charles VIII marched the length of Italy to conquer Naples, only to see victory melt away as his army, decimated by malaria, was forced into an ignominious retreat. In 1538, when Charles communicated a secret plan to lead an armada against Istanbul, the very citadel of the Grand Turk, Mary of Hungary besought him to think how he would answer before God for what might befall Christendom, not to mention his own family, if such an expedition were to meet disaster. In 1543, learning of Charles's decision to lead his troops into battle in the Rhineland, Mary again begged her brother to consider how much depended on the safety of his person. Charles's reply was nicely attuned to the fighting spirit of a woman who, during the previous campaign season, had done everything but mount a horse and lead men into the fray herself: "I promise you I will do nothing you would not do, if you were in my place."[52]

Charles faced competing demands. On one hand, the Consejo de Estado in Valladolid threw cold water on almost any scheme that would have Castile's monarch gallivanting off to foreign parts.[53] On the other hand, his presence was insistently required wherever a Habsburg realm suffered enemy invasion. For example, in 1538, Mary of Hungary withheld the just-mentioned letter about Charles's plan for Istanbul from her Council of State, lest councillors "despair" when they grasped that Charles would not be coming to the Low Countries to lead them in repelling the French. In November 1542, having turned back a French invasion but expecting another in the spring, Mary shamed Charles into promising to come the

---

the *Landsknechte* were or were not acting under orders from Charles, see John Headley, *The Emperor and His Chancellor: A Study in the Imperial Chancery under Gattinara* (Cambridge, 1983), 110–113.

[52] Margaret to Charles, 26 May 1529, Lanz, Letter 117, I, 302–303; Mary to Charles, August 1538, *Staatspapiere*, Document LIIV, 265–266 (the planned expedition against Istanbul never took place); Mary to Charles, 29 October 1543, Lanz, Letter 513, II, 404; Charles to Mary, 30 October 1543, Lanz, Letter 514, II, 405. For Mary's conduct of the defense of the Low Countries against simultaneous invasions from France and the Rhineland in 1542, see Doyle, "The Heart and Stomach of a King but the Body of a Woman," chap. 7.

[53] E.g., Consulta of the Consejo de Estado, 1 May 1538, Estado 637, 94: it would be "dangerous" for Charles to go to Germany to hold an imperial diet, as the Roman Curia wanted him to do.

following year by reminding him of his pledge to deputies of the provincial states: "They say you promised them that if we sustained the first shock of combat, you would not fail to come to their aid with all your strength." At the end of 1544, hobbled by gout and preoccupied by the affairs of Germany, Charles wiggled out of a written promise to the Hungarian Diet to join Ferdinand in a campaign against the Turks the following summer, instructing his emissary, Geraard Veltwijk, not to say anything that might bind him to come in person. But Ferdinand gave Veltwijk strict orders "not to say a word to anyone" about this article of his instructions, fearing that any report that Charles was not coming might prompt Hungary's magnates to shift their allegiance to the sultan.[54]

How were these conflicting priorities of the various Habsburg realms to be sorted out? Charles seems to have given special weight to two issues. The first was his sense of the needs of the dynasty. He was eager to go to Italy in the 1520s, not just because of Gattinara's exalted conception of Italy's place in the world, but because according to medieval tradition an emperor-elect could only be crowned by the pope, in Italy. As he explained to his brother, one could not think of securing Ferdinand's position in Germany by getting him recognized as King of the Romans (heir apparent) until Charles himself was crowned.[55] The second consideration, complicated enough to require separate discussion, involved the emperor's sense of his own honor and reputation.

"Honor and Reputation"

While Charles was campaigning in Provence in 1536, the Consejo de Estado deliberated on what he ought to do in the coming weeks: if Francis I should invade Italy, even more if he should invade Spain, Charles's "honor" required confronting his enemy on the field of battle; if not, he should return to Spain, the sooner the better. In 1542, hearing that Francis was leading an army against Perpignan, to be supported from the sea by Turkish galleys, Charles wrote Tavera, "I have determined to put my own person at risk" to oppose him (in the event, he did not). In 1543, on the point of departing for a campaign against the imperial princes in the Rhineland who had joined with France in attacking the Low Countries, he explained his reasoning in a secret instruction for Philip:

---

[54] Mary to Charles, August 1538, cited in note 52; Mary to Charles, 28 November 1542, Aud. 53, 342v–343; Veltwijk to Charles, 11 December 1544, Lanz, Letter 529, II, 419–420, and Charles to Ferdinand, 15 January 1545, HHSA-B, PA 5, Konvolut 1.

[55] Charles to Ferdinand, 26 March 1525, *Familienkorrespondenz*, Letter 133, I, 178; Consulta of the Consejo de Estado, November 1526, *Corpus Documental*, Letter XXIV, I, 117–118. Fernández Alvárez notes that the crusade motif was stressed in official explanations for the journey to Italy Charles eventually did make in 1529: Charles's "poder" for Isabella to govern in his absence, 8 March 1529, *Corpus Documental*, Letter XXXV, I, 143–147.

I undertake this journey against my will, for the sake of honor and reputation [*honra y reputacion*], for if our vassals will not serve us, one cannot sustain the burden of governing.... This voyage is full of danger for my honor and reputation, for my life and for my house; and may it please God it is not dangerous also for my soul, as I trust it is not, for I undertake it with good intention, to provide a remedy for preserving what has been given me, and not to leave you, my son, poor and robbed of authority.... Believe that what I do has been forced upon me to preserve my honor, for without it my ability to govern and your inheritance will be diminished.[56]

The same logic applied to Charles's understanding of his position as Christendom's anointed leader in the age-long struggle against Islamdom. In April 1532, writing from Regensburg, Charles outlined for Isabella a scenario that would delay his return to Spain: "In view of my obligation to defend the faith and the Christian religion, and finding myself here [in Germany], I have decided that if the Turk comes in person, which he can only do at the head of a great force, I will go forth with all the forces I can find to resist him." In the ensuing months Sultan Suleyman did in fact lead a large army against Austria. True to his word, Charles joined Ferdinand at the head of a huge Christian war flotilla that embarked at Regensburg for the voyage downriver to Vienna, only to find that the Ottoman army had already withdrawn (see Chapter 7).[57] In the summer of 1534 Kheir-ad-Din Barbarossa, captain general of the Ottoman fleet, commanded a fleet of seventy galleys that raided at will along the north coast of Sicily and the west coast of Naples before turning south to occupy Tunis, which Barbarossa clearly intended to use as a base for further operations. It was the humiliation dealt him by Barbarossa's voyage that led Charles to take personal command of the armada against North Africa that had been discussed for several years and was now to be directed against Tunis (1535; Chapter 7).[58]

In the sixteenth century, subjects all across Europe groaned under the weight of war taxation. Historians doubt that the cumulative fiscal burden was in fact greater than it had been in the past, adjusting for inflation,[59] but there is no mistaking the resentment and sense of hardship provoked

---

[56] Consulta of the Consejo de Estado, October 1536, Lanz, Letter 446, II, 263–267; Charles to Tavera, 26 July 1542, *Corpus Documental*, Letter CCXLIV, II, 78–79; Charles's secret instruction for Philip, 6 May 1543, *Corpus Documental*, Letter CCLII, II, 105 (unlike the "ostensible instruction," to be shared with the Consejo, this document was to be kept by Philip under lock and key, to be seen by no one, except in the event of Charles's death, in which case it was to be read aloud to the Cortes).

[57] Charles to Isabella, the second of two letters dated 6 April 1532, *Corpus Documental*, Letter CXXXVIII, I, 350–351.

[58] Morial, *El Virrey de Napoles Don Pedro de Toledo*, 99–100, 169–172.

[59] Juan Gelabert, "The Fiscal Burden," in Bonney, *Economic Systems and State Finance*, 539–576, especially, the section on "The Fiscal Burden in the Sixteenth Century," 557–564.

by taxes that were at least nominally higher. Yet subjects complained even more about a ruler who suffered his territory to be invaded with impunity. "Honor and reputation" was thus a precious asset for the ruler and his lands, not a mere chivalric fantasy. It was, in effect, the keystone in a conceptual arch forming the grand strategy that guided Charles and his advisers.

Chapter 2

The Habsburg-Valois Struggle: Italy, 1515–1528

Gattinara's outline of Habsburg grand strategy (1523) called for preserving the Kingdom of Naples, and keeping Italy in good order, through ensuring that the two key northern centers, Milan and Genoa, remained in friendly hands. But this seemingly simple plan for control of the peninsula faced three formidable obstacles: the political instability of northern and central Italy as a whole; the delicate equilibrium of hostile factions in each of the two great cities, Milan and Genoa; and, most important, the ambition and great wealth of France, Europe's most populous kingdom.

For hundreds of years, towns in northern and central Italy – except for Venice[1] – had been divided by rivalries between noble clans loosely identified with Italy's pro- or antiimperial factions, known since the early thirteenth century as the Ghibellines and the Guelphs. In the high and late Middle Ages, during periods of open warfare between the papacy and the Holy Roman Empire, families like the Orsini of Rome and the Este of Ferrara rallied to the papacy, while the Colonna of Rome and the Gonzaga of Mantua defended the imperial cause. During Charles V's reign, the Orsini and the Este could still be counted on (most of the time) to fight for France,[2] while the Colonna and the Gonzaga were, like their ancestors, fairly dependable allies of the emperor.[3] In many towns this conflict among the great families was overlain by another, which pitted the *popolo* – families connected with the merchant or craft guilds – against the arrogant behavior of the magnates. As any reader of Dante's *Comedy* knows, families who lost out in these struggles were not just deprived of

---

[1]   Hence the proud title Venice claimed for itself: La Repubblica Serenissima. Modern historians have qualified but not overturned Venice's reputation for freedom from factionalism.

[2]   Italy's loose coalition of local Guelph factions, originally propapal, became pro-French when the popes bestowed the Kingdom of Naples on the House of Anjou.

[3]   For Italian politics of this period, see Francesco Guicciardini, *Storia d'Italia* (5 vols., Bari, 1929), or the abbreviated English version, *The History of Italy*, tr. Sidney Alexander (New York, 1969).

office, they were often deprived of their property and driven from the city. Hence Italy's towns were filled with men eating the bitter bread of exile, hoping for a chance to raise an army and strike back, to reclaim their patrimony and their native place. How could any external power, however great, hope to impose a stability of its own making on a country where every important town harbored well-connected families working tirelessly to overturn existing political arrangements somewhere else?

In different ways, Milan and Genoa were special instances of this larger pattern. Milan's Visconti rulers (1302–1451) built a large and prosperous state, extending its boundaries to threaten the Venetian Republic in the east, Florence in the southwest, and, at Bologna, the Papal States in the southeast. Indeed, Giangaleazzo Visconti (d. 1402) made Milan a fief of the empire by purchasing from Emperor Wenceslaus IV the title of duke. But Visconti might also provoked a reaction: Venice abandoned its aloofness from mainland politics in order to carve out a large Terraferma dominion, extending as far inland as Padua. There was also a more basic problem, as Italian historians have noted:[4] Milan's power was built on sand, for as each duke died, his successor had to spend several years reconquering the formerly independent city-states that had taken the occasion to reclaim their liberty. After an unhappy interlude in which Milan's citizens tried with little success to govern themselves as a republic (1451–1454), Francesco Sforza, a mercenary commander, founded a new ducal dynasty that was to last into Charles's reign. But, as before, he who controlled Milan could not be sure of controlling Cremona or Pavia. And if fifteenth-century Venice had reacted with force to a too powerful duke of Milan, how might sixteenth-century Venice respond to a foreign potentate who claimed Milan?

More than most Italian cities, Genoa's history is marked by a double rivalry between Guelph and Ghibelline nobles, on the one hand, and between the *popolo* and noble clans as a group, on the other. In theory, Genoa was governed by a fourteenth-century constitution, the Regolae, which provided that every magistracy should have an equal number of Guelphs and Ghibellines. At the top, there was a doge elected for life, who had to come from the *popolo*. In practice, the city's political life was bedeviled by an ongoing struggle between Guelphs and Ghibellines to secure the election of the right man from the two families that came to dominate the dogeship: the Fregoso, loyal to the Guelphs, or the pro-Ghibelline Adorno. This arrangement was also an invitation for outside powers to throw their weight behind one candidate or another. For example, Ottavio Fregoso ruled as doge with French support (1513–1522), only to be supplanted in a coup led by the Adorno, who took advantage of a Habsburg victory

---

[4] Federico Chabod, *Machiavelli and the Renaissance* (New York, 1954).

over the French near Milan. But Charles's ambassador, Lope de Soria, offended leading Genoese by his tendency to conduct himself more as a proconsul than as the envoy to an independent republic. Hence it was not difficult for Andrea Doria, Genoa's great admiral, to spark a countercoup by bringing his war galleys into the harbor (1528).[5] Genoa was again under a government friendly to France – but for how long?

Charles's grandfather, Emperor Maximilian I, had ambitions in Italy, but he lacked the resources to maintain an army south of the Alps for any length of time. Hence it fell to France to nurture dreams of grandeur in Italy. Having inherited a claim to Naples, tracing back to the Angevin dynasty that had been deplaced by Alfonso V of Aragón (d. 1458), France's King Charles VIII (r. 1484–1498) led an army across the Alps in 1494. He in fact conquered the Kingdom of Naples and held it briefly.[6] But later French ambitions focused more on the duchy of Milan. The childless Charles VIII was succeeded by Louis XII (r. 1498–1514), a prince of the house of Orléans, who had a claim to Milan by virtue of his descent from the Visconti. In 1498 Louis's army overwhelmed the defenses of the Sforza duke of Milan, Lodovico il Moro. Milan was to be French for some years. But Pope Julius II (1504–1513) organized a coalition that included Emperor Maximilian I, King Ferdinand of Aragón and Naples, and the Republic of Venice; the French were expelled from Milan, and a subsequent attempt to recapture the city was also defeated (1512–1513). Had these powers remained united, they might have maintained the status quo in northern Italy. But if French rule could not provide stability for northern Italy, a coalition of this type, based on a fleeting common interest, was even less likely to do so.

From Marignano to Pavia, 1515–1525

The immediate background to Charles's wars in Italy begins with the advent of his great rival, Francis I. Francis sought to begin his reign in the same glorious way as Louis XII, his cousin and predecessor. Leading an army that included 8,000 Gascon "adventurers"[7] and 23,000 south German *Landsknechte*, he crossed the Alps in July 1515. French diplomacy had won over Venice, but Pope Leo X (1513–1521), Ferdinand of Aragón and Naples, and Emperor Maximilian helped pay for the thousands of Swiss who defended Milan for Massimiliano Sforza, Lodovico's

---

5   Pacini, *La Genova dell'Andrea Doria nell'impero di Carlo V*, 51, 77–78.
6   The House of Anjou, a branch of France's royal family, ruled in Naples from 1268 to 1441.
7   Knecht, *Renaissance Warrior and Patron*, 69–70: the *aventuriers* were "volunteers recruited by captains holding a royal commission"; they served not for regular pay, but for the chance of booty.

son. French agents offered the Swiss 1 million crowns to change sides, but the proposed treaty was accepted only by contingents from the western-most cantons. The rest, led by a pro-Habsburg cardinal,[8] marched out of Milan to seek the French army, entrenched at Marignano, to the southeast. For two days of equal and unusually bloody battle, three squares of Swiss pikemen, 7,000 men each, measured their valor against Francis's Gascons and *Landsknechte*; the arrival of Venice's army turned the tide and delivered Milan to France (10–11 September 1515). Maximilian I sought to reverse this decision by a descent into Italy the next spring, but lack of funds forced him to abandon his mercenary army and return ignominiously to Austria. French diplomats now made a bargain with the Swiss Confederation: for a war indemnity of 700,000 crowns, plus an annual subsidy of 2,000 crowns per canton, the Swiss agreed not to fight against France. Meanwhile, Doge Ottavio Fregoso ensured that Genoa's port facilities, including the satellite town of Savona, would be available for France as needed.[9]

Charles's election as emperor (June 1519) portended a new round of war, because tradition required the emperor-elect to be crowned by the pope in Italy. Francis expected Charles to use the occasion to challenge his position in Milan, a fief of the empire. Efforts at reconciliation, including a meeting between the two sovereigns at Guînes in northern France (June 1520),[10] brought no result. The next year Francis arranged an attack on Luxemburg, and an invasion of Navarre that ended with the capture of the important town of Fuenterrabía (October 1521). Meanwhile, Charles made his own plans, winning the adhesion of Leo X through a secret treaty promising that Parma and Piacenza would be detached from the duchy of Milan and incorporated in the Papal States. Charles's captain general in Lombardy, Prospero Colonna (d. 1523), marshaled men from the Spanish garrisons of Naples, German *Landsknechte* sent by Ferdinand, and Swiss mercenaries fighting under the papal banner; in November the imperial army occupied Milan in the name of Francesco Sforza, brother and heir of Massimiliano. In reply, Francis I sent a large contingent of Swiss across the Alps under Odet de Foix, lord of Lautrec. As the two armies skirmished along the Po valley, the Swiss, with pay overdue and rations short, demanded a decisive engagement. Against his will, Lautrec attacked the well-fortified imperialist camp near Monza, on the grounds of a country estate known as La Bicocca. Charging with the ardor that had won so many victories in the past, Swiss pikemen were mowed down by field artillery, and by *arcabuceros* positioned on the flanks of Spanish infantry

[8] Matthaeus Schiner (c. 1465–1522), cardinal-bishop of Sion in the Swiss canton of Valais.
[9] Knecht, *Renaissance Warrior and Patron*, 62–87; Hermann Wiesflecker, *Kaiser Maximilian I* (5 vols., Munich, 1971–1986).
[10] The Field of the Cloth of Gold, orchestrated by England's Cardinal Thomas Wolsey.

units (27 April 1522). As Lautrec retreated across the Alps, Colonna moved
on to Genoa, which his men entered in May; at this point the pro-imperial
Antoniotto Adorno now replaced Fregoso as doge.

The next summer Swiss and Gascon infantry crossed the Alps once
more – Spanish sources estimated their number at 30,000 men – led by
Guillaume de Gouffier, lord of Bonnivet and admiral of France (September
1523). Bonnivet encircled Milan, but could not penetrate imperialist defenses either here or at Pavia. The imperialists were now joined by Duke
Charles of Bourbon, a rebel against his liege lord,[11] and by the new viceroy
of Naples and captain general, Charles de Lannoy. With reinforcements
from Spain and Germany, Lannoy marched out of Pavia but declined
Bonnivet's offer of battle, calculating that a lack of money would cause
the French army to break up. In fact, Bonnivet withdrew to France a few
weeks later (May 1524).[12]

Now began a sequence of events that led to the greatest imperialist
victory of the Italian wars. As Lannoy and Bourbon were mustering out
some of their German infantry, they received instructions from Charles to
carry the war into France with an assault on Marseilles, the chief city of
Provence. Leaving Lannoy at Asti to guard Italy's Alpine frontier, Bourbon
and the marquess of Pescara[13] crossed the Alps in June 1524. From Asti,
fourteen siege cannon were brought by boat up the Tanaro River as far
as possible and thence down through the mountains to Savona, to be
loaded on seventeen galleys commanded by Hugo de Moncada, viceroy
of Sicily, and Rodrigo de Portoundo – the combined fleets of Naples,
Castile, and Sicily.[14] The galleys offloaded the siege guns at Antibes but
could not support the siege of Marseilles, defended by a larger French fleet
commanded by Andrea Doria; instead they occupied the port of Toulon,
from which they sent Bourbon more guns. Bourbon bombarded Marseilles
on 23 August and again a few weeks later, with the added guns from Toulon.
Although breaches were made in the medieval curtain walls, "the ascent
remained difficult, because those within had piled up a mound of dirt two
stories high, which the artillery could not bring down." Marseilles' garrison
commander, Lorenzo Orsini (known as Renzo da Ceri), had adopted the

---

[11] Mainly owing to a dispute over inheritance rights to important lands controlled by the Bourbon,
a branch of France's royal family; Francis I recognized the claims of his mother, Louise of Savoy,
thus setting aside the duke's claim, before the Parlement of Paris had rendered a decision.

[12] Karl Brandi, *Emperor Charles V*, tr. C. V. Wedgwood (New York, 1938), 154–160, 201–216; Knecht,
Renaissance Warrior and Patron, 62–88, 165–184. Bonnivet's infantry is estimated at 30,000 men both
by Mexia, *Historia del Emperador Carlos V*, 331, and by Santa Cruz, *Crónica del Emperador*, I, 67.

[13] Ferrante d'Avalos, uncle of Alfonso d'Avalos, marquess of Vasto; for this family's position in Naples,
see Chapter 13.

[14] For a copy of Portoundo's asiento as captain general of Spain's fleet of eight galleys, dated 21 August
1529, see Gómara, *Crónica de los Barbarrojas*, appendix 26, 493–503.

defense against artillery bombardment developed by Italian engineers some twenty years earlier: a dirt mound or *retirata*, thrown up behind the point at which enemy guns were making a breach, was indeed better that stone or brick walls at absorbing incoming fire.[15] Hearing that the king was forming a large French army, Bourbon raised the siege (29 September) and retreated to Lombardy.[16]

As Francis I began his march across the Alps, the imperialists decided that Leyva would hold Pavia, while Lannoy and Pescara, leaving Milan undefended, fortified Lodi and Cremona; Bourbon went to Germany to bring back the 10,000 or so *Landsknechte* Charles had ordered to be raised.[17] Knowing that Leyva was desperately short of cash, Francis had his army begin an encirclement trench around Pavia (28 October 1524), save on the side where the city walls ran along the Ticino River. To defend against an imperialist relief force from the direction of Lodi and Cremona, he also ordered a defensive trench or countervallation, from the Ticino to the Park of Mirabello, a fortified palace outside Pavia. Within Pavia, Leyva contented his men by seizing church plate to coin money. In late October, Fernando Alarcon reached Lombardy with 5,000 Spaniards and 700 heavy cavalry from Naples, while Ferdinand's government in Innsbruck was mobilizing the *Landsknechte* for Bourbon.[18] When Bourbon and his men reached Lodi, the combined imperialist army set out for Pavia, where it encamped opposite the French defensive trench, offering battle. Francis I declined, apparently expecting that his enemies would run out of money. He was not far wrong: it was a shortage of funds that determined Lannoy to attack, even though his force may have been somewhat smaller. On a midnight march, the imperialists moved their siege guns opposite the fifteenth-century wall of the Park of Mirabello – easier to batter down than the solidly built French countervallation. While Leyva's men cut the Ticino bridges to prevent a French retreat, Lannoy's cannon opened several breaches in the Mirabello wall, and his units charged through. From his

[15] Mexia, *Historia del Emperador*, 348–349, 354–357 (for the quote, 356); Santa Cruz, *Crónica del Emperador*, 82–84. In keeping with a tendency to avoid imputing to his hero aggressive designs against France, Santa Cruz has Lannoy, Bourbon, and Pescara take the decision to invade Provence after having read letters from Charles and from his then ally, King Henry VIII. For the *retirata*, see Duffy, *Siege Warfare*, 16–17, 52.

[16] Knecht, *Renaissance Warrior and Patron*, 211–215; Mexia, *Historia del Emperador*, 353–357; Santa Cruz, *Crónica del Emperador*, II, 82–86.

[17] According to Mexia, *Historia del Emperador*, 359, 5,000 Germans, 1,000 Spaniards, and 1,200 cavalry; according to Santa Cruz, *Crónica del Emperador*, II, 87, 2,000 Spaniards, 5,500 Germans, and 300 cavalry.

[18] Ferdinand to Charles, from Vienna, 1 and 24 November 1524, *Familienkorrespondenz*, Letters 103 and 106, I, 232–234, 238: the first letter reports Alarcon's arrival, and Ferdinand's orders to the Austrian government at Innsbruck; the second reports that he will leave for Innsbruck in two days to hasten the levy of the 10,000 *Landsknechte*.

camp near the opposite end of the Park, Francis led his men-at-arms in a counterattack that seemed about to succeed, until 1,000 Spanish *arcabuceros*, concealed by Pescara in a copse, opened fire with devastating effect. Francis I had to surrender his sword, thousands of his men were killed or drowned in the river, and some 10,000 more were taken captive (24 February 1525).[19]

Turnabouts: From the Treaty of Madrid to the Siege of Naples

Charles could scarcely have hoped for a greater day. The captive king was taken to Spain by Lannoy. Charles treated his enemy with courtesy but would not give him his freedom until Francis signed a humiliating capitulation, abandoning, in addition to all his claims in Italy, the duchy of Burgundy, the patrimony of France, and also of the emperor's Burgundian ancestors (Treaty of Madrid, January 1526). Yet in demanding Burgundy, which to him seemed the rightful fruit of his great victory in Italy, Charles demanded too much. He saw no problem in the fact that the treaty required Burgundy's parliament or estates to countenance the separation of their province from France. Burgundy was to prove the hinge that allowed Francis to turn his humiliation into a new anti-Habsburg coalition that fell just short of achieving a great triumph.

Francis's two sons came to Spain as hostages for ratification of the treaty by the Parlement of Paris and by the provincial estates of Burgundy. But the day before signing the treaty, Francis had summoned his advisers to swear a solemn oath that he was acting under duress. Once the king had returned home, the rejection of the treaty by the estates of Burgundy, in a spirit of French patriotism, gave Francis an excuse to delay ratification while his diplomats were busy in capitals whose rulers had reason to fear Habsburg preeminence. Giuliano de Medici, Pope Clement VII (1523–1534), joined with France in the League of Cognac (May 1526), both for the Papal States and for Medici Florence. Other signatories included the Republic of Venice, the duke of Ferrara, Ercole II d'Este (d. 1559), and Duke Francesco Sforza, newly restored in Milan by the victors at Pavia, yet suspicious of Habsburg power.[20]

When armies of the league began operations in Lombardy, Charles requested Ferdinand to send as many as 12,000 *Landsknechte* across the Alps under Georg von Frundsberg, a respected "colonel" or mercenary commander. In Milan, Bourbon had been having trouble with his Spaniards;

---

[19] For the most recent discussion of the battle of Pavia, with an evaluation of the pertinent sources, Faustino Gianini, *Mirabello di Pavia. Il parco, La battaglia, La parrochia* (Pavia, 1984), "La Battaglia," 137–158.

[20] Knecht, *Renaissance Warrior and Patron*, 239–260.

they would not quit the city until he allowed them to sack Milan's monasteries to make up for their arrears in pay. Frundsberg's arrival brought no relief, because he too had not received remittances promised by Charles. Leaving Leyva to defend against an expected French invasion, Bourbon and Frundsberg set out for Medici Florence, "in hopes of a sack, as the soldiers desired."[21] Meanwhile, in order to strike at the Papal States from the south, Charles ordered Lannoy (still in Spain) to bring to the Kingdom of Naples the 4,000 Germans who had been defending the Pyrenees frontier, as well as 6,000 newly recruited Spaniards. Landing in Gaeta, just above Naples, Lannoy invaded the Papal States, ignoring a truce with the pope made by another Habsburg commander. After a futile siege of a small hill town, however, he too entered into negotiations; in this second truce (March 1527) Clement VII agreed to provide 60,000 ducats to help keep Bourbon's army at bay. Lannoy's envoy, Cesare Ferramosca, reached Bourbon's camp with news of the truce and some of the pope's 60,000 ducats in late March. Because the truce had been concluded by Lannoy as viceroy of Naples, the marquess of Vasto immediately withdrew his Neapolitan levies from Bourbon's camp. But Bourbon, according to Ferramosca's report to Charles, lacked the authority to decide things for the men under his command. Instead, he referred the matter to the twelve elected spokesmen for his infantry, who were adamant about continuing their march.[22] While Ferramosca presents Bourbon as no longer in control of his army, one can also argue that the Constable saw the fury of his men — including the many Protestants among Frundsberg's *Landsknechte* — as a useful instrument for punishing Clement VII, and that Charles himself was of the same opinion.[23] In any event, Lannoy himself reached Bourbon's

---

[21] The quotation is from Santa Cruz, *Crónica del Emperador*, II, 285; for evidence supporting this view, see Judith Hook, *The Sack of Rome* (London, 1972), 122, and the sources cited in her note 22.

[22] Ferramosca to Charles, 4 April 1527, Lanz, Letter 99, I, 230–234, stressing the mutinous character of the men, especially the German infantry, who, he says, wanted to kill him because he was attempting to halt their march. For hostility between Bourbon and Lannoy, fanned by Ferramosca for purposes of his own, Santa Cruz, *Crónica del Emperador*, II, 167.

[23] Hook, *The Sack of Rome*, 141, citing a report from the Venetian ambassador in Spain: 12 May, before news of the Sack can have reached Spain, Charles expressed publicly his displeasure with the truce concluded by Lannoy. Santa Cruz, not cited by Hook, is of the same opinion (*Crónica del Emperador*, II, 286–287), but I have not found confirmation for his assertion that an envoy from Clement VII brought Bourbon a copy of a letter from Charles endorsing the truce. In Santa Cruz's account, Bourbon said he could not turn back unless he saw the original letter; he did this because he could see from the text that "what [Charles] had written about complying with the truce was written more for the sake of compliance than because the truce was to be kept" (cf. the roughly contemporary Spanish saying, "obedesco, pero no cumplo"). Hook also endorses (p. 138) "the accepted contemporary viewpoint" that Lannoy and Bourbon (despite their known hostility: see previous note) were in collusion to deceive the pope with a false truce. But Vasto's withdrawal of the Neapolitan levies from Bourbon's camp indicates to me that Viceroy Lannoy wanted the truce observed.

camp a few weeks later with additional money, and word that the pope had promised a good deal more. But he soon departed, either because the troops had increased their demands, or because (as Lannoy later reported to Charles) it was not "seemly" (*honnête*) to march in the company of such a disorganized rabble.[24] Finding the road to Florence blocked by unseasonable snows, Bourbon and his men turned aside into Romagna, intending now to march on Rome itself. They left their siege artillery behind, judging that ladders would be enough to surmount the papal city's weakened defenses, as indeed they were.

The infamous Sack of Rome (6–12 May 1527) is described by a recent historian as "one of the most horrible in recorded history."[25] Civilians were slaughtered in great numbers (estimates of 8,000 to 10,000 are common); countless women were raped; countless churches, palaces, and homes plundered.[26] Charles's military position in Italy was never so strong as now, but his European reputation was never so low. Although his pamphleteers initially claimed credit for a glorious victory over a perfidious pope, as the horror of the sack began to sink in, they switched tactics, arguing that runaway soldiers had transgressed the emperor's will.[27]

The military situation changed almost as quickly. Pierre de Veyre, Charles's new ambassador in Italy, arrived in Genoa (September 1527) thinking that the wages of imperial armies in the peninsula were paid. In fact, they were owed arrears totaling 400,000 scudi (373,360 ducats). Pope Clement VII had delivered only 150,000 of the 400,000 scudi he had promised just prior to the sack, and of the 300,000 promised by the Republic of Florence not a sou had been paid.[28] Meanwhile, the League of Cognac was growing stronger, as Lautrec led yet another French army across the Alps (August 1527), while Andrea Doria seized control of Genoa. Lautrec conquered and sacked Pavia, but instead of challenging Leyva's defenses at Milan he struck south into Apulia; by this time he had as many as 50,000 men, 22,000 mercenaries, and the rest *aventuriers*. The quick surrender of Aquila (February 1528) and the conquest of Sulmona prompted anti-Spanish rebellions in other towns of the kingdom, even as Venice occupied key ports along the Adriatic. Meanwhile, Philibert de Châlons, prince of Orange and viceroy of Naples (1527–1530), had with

---

[24] Lannoy's long instructions for Durant's mission to Charles, 17 May 1527, see Lanz, Letter 284, on this issue I, 702–705.

[25] Hook, *The Sack of Rome*, 167.

[26] Save as noted, this paragraph is based on ibid.

[27] De Veyre to Charles, 30 September 1527, *Lanz*, Letter 101, I, 249–251; Charles to Ferdinand, 27 November 1527, *Familienkorrespondenz*, Letter 130, II, 148–152. For the ensuing propaganda war, focusing on whether the *Landsknechte* were or were not acting under orders from Charles, Headley, *The Emperor and His Chancellor*, 110–113.

[28] De Veyre to Charles, 30 September 1527, Lanz, Letter 101, I, 251–252.

great difficulty gotten the remnants of Bourbon's[29] army to leave their Roman encampment to march against Lautrec. But Vasto persuaded him not to hazard battle: their only hope was to withdraw on the capital. As Doria drew up his galleys for a blockade by sea while Lautrec's army dug in on the heights above Naples, it seemed the days of the Habsburg Kingdom were numbered.

Yet the fortunes of war now changed again, even more dramatically than after the Treaty of Madrid. During the periods when French influence in Genoa was paramount, Francis I had in effect divided in two the traditional territory of the Republic of Genoa, keeping for himself the Riviera di Ponente and the port of Savona. If the city's leading men did not like being given orders by Lope de Soria, Charles's ambassador, they liked even less the prospect that Savona would be turned into a French port to rival the shipping of their own harbor. Lannoy, captured in battle, had gotten word to Orange that Doria was deeply troubled by France's plans for Savona. In consequence of the fact that he now agreed to begin negotiations with Orange, through intermediaries, Doria suddenly withdrew his fleet (4 July 1528). The defenders of Naples took heart immediately, while the besiegers, weakened by malaria, were soon in retreat. In August Doria signed a momentous agreement to transfer his galleys – at the time, twelve – to the payroll of Charles V.[30]

Soon afterward Doria again drew up his galleys before Genoa, this time in support of a movement that overthrew the city's pro-French regime. At an assembly of the citizens convened by Doria's allies (13 September), it was agreed to appoint a commission to draft a new constitution, the Reformationes Novae, which went into effect in October. All existing divisions among citizens, like that between Guelphs and Ghibellines, were henceforth abolished. Instead, all of the city's "noble citizens" were to form "a single order" made up of twenty-eight houses (alberghe), each of which was to have a proportionate share in legislative bodies (a Council of Four Hundred and a Council of One Hundred). At the top of the administrative hierarchy there was to be a doge chosen for two years, advised by a board of eight governors, also chosen for two years. The new constitution achieved its objectives: it ended the worst features of factionalism and united most leading families behind the cause of reclaiming for the Republic of Genoa the parts of its traditional territory that were now occupied by French garrisons or by local nobles. At the same time, Genoa was now firmly in the imperial camp, even if Charles was to find the doge and his governors

---

[29] Bourbon himself was killed in the assault on Rome.

[30] For Lautrec's campaign and the siege of Naples, Tommaso Pedio, *Napoli e Spagna nella prima meta del cinquecento* (Bari, 1971), 70–108; for Doria's complaints about French plans for Savona, Santa Cruz, *Crónica del Emperador*, II, 408–409.

rather prickly at times, as when they refused to accept Lope de Soria for a second term as his ambassador.[31] For the story to be told in this book, it is almost impossible to exaggerate the importance of Genoa's subsequent backing of the emperor's plans: all of his naval campaigns and some fought on land would not have been possible without Doria's fleet; and, especially in the latter years of the reign, the credit arrangements that kept his armies on the march would not have been possible without Genoa's bankers.

Of course, the immediate impact of Andrea Doria's change of allegiance was that it broke the French siege of Naples, certainly the gravest threat thus far to any of the Habsburg dominions. Reflecting on this turn of events some years later, Charles's official geographer and chronicler, Alonso de Santa Cruz, adopted a homiletic tone:

> [Charles] was short of funds, and could not send help to his army in Naples by land or sea, because Andrea Doria patrolled the coast of the kingdom. Indeed, considering the great strength of the one army and the weakness of the other, no one can have believed that the emperor would not soon be conquered and dispossessed of all he had in Italy. But it was pleasing to God's will that things should turn out much differently than men expected.[32]

The vicissitudes of war in Italy would indeed have made a fit subject for sermons on the flimsiness of all human plans. What were Charles's thoughts? If one may judge by his subsequent actions, the emperor seems to have reflected less on how close he came to losing Naples, and more on the events leading up to the Sack of Rome: if he took personal charge of his armies, bankers would be more cooperative, and his troops, with wages paid in advance, would do as they were told. In other words, he had to become, himself, an impresario of war.

---

[31] Pacini, *La Genoa dell'Andrea Doria nell'impero di Carlo V*, chaps. II and IV.
[32] Santa Cruz, *Crónica del Emperador*, II, 401.

Chapter 3

The Search for Revenue, I: The Hard Roads of Fiscal Reform

Every European prince had his "domain" or "ordinary income," that is, the miscellaneous crown rights inherited from his remote predecessors, including tolls and especially agrarian dues of various kinds. Even in Brabant, one of the highly urbanized core provinces of the Low Countries, the prized Antwerp Toll brought in far less than a collection of mainly rural rights and fees scattered throughout Brabant.[1] In predominantly rural Naples, transhumance grazing was a royal monopoly; domain officials collected a toll for use of royal pastureland, the so-called Dogana di Foggia, that still accounted for 6% of the kingdom's gross income as late as 1550. In Castile the king had toll receipts but virtually no domain income in the usual sense of landed revenue. But Castile's crown had other "ordinary income" (*rentas ordinarias*) that rival sovereigns might envy. Its principal component was the *alcabala*, a sum collected by tax farmers for each town and its dependent countryside.[2] *Alcabala* was apparently the Arabic form of the Latin *gabella*, a general sales tax of 5% known in Iberia in Roman times. One by one, the towns of fourteenth-century Castile agreed to have sums equal to 5% of the value of sales within their jurisdictions collected by the tax farmers.[3] To subjects having to pay tolls, or fees for pasturing their flocks, or a 5% sales tax, it must have seemed that their sovereigns were so rich that any further demand for money would be unconscionable. But precisely because these revenues had been collected for centuries, they

---

[1] Aud. 868, 62–70v, a summary of income and expenses for the domain revenues of Brabant for 1535. Total income was 72,408, of which only about a third (24,300) came from the Antwerp collection district, including the toll. After subtraction for standing charges, the net (*cler*) was 23,207.

[2] Tracy, *A Financial Revolution*, 31; Alan Ryder, *The Kingdom of Naples under Alfonso the Magnanimous* (Oxford, 1976), 359–362, and Antonio Calabria, *The Cost of Empire: The Finances of the Kingdom of Naples in the Time of Spanish Rule* (Cambridge 1991), 8–9. I. A. A. Thompson, "Castile: Polity, Fiscality, and Fiscal Crises," in Philip Hoffman and Kathryn Norberg, eds., *Fiscal Crises, Liberty, and Representative Government* (Stanford, 1994), 140–180.

[3] Carande Thobar, *Carlos V y sus banqueros*, II, 221–222.

were also heavily burdened with standing charges and debts.[4] For a ruler, there was never enough money, especially not when war was in the offing. This chapter examines various ways of trying to make traditional revenues go farther.

The Low Countries

Charles inherited here a sound fiscal administration built up by the dukes of Burgundy (1384–1477). Each province had a number of collection districts for domain income, and a separate, provincewide receiver for subsidy income (see Chapter 4), all under the supervision of a receiver general. The Council of Finance in Brussels prepared a budget (*état*) for each year, and each province had auditors to scrutinize the accounts prior to verification by the Chamber of Accounts in Lille. Only then did the receiver general's clerk make a general summary account for the year.[5] As late as 1531 Charles had naive expectations about what he could get from the Low Countries. In January of that year he promised to assign to his brother, on future subsidies of the Low Countries, a debt of 235,000 Rhine gulden, which Ferdinand had not been able to collect from previous assignations. In fact, the revenues of the Low Countries offered no such leeway. The ten-year summary of income and expenditures that was prepared for the emperor's perusal the next month (February 1531) showed only a slight deficit – indeed, so slight (.003% for a ten-year total income of 15,111,493 Carolus gulden) that it gave a false picture of the real state of affairs. For example, there was no mention of outstanding claims, like back wages for infantry on garrison duty and for the standing cavalry units, the *compagnies d'ordonnance*. When Charles planned a short trip to Germany to attend the Diet of Speyer (July 1531), he had to wait until money could be found to pay the "very great" arrears of the mounted companies that refused to accompany him unless paid something of what they were owed. Nonetheless, as he wrote Ferdinand at this time, Charles was satisfied that complaints against his financial officials were based mainly on hearsay and "contained more passion than truth." The real problem, he thought, was political: in the Low Countries,

---

4 For the domain revenues of Brabant in 1535, see note 1; in Flanders, gross domain income for the same year was 107,300 Carolus gulden, but net income was only 24,267, or 22.6% of the gross; in Holland the picture was brighter: 44,398 of 76,300 gulden, or 58.2%, was still available to the government: Aud. 868, 73–73v, 83–85v. In Castile, in 1522, 36.6% of the *rentas ordinarias* were pledged for payment of annual interest on bonds or *juros* issued by the treasury: Carande Thobar, *Carlos V y sus banqueros*, I, 91. In Naples, annual income for the Dogana di Foggia in 1498 was 3,434 ducats, of which only 768 remained for the government to spend: Coniglio, *Consulte e bilanci del Viceregno di Napoli* Document 1.

5 For a comparison for 1520–1530 of domain receipts (2,509,044 gulden) and subsidy receipts (10,130,757), see Aud. 873,1–21. For an overview, Tracy, *A Financial Revolution*, chap. 2.

Map 3.1. The core provinces: Flanders, Brabant, and Holland

"everyone demands privileges that are contrary to my sovereignty [*hauteur*], as if I were their companion and not their lord."[6]

Before departing for a longer stay in Germany, Charles met with Mary of Hungary and her Council of Finance (December 1531) to agree on a projection of income and expenditures over the next six years. Within a month, however, Mary had to remind her brother there was no money in the budget for the new pensions he was already promising to important men in Germany. Two months later (March 1532) she sent him a copy of a certain "resolution that the Council of Finance and I have taken after a long discussion on how to avoid the interest charges arising from past or future loans by the merchants in Antwerp." There was a similar message in 1534, explaining that a more correct calculation of the expenditures that Charles had approved in December 1531 would have shown that revenues projected for the six years would be exhausted in at most four years, not six, even if it had not been for 350,000 gulden in unplanned expenses for 1531–1534 (many ordered by the emperor himself).[7] Mary tried to save money by suppressing all annual pensions save those that were absolutely necessary; some optimistic projections for the years 1534–1536 actually showed slight surpluses, by dint of suppressing approximately 950,000 gulden in pension charges.[8]

Despite such measures, Mary and her Council of Finance were forced to rely on credit, contravening Charles's direct instructions; to keep interest charges a bit lower, they borrowed 120,000 gulden from the government's own receivers of subsidies,[9] not from the Antwerp bankers. The money was needed, again, to pay at least some of the arrears for the six *compagnies d'ordonnance*, whose annual wages amounted to 338,592 gulden. For the coming year, 1535, they projected income of 852,038 gulden, and expenses of 922,598, meaning a deficit of 70,560; when various other obligations were added, including loans to be repaid in 1535 and a deficit of 138,534 pounds projected for 1534, the total shortfall was 500,244, or 58.7% of the expected net income.[10] Mary could not force her ordinary or peacetime expenses to fit within the constrains of normal annual income, and neither could Charles. Around this time, the emperor seems to have recognized that his Low Countries provinces could not fully provide for their own military

---

[6] For the summary, see note 8; Charles to Ferdinand, 13 January, 21 July, and 1 October 1531, *Familienkorrespondenz*, Letters 446a, 521, 548, III, 3–5, 218, and 286–288.

[7] Mary to Charles, 21 January and 23 March 1532, Aud. 52, 1, 44; for the message to be sent to the emperor in 1534, Aud. 868, 1–12.

[8] Aud. 875, a dossier of 175 folios containing budget summaries for the years 1531–1536, with accompanying memos explaining to Charles how various unanticipated expenses had derailed plans to achieve solvency.

[9] For these officials, see Chapter 12.

[10] Aud. 868, 1–2, 3–18, 19–46, 97–104.

needs, much less those of other Habsburg lands. When war threatened during the 1530s, he had funds remitted to Mary from Spain: 120,000 ducats (roughly 219,509 Carolus gulden) in December 1535, and a total of 250,000 ducats in March and August 1537.[11] During the 1540s and 1550s these transfers from Spain would increase dramatically.

Naples

The fundamental fact of life in Naples was that the crown controlled only about 4% of the kingdom's communities. To be sure, the capital city, with nearly 10% of the kingdom's population,[12] was a community of the royal domain, that is, ruled directly by the crown, as were most of the sizable towns. But at the time of Charles's accession there were in all 1,551 *università* or town and village communes. According to a report by Charles Leclerc, all but a few of these could be grouped under eight categories of lordship:[13]

domain	60
4 princes	98
16 dukes	333
13 marquises	59
50 counts	318
538 barons	519
churches	120
towns	32

This pattern of baronial control was deeply rooted in the kingdom's history. Under the Angevin dynasty (1268–1442),[14] related to France's royal house, kings and queens of Naples raised money by selling parcels of royal domain to their vassals. Traditional rules prevented alienation of towns with fortresses, but by the early years of the reign of Alfonso V, the first king of the Aragonese dynasty (1442–1478), only 134 of the kingdom's 1,551 *università* were under direct royal rule. Most barons exercised civil

---

[11] Charles to Mary, Aud. 48, 111, as cited by Fernández-Alvárez apropos of *Corpus Documental*, Letter CLXXXII, I, 444–446; Charles's ostensible and secret instructions for Horton's mission to Mary, 15, 19 March 1537, Lanz, Letters 665, 666, II, 570–572 (the first, to be read in council, bids Mary not use the 100,000 ducats carried by Horton except in case of necessity; the second, for Mary's eyes only, reveals that Horton is carrying 200,000 ducats); Charles to Mary, 19 August 1537, Lanz, Letter 691, II, 679–680, he has sent a further 50,000 ducats.

[12] For 1532, the estimates of Hernándo Sanchez, *Castilla y Napoles*, 243, are: 150,000 for the capital, 1 million for the kingdom.

[13] Leclerc, "Rapport et Recueil," chap. x, 5–59v, chap. xxiii, 88–94. Leclerc also mentions twelve "subfiefs," without saying to whose lordship they pertained. Counting these twelve, his numbers add up to 1,551 *università*.

[14] With papal support, Charles, duke of Anjou, a younger brother of France's King Louis IX, conquered Naples from its Hohenstaufen ruler in 1268.

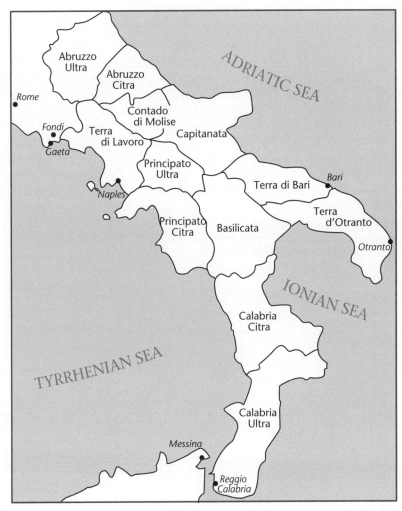

Map 3.2. The Kingdom of Naples

jurisdiction in their baronies, as well as criminal jurisdiction ranging from
petty to capital crimes. Their privileges included the right to levy "feudal aides" in the three traditional cases[15] and the right to prohibit their
subjects from keeping mills, baking ovens, inns, or washing stations for the
preparation of newly woven cloth. Ferrante I (d. 1495), who ruled first for
his absent father Alfonso and then in his own name, attempted to break
down these baronial monopolies. He recognized all subjects as entitled to
sell their goods freely, without interference from their lords (1466), and
mandated the tearing down of baronial inns, to allow subjects to set up as

[15] Ransom of the lord from captivity, knighthood of his eldest son, marriage of his eldest daughter.

innkeepers (1483). But barons generally ignored these provisions, especially after a French invasion had removed Ferrante.[16]

Subjects of the barons still supported the royal fisc, for the hearth tax or *focatico*. This tax was initially approved by the Parlamento of the kingdom under Alfonso (1442), but by the sixteenth century officials collected it routinely, without further recourse to the kingdom's representative assembly (see Chapter 13). Each of the *università* had to pay an annual sum, eventually fixed by royal officials at 1.55 Neapolitan ducats[17] per hearth. Excluding the metropolis of Naples, exempt from the enumeration as well as the hearth tax, the number of hearths in the kingdom was reckoned at 262,215 in the early years of the sixteenth century, which meant a nominal *focatico* yield of approximately 400,000 ducats. The actual yield was much lower. For the fiscal year 1507–1508 (1 September–31 August), it was found that the kingdom had expenses of 483,845 ducats, as against a total income of only 218,568.[18] Some *focatico* income was lost (about 15,000 scudi or Neapolitan ducats) through "conventions" that permitted major towns to reduce the sums they owed by a fixed percentage, often more than 50%. Larger sums were lost through alienation-in-perpetuity of the hearth taxes of particular localities to ecclesiastical corporations and private individuals (80,749), and through revenues pledged to a banker named Paolo de Tholosa for repayment of his loans (25,032).[19]

Lax enforcement of rules meant to prevent barons from cutting into the taxpaying capacity of their subjects was a more basic problem; for example, barons required subjects to pay a fee for the privilege of trading outside the barony, despite Ferrante I's edict guaranteeing freedom of trade. Laws had to be enforced to be effective, but officials of the Sommaria (Treasury) and the Scrivania di Ragione (Secretariat of Accounts) were often brothers and cousins of the barons whose monopolistic ambitions they were expected to curb. They also tended to view their offices as "fiefs," or properties to be exploited for maximum gain. Whenever the Sommaria sent out quotas for a new levy on each hearth, many of the *università* sent delegates to the capital

---

[16] Benedetto Croce, *Storia del regno di Napoli* (6th ed., Bari, 1965), 85.

[17] I.e., 15 carlins (10 carlins to a Neapolitan ducat, worth .9334 Spanish ducats) and 1 grain (20 to a carlin) per hearth; for monetary units and weights and measures, see the introductory matter in Calabria, *The Cost of Empire.*

[18] Pedio, *Napoli e Spagna*, 412; Coniglio, *Consulte e bilanci del Viceregno de Napoli*, Document 21, 318–321.

[19] Leclerc, "Rapport et Recueil," chap. xxxviii, 109–110v, "Estat de revenu dudit royaulme tel que se trouvoit au jour du trespas du feu roy catholique [Ferdinand]," and chap. xxxix, 111–163v, "De la raison en particulier de tant de revenu et des charges dudit royaulme de Naples avec lestat dicelle pour lannee finie a dernier daoust 1521." The yield on 262,215 hearths at 1.55 ducats would be 406,433, but Leclerc gives the figures as 496,371 for the year of Ferdinand's death [1516], and 396,371 for 1521. One might be tempted to regard the former figure as a mistake in recording, save for the fact that income and expenses for 1516 do not balance without the error.

to explain why they could not pay as demanded; full credit was often given for part payment, and it seems that understanding officials received a suitable reward. When the Sommaria dispatched commissioners to conduct a new hearth census, they sometimes found townsmen or villagers had barricaded the entrances to their streets; surely it was hard not to write down the same number of hearths as in the previous census, while accepting a small gift.[20]

Finally, the kingdom had no strong government after 1494. In that year, as seen in Chapter 2, France's King Charles VIII, alleging rights bequeathed to him by the last Angevin claimant, drove Ferrante I from his throne and briefly occupied the kingdom. Ferrante II (r. 1495–1503), son of Ferrante I, was deprived of his crown for good and all when Gonsalvo de Córdoba conquered Naples in the name of Ferdinand of Aragón, Alfonso V's grandson. From this time on, the kingdom was ruled not by members of the dynastic family, as in the Habsburg Netherlands, but by viceroys, first Gonsalvo de Córdoba (1503–1507), then Ramón de Cardona (1509–1522). Foreign viceroys could never command the same authority as a "natural" or native prince; hence barons, bureaucrats, and town councils in the domain cities all found ways of appropriating royal revenue for their own use. For example, a later investigation discovered that since the accounts of local receivers were not audited for the years 1520–1525, a good portion of the money had simply been pocketed by officials.[21]

Archduke Charles became king of Naples upon the death of his grandfather Ferdinand in 1516. His Burgundian advisers, full of ambitious plans for their young master, knew enough about Naples to realize that something had to be done to make the kingdom yield disposable revenue. The president of the Council of State, Guillaume de Croy, lord of Chièvres, sent Charles Leclerc, president of the Chamber of Accounts in Lille, to Naples for a proper tally of all revenues and expenses. Leclerc's instructions as commissioner general for Naples were dated 24 January 1517. With the cooperation of Viceroy Cardona and the Sommaria, he was to prepare balances both for the year of Ferdinand's death and for the subsequent period. He was also to determine if the barons of the kingdom were abusing their subjects by levying unauthorized taxes, and to make sure that money was "reserved" for the 100,000 crowns Charles had to pay the king of France in June 1517, according to the terms of a treaty concluded the previous year.[22]

[20] Coniglio, *Consulte e bilanci del Viceregno di Napoli*, 22–38.

[21] Ryder, *The Kingdom of Naples under Alfonso the Magnanimous*, 210–217; Giuseppe Coniglio, *Il regno di Napoli al tempo di Carlo V* (Naples, 1951), 22, 30, 99, 217.

[22] Leclerc, "Rapport et Recueil," instruction of 24 January 1517, folios 8–14v; Knecht, *Renaissance Warrior and Patron*, 84: according to the August 1516 Treaty of Noyon, Charles agreed to pay Francis I an annual tribute of 100,000 crowns, in implicit recognition of France's claim to the Kingdom of Naples.

As might be expected, Leclerc's mission met resistance from the chief
officials of the kingdom, especially the conservator of the royal patrimony,
count of Cariati, Giambattista Spinelli, a member of the Genoese banking
family. Spinelli managed to get himself appointed commissioner general
in Leclerc's place, causing the latter to go to Saragossa for a meeting with
his patron, Chièvres (September 1518). Leclerc returned to Naples with
a fresh appointment and fresh instructions, including Charles's demand
that the kingdom provide 200,000 ducats "for defense against the Turks,
and for the expenses of our election as Holy Roman Emperor." In time,
Leclerc summoned the barons and cities of the kingdom for a Parlamento[23]
(April 1520). The assembly duly agreed to a "gift" or *donativo* of 300,000
ducats, in the form of a temporary extra levy on each hearth, but with
a catch: in return for granting 100,000 ducats in excess of the 200,000
that had been asked, the Parlamento stipulated, for the first time, that the
money had to be spent within the borders of the kingdom. In fact, it seems
that money to help repay the loan for Charles's election had to be found
from another source.[24] Leclerc's difficulties with high officials in Naples
persisted. Following the death of Chièvres (May 1521), he could not make
headway at Charles's court against the friends his enemies had there; in
May 1522 he was discharged a second time from his post as commissioner
and told not to meddle further in the affairs of Naples.[25]

Leclerc did produce a detailed summary of expected income and expenses for the year ending 31 August 1521. But the fact that his sums
come out even – with approximately 760,000 ducats in income as well as
expenses – shows that ferreting out the kingdom's fiscal problems was not
this experienced auditor's real purpose in Naples. What Leclerc accomplished during his second term of office as commissioner was to "recover"
276,000 ducats, mainly by the sale of domain cities and villages, and by
"compositions" in which various barons and officials settled any claims
that might be made against them by the crown. Money brought in by
these means was paid out to Charles's bankers, apparently for the imperial
election loan (106,000); to Antoine de Lalaing, count of Hoogstraten and
head of the Council of Finance in the Low Countries, "by special account
rendered to him" (47,500); to Chièvres, Hoogstraten, and other members

[23] For the Parlamento, see Chapter 13.
[24] See note 25.
[25] Pedio, *Napoli e Spagna*, 418–429, for a summary of Leclerc's mission, and 439–461, for a summary of
his report. On the Parlamento of 1520, D'Agostino, *Parlamento e società nel regno di Napoli*, 209. It is
tempting to see the 103,500 ducats Leclerc describes as paid "to the marquis of Aarschot [Chièvres]
into the hands of the Welsers" as a partial repayment for the Welser portion of Charles's imperial
election loan (for the loan, see Chapter 5): "Rapport et Recueil," chap. xli, 170–172v, "Declaration
des deniers que ledit commissaire a par ses diligences recouvres et a lordonnance de sa maieste paye
durant ladit commission."

of the Council of State (30,947); and to Chièvres himself, for the sale of the offices Charles had given him as grand admiral and captain general of the sea in Naples (34,500).[26] Thus the young emperor did well enough from Leclerc's mission, but Chièvres and his friends did better.

Mercurino Gattinara, the rising star of Charles's inner circle, was not fooled by the fictive balances Leclerc accepted. While Charles met with Germany's princes at the Diet of Worms (January–May 1521) – where Martin Luther refused to recant and was declared an outlaw – Gattinara pored over copies of the accounts for recent years, which one of the secretaries of accounts had been requested to bring in person to Worms. While Charles met with Henry VIII and Francis I at a peace conference arranged by Cardinal Wolsey (Calais, October 1521), Gattinara finished a lengthy memorandum on what was wrong in Naples. The simple truth, as he saw it, was that direct orders from Charles had been set aside by the viceroy and the Sommaria, in favor of local priorities not always reported in the accounts. Because the great nobles of the Kingdom monopolized the administration of justice and finance, they were at liberty to divert crown revenues to their own profit, and to terrorize anyone incurring their displeasure. Some modern scholars have argued that Gattinara's picture of things was too harsh. For example, if Viceroy Cardona took money earmarked for Charles's use and gave it to local garrisons instead, it was to stop their extorting unpaid wages from townsfolk whom they were supposed to be protecting.[27] But Gattinara was surely right in thinking there could be no fiscal reform in Naples unless the great barons of the kingdom were subjected more firmly to Spanish rule.

For the moment, however, the greatest need was for a viceroy who could effectively represent Charles's overall interests in Italy. Charles de Lannoy (r. 1522–1527) served the emperor well at the battle of Pavia (1525). In 1528 Viceroy Philibert de Châlons, prince of Orange (r. 1527–1530), bouyed by Andrea Doria's defection to the imperial cause, turned back a massive revolt in which barons and cities made common cause with French and Venetian troops in an effort to throw the Spaniards out of Naples. In 1529–1530, Orange commanded the long and ultimately successful siege of Florence, in which he himself was killed, leaving the kingdom for

[26] "Rapport et Recueil," chap. xxxix, 111–163v, "De la raison en particulier de tant le revenu et des charges dudit royaulme de Naples avec lestat dicelle pour lannee finie au dernier daoust 1521"; and chap. XII.

[27] D'Agostino, *Parlamento e società nel regno di Napoli*, 206–207; Giuseppe Galasso, "Trends and Problems in Neapolitan History in the Age of Charles V," in Antonio Calabria and John A. Marino, eds. and tr., *Good Government in Spanish Naples* (New York and Frankfurt, 1990), 13–78, here 23–30. For Gattinara's memorandum, Karl Lanz and Franz Cheml, eds., *Actenstücke und Briefe zur Geschichte des Kaisers Karls V*, in *Monumenta Habsburgica* (6 vols., Vienna, 1853–1858), IV, 401–418.

a time to his lieutenant, Cardinal Pompeo Colonna (1530–1532).[28] But once a peace favorable to the Habsburgs was established in Italy, the main preoccupation of the government in Naples was finding money to pay for the debts of recent wars. For 1530, when the kingdom's income cannot have been more than 300,000 ducats, there was a total of 1,194,117 ducats in "changes" or *cambi* payments that bankers made on the treasury's behalf outside the kingdom. When Pompeo Colonna coaxed a huge *donativo* – 600,000 ducats – from the Parlamento of 1532, it seems the money went to pay debts stemming from the siege of Florence.[29] Meanwhile, treasury officials ignored payment orders for nonessential matters, like Ferdinand's annual pension of 60,000 ducats, which Charles had assigned on Naples; as of 1528 it had not been paid for two years, so that the Fugger bank, to which Ferdinand reassigned this income in payment of a loan, remitted the debt elsewhere, at Charles's expense.[30]

In 1529 Charles sent to Naples Iñigo Lopez de Mendóza, bishop of Burgos, with instructions to oversee confiscation of the properties of barons implicated in the recent rebellion. Alarmed by the state of the kingdom as he found it, Lopez in turn sent Treasurer Alonso Sanchez to Spain with instructions to urge upon Charles the need for a Spanish viceroy, with full authority to stop the barons from exercising "tyranny" over their subjects. Sanchez either brought with him or sent after his return a fiscal summary for the period 24 March–1 December 1529, showing income of 1,146,963 ducats. But Sanchez's "income" included bankers' loans or *cambi* (676,033), alienations of domain, and other loans; hearth tax and toll income amounted to no more than 303,718.[31] Charles and his advisers were not fooled. Sanchez was told in no uncertain terms to report as income only real revenues, as he in fact did in a balance for the year 1 September 1530 through 31 August 1531. This time, income was listed at 283,897, as against 284,969 in ordinary expenses, 97,694 in extraordinary expenses, 206,230 counted as income for the year, even though assigned to various creditors, 219,544 in bankers' loans, not counting interest, 638,538 in unpaid debts that had accumulated since the beginning of the revolt (1527), and 246,876 in assignations by Charles on Naples (including what he still owed to Ferdinand) that could not possibly be met. These figures – 284,969 in income and 1,693,851 in debts and expenses – finally give a plausible

---

[28] See Chapter 6; for a full account, Pedio, *Napoli e Spagna*, 67–108.

[29] See Chapter 6; Coniglio, *Il regno di Napoli*, 113–114, 243–245; Pedio, *Napoli e Spagna*, 297.

[30] Galasso, "Trends and Problems in Neapolitan History," 33–35; Hernándo Sanchez, *Castilla y Napoles* 184–190; Charles to Ferdinand, in response to Ferdinand's instructions for Sanchez's mission to Spain, 8 November 1528, *Familienkorrespondenz*, Letter 240, II, 323–324; Pölnitz, *Anton Fugger*, I, 570–571.

[31] Coniglio, *Consulte e bilanci del Viceregno di Napoli*, Document 35, 387–389, Lopez de Mendóza's instruction to Sanchez; Document 38, 409–413, Sanchez's report.

picture of how bad things were. What was to be done? The instructions that Charles gave Sanchez on his return to Naples proposed convening the Parlamento to ask approval for a new kind of tax large enough to remedy the kingdom's inveterate deficits. The large *donativo* for which Pompeo Colonna won approval in 1532 was at least a partial response to Charles's instructions. But full implementation of the emperor's wishes for Naples would await the appointment of a "Spanish viceroy" of the House of Alba, Pedro Alvárez de Toledo (r. 1532–1553).

The reform proposals put forward by Leclerc and Gattinara[32] were not forgotten, as may be seen from edicts issued by the new viceroy between 1532 and 1536, curbing various abuses by the barons.[33] Toledo also decreed (1539) that the provincial auditors (*uditori*) who presided over appellate courts should receive an annual salary, instead of having these offices farmed out to the highest bidder.[34] But the real chance for reform in Naples came during and just after Charles's visit, from October 1535 to March 1536,[35] when he reestablished the dormant office of conservator of the royal patrimony. His choice fell on Bartolommeo Camerario of Benevento (1497–1561), a doctor of civil and canon law who had taught in the law faculty at the University of Naples, and who had also served for a time as one of the presidents of the Sommaria. Camerario's reports shed a harsh light on how officials were cooking the books. If the Secretariat of Accounts had recorded for the fiscal year 1 September 1535 through 31 August 1536 a net disposable income of only 76,290 scudi, Camerario found that the actual figure was 338,858 scudi; the difference went for expenditures that officials did not care to report to their Spanish sovereign. The Sommaria regularly accepted bribes from *università* slow in making hearth tax payments, and tried to keep Spain in the dark by forwarding budgets for the coming year rather than actual accounts for a year just completed; when accounts were demanded they counted expenses twice to make the sums come out right. At Alonso Sanchez's treasury, officials invested government funds for their own profit. Finding a sum of 100,000

---

[32] See Chapter 13.

[33] Coniglio, *Il regno di Napoli*, 22–25; Hernándo Sanchez, *Castilla y Napoles*, 229–231.

[34] Francesco Caracciolo, *Uffici, difesa e corpi rappresentativi nel Mezzogiorno in eta spagnola* (Reggio Calabria, 1974), 19. Toledo's reform lasted only until 1582, when a fresh investigation determined that salaried auditors were guilty of the same corrupt practices Toledo had complained about decades earlier.

[35] Following his failed campaign in Provence, Charles brought copies of the Neapolitan treasury accounts back to Castile for examination by Spanish officials. It was at this time that Juan de Figueroa unearthed evidence that, as noted earlier, barons and town councils had simply pocketed large sums during the years 1520–1525, when the accounts of local collectors were not being audited: Coniglio, *Il regno di Napoli*, 22, 66, 74, 92, 99, 189, 210, 217, 221–231; Hernándo Sanchez, *Castilla y Napoles*, 218; Morial, *Il Virrey de Napoles Don Pedro de Toledo*, 36–39, 127.

ducats lost through fraud, Camerario "recovered" a like amount from a tax farmer, Girolamo Pellegrino, to whom the Secretariat of Accounts had granted the "favor" of not auditing his accounts for the last twelve years.[36]

But Charles had no sooner departed from the kingdom than Camerario was sending complaints about certain persons who were trying to sow enmity between him and the viceroy. In fact, the cause of reform depended entirely on Toledo, and he seems to have shielded Camerario from his critics for a few years. By 1539, however, either the viceroy withdrew his protection or the clamor had become too loud. Charles suppressed the office of conservator of the patrimony, compensating Camerario by naming him as one of the presidents of the Sommaria. In 1540, when Toledo issued an edict requiring that all officials perform their duties in person, without using substitutes, Camerario made public a reply in which he asked why the viceroy himself spent so much time at his villa in Pozzuoli, some distance from the capital; from this time, according to the chroniclers, Camerario was known by local wits as "Temerario" (the rash). In 1543 the viceroy announced that Camerario was being suspended from his post at the Sommaria while one Bratuccio (a reputed enemy) investigated charges of malfeasance that had been made against him. Traveling to the Diet of Speyer to plead his case before Charles V in person (1544), Camerario got himself restored to office and had Bratuccio removed from the investigation. Back in Naples, however, his fellow presidents – said to be in league with Toledo – refused to accompany him as they walked to the viceregal palace or to show him any other sign of respect. Camerario managed to collect his family and move them to Linz (Upper Austria) a few months before the tribunal to which his case had been entrusted (in which Bratuccio was again involved, at least informally) pronounced him guilty as charged and sentenced him to death in absentia (February 1547). The would-be reformer ended his days in Rome, writing theological treatises against Protestant doctrine and lending his support to plots by Neapolitan exiles to overthrow Habsburg rule in the kingdom.[37]

Camerario's fall from grace has been variously interpreted. One scholar assumes he was guilty as charged, having fallen into the evil ways he condemned in others.[38] Another sees Toledo's enmity as rooted in Camerario's involvement with a group of Neapolitan humanists whose membership partially overlapped that of the circle of the Spanish theologian

---

[36] Coniglio, *Il Regno di Napoli*, 221–232; Caracciolo, *Uffici, difesa e corpi rappresentativi*, 19, 70; Hernándo Sanchez, *Castilla y Napoles*, 218–221.

[37] Carlo di Frede, "Il processo di Bartolommeo Camerario," in *Studi in onore di Ricardo Filangieri* (2 vols., Naples, 1959), II, 329–344.

[38] Caracciolo, *Uffici, difesa e corpi rappresentativi*, 71, who cites but seems not to have read the article by Di Frede.

Juan Valdés (1500–1541), some of whose disciples were convinced Protestants.[39] A third, more inclined to credit the chroniclers, blames the quarrel on the viceroy's wounded *amour propre*, stemming from the incident in 1540.[40] The deeper reason lies in the inherent loneliness of the fiscal reformer's path. Camerario delved more thoroughly than Leclerc into the irregularities of the Neapolitan accounts. His reward was to be not merely dismissed from office but also sentenced to death. Despite the language of reform in Toledo's 1532 instructions, the battle against baronial tyranny and bureaucratic corruption was never meant to be his highest priority. His real task in the fiscal sphere was to find in Naples at least some of the money Charles needed for his far-ranging plans. To this end, he had to conciliate the great men of the kingdom, not alienate them by overzealous inquiries (see Chapter 13).

Castile

As a Christian nation, Spain was created by the long struggle to reclaim the Iberian peninsula from the heirs and successors of the Moorish conquerors of the early eighth century, culminating with the conquest of Granada in 1492. As a unified nation, Spain was created by the marriage in 1469 of the so-called Catholic Kings, Ferdinand II of Aragón (r. 1479–1516) and Isabella of Castile (r. 1474–1504). Upon the death of Isabella's half-brother, King Henry IV, her claim to the crown was contested by armed partisans of the late king's daughter. Following a long civil war (1474–1479), Isabella had solid backing from the Cortes for a program of reform: she streamlined the administration of the kingdom, reduced expenditures by eliminating needless pensions, and created a civil guard to police the kingdom. This was to be the nucleus of the army Ferdinand formed for his wars in Italy. Isabella increased the rate for the *alcabala* from 5% to 10%, and the treasury profited also from the growth of internal trade during long decades of peace.

But if the Catholic Kings bequeathed a strong treasury to their grandson, the fisc was never to recover from damages suffered at the beginning of Charles's reign. A large portion of the massive imperial election loan, provided by Augsburg bankers, had been assigned for repayment on a *servicio* that Charles extorted from his Cortes just before sailing off in September 1520 to claim the imperial crown. When this subsidy was in effect nullified by the ensuing Revolt of the Comuneros (see Chapter 14),

---

[39] Hernándo Sanchez, *Castilla y Napoles*, 219, 497–502; on one of Camerario's friends, a humanist and law professor whom Toledo deprived of his lectureship at the law faculty in 1543, Elias de Tejada, *Napoles hispanico* (4 vols., Madrid, 1958), II, 297–302; on Valdés, see A. Gordon Kinder, "Juan de Valdes," *Encyclopedia of the Reformation* (4 vols., New York, 1996), IV, 212–214.

[40] The view of Di Frede, "Il Processo di Bartolommeo Camerario."

Map 3.3. The Kingdom of Castile

there was no income on which to assign the loan, and no more credit for the new emperor.[41] When Charles prepared to return to Spain in 1522, after loyalist nobles had put down the rebellion, he stopped in England at the court of Windsor, where commissioners of the Augsburg firms embarrassed him by demanding new assignations for their loans. Ramón Carande Thobar, the premier historian of Castile's finances, was not able to determine if the Fugger of Augsburg, to whom the greatest debt was owed, ever did receive complete payment. In January 1523 Charles was amazed to be told by his chief auditors (*contadores mayores*) that the crown's annual obligations were "much greater than the portion of royal incomes that remains at my disposal." In fact, all income expected for 1524 was already pledged for expenses of 1523.[42]

---

[41] See Chapter 14.

[42] Manuel Fernández Alvárez, *Charles V, Elected Emperor and Hereditary Ruler*, tr. J. A. Lalaguna (London, 1975), 23–36; Carande Thobar, *Carlos V y sus banqueros*, II, 61, 536–537, III, 46–49;

Charles and his officials tried everything they could think of to shore up the kingdom's finances, starting with a reorganization of financial administration along lines familiar in the Netherlands. Previously, there had been two Chambers of Account (for income and expenses), linked to king and council only by a secretary for the Hacienda, a post filled since 1517 by Francisco de los Cobos. Charles now created a new board of three officials (including Cobos), soon to be known as the Consejo de la Hacienda, for supervision of both revenues and expenditures, like the Council of Finance in the Low Countries. This change provided a clearer picture of the state of royal finances, but did not improve the deficit, partly because plans for creating a unified treasury were never carried out.[43] Meanwhile, to shore up the crown's credit, he approved in March 1524 a contract by which administration of the lands of Castile's military orders,[44] annexed to the crown, was farmed out for the years 1525–1527. Terms of the contract permitted the Fugger to make deductions against the approximately 135,000 ducats they were to pay each year for the 200,000 ducats they claimed were still owing to them from the imperial election loan. Contracts like this one, renewed in subsequent years, led the Cortes to complain that foreign bankers, by administering the kingdom's revenues, were siphoning off the profits from a growing economy that would otherwise have accrued to the crown. Modern scholars are not so sure. The Fugger apparently did not submit the required reports on actual *maestrazgo* income prior to 1542, but accounts for the 1538–1542 contract show that their claim of a shortfall was eventually honored by the crown.[45]

The only real improvement in Castile's finances for which Charles was responsible[46] came from his ongoing negotiations with successive popes. In recognition of the role he claimed as the champion of Christendom against its foes, and for helping individual popes with their political problems in Italy,[47] he won prolongation of important privileges dating from an earlier time. The *cruzada*, originally granted by Pope Innocent VIII in anticipation of the campaign against Muslim Granada, funneled to the treasury sums the faithful paid for indulgences promoted by licensed preachers. This

Pölnitz, *Anton Fugger*, I, 512–513. It may be that Jacob Fugger contracted to deliver his portion of Charles's election loan in conditional installments, each one dependent on repayment of principal and interest from the previous installment (a later contract of this kind, a loan by the Welser in 1535, is discussed in Chapter 7). This may explain why the empire's electors were still owed some 300,000 ducats for the portion of their promised bribes (with interest) they still had not received at the time of Ferdinand's election as King of the Romans in 1531 (Chapter 7).

43 Carande Thobar, *Carlos V y sus banqueros*, 62–82.
44 The maestrazgos or masterships of the three military orders are discussed in Chapter 5.
45 Hermann Kellenbenz, *Die Fuggersche Maestrazgopacht (1525–1542)* (Tübingen, 1967), 6–9, 98–102; Carande Thobar, *Carlos V y sus banqueros*, I, 263, II, 378–402.
46 I.e., not counting the flow of gold and silver from the Indies, discussed in Chapter 5.
47 This is especially true of the conquest of Florence by imperial armies for the Medici pope, Clement VII, in 1529–1530: see Chapter 6.

revenue too was administered by bankers: for 1523–1525, the contractors agreed to pay the crown 150,000 ducats per year. Charles hoped for more from the clerical *subsidio*. In 1519 Pope Leo X directed Castile's clerics to give the crown a fourth (*quarta*) of their income instead of the usual 10%, but it is not clear the crown actually received this added revenue, not even during the brief pontificate of Adrian VI (1522–1523), who in his days as a theology professor at the University of Louvain had also been Archduke Charles's tutor. In advance of his meeting with Charles at Bologna in 1530, Pope Clement VII sent to Spain letters requiring payment of the full *quarta* over a period of three years; Empress Isabella was able to use the pope's letters to negotiate a loan contract for 400,000 ducats.[48] Finally, Clement also authorized Charles to transfer to crown ownership properties of the three military orders (*maestrazgos*) having a total income of up to 80,000 ducats a year; these properties – usually villages with their lands – could then be sold to the highest bidder. Although buyers could not always be found, there were occasions when funds raised in this way helped the *Consejo de la Hacienda* out of a tight corner.[49]

* * *

At best, these measures helped increase income at a rate comparable with the increase in deficits. Even in Castile, where important new revenues were created through Charles's negotiations with the papacy, estimates for the 1530s paint a picture no better than that given by the contadores mayores in 1523. According to a projection for 1539, for example, the crown had income sufficient to cover 1,030,000 ducats in expenses, leaving obligations of 865,000 ducats that could not be paid. This the bankers had to cover, their loans paid off bit by bit, or rolled over in new contracts. Any unplanned expenses, like those involved in contesting France's claims in northern Italy, could only be met by still further loans.[50] In fact, the loans required were of a size that could only be supported by revenues not yet discussed, including gold and silver from Spain's conquests in the Americas. Had Charles been limited to the borrowing that was supportable by his regular and predictable revenues, he might never have left Spain.

---

[48] Charles to Isabella, c. January 1530, *Corpus Documental*, Letter LIII, I, 188–190; Brandi, *Emperor Charles V*, 282–288.

[49] Carande Thobar, *Carlos V y sus banqueros*, II, 435–486; Helen Nader, *Liberty in Absolutist Spain: The Habsburg Sale of Towns, 1516–1700* (Baltimore, 1990), 2, 100.

[50] Carande Thobar, *Carlos V y sus banqueros*, II, 96–100, III, 72.

Chapter 4

The Search for Revenue, II:
Parliamentary Subsidies

Representative assemblies convened by the prince to request subsidies were a distinctive feature of medieval Europe's political landscape, hitherto unknown in any other part of the world. Some such bodies (like the Cortes of León, the predecessor of the Cortes of Castile) dated from as early as the twelfth century, but others, like the Parlamento of Naples, appeared only in the fifteenth century. The subsidies they granted usually ran for a term of two or more years, and were based on some kind of repartition or wealth-estimate.[1] In Castile and in separate Low Countries provinces, rulers could expect the grants to be renewed (albeit with some bargaining) when the current subsidy had expired. In Naples, by the early sixteenth century government officials were collecting the *focatico* without any further consultation of the kingdom's Parlamento.[2] By this time, the annual subsidies had come to be seen as "ordinary," and rulers pressed for "extraordinary" subsidies, to which they claimed to be entitled in time of invasion or other emergencies. Without using the same terminology, officials in Naples did the same thing: they convened the Parlamento to demand "gifts" or *donativi* that were, in effect, extraordinary subsidies.[3] Whatever the names that were used, extraordinary subsidies, and higher ordinary subsidies, could mean new money for cash-strapped Habsburg governments – provided that the parliaments were willing to cooperate.

[1] Calabria, *The Cost of Empire*, 39–40 (note that the *focatico* did not require periodic reapproval by the Parlamento); Carande Thobar, *Carlos V y sus banqueros*, II, chap. XII; Tracy, *A Financial Revolution*, 32–33.

[2] Calabria, *The Cost of Empire*, 40–43; Carande Thobar, *Carlos V y sus banqueros*, I, 536–537; Tracy, *A Financial Revolution*, 32; Ryder, *The Kingdom of Naples*, 210–213.

[3] Calabria, *The Cost of Empire*, 40, 57; Carande Thobar, *Carlos V y sus banqueros*, I, 536–537, 511; James D. Tracy, "The Taxation System of the County of Holland during the Reigns of Charles V and Philip II, 1519–1566," *Economisch- en Sociaal-Historisch Jaarboek* 48 (1984), table I, 108–109.

The Low Countries: "People of Evil Disposition" versus a Government "Colluding" with Its Enemies

Counting only towns of 10,000 or more, the population of present-day Belgium (including Flanders and most of Brabant) was 21% urban in 1550, and the present-day Netherlands (including Holland and the northern part of the old duchy of Brabant) was 15.8%; by comparison, present-day Italy was 15% urban. If towns of 5,000 or more are counted, Flanders was 36% urban by 1500, and south Holland,[4] with its many small towns, 54%.[5] The core provinces were precocious also in the emergence of representative assemblies, prototypes of which appeared in Flanders, as in Léon, as early as the twelfth century. Because each of the territories that made up the Burgundian Low Countries had previously been ruled by separate dynasties, the dukes of Burgundy (1384–1477)[6] had to respect their distinctive institutions. In Flanders, the representative assembly consisted for practical purposes of its third estate, known as the Four Members of Flanders: the cities of Ghent, Bruges, and Ypres, and the so-called Franc of Bruges, a federation of small towns and rural castellanies. In Brabant the abbots of twelve great monasteries made up the first estate, the nobles the second, and four "great cities" the third: Antwerp, Brussels, Louvain, and 's Hertogenbosch.[7] The clergy had no part in the States of Holland, which consisted of the college of nobles (having one vote) and six "great cities": Dordrecht, Leiden, Haarlem, Delft, Amsterdam, and Gouda.[8] Whereas ducal officials fixed the subsidy quotas for each province, the provinces had their own systems of internal allocation, based on assessments of taxable wealth that were renewed only at great intervals. According to the *transport* of Flanders (1517), rural districts were assessed for 56% of the

---

[4] From the Maas to the Zuider Zee, roughly equivalent to the modern province of Zuid-Holland; Noord-Holland was more rural, then and now, though it too had a number of small towns.

[5] Walter Prevenier and Wim Blockmans, *The Burgundian Netherlands* (Cambridge, 1986), 28–33; Jan De Vries, *The Dutch Rural Economy in the Golden Age* (New Haven, Conn., 1974), 81.

[6] Philip the Bold (1364–1404), John the Fearless (1404–1419), Philip the Good (1419–1467), and Charles the Rash (1467–1477).

[7] Often called in English by the French rendering of its name, Bois-le-Duc.

[8] W. Prevenier and W. P. Blockmans, *Handelingen van de Leden en Staten van Vlaanderen-Commision Royale d'Histoire de Belgique, Publications in Quarto*, vols. 58, 64, 67, 72 (Brussels, 1961–1982); W. P. Blockmans, *De Volksvertegenwoordiging in Vlaanderen in de Overgang van de Middeleeuwen naar de Nieuwe Tijd (1384–1506), Verhandelingen van de Koninklijke Akademie van Wetenschappen, Letteren en Schoone Kunsten van België, Klasse der Letteren*, 90 (Brussels, 1978); W. P. Blockmans, "Typologie van de Volksvertegenwoordiging in Europa tijdens de Late Middeleeuwen," *Tijdschrift voor Geschiedenis* 87 (1974): 483–502; W. P. Blockmans, "De representatieve instellingen in het Zuiden, 1384–1483," and P. H. P. Leupen, "De representatieve instellingen in het Noorden, 1384–1482," in D. P. Blok et al., eds., *(Nieuwe) Algemene Geschiedenis der Nederlanden* (15 vols., Haarlem, 1977–1983), IV, 156–163, 164–171.

total, the cities for only 44%, including 14.4% for Bruges, 14.1% for Ghent, and 7% for Ypres. In the Holland *schiltal* of 1514, the countryside was to pay for 37.46% while the cities paid for 59.38%, including 5.58% for Dordrecht, 8.07% for Leiden, 6.33% for Haarlem, 8.52% for Delft, 8.02% for Amsterdam, and 5.54% for Gouda.[9]

At the same time, strong Burgundian rulers molded inherited consultative procedures to their own purposes. For example, instead of dealing with the various urban and rural assemblies convened by his predecessors as counts of Holland, Duke Philip the Good (1419–1467) induced his subjects to send delegates to a single assembly, known henceforth as the States of Holland. Toward the end of his reign, Philip also persuaded the provincial states to send deputies to an assembly soon known as the States General, to hear a "general proposition" stating the government's demands.[10] The restriction of town voting rights to a few so-called great cities was also due to pressure from above. In sixteenth-century Holland, the six great cities encouraged smaller towns to send delegates to certain meetings of the states, on the principle that "broader representation means greater authority" in negotiations with the government. But rather than enlisting the small towns against the tax-evasion strategies of the great cities,[11] as she might have done, Mary of Hungary apparently preferred dealing with as few town governments as possible: she scolded provincial officials for inviting towns that had "no business" at meetings of the states.[12]

The parliaments of the separate Low Countries provinces met more frequently than in any other part of Europe; this is certainly because of the fact that distances were not so great as in large kingdoms like Naples

---

[9] Maddens, *De Beden in het Graafschap Vlaanderen,* 13–16; Tracy, "The Taxation System of Holland," 89, based on GRK, no. 3441, Willem Goudt's account of totals due for an extraordinary subsidy of 100,000 Carolus gulden (1542).

[10] Leupen, "De representatieve instellingen in het Noorden." See also W. Prevenier, and J. G. Smit, eds., *Bronnen voor de Geschiedenis der Dagvaarten van de Staten en Steden van Holland voor 1544,* vol. I (The Hague, 1987).

[11] See my subsequent discussion of the "graces" or rebates demanded by the great cities in all three provinces; the small towns and the countryside often had to make up the difference.

[12] *RSH* 24 March 1542: the advocate, Aert van der Goes (compiler of the first volume of *RSH*), reports that Lodewijk van Schoer, president of the Council of State, questioned him sharply in Mary's presence as to why representatives of several smaller towns were in attendance at a meeting of the states in Brussels. They always come, was the advocate's reply; Mary herself then told him they had "no business here." For the principle that may be involved, AJ 23 August 1523: Dordrecht prefers not to join with other cities in their firm opposition to the territorial inquisition newly established by Charles V's government, but if the other cities send a delegation to Brussels, Dordrecht will join in, "since broader representation may give greater authority" (indien frequentior senatus breeder last gaefve). Delegates of six smaller cities were also present for this meeting, but because the territorial inquisition had not been mentioned in their writ of summons, they refused to given an opinion on the issue without consulting their principals.

and Castile. It may also have been a function of the fact that deputies were tightly controlled by their principals, the town governments. When the states were asked for extraordinary subsidies, deputies might shuttle back home three or four times[13] before returning an answer acceptable to government officials. Duke Charles the Bold (1467–1477) attempted to break down this tradition of town control. Following a "general proposition" explaining the duke's needs to the States General, it was customary for the deputies of each province to be told separately what their quota was; they then returned to their cities, and met again at the provincial level before returning a common response to the next meeting of the States General. Starting with the States General of 1471, the imperious Duke Charles demanded an immediate response from each province, without further consultations. Deputies lacked the courage to say no, even though the duke also demanded subsidies at levels not seen before, to support ambitious plans for conquest in Alsace and Lorraine. For a few years, the States General functioned as a tame national parliament.[14]

Everything changed when Charles's dreams of glory ended with his death in battle at Nancy (Lorraine, January 1477), leaving his daughter Mary as heiress. Charles's great foe, King Louis XI of France (1460–1484), repossessed himself of the duchy of Burgundy[15] – this was the loss that Charles V would try to make good with the 1526 Treaty of Madrid. Meanwhile, the States General recognized Mary as their ruler, but only after she issued a "Great Privilege" nullifying many of her father's centralizing measures. Henceforth, the States General was merely a forum at which provincial deputies heard the government's "general proposition" before returning home to the serious business of considering the "particular proposition" to their province. There were also separate "Great Privileges" for Brabant, Flanders, Holland, and other provinces: in defiance of the principle of majority rule, individual towns with voting rights were now authorized to refuse any tax to which their deputies had not consented. Maximilian of Habsburg, whom Mary had chosen as her husband and her defender against France, was soon forcing the French to withdraw from places they had occupied. But Flanders, fearing that Maximilian would prolong the war in hopes of recovering the duchy of Burgundy,

---

[13] A practice known in Netherlandish as *ruggespraak* (backspeak).

[14] J. A. van Houtte et al., eds., *Algemene Geschiedenis der Nederlanden* (11 vols., Utrecht, 1949–1958), III, 269; Richard Vaughan, *Charles the Bold* (London, 1973), 185–189, 205–210, 414–415; H. G. Koenigsberger, "The Powers of Deputies in Sixteenth-Century Assemblies," in his *Estates and Revolutions* (Ithaca, N.Y., 1971), 176–210.

[15] The duchy of Burgundy was the apanage granted to Duke Philip the Bold (1368–1404) by his older brother, France's King Charles V. When Charles V demanded the return of the duchy as part of the 1526 Treaty of Madrid (see Chapter 2), he pursued an ambition cherished by his dynasty ever since the disaster of 1477.

refused to accept him as regent in Flanders for the couple's infant son, Archduke Philip the Fair. Maximilian's relations with Flanders worsened following Mary's premature death in 1482. From 1485 there were periods of open civil war, with Maximilian suffering at one point the indignity of being placed under arrest by the burghers of Bruges (1488). In the end, his German mercenaries were more than a match for the civic militias of Ghent and Bruges; the 1492 Peace of Cadzand imposed terms on Ghent, the last holdout, and nullified the Great Privilege of Flanders. When Maximilian was elected Holy Roman Emperor (1495), Philip the Fair made the obligatory "joyful entry" tour of all his major towns, so he could swear to uphold the privileges of each province and be acclaimed as duke of Brabant, count of Flanders, count of Holland, and so forth (Charles would do the same when he was declared of age in 1514).[16] As Philip swore to uphold Holland's privileges, his councillors were careful to omit from the oath the terms of that province's Great Privilege of 1477.[17] From this time forward, government officials – if not the towns themselves – operated on the assumption that the vital principle of majority rule in the provincial parliaments had been reestablished.

Outside of Flanders, Maximilian had remarkable success in winning over the great noble families that had supported Burgundian rule, like the Croy of Hainaut, the Lalaing of the Douai region, the Brabant branch of the Nassau family (based in Breda), and the Egmont in Holland. Grouped together in the Order of the Golden Fleece, the families undertook to hold the country together for the new Habsburg dynasty. When Archduke Philip died unexpectedly of sweating sickness in 1506, they gave their loyalty to Philip's sister, Margaret of Austria, the widowed duchess of Savoy, whom Maximilian named as regent for his six-year-old grandson, the future Charles V.[18]

During her two terms as regent (1506–1514 and 1517–1530), Margaret found that, majority rule or not, towns that had given their consent to a subsidy would not pay unless all their sister cities paid. For example, when the States of Brabant were asked for 85,000 Rhine gulden (1510), the clergy, the nobles, and three of the four cities assented to 70,000. But the

---

[16] There never was a general territorial title by which rulers of the Burgundian and Habsburg Netherlands were recognized.

[17] Walter Prevenier and Wim Blockmans, *The Promised Lands: The Low Countries under Burgundian Rule, 1369–1530*, tr. Elizabeth Fackelman (Phildelphia, 1999), 199–212; P. J. Blok, *Geschiedenis eener Hollandse Stad* (4 vols., The Hague, 1910–1918), II, 25–27; A. G. Jongkees, "Het Groot Privileg van Holland," in W. P. Blockmans, ed., *Het Algemeen en de Geswestelijke Grote Privileges van Maria van Bougondië* (Heule, 1985), 145–235.

[18] The best study of these families as a group remains Paul Rosenfeld, "The Provincial Governors from the Minority of Charles V to the Revolt," *Standen en Landen/Anciens Pays et Assemblées d'État* 17 (1959): 1–63.

agreement collapsed because 's Hertogenbosch refused to pay anything.[19] In practice, Margaret's commissioners had to negotiate separately with each voting great city.[20] Although towns sometimes had legitimate reasons for not meeting their quotas, magistrates were very good at special pleading. The cumulative effect of government concessions over the years may be seen in calculations for the first year of Mary of Hungary's regency (1531), which was also the first year of a six-year ordinary subsidy approved by all three core provinces. In Brabant, the clergy paid a third of its assessment, Louvain slightly less; Brussels and 's Hertogenbosch paid more than half, while wealthy Antwerp, expecting other favors from the government, did not demand any "graces" or rebates. In Flanders, however, Bruges paid but 6.94% of its quota; Ghent, 11.91%; Ypres, 8.54%; and the Franc of Bruges, 14.85%. The nominal value of the ordinary subsidy in Flanders was reduced in this way by 34.82%, with the Four Members – which alone had voting rights – claiming 96.9% of the quota reductions. In Holland, prosperous Amsterdam, like Antwerp, expected other favors and paid five-sixths of its quota, but Leiden paid only 33.33%; Dordrecht, 35.82%; and Haarlem, 39.47%. Thus, graces ate away 35.24% of Holland's subsidy, with the six great cities enjoying 61.8% of the benefit.[21] In effect, magistrates were trying to achieve for their burghers the enviable status already enjoyed by the clergy and the nobles, who in some provinces had the privilege of voting taxes to be paid by others. But government officials believed it was only a matter of time before country people would rise in wrath against the selfishness of the great towns,[22] much as the burghers of 's Hertogenbosch had risen against the tax exemptions of their clergy in 1525.[23]

Margaret also had to deal with long-standing quarrels[24] that divided one province from another, all the more so because military threats to the

---

[19] 's Hertogenbosch complained that it had already spent a large sum to have its militia recapture a castle that had been occupied by troops from Guelders.

[20] Antoine de Lalaing, count of Hoogstraten and *Stadtholder* of Holland, to Mary of Hungary, 15 May 1532, Aud. 1525: Vanden Dale, Mary's commissioner, failed to get the States of Holland to agree to a subsidy because he rejected the advice to negotiate separately with deputies from each town.

[21] Aud. 875, "Etat des revenus et charges, 1531–1536," folios 1–40 for 1531.

[22] E.g., AJ 10 September 1523, 26 May 1525, 25–27 June 1536; Gerrit van Assendelft, first councillor of the Council of Holland, to Hoogstraten, 5 January 1537, Aud. 1530.

[23] Albertus Cuperinus, *Chronicke*, in C. R. Hermans, *Verzameling van Kronyken, Charters en Oorkonden betrekkelijk de Stad en Meerij van 's Hertogenbosch*, vol. 1 ('s Hertogenbosch, 1848), 90–91. The contemporaneous German Peasants' War had a strong anticlerical thrust.

[24] For example, Flanders and Holland were frequently at odds over rules governing the herring fishery, and even more over commercial relations with the Hanseatic League; Bruges was one of the main entrepôts for Hanseatic merchants, but the principal obstacle to Holland's commercial penetration of the Baltic was Lübeck, the dominant power among Hanseatic cities: James D. Tracy, "Herring Wars: Efforts by the Government of the Habsburg Netherlands to Achieve Strategic Control of the North Sea, ca. 1520–1560," *Sixteenth Century Journal* 24 (1993): 249–272; Klaus Spading, *Holland und die Hanse im 15en Jahrhundert* (Weimar, 1973).

Low Countries came from different directions. From the south, French armies could enter Artois, Hainaut, Namur, or Luxembourg without having to cross any natural barrier. Flanders lay just north of Artois; southern Brabant, just north of Hainaut and Namur. From the east, armies from the duchy of Guelders had to cross only one river to strike at Limburg, northern Brabant, or Holland.[25] Government officials naturally expected all the provinces to help "put out the fire" wherever it struck, but each province had vivid memories of having been left in the lurch by the others in its time of need.[26] Meeting at Ghent (Flanders) in 1508, the States General declared that the war against Guelders was a "particular" affair of Brabant and not a matter of general concern to "Burgundian" lands as a whole. In 1512 Brabant, Holland, and Hainaut agreed to their quotas in an extraordinary subsidy for war against Guelders, but Flanders, Lille, Douai, and Orchies refused. In December 1523 it was Holland's turn to refuse to contribute anything for the defense of Hainaut, ravaged by the French; Hainaut still had its farmland, Hollanders insisted, but the Baltic commerce that sustained their province was utterly ruined by the current war against Lübeck and her Hanseatic allies. In April 1524, when the States of Brabant were asked to form a "Union" with Holland to prosecute the war against Guelders, Antwerp and 's Hertogenbosch agreed, but Brussels and Louvain refused, citing the contributions they were expected to make toward the defense of Hainaut and Luxemburg.[27]

Clashes between court factions highlighted this geographical fault line. Noble families with extensive holdings in French-speaking provinces – including Guillaume de Croy, lord of Chièvres, first chamberlain for young Archduke Charles – did not see why minor skirmishes in the northeast should impede the important business of keeping the peace with France. Moreover, because the Four Members of Flanders nurtured old suspicions about Maximilian and his loyal daughter Margaret, the emperor had difficulty rallying the States General behind his own long-standing grievances against the perfidious French.[28] But other nobles had extensive holdings

25 Utrecht and Overijssel lay between parts of Guelders and the main part of Holland, but these lands did not come under Habsburg rule until 1527, when the prince-bishop of Utrecht, invaded from Guelders, renounced his temporalities in favor of Charles.

26 Thus in 1508 the States General declined to help pay for an army to respond to the invasion of Brabant by Guelders; in 1512, while other provinces agreed to a request for 150,000 Rhine gulden to aid Brabant after another invasion from Guelders, Flanders, Lille, Douai, and Orchies would only consent to 60,000: Alexandre Henne, *Histoire du règne de Charles-Quint en Belgique* (10 vols., Brussels, 1858–1860), I, 176–177, 293–294.

27 Ibid., I, 249, 294; AJ 29 December 1523, 25 April 1524 (cf. 12 May 1528: Antwerp and 's Hertogenbosch again agree to form a union with the States of Holland, but Brussels and Louvain again refuse).

28 In addition to Burgundy (note 15), Maximilian lost a wife to France. In 1491, when he was betrothed to Anne of Brittany and France's Charles VIII was betrothed to Maximilian's daughter Margaret of

in areas frequently ravaged by Guelders, including Count Hendrik van
Nassau in Brabant, and, in Holland, Floris van Egmont, count of
IJsselstein. With their backing, and that of towns in Holland and northern
Brabant, Margaret was able to press the fight against France's ally, the duke
of Guelders, if not against France itself.[29]

Had Margaret's commanders covered themselves in glory, she might have
won the gratitude of subjects who feared Guelders, and the respect of those
who feared France. Instead, their repeated failures fanned dangerous suspicions. Certain broadsides in "derision and contempt" of Margaret were
affixed to church doors; in Bruges a man had part of his tongue cut out for
saying in public that Margaret would "destroy everything if we don't do
as she wishes." In his Latin *Deeds of the Dukes of Brabant* (1526), Adrianus
Barlandus, a humanist professor at the University of Louvain, presented
a government that schemed against its own subjects. Thus the sack of a
Brabant town by forces from Guelders in 1507 was due to the sinister motives of a Habsburg commander who waited passively nearby (in fact, he
had orders not to risk his precious mercenary army in a field engagement).
Erasmus of Rotterdam took suspicions like those of his friend Barlandus
to a level that can only be called political paranoia. When a German mercenary company known as the Black Band rampaged through Holland
in 1517, burning Alkmaar in the north and Asperen in the south, Erasmus
knew why: "Because the Hollanders were complaining" about the government's demand for an extraordinary subsidy, "this tempest was loosed upon
them by design." Erasmus believed that princes and nobles "colluded" with
their apparent enemies, the better to milk the wealth of their subjects.[30]

These not-so-cloistered scholars echoed conspiracy theories common
among their countrymen. In October 1523 the States of Holland accused
the provincial governor or Stadtholder – Antoine de Lalaing, count of
Hoogstraten – of failing to live up to his promises to "avenge the emperor's
honor" by invading Guelders. The deputies suggested sarcastically that they
might have misunderstood the purpose of a recently granted war subsidy;
perhaps there was truth in "what people said, that if the subsidy had not
been promised, peace would have been made." During another heated
exchange with Hoogstraten, deputies explained why their constituents[31]
would not suffer paying more taxes:

Austria, Charles repudiated Margaret, intercepted Anne on her journey to join Maximilian, and
   forced Brittany's heiress to marry him instead.
[29] J. E. A. L. Struick, *Gelre en Habsburg, 1492–1528* (Arnhem, 1960); for conflicts with France, Andreas
   von Walther, *Die Anfänge Karls V* (Leipzig, 1911), and Henne, *Histoire du règne de Charles-Quint*.
[30] Henne, *Histoire du règne de Charles-Quint*, I, 248, 309–310; Adrianus Barlandus, *Historia Rerum
   Gestarum a Brabantiae Ducibis* (Brussels, 1585), 169, 171; James D. Tracy, *The Politics of Erasmus: A
   Pacifist Intellectual and His Political Milieu* (Toronto, 1978), chap. 4.
[31] Constituents in an indirect sense: the magistrates of Holland's towns formed oligarchies recruited
   by co-option, not popular election. But because towns often paid their subsidy quotas from the

The common man [*gemeen man*] murmurs greatly, and cannot understand why men from Guelders crossed the Vaart [near Utrecht] and came into our land immediately after our soldiers withdrew, or why houses and fields at Naarden were burned by the enemy two or three days after the eighty cavalrymen stationed there were called away to Brabant; the people are in an evil mood, thinking all is trickery, and there is danger of an uprising.

In Brussels the next month, Amsterdam's town secretary conveyed the same message to Jean Carondolet, archbishop of Palermo, and president of the Council of State: "One cannot induce people to consent to further taxes because they think it will be the same old story; one can expunge this infamy from the hearts of men only by carrying the war into the land of Guelders."[32]

Public mistrust stemmed in part from unwillingness to accept the brutal logic of contemporary warfare. Deputies to the provincial states had no illusions about their civic militias; they usually endorsed the common belief that townsmen were no good at fighting any distance beyond their city walls.[33] Because mercenaries were the obvious alternative to militiamen, the government's military planning was at the mercy of the utter opportunism of companies of professional soldiers, mostly from Germany.[34] The "common man" could not understand why his majesty's subjects should suffer unspeakable atrocities at the hands of mercenaries who had formerly served under the Habsburg banner, as the Black Band did before its rampage through Holland 1517.[35] Indeed, how could one persuade hardworking peasants and craftsmen that yet more money was needed, and right away, to prevent men who signed on to fight in Charles's name from defecting to the enemy as soon as they arrived in the Low Countries; or to give the government's commander in Holland enough of what his men were owed so that they would not "go over" when he returned empty-handed to their camp? Not even a truce brought relief,

---

receipts of local excise taxes that bore most heavily on those least able to pay, magistrates could endanger their own position by giving way too freely to the government's demands.

[32] AJ 25 October, 28 December 1523, 18 January 1524.

[33] AJ 25 September, 8–12 December 1523 (but also 21–23 November 1523: Dordrecht's deputies say, give us the money and we will defend ourselves), and *RSH* 16 June 1528.

[34] Men of fighting age had too many opportunities to chose from in the prosperous core provinces: *RSH* 16 June 1528, Delft's deputies assert that local men will not sign on as soldiers for less than six to ten silver stuivers per day (that is, nine to fifteen Carolus gulden for a month of thirty days; six years later (*RSH* 14 March 1533) the going rate for "foreign" knechten was said to be five Carolus gulden per month.

[35] AJ 30 July 1523: alleging the need for more funds to keep troops fighting under the Habsburg banner in neighboring Friesland, Margaret's commissioner, Gerard Mulart, reminded the deputies what had happened to Alkmaar "propter non solutionem," that is, because the government had run out of money to keep the Black Band on its payroll.

because still more money was needed to persuade the mercenaries to go home, without "eating" the lands of their employer.[36]

Habsburg officials grasped the problem in a general way. Mercurino Gattinara, who earned his stripes as an adviser to Margaret of Austria during her first regency in the Low Countries, passed on some useful advice to Charles: "Seeing all their sacrifices end in a truce, peoples will not resign themselves to more, for they believe the semblance of war is a pretext for taking their money."[37] But one may doubt how well the French-speaking aristocrats like Gattinara and Hoogstraten understood the Netherlandish-speaking burghers who confronted them in the provincial states. Reared in the belief that only persons of noble birth could understand matters of honor and high politics, they saw clearly enough how tenacious the deputies were in defending the material interests of their towns, and of the mercantile elite. What they sometimes failed to see was that burghers were also willing, under the right circumstances, to make sacrifices for the "Burgundian" cause. When the States of Brabant refused a proposal to hire troops to guard the frontier with Guelders, it was because they preferred to back an invasion of enemy territory and saw it as a waste of money to station soldiers along a boundary that could be crossed at many points. But Margaret of Austria dismissed the Brabanders as "people of an evil disposition."[38] Because Gattinara knew of the factionalism that had caused civil wars in Holland for more than a hundred years, ending in 1492, and because he knew also that the nobleman most identified with the war against Guelders was from a family strongly identified with one of the two factions, he feared that Holland as whole might go over to the duke of Guelders in order to have peace; here too one may speak of political paranoia.[39]

Both the government and the burghers had things to learn about how to wage war in a society whose military budget depended upon the consent of the governed. In this respect, as Chapter 12 will show, the wars of Charles V's reign would be a harsh but effective teacher.

The Parlamento of Naples

The Parlamento of Naples mirrored in its structure the power of the baronage. Meeting by tradition in the Franciscan cloister of San Lorenzo in Naples, each of the three chambers gave its vote separately on the government's proposition: the titled nobility (princes, dukes, marquises,

[36] AJ 9 October 1523, 25–28 January, 15–23 March, 7 June 1524.
[37] Gattinara's "ten commandments of war," Lanz, Letter 49, I, 89–90.
[38] Henne, *Histoire du règne de Charles-Quint*, I, 287; AJ 25 September, 8–12 December, 17–18 December 1523; *RSH* 16 June 1528, 20 September 1534.
[39] Tracy, *The Politics of Erasmus*, 79; for the Hoek and Kabeljauw (Hook and Codfish) wars, Michiel Brokken, *Het Ontstaan van de Hoekse en Kabeljauwse Twisten* (Zutfen, 1982).

and counts), the untitled nobility, and the cities of the royal domain, excluding Naples. As viceroys gained control of the process by which urban
deputies to the Parlemento were chosen, domain cities were less and less
inclined to bear the expense of sending representatives to a distant capital.
In effect, Naples spoke for the kingdom's towns, even though it was not
represented in the Parlamento, because it was exempt from the hearth
census as well as the ordinary hearth tax. Naples itself was governed by
the deputies of six neighborhood corporations known as *seggi* (seats); the
city's mayor or *sindico* was chosen by turns from the six *seggi*. The five
seggi in which membership was limited to the nobility were dominated by
the kingdom's great nobles, who had palaces in the capital; the sixth was
the *seggio del Popolo*, created in 1495. At sessions of the Parlamento, the
heads of the six *seggi* collected the votes of each of the three chambers.
A "deputation" then presented the viceroy with the Parlemento's response,
together with certain requests or *capitoli* for his consideration. By 1536 the
deputation had a fixed composition: six titled barons, six untitled barons,
and two representatives from each of the six *seggi* in Naples. Earlier in the
sixteenth century, the deputation seems to have been made up of no more
than four to six men, who represented in some sense the same important
constituencies. From 1511 the *sindico* of Naples had the right of speaking
in behalf of the deputation.[40]

Parlamentos of the sixteenth century were on occasion called upon
to approve a special form of direct taxation, the gift or *donativo*. One-
fourth was paid by the baronage (in lieu of a tax on the income of their
feudal properties, which was otherwise collected annually); the other three-
fourths was apportioned among the *università* and collected as an add-on
to the annual hearth tax. Ferdinand the Catholic set the precedent when
he summoned a Parlamento (1507–1508) solely to consider his request for
a *donativo* of three carlins per hearth (.3 scudi) for each of the next seven
years, to compensate him for what he had spent in expelling French armies
from the kingdom. The deputation brought back an affirmative response,
together with *capitoli* requesting that only natives be appointed to office in
the kingdom, to which the king agreed. This grant, with a gross value of
80,200 scudi or Neapolitan ducats per year, was followed by further *donativi*
in 1510 (4.7 carlins per hearth for the marriage of Ferdinand's daughter) and
1518 (110,000 ducats in all for the marriage of Charles's sister, Eleanor).[41]

These reasons given for these requests bear a close relationship to the
traditional ideas about the circumstances in which a lord might lawfully

[40] D'Agostino, *Parlamento e società nel regno di Napoli*, 18–35; Aurelio Cernigliaro, *Sovranità e feudo nel
regno di Napoli* (2vols., Naples, 1983), I, 198–201; Elena Croce, "I parlamenti napoletani sotto la
dominazione spagnola," *Archivo Storico per le Provinze Napoletane*, n.s., 22 (1936): 341–358.

[41] Coniglio, *Il regno di Napoli*, 181–183; Caracciolo, *Uffici, difesa e corpi rappresentativi*, 194, 201, 209.

demand "feudal aides" of his vassals.[42] Archduke Charles's Burgundian advisers, familiar with the idea of extraordinary subsidies in the Low Countries, saw a wider scope for *donativi* in Naples. Charles Leclerc's instructions for his first mission to Naples (January 1517) included asking "the estates of the realm" for a grant of 807,000 ducats over five or six years, to buy back at a capitalization ratio of 1:10 the proprietary rights of various barons and ecclesiastics over hearth tax receipts in their districts, with an estimated annual value of 80,629 ducats.[43] But no Parlamento was actually summoned until 1520, when, according to the instructions for his second trip to the kingdom, Leclerc was to ask for a *donativo* of 200,000 ducats "for defense against the Turks, and for the expenses of our election as Holy Roman Emperor." This Parlamento was precedent-setting in a different way. The deputation promised a grant of 300,000 ducats payable over three years, 100,000 more than had been requested. But at the instance of Lodovico di Montaldo, a deputation member who was also one of the three regents of the Chancery serving on the Collateral Council, they also presented a single *capitolo* stipulating that all of the money should be expended for needs within the kingdom. If Charles's government was demanding that *donativi* have the open-ended character of extraordinary subsidies, the Parlamento was, for the first time, insisting that agreements of this kind had a reciprocal character: there was to be no grant of money unless the representatives of the sovereign agreed to the conditions for its use.[44] In fact, it seems that the money Charles needed to pay off part of the loan for his imperial election came not from this *donativo*, but from sums "recovered" by Leclerc by other means.[45]

From 1522 to 1527, while the viceroy, Lannoy, was preoccupied by Charles's affairs elsewhere in the peninsula, the kingdom's finances suffered from neglect.[46] In the fall of 1528, just after the French had been expelled, the Parlamento alleged three reasons for refusing the *donativo* requested by Orange's lieutenant, Pompeo Colonna: the kingdom was just beginning to recover from civil war, arrears from the *donativo* of 1520 were still being collected, and the *capitoli* (presumably also those of 1520) had never been confirmed by the sovereign. Nonetheless, with the help of Colantonio Caracciolo, marquess of Vico, and Girolamo Pellegrino, *eletto*

[42] Chapter 3, note 15.
[43] Leclerc, "Rapport et Recueil," folio 9v. Leclerc's tally of the hearth tax rights held by barons and ecclesiastics was virtually the same: 80,749.
[44] I follow here the interpretation of D'Agostino, *Parlamento e società nel regno di Napoli*, 206–210; Coniglio, *Il regno di Napoli*, 189.
[45] Chapter 3, note 25.
[46] Chapter 3, note 35: Figueroa's finding that the accounts of many revenue collectors had not been audited for the years 1520–1525.

or chief magistrate of the Seggio del Popolo in Naples, Colonna obtained agreement for an immediate levy of 50,000 ducats and the promise of 100,000 to 200,000 more if certain conditions were met. In return for a grant total of 200,000 in Charles's name, Orange agreed to the deputation's conditions, including a demand that Spanish troops garrisoned in Naples and other cities be sent out of the kingdom as soon as possible.[47]

In 1529 the kingdom's treasurer, Alonso Sanchez, returned from Spain with a "secret instruction"[48] from Charles for convening the Parlamento to ask approval for a new tax of unprecedented size, large enough to cleanse the kingdom's ledgers of debt. The unknown author of the memorandum carried by Sanchez assumed a total of 350,000 potentially taxable hearths for the whole kingdom: 300,000 in the hearth census, another 100,000 for the city of Naples (not included in the *focatico* census), with a subtraction of 50,000 for exempt persons (barons and clergy) and for hearths abandoned in the last war. Assuming further than one *tomolo* of grain (approximately 55.3 liters) was sufficient for the needs of seven hearths for one day, the author calculated that the taxable population consumed 50,000 *tomoli* per day, or more than 18,000,000 during the course of a year. A tax of only one grain (one-twentieth of a ducat) per *tomolo* would thus yield 900,000 ducats per year, or, "if one assumes that people eat less," 800,000. To be sure, the very mention of an annual levy of this size would evoke resistance, but "the people need not know the total sum, for one need not mention it in the Parlamento; one need only propose the grain tax [*dacio*] as a revenue for the crown, and leave the hearing of accounts to those who know how to do this."[49]

The Spanish official who drafted this proposal was naive if he believed the Parlamento would approve a tax without demanding to know the total sum. But in a time of desperate need, following the recent rebellion, officials in Naples seemed willing to accept the idea of looking to the Parlamento for new revenues. In July 1530 Sigismondo Loffredo, one of the regents of the Chancery, wrote to Charles concerning the different ways badly needed sums might be raised. One must not sell any more domain towns, he argued, for there were now only forty-five, even fewer than at

[47] D'Agostino, *Parlamento e società nel regno di Napoli*, 217–218. This was the same Pellegrino from whom Camerario was later to collect 100,000 ducats, in consideration of the fact that his accounts as a revenue collector had not been audited for twelve years: Chapter 3, note 36.

[48] As was common on diplomatic missions of the period, Sanchez was given "instructions," to be used as his credentials, and also "secret instructions," to be shared only with those designated; see Coniglio, *Consulte e bilanci del Viceregno di Napoli*, Document 36, 391–407.

[49] Ibid., 405–406. The text does not mention a rate of one grain per tomolo, but it makes the numbers come out even (50,000 tomoli per day times 365 days a year = 18,250,000 tomoli times .05 ducats = 912,500 ducats). In regard to the hearing of accounts, I read the text's "echar" as "escuchar."

the beginning of Charles's reign. Instead, Viceroy Philibert de Châlons, the prince of Orange, should summon a Parlamento as soon as he had successfully completed his siege of Florence and returned to Naples. In fact, Orange was killed before Florence. But Charles sent orders in keeping with Loffredo's advice,[50] and Orange's successors did indeed turn to the Parlamento for help, albeit not in the terms proposed in Sanchez's instructions.

In light of these precedents, it would not seem that prospects were good for a parliamentary grant as large as 800,000 ducats, as had been suggested by Charles's officials in the instructions for Leclerc, and again in the memorandum carried by Sanchez. Owing to Orange's death, it fell to his lieutenant, Colonna, to carry out Charles's order to summon a Parlamento. Colonna informed the emperor that no assembly could be called for now, because Spanish troops had yet to vacate the kingdom, as was stipulated in the *capitoli*. When the Parlamento did convene (summer 1531), Colonna made an unprecedented demand for a *donativo* of 600,000; moreover, he wanted this sum collected not over a term of years, as was customary, but within one year.[51] Many observers no doubt thought that Colonna, who was ambitious for appointment as viceroy but heartily disliked by the barons, had overplayed his hand. Nonetheless, Colonna's proposal, accepted by the Parlamento in 1532, marked the beginning of a new era of parliamentary subsidies in Naples, a fact that was to be of no small importance for the financing of Charles's wars. The reasons for this turnabout are the subject of Chapter 13.

The Cortes of Castile

Like Aragón and Portugal, Castile grew out of the Reconquista. After Moorish invaders overwhelmed the Visigothic kingdom of Spain in 711, Christian princes held only the northern rim of Iberia, beyond the Cantabrian Mountains. In the course of intermittent warfare against Muslim states, the Cantabrian principality of Asturias expanded south across the mountains, forming the Kingdom of León. The addition of Old Castile, including key cities like Valladolid, Segovia, Salamanca, Ávila, Guadalajara, and Madrid, created the Kingdom of León and Castile, soon known simply as Castile. Estremadura, south of the Duero, had fewer important towns, as did New Castile, south of the Tagus River, save for Toledo. Last of all came Andalusia, the garden of Muslim Spain. The "kingdoms" of Córdoba, Jaen, and Seville were conquered in the first half of the thirteenth century, but Granada, the last remnant of Muslim Spain,

[50] D'Agostino, *Parlamento e società nel regno di Napoli*, 218.
[51] Ibid., 219-231.

did not surrender until 1492, only eight years before Charles's birth. This secular struggle against Islam kept the traditions of Crusade warfare alive in Castile; fighting men of noble rank enjoyed here a social prestige not to be found anywhere else in Europe.

In contrast to Naples and the Low Countries, the distinct regions of old-regime Castile were never organized as provinces. Every bit of land, whether under royal or seigneurial jurisdiction, was incorporated within the boundaries of a municipality.[52] Cities (*ciudades*) had a certain honorific priority,[53] but towns (*villas*) had the same status as governing centers for patches of countryside, small or large. Castile's "few hundred"[54] town-states varied greatly in size, generally along a north–south line reflecting the course of the Reconquista. In the far north, villages sometimes joined together to form a town of their own. In New Castile, Toledo controlled a rural territory embracing seventy villages (*pueblos*) and approximately 6,150 square kilometers, or 2,330 square miles[55] – about the size of the province of Holland. In Andalusia, the "kingdom" of Córdoba included sixty-two villages and approximately 13,718 square kilometers or about 5,220 square miles.[56]

Some villages escaped the control of their municipality: Castile's kings over the centuries alienated royal lands (*realengo*) by granting town charters to villages held by powerful nobles, or favored ecclesiastical corporations.[57] But most were subject to taxes and crop-marketing rules decreed by their principal towns. Hence "the real tension in this society was not between monarch and nobles, nor between lords and their subjects, but between municipalities, and especially between towns and their subject villages."[58] Isabella the Catholic (r. 1474–1504) saw in this tension an opportunity. Instead of granting town charters to villages controlled by her favorites, she sold charters to villages controlled by her enemies among the nobles.[59]

[52] For this paragraph, save as noted, Nader, *Liberty in Absolutist Spain,* 1–12.

[53] Jean-Pierre Dedieu, *L'Espagne de 1492 à 1808* (Paris, 1994), 102; Nader, *Liberty in Absolutist Spain,* 74: cities, but not towns, enjoyed judicial autonomy (e.g., royal judges entered a city only by invitation of the city government), because towns, but not cities, always had a lord, either one of the great nobles, or the king himself.

[54] Dedieu, *L'Espagne de 1492 à 1808,* 107.

[55] Antonio Dominguez Ortiz, *El Antiguo Régimen: Los reyes catolicos y los Austrias* (Madrid, 1973), 129; Julian Montemayor, *Tolède entre fortune et déclin (1530–1640)* (Limoges, 1996), 92–100.

[56] José Ignacio Fortea Perez, *Córdoba en el siglo XVI: Las bases demográficas y económicos de una expansión urbana* (Córdoba, 1981), 64–124.

[57] Montemayor, *Tolède entre fortune et déclin,* 100, calculates that about 10% of Toledo's rural *tierra* had "escaped" the control of the city in this way.

[58] Nader, *Liberty in Absolutist Spain,* 6.

[59] Ibid., 71, 83–84. In Castile's civil war, one faction supported Isabella, while the other backed Enrique IV's daughter, whom Isabella's partisans styled "La Beltraneja," believing her to be the daughter of the queen's alleged lover, Beltrán de la Cueva.

Charles V was not deaf to the appeals of villages willing to pay for the coveted privilege of being a town, though in such cases he offered the town a chance to make a higher bid to keep its territory intact.[60] Over the long run, the same Spanish monarchy that raised money in Naples by selling towns to private lords raised money in Castile by selling urban charters. If 60% of the kingdom's organized communities were classed as villages in 1500, by 1700 75% were classed as municipalities.[61]

This new focus by historians on municipalities[62] fits into a broader reinterpretation of the balance of power in early modern Castile. Liberal historians of the early nineteenth century saw in the Cortes of Charles's reign an assembly representing the people and their interests.[63] By contrast, historians of the late nineteenth century saw the reigns of Isabella and of Ferdinand of Aragón (1479–1516) as marking the transition from a weak monarchy dependent on its nobility to an "absolute" monarchy that allied with the urban middle classes to humble Castile's grandees. In this view, Castile's tame Cortes had nothing in common with England's proud tradition of parliamentary independence, especially from Charles V's reign, when the assembly meekly granted the *servicios* demanded, and only then presented petitions for the king to consider at his good pleasure.[64] But the idea that the Catholic kings used burgher support to undermine the position of the great nobles has now come to be seen as nothing more than a "stubborn legend."[65] Some usurpations of jurisdiction by the nobles during the civil wars of the 1470s were indeed overturned by Ferdinand and Isabella, but many more were tacitly accepted, and supporters of the crown were rewarded with new privileges. The Mendóza clan, for example, achieved control of Guadalajara: "by unwritten law" the duke of Infantado, the head of the family, now had the right to control the city council and, with it, Guadalajara's vote in the Cortes. Isabella did indeed provide *corregidores* or royal governors for the

[60] Ibid., 7, 99–101 (Charles also preferred to take advantage of papal permission to detach lands from the control of Castile's military orders, for sale to noble families seeking to expand their holdings); Montemayor, *Tolède entre fortune et déclin*, 97: in 1537, Toledo obtained from Charles a privilege by which its villages were prohibited from seeking town charters.

[61] Nader, *Liberty in Absolutist Spain*, 3.

[62] Ibid., 12, identifies as the first study to reflect a real understanding of the relationship between town and countryside Carla Rahn Phillips's *Ciudad Real, 1500–1750: Growth, Crisis, and Readjustment in the Spanish Economy* (Cambridge, Mass., 1979). (1979).

[63] One work criticized by Carande Thobar, *Carlos y sus banqueros*, II, 504–508, is Francisco Martínez Marina, *Téoria de las Cortes de los reinos de Léon y Castilla* (2 vols., Madrid, 1813).

[64] For this view of the Cortes during Charles's reign, Colmeiro, *Cortes de los antiguos reinos*, Introduccion, II, 101, 129, 140. The most recent defender of the thesis of a strong monarchy and a weak Cortes during the reign of the catholic kings is Juan Manuel Carretero Zamora, *Cortes, monarquía, ciudades. Las Cortes de Castilla a comienzos de la epoca moderna (1476–1515)* (Madrid, 1988).

[65] Dominguez Ortiz, *El Antiguo Régimen*, 13.

towns, but this was a way of keeping peace between urban factions, not a strategy of royal centralization. The *corregidor* presided over meetings of the *ayuntamiento* or town council, but could not control its deliberations; the town, not the crown, paid his salary.[66] Finally, just as the absolute-monarchy thesis depended on the idea that there was a fundamental clash of interests between nobles and burghers,[67] the new picture of a balance of power among crown, nobles, and towns rests on a contrary insight: towns remained politically important precisely because they came to be dominated by a sector of the nobility whose wealth and prestige continued to grow.

Among Castile's noble families, the grandees, recognized as such from the beginning of Charles's reign, stood out by virtue of their vast estates, usually in Estremadura, New Castile, or Andalusia; they often held the title of duke and claimed the right to stand "covered" (with their caps on) in the presence of the monarch. *Caballeros* (horsemen)[68] were, as the name implies, required by law to maintain a horse of a certain quality, together with armor and weapons, and to hold themselves ready (until age sixty) for a summons to war in the king's name. As late as the fifteenth century, *caballeros* had to appear in arms at periodic regional musters. Finally, *hidalgos* (sons of somebody) had no legal obligation to keep horse and arms; instead they had to be able to prove, by the testimony of neighbors, that their fathers and both grandfathers were recognized as *hidalgos*, meaning that they enjoyed exemption from taxes that commoners had to pay. Kings could issue grants of *hidalguia* – Isabella's brother and predecessor, Enrique IV, was prodigal in this regard – but *hidalgos* "by blood" did not readily accept these nobles-by-decree. In 1523 Charles V revoked all previous grants of *hidalguia*; there were other ways the crown could profit from the ambitions of social climbers.[69]

No other country in Europe had such a high percentage of nobles. According to a census for Castile completed between 1528 and 1536, there were 784,624 households of lay commoners, and 108,358 of *hidalgos*; in a total population estimated at 5 million, there were about 541,790 people

[66] Ibid., 13–15; Marie-Claude Gerbet, *Les nobles dans le royaume de Castile: Étude sur les structures sociaux en Estremadure 1454–1516* (Paris, 1979), 126; Henry Kamen, *Spain, 1469–1714: A Society of Conflict* (2nd ed., London, 1991), 24–26.

[67] An assumption grounded not merely in classical Marxist historiography but in its mirror image, the liberal historiography of the late nineteenth and early twentieth centuries, of which the works of the great Belgian historian Henri Pirenne may be taken as representative.

[68] Compare similar terms with the same dual meaning in other languages: *eques* in classical and medieval Latin, *chevalier* in French, *cavaglieri* in Italian, *ridder* in Dutch, *Ritter* in German. The English term "knight" is an exception to the pattern.

[69] Dominguez Ortiz, *El Antiguo Régimen*, 105–116; Gerbet, *Les nobles dans le royaume de Castile*, 107–137. For the sale of urban magistracies during Charles's reign, see note 80.

recognized as being of noble descent, or 10.8%.[70] The density of noble
families varied greatly, along the same north-south line mentioned earlier.
Nearly half of the *hidalgos* lived in the Cantabrian mountain zone, including
the Atlantic coast. South of the mountains, one could find in rural Castile
hidalgos who struggled to keep up appearances – Cervantes' impecunious
gentleman of La Mancha was not just a literary invention.[71] *Caballeros* were
to be found in the towns of Old Castile, New Castile, Extemadura, and
Andalusia; although they were usually important landholders, they almost
always resided in the principal town of the district. In Seville they were
heavily involved in overseas trade, as were the numerous grandee families
resident there. The *caballeros* of Estremadura, found only in the major
towns, formed a homogeneous social group defined by long residence and
pronounced endogamy.[72]

By the fifteenth century most towns had a council (*ayuntamiento*) whose
members served for life, as well as an assembly whose members were
elected annually, either by the parishes or at a town meeting open to all
heads of household.[73] Not long after Muslim Córdoba was conquered by
Castile (1239), each of the city's fifteen parishes elected *jurados* or sworn
men for annual terms. During the second half of the fourteenth century,
the crown created an *ayuntamiento* consisting of twenty-four *regidores* or
aldermen. *Jurados* could present petitions at meetings of the *ayuntamiento*,
but only *regidores* had a vote.[74] In Toledo, conquered in 1232, it seems
the earliest equivalent of a town council was an informal gathering of all
caballeros who had settled in the town. Not until 1421 was there a council
of twenty-four *regidores* appointed by the crown. Here, too, *jurados* elected
by the parishes had an assembly of their own and could present petitions
to the twenty-four.[75] As *regidores* died out, it seems that replacement by
co-option was common. In Valladolid, where Charles V kept court, ten
noble families, divided into two lineages, had shared local offices among

[70] Fernández Alvárez, *Carlos V, el César y el hombre*, 190–191; Dominguez Ortiz, *El Antiguo Régimen*,
76ff., 110: a census of 1591, which put Castile's population at 6,145,000, indicated the same percentage of families as enjoying the status of *hidalguia*. Both historians assume a multiplier of five in
calculating the number of persons per hearth.
[71] By a quirky Castilian interpretation of Basque law, anyone who could prove he was born in the
Basque provinces was treated as an *hidalgo*.
[72] Ruth Pike, *Aristocrats and Traders: Sevillian Society in the Sixteenth Century* (Ithaca, N.Y., 1972), 26–
35; Gerbet, *Les nobles dans le royaume de Castile*, 136–137; Domingeuz Ortiz, *El Antiguo Régimen*,
111–114.
[73] For the annual town meeting or *concejo abierto* (open council), held even in very small towns, see
Nader, *Liberty in Absolutist Spain*, 32–33.
[74] John Edwards, *Christian Córdoba: The City and Its Region in the Late Middle Ages* (Cambridge, 1982),
24–57.
[75] Montemayor, *Tolède entre fortune et déclin*, 285–295.

themselves since the eleventh century. In Medina del Campo, known for its merchant fairs, the seven *regidores* were each chosen by one of the city's seven ancient lineages.[76]

Nobles were increasingly loath to submit to the orders of mere commoners. The *procuradores* who spoke for Castile's municipalities in the Cortes were almost always nobles and certainly represented the men of their caste. At the Cortes of Toledo (1525), the procurators asked the crown to annul "ancient customs" by which some communities prohibited *hidalgos* from serving in certain offices, alleging that "*hidalgos* are of better quality than *pecheros* [commoners]".[77] At the Cortes of Madrid (1534), they asked that *hidalgos* be permitted to enter town councils, any privileges to the contrary notwithstanding, because "to [*hidalgos*], more than to others, is owed governance and the administration of justice."[78] Commoners vigorously opposed such efforts, especially in the high country between the Cantabrian mountains and the Tagus River, where urban *hidalgos* clamored for access to office as a way of supplementing their sometimes meager incomes. In Logroño, a midsized town in Old Castile, commoners paid the crown a substantial sum to have their *ayuntamiento* popularly elected, not chosen from within the oligarchy.[79]

As much as anything else, the crown's perennial need for money tipped the scales in favor of the nobility. In Córdoba, in addition to the traditional twenty-four *regidores*, the crown by 1469 had created by sale as many as ninety new positions. Isabella and Ferdinand reduced the number of "extra" *regidurias* to ten, but they also kept the practice of selling to *regidores* the right to transmit their positions to a chosen heir. During the difficult fall of 1544, if not earlier, Charles V approved "increases" (*ampliaciones*) in the number of urban offices as a means to raise desperately needed cash. The proposal he endorsed called for new *juraderias* as well as *regidurias* and notarial licenses.[80] From the 1540s the parish elections

---

[76] Bartolomé Bennassar, *Valladolid au siècle d'or* (Paris, 1967), 407–411; Dominguez Ortiz, *El Antiguo Régimen*, 197; Modesto Ulloa, *La hacienda real de Castilla en el reinado de Felipe II* (Madrid, 1977), 46.

[77] Literally, those who carry a fiscal burden (*pecho*; for this sense of the word, cf. Latin *pecus*), i.e., taxation.

[78] Dominguez Ortiz, *El Antiguo Régimen*, 105; Colmeiro, *Cortes de los Antiguos Reinos*, Introduccion, II, 135, 172.

[79] Dominguez Ortiz, *El Antiguo Régimen*, 106–107; I. A. A. Thompson, "Castile: Absolutism, Constitutionalism, and Liberty," in Hoffman and Norberg, *Fiscal Crises*, 46.

[80] Edwards, *Christian Córdoba*, 34–43. Charles's instructions for Isabella, 8 March 1529, *Corpus Documental*, Letter XXXVIII, I, 151–154: so that Charles can have something to reward the gentlemen who follow him to Italy, he asks her to reserve to him the granting of all notarial licenses (*escribanias*) worth more than 50,000 maravedises (133.33 ducats) per year, as well as all offices in the cities of Toledo, Seville, Burgos, Granada, Córdoba, Valladolid, Segovia, Salamanca, and Jaen. Cobos to Charles, 7 August 1543, *Corpus Documental*, Letter CCLX, II, 157–158: to raise

by which *jurados* in Toledo had traditionally been chosen were no longer held. The process by which urban officeholders became a hereditary caste was completed at some point during the sixteenth century, with *caballeros* in particular monopolizing the higher levels of the magistracy.[81] They were, as some historians put it, the "patriciate" or "urban middle class" of sixteenth-century Castile.[82]

Scholars also call attention to close ties between the crown and urban *procuradores* to the Cortes. *Corregidores* did their best to see that loyal men were chosen, and many of those selected were also royal officials; moreover, *procuradores* depended on the crown, not on the towns, for their salaries and travel expenses. It was also common for the *procuradores* who voted for a *servicio* to serve as collectors for their town and its region, taking a percentage of the total for their pains.[83] At the Cortes of Valladolid (February 1544), the procurators petitioned Philip for permission to make the offices they held hereditary, without the usual ceremony of a special oath to the king; Charles instructed Philip to grant them this, because they had served him well at the Cortes.[84]

Venal and submissive though these men may have been, however, they were still mandatories of the towns. The one study available for Charles's reign shows the *ayuntamiento* watching closely to ensure that procurators voted on *servicio* requests exactly according to their written instructions.[85] Though some petitions raised issues of special interest to the *procuradores*, the vast majority dealt with the concerns of litigants (speedier justice at the royal courts, curtailing fees demanded by petty officials), town councils (limiting the cases in which the verdicts of town courts could be appealed to royal courts, restricting the privileges of the clergy), or native merchants

funds, the Consejo de la Hacienda has proposed increasing the number of "regimientos, juraderias, y escribanias," as well as selling privileges by which annual offices would be held for life. Charles to Philip, 6 July 1544, *Corpus Documental*, Letter CCLXXX, II, 244: Charles hesitates to approve the recommended "ampliaciones de regimientos y otros oficios que no tienen jurisdicion," but notes there is already a "poder" for doing so dating from his first trip to Italy (although such a "poder" is not mentioned in the instructions for Isabella cited earlier), wonders whether unsuitable persons might not be promoted to responsible positions, and asks for an estimate of how much might be raised in this way. Philip to Charles, 17 September 1544, *Corpus Documental*, Letter CCLXXXVII, II, 273–274: having consulted with his councils, Philip has decided to proceed, though no great sum can be expected, for "las necesidades son tan grandes"; he will have the names of prospective purchasers screened by the *corregidores* and by current *regidores*, who would not give their approval to men lacking the right qualities.

[81] Montemayor, *Tolède entre fortune et déclin*, 287–288; Pike, *Aristocrats and Traders*, 33–52; Benjamín González Alonso, *Sobre el estado y la administración de la corona de Castilla en el Antiguo Régimen* (Madrid, 1981), 57–84; Kamen, *Spain, 1469–1714*, 23.

[82] Dedieu, *L'Espagne de 1492 à 1808*, 77–79; Dominguez Ortiz, *El Antiguo Régimen*, 111.

[83] Carretero Zamora, *Cortes, monarquía, ciudades*, 9; Colmeiro, *Cortes de los Antiguos Reinos*, II, 100–104.

[84] Charles to Philip, third letter of 6 July 1544, *Corpus Documental*, Letter CCLXXX, II, 244.

[85] Juan Sanchez Montes, *Agobios carolinos*, 109–131; Carretero Zamora, *Cortes, monarquía, ciudades*, 14.

(enforcing the laws against export of specie, ending the monopolies in certain commodities obtained by the Genoese).[86] In sum, *procuradores* also stood for the interests of Castile's important towns.

The Cortes of León and Castile, dating from 1188, had clerical and noble as well as municipal "arms" (*brazos*).[87] Although as many as 180 towns were summoned to send two *procuradores* to at least one Cortes between 1295 and 1315,[88] by 1435 this number had dwindled dramatically.[89] Of the towns that now had permanent voting rights, eleven were to be found in León and Old Castile, including León itself; Burgos, the capital of Castile's wool trade; the university town of Salamanca; and Valladolid, Madrid, and Guadalajara.[90] Toledo and Cuenca spoke for all of New Castile, Murcia for the southeast corner of the kingdom. The capitals of Andulasia's former "kingdoms" rounded out the assembly: Córdoba, Jaen, Seville. Granada was added to the list in 1498, making eighteen in all, and in 1512 Ferdinand the Catholic accepted a petition from the Cortes not to extend voting rights to any other cities.[91] Measured by *alcabala* returns from the 1530s, these eighteen cities and their rural districts encompassed only about 40% of Castile's taxable wealth.[92]

From 1480 to 1498 Isabella and Ferdinand did not summon a Cortes, preferring to gain the needed approval for taxation through negotiations with a newly created federation of towns known as the Holy Brotherhood (Santa Hermandad). When meetings of the Cortes resumed in the early sixteenth century, urban procurators no longer insisted, as they once did, on strict controls over how monies granted by the assembly were

[86] Cf. the 119 petitions presented by the Cortes of Segovia in 1532 (Colmeiro, *Cortes de los Antiguos Reinos*, IV, 525–579). Only one dealt with the special concerns of *procuradores* (no. 118, their lodging expenses). Another (no. 106) was the proposal for a "general capitation" of the *alcabala*, discussed later. Four general topics come up more frequently than others: requests for speedier justice at royal courts, 24 petitions; restricting the privileges of the clergy, 12; limiting appeals from town courts, 11; and regulation of trade, 11.

[87] The clerical estate of the Cortes – Castile's thirty-three bishops plus a number of abbots – is not to be confused with the assembly of the clergy convened to approve collection of the clerical *subsidios* granted by the papacy. See Sean T. Perrone, "The Castilian Assembly of the Clergy in the Sixteenth Century," *Parliaments, Estates and Representation* 18 (1998):53–70: after 1505, the assembly was made up of representatives from the cathedral chapter of each diocese. I am grateful to Professor Perrone of St. Anselm College (Manchester, New Hampshire) for a copy of his article.

[88] Joseph O'Callaghan, *The Cortes of León and Castile, 1188–1350* (Philadelphia, 1990), 48–58.

[89] Cf. the emergence (as noted earlier) of the so-called great cities, which alone had voting rights in the parliamentary assemblies of Brabant and Holland.

[90] The others were Ávila, Segovia, Soria, Toro, and Zamora.

[91] Carretero Zamora, *Cortes, monarquía, ciudades*, 4–6.

[92] Carande Thobar, *Carlos V y sus banqueros*, II, 235, 245: the gross value of the *alcabala* and *tercia* for 1534 was calculated at 847,924 ducats, while in 1536 the yield of both revenues in seventeen of the eighteen voting cities (not counting Soria) was estimated at 323,127 ducats, or 38.1%.

spent.[93] But if young Charles imagined that the Cortes might be managed by a show of authority, his first sojourn in Castile (November 1517–
May 1520) taught him a different lesson. Charles's position was delicate,
because his mother, Juana "the mad," was still the queen of Castile,
despite her affliction; also, many in Castile and Aragón would have preferred as their king Charles's brother Ferdinand, who had been raised
here and spoke Spanish. Finally, his Burgundian councillors were indecently ostentatious in claiming the perquisites of power; for example,
Guillaume de Chièvres procured for his young nephew the archbish-
opric of Toledo, Castile's primatial see. Reactions were soon evident, as
at the Cortes of Valladolid (1518), where Charles had to swear to uphold the laws of the realm before the assembly would swear allegiance
to him as king. In petitions that used a traditional formula referring
to new sovereign as "our paid servant" (*nuestro mercenario*), Charles was
asked to learn Spanish, not to leave the kingdom until he had married, and keep Ferdinand in Spain – in fact, he sent him to Austria as
soon as possible. Before presenting the petitions, however, the procurators
granted a *servicio* with a nominal[94] value of 181,333 ducats for each of the
years 1519–1521, an increase of 33% over sums granted to Ferdinand and
Isabella.[95]

Charles did begin learning Spanish and dressing in the Castilian manner,
but as soon as he learned of Maximilian's death (February 1519), he and
Chièvres made plans to claim the Habsburg imperial inheritance. For their
loans for the election, the Fugger and Welser firms demanded appropriate
guarantees. The Welser accepted assignation on the revenues of Naples, and
Charles Leclerc seems to have gotten them their money (Chapter 3). The
Fugger looked to Castile for payment, and some portion of what they were
owed was eventually cleared by giving the firm its first *maestrazgo* contract
in 1523.[96] But it seems the original idea was to assign this debt to a new
servicio, for which Charles called a meeting of the Cortes for March 1520
in Santiago de Compostella (Galicia), a point convenient for his intended
voyage to Flanders. The royal summons caused an uproar: the king who
had been asked to remain in the kingdom was leaving in unseemly haste;

[93] Carretero Zamora, *Cortes, monarquía, ciudades*, 61–68, 78–79; the same points are made by
   Thompson, "Castile: Polity, Fiscality," 165–166, who, however, takes a more positive view of the
   constitutional position of the Cortes during Charles's reign.
[94] For Charles's reign, I have not seen any attempt to calculate the net value of *servicios*, after subtracting
   for reductions of the kind that Carretero Zamora describes for the period prior to Ferdinand and
   Isabella: *Cortes, monarquía, Ciudades*, 71. At least for some purposes, royal auditors in Charles's time
   counted the *servicios* at face value (see Table 9.1).
[95] Fernández Alvárez, *Charles V*, 23–27; Colmeiro, *Cortes de los Antiguos Reinos*, II, 92–96; Carande
   Thobar, *Carlos V y sus banqueros*, II, 536–537; Carretero Zamora, *Cortes, monarquía, ciudades*, 72–73.
[96] Chapter 3, note 45.

he was violating custom by requesting a new *servicio* while the current one was still being collected; and no Cortes within memory had assembled in such an out-of-the-way part of the kingdom. Charles and his retinue had to evade efforts by the citizens of Valladolid to detain him forcibly within its walls. In Santiago, his councillors made no headway with the *procuradores* of the sixteen towns grudgingly convened. In another slap at custom, Charles announced that he would leave behind as his regent a foreigner, Cardinal Adriaan Floriszoon of Utrecht.[97] Only after the assembly had been prorogued and reconvened in the port of La Coruña did the emperor-elect's men wring from it the narrowest of majorities for another *servicio* equivalent to 181,333 ducats a year, to run from 1522 through 1524.[98]

This grant was nullified by events. Whether the *servicio* approved at Valladolid in 1518 was actually collected during the tumultuous years of 1520 and 1521 is not clear, but there was no new subsidy for the bankers to deal with until the Cortes of Valladolid (1523) granted one.[99] Even before Charles had boarded his ship at La Coruña, Toledo expelled its *corregidor*, the symbol of royal authority, while citizens of Medina del Campo battled royal troops for control of the town's artillery. Municipalities all over Castile sent delegates to Ávila to form a Holy Union (Santa Junta) to oppose the crown's demands. In September 1520, as Charles was acclaimed by the empire's electors in Aachen, rebel forces seized Tordesillas, where Queen Juana kept her residence. In some areas peasants rose in arms against their noble lords, for their own reasons, but also in sympathy with *los Comuñeros* (the commoners), as the insurgents were called. Giving heed to Spanish advisers, Charles named two leading grandees as "coregents" with the cardinal of Utrecht. The triumvirate issued special appeals to likely supporters. Burgos, first in order of precedence among cities in the Cortes, rallied to the royalist cause, in part because Toledo, the number-two city, was playing a leading role in the rebellion. Many grandees and *caballeros* came to Charles's aid because they feared the movement's populist dimensions. Royalists recaptured Tordesillas before the year was out and in April 1521 dealt the main rebel army a decisive defeat at nearby Villalar.[100]

When he landed at Santander on his return to Spain (July 1522), the emperor seemed to think he was in a position to exploit his victory. In the

---

[97] A Louvain theologian, Charles's onetime tutor, and the future pope Adrian VI (1522–1523).

[98] Colmeiro, *Cortes de los Antiguos Reinos*, II, 103–114.

[99] Carande Thobar, *Carlos V y sus banqueros*, II, 536–537, has no *servicio* approved for collection during 1522. The Cortes of Valladolid (1523) approved a grant of 410,666 ducats over a period of three years, beginning that year: Colmeiro, *Cortes de los Antiguos Reinos*, II, 115–117.

[100] Fernández Alvárez, *Charles V*, 39–43. For full treatments, Stephen Haliczer, *The Comuneros of Castile: The Forging of a Revolution, 1475–1521* (Madison, Wis., 1981), and José Antonio Maravall, *Las comunidades de Castilla* (Madrid, 1979).

past, it had been customary for municipal councils to give their *procuradores* limited mandates, which prevented them from responding to the king's demands in any way other than instructed. In contrast, Charles's summons for a Cortes at Valladolid early the next year stipulated that the mandates must this time be "general," so that *procuradores* might respond appropriately to the proposition to be presented in detail at Valladolid.[101] But in broad terms one may say that the town councils with whom Charles had to deal represented the nobles who had won the civil war, not the commoners who had lost. Thus while the *procuradores* came to Valladolid with "general" mandates, as Charles had insisted, they also carried instructions stipulating that no *servicio* be voted until the emperor had heard and responded to their 105 petitions. As Charles correctly noted, this would have been contrary to custom, for parliaments had always voted grants before hearing the reply to their petitions – and not just in Castile.[102] When he promised not to dismiss the Cortes before responding to all of the petitions, the *procuradores* relented. But the *servicio* they voted was for 136,889 ducats a year for three years, the level that had been customary under Ferdinand and Isabella, not the 181,333 ducats a year granted at Valladolid in 1518.[103] After a revolt that had imperiled Charles's crown, this was a new beginning, if not an auspicious one. Chapter 14 will show how the *procuradores* would open their purse strings more widely only after Charles agreed to accommodate the interests of the towns and their noble magistrates.

[101] According to the "absolutist" interpretation of Castile's constitutional history mentioned earlier, this directive is a clear indication that the Cortes that was left to face Charles in the aftermath of the rebellion – especially its urban "arm" – was only a shadow of the powerful parliamentary assemblies of earlier centuries. Cf. Colmeiro, *Cortes des los Antiguos Reinos*, II, 117, 129–130.

[102] Meeting in Charles's presence in Brussels, the States of Holland made the same demand, and got the same reply, perhaps rather more brusquely: "I want to be trusted, and will not bargain with my subjects" ; let the States agree to renew the ordinary subsidy as demanded (they did), and trust him to deal with their complaints (*RSH*, 29 March 1531). Older views of the weakness of Castile's Cortes were influenced by an implied contrast with England's Parliament, but the newer view is that in England too there was no "redress before supply" until the seventeenth century: Stanford E. Lehmberg, *The Later Parliaments of Henry VIII, 1536–1547* (Cambridge, 1977), 95, 175–180.

[103] Colmeiro, *Cortes de los Antiguos Reinos*, II, 117–130; for the 105 petitions and Charles's responses, IV, 364–402.

Chapter 5

The Search for Credit: Charles and His Bankers

Long-term borrowing, through bonds or annuities sold to the public, did less harm to the fisc than the high-interest loans for which bankers demanded repayment within a year or two. Charles was fortunate in that each of his key realms had procedures for marketing bonds secured by the annual receipts of specified crown revenues. For *rentes* on the domain revenues of the Low Countries, investors accepted rates as low as 6.25%, because they knew that collectors of the revenues in question had standing instructions to pay bondholders before meeting any other expenses assigned on their receipts.[1] Domain revenues in the two wealthiest provinces, Brabant and Flanders, were already heavily pledged at the time of Charles's accession, but when Mary of Hungary and her Council of Finance examined domain accounts in the 1530s,[2] they found important unpledged revenues in Holland, as well as in the recently acquired provinces of Friesland (1515–1517) and Utrecht and Overijssel (1528). Focusing on these northern regions, Mary's government raised 755,541 pounds through sales of *rentes* on the domains between 1534 and 1540, roughly three times what had been raised in this way all during the 1520s. Mary's officials also negotiated contracts with the city government of Antwerp for loans of 104,309, 344,517, and 488,825, all of which were assigned for repayment on selected domain receipts of various provinces over periods of fifteen to twenty years.[3]

In Naples "incomes" were sold on the receipts of tolls and other revenues.[4] Castile's long-term debt dated from Isabella the Catholic; in return

---

[1] This was a common rate for *rentes* that could be redeemed at will by the government, or passed on to one's heirs if not redeemed.

[2] Aud. 868, 62–95v.

[3] Lille B, nos. 2363 (1531), 2369 (1532), 2380 (1534), 2386 (1535), 2392 (1536), 2398 (1537), 2404 (1538), 2419 (1539), 2418 (1540), on microfilm at the Archives Généraux du Royaume/Algemeen Rijksarchief, Brussels.

[4] Leclerc, "Rapport et Recueil," chap. xxxviii, 109–110v, "Estat de revue dudit royaulme tel que se trouvoit au jour du trespas du feu roy catholique," for "rentes sallaires et offices" charged against the

for their capital, investors received *juros* or "rights" to annual interest payment from one or another of the crown's *rentas ordinarias*. As in the Low Countries, rates were lower for hereditary *juros* than for life *juros* extinguished by the death of the beneficiary. In 1522 the crown's "ordinary income" amounted to 1,002,672 ducats – more than seven times as much as the domain revenue for all of the Low Countries provinces.[5] Because only 36.6% of this total was pledged (*situado*) to the payment of *juro* interest,[6] Castile's *rentas ordinarias* afforded Charles an even better opportunity for relatively cheap credit than did the domain revenues of the Low Countries.

But long-term credit also came in dribs and drabs, as investors put up sums that were considerable to them, but paltry when measured against the needs of the fisc. When money was required quickly, only the great banking houses had the resources to raise large sums, and the contacts that allowed them to remit money in the currency desired. For example, to meet a French invasion of the Low Countries in 1543, the emperor, then in Germany, ordered Cobos in Valladolid to send money to Antwerp. Having 160,000 ducats at his disposal, Cobos sent the cash by galley to Genoa, whence it was remitted to Antwerp by letters of exchange. The exchange charges were considerable, Cobos explained, but it would cost more to have money "changed" directly to the Low Countries, or to convoy specie through the waters bordering France.[7]

Each of Charles's realms also had established relations with favored bankers. In the Low Countries, he needed their help to enter into his inheritance. Emperor Maximilian demanded 150,000 gulden in order to acquiesce in his grandson's being declared of age (1514), and Charles's "Joyful Entry" tour of the provinces was expected to cost a further 100,000. For these contingencies Chièvres and the Council of Finance negotiated loans in Antwerp; for example, Bernhard Stecher, factor for the Fugger of Augsburg, advanced the 150,000 for Maximilian.[8] During three years of

income from "douanes, fundiques et salmes," 25,959 ducats; chap. xxxix, 111–163v, "De la raison en particulier de tant le revenue et des charges dudit royaulme de Naples avec lestat dicelle pour lannee finie au dernier daoust 1521," under expenses, entry for charges against customs revenue, "rentes a vye" and "rentes a rachat."

5   Again, see my subsequent discussion for a comparison of the structure of revenues.
6   Pilar Toboso Sanchez, *La deuda pública castellana durante el Antiguo Régimen (Juros) y su liquidacion en el siglo XIX* (Madrid, 1987), 26–62.
7   Cobos to Charles, 7 August 1543, *Corpus Documental*, Letter CCLX, II, 153.
8   For the 150,000 Holland pounds (Low Countries gulden) for Maximilian, see Wiesflecker, *Kaiser Maximilian I*, V, 190. The basic work on Netherlands government borrowing for this period (regrettably not published) was done by Dr. Ghislaine Bellart, archivist for the Pays du Nord, who in 1980 was kind enough to let me examine her notes on loans for 1516–1530, in her office in Lille. See Fernand Braudel, "Les emprunts de Charles-Quint sur la place d'Anvers," in *Charles-Quint et son Temps*, 191–201, p. 191: "Le présente communication, pour l'essentiel, est l'ouevre de Mlle. Ghislaine Bellart."

Figure 5.1. Jan Ossaert, *Francisco de los Cobos,* Getty Museum, Los Angeles.

war against France and Guelders (1521–1523) Margaret of Austria borrowed at levels equal to the Chièvres era, but she was nonetheless loath to take on debt, and made little use of the bankers during the relatively quiet years that followed.[9] When she borrowed 126,000 gulden from the Augsburg

---

[9] "Deniers prins au frait" is an item always listed in the income part of Low Countries fiscal accounts of this era, meaning that the government still has the use of the money until it is paid back.

firm of Ambrosius Hochstetter for the campaign of 1528, to be repaid in installments of 40,000 pounds per year over five years, she was at pains to justify this loan and its expense to her nephew.[10]

In Naples, the position of conservator of the royal patrimony was held by Giambattista Spinelli, a member of the Genoese banking family, while the treasury's creditors included the Lomellini, another Genoese firm, and a banker named Paolo de Tholosa.[11] In Spain, Ferdinand had turned to Jewish bankers to finance the conquest of Granada (1492). But Jewish firms were thrust aside amid the anti-Semitism that accompanied Isabella's creation of a special royal tribunal, the Spanish Inquisition (1492), for detecting those among Castile's New Christians who were secretly practicing the Jewish beliefs of their ancestors. In their place, Genoese firms, already trading in the products of Andulasia's orchards and vineyards, now developed closer ties with the crown. For example, from 1521 through 1523, the Centurione and the Grimaldi had the contract for administering the lands of the three military orders that had been annexed to the crown.[12]

The young Charles expected that a Holy Roman Emperor should be able to borrow on the strength of his personal bond. But bankers made it clear that his signature on a piece of paper was worthless, unless backed by guarantees they trusted.[13] High officials and great nobles were called upon to interpose their personal wealth between the sovereign and his creditors. Yet Charles could not compel even his closest councillors to keep on lending when the incomes earmarked to repay their previous loans were devoted instead to other needs.[14] Quite apart from guarantees, how was

---

[10] See the curve for "short-term loans" in table 1 of Braudel, "Les emprunts de Charles-Quint," based on the work of Mme. Bellart (note 8). Aud. 873, 53v–57v: this lengthy summary of income and expenditures for 1520–1530 is described at the end (folio 315v) as "Presented by [Antoine de Lalaing, count of] Hoogstraaten [leading member of the Council of Finance] and the receiver-general for all finances [Jean Micault] to the emperor in Brussels at the end of February 1531, and examined by him during March, in the presence of the archbishop of Palermo [Jean Carondolet, president of the Council of State] and the audiencer [Laurent Dublioul – the Audience was the government secretariat]." Aud. 867, 132–137, copy of Margaret's instructions for Rosimbos and Barres on their mission to Charles, April 1529. The Hochstetter loan was signed over to the Fugger when Ambrosius and his firm suffered bankruptcy: Pölnitz, *Anton Fugger*, I:1, 144–145.

[11] For debts to Paulo Tholosa and Augustino Lomellino, see Coniglio, *Consulte e bilanci del Viceregno di Napoli*, Document 9; for Spinelli, Chapter 3, note 25.

[12] Carande Thobar, *Carlos y sus banqueros*, II, 91, 221–226; Toboso Sanchez, *La deuda pública castellana*, 26–62; Gabriella Airaldi, *Genova e la Liguria nel medioevo* (Turin, 1986), 63–66.

[13] Charles to Margaret of Austria, 31 October 1522, Lanz, Letter 40, I, 72.

[14] E.g., Cobos to Charles V, 7 August 1543, those at court in Valladolid will not lend more, now that Charles has taken for his own purposes the gold and silver from the Indies on which their previous loans were assigned: *Corpus Documental*, Letter CCLX, II, 157–158.

the loan itself to be repaid? In most cases, the successful completion of a loan contract required treasury officials to set aside for the emperor's immediate priorities revenues that (in their view) might better have been assigned to outstanding debts or other needs of the realm. This chapter explores the credit arrangements Charles had to accept in order to finance his wars: the bankers who took the risk of trusting his promises to repay; the kinds of revenue on which they wanted their loans assigned; and the struggle between bankers and treasury officials over the allocation of choice revenues.

Genoa, Augsburg, and Antwerp

Of the seven most important banking centers that had developed in Europe since the thirteenth century, three of these were effectively closed to Charles, and one was not as useful to him as it might have been. In Venice, the republic paid for its wars by forced loans levied on the citizens, and bankers stayed away from state debt.[15] Moreover, the Serene Republic was not friendly to Habsburg hegemony in Italy, and it also had unresolved territorial conflicts with Habsburg Austrian lands on its northern border.[16] When King Louis XI (d. 1484) established quarterly merchant fairs in Lyons to compete with those of nearby Geneva, Lyons became France's financial hub, attracting branches of the major Tuscan banking houses. This connection was strengthened when Catherine de Medici, last legitimate descendant of the branch of the family that had founded the Medici bank, married the duke of Orléans, the future King Henry II, in 1533. For his wars against Charles V, Francis I accumulated, by 1546, a debt of 6,860,844 livres tournois or 3,049,264 French crowns on the Lyons exchange.[17] Using a Florentine exile as his broker in Lyons, Henry II had loans outstanding for 3,658,400 livres by Easter 1553. Even if banking

[15] Frederick C. Lane, *Venice, a Maritime Republic* (Baltimore, 1973), 147–148: Venetian bankers developed "a distinctive style which we associate with the name giro-bank. The main function of a Venetian banker was not making loans, but making payments on behalf of his client." Venice was able to retire its state debt (based on forced loans) by the end of the sixteenth century: Luciano Pezzolo, *L'oro dello stato. Società, finanza e fisco nella Repubblica veneta del secondo '500* (Treviso, 1990). Cf. Hamon, *L'argent du roi*, 141: among the 124 lenders to the French crown on the Lyons exchange who can be identified, there were eighty-seven Italian bankers, including forty-five Florentines and seventeen Lucchesi, but not a single Venetian.

[16] Cf. Mary to Charles, August 1538, *Staatspapiere*, LIV, 263–268: Charles should especially remember that "not everyone would wish to see you greater, especially the Venetians, for they are but a republic, meaning they have little constancy, and care only for their own particular interest" (my translation).

[17] About 1,829,558 Spanish ducats, since the 2 million crown ransom for Francis I's two sons was valued at 1.20 million ducats (Chapter 2).

houses sometimes hedged their bets by lending to rival princes,[18] Lyons was not the place for Charles V to seek funds. Florence, which gravitated into the Habsburg orbit under Duke Cosimo I, was itself a major capital market; Florentine banking houses, active in the Kingdom of Naples for centuries, continued making loans to the Habsburg government there.[19] But many leading Florentine firms carried on their business from exile, owing to their anti-Medici (and hence anti-Habsburg) politics. The Strozzi and other firms active in Lyons were major backers of the French crown. Of the 124 bankers who can be identified as joining in loans to the French crown on the Lyons exchange, 45 were Florentines.[20]

In Castile, Seville was poised to become a banking center because of the flow of New World gold and silver registered at the House of Trade (Casa de la Contratacion). But Charles V inhibited the growth of banking here by his frequent sequestrations of private treasure (see Chapters 7 and 11). By default, the traditional quarterly fairs of Medina del Campo in northern Castile, not far from the center of the wool trade in Burgos, remained Spain's leading source of commercial credit.[21] Local bankers, together with agents of some Italian firms, accepted merchant loans at the usual low interest in order to relend at higher rates to Castile's impecunious sovereign. The sums were often impressive,[22] yet not as impressive as they might have been. Medina's fairs were timed to fall in the intervals between Antwerp's fairs, for the convenience of merchants traveling or remitting payments from one country to the other. Many of the family firms active in both centers were New Christians, descendants of the Spanish Jews who had converted to Catholicism in the fourteenth and fifteenth centuries. When charges of Crypto-Judaism were brought against New Christians trading on the Antwerp exchange, resulting in sequestration of their property, Charles turned a deaf ear to pleas for intervention on

---

[18] For loans to the French crown by the Welser of Augsburg, Knecht, *Renaissance Warrior and Patron*, 344–345, 504–505; Frederic Baumgartner, *Henry II, King of France, 1547–1559* (Durham, N.C., 1988), 84–85.

[19] On the Acciaiuoli in Naples, see Pölnitz, *Anton Fugger*, II-i, 515. On Carande Thobar's list of lenders to the treasury of Castile, "Rafael Achioli" (*Carlos V y sus banqueros*, III, 210) looks to be a member of this family, and "Reinaldo Strozzi" (II, 555) was probably of the Florentine family of that name.

[20] Frederic Baumgartner, *France in the Sixteenth Century* (New York, 1995), 77–78; Martin Wolfe, *The Fiscal System of Renaissance France* (New Haven, Conn., 1972), 106–109; Richard Gascon, *Grand commerce et vie urbaine au XVIe siècle: Lyon et ses marchands* (2 vols., Paris, 1971). On Pietro Strozzi, a leading anti-Habsburg political figure as well as a banker, see Knecht, *Renaissance Warrior and Patron*, and the references in Pölnitz, *Anton Fugger*, II-i. See note 15.

[21] Carla Rahn Phillips and William D. Phillips, *Spain's Golden Fleece: Wool Production and the Wool Trade from the Middle Ages to the Nineteenth Century* (Baltimore, 1997), 95.

[22] See Table 5.1: of the 2,035,674 ducats in loans by "Spanish bankers," Rodrigo de Dueñas brokered loans for 1,094,267, slightly more than half.

behalf of the accused. This may be a reason why New Christian bankers played almost no role in lending to the crown during Charles's reign – in sharp contrast to the leading position their descendants assumed in Castilian royal finance in the late sixteenth and especially the seventeenth century.[23]

In effect, Charles had to satisfy his borrowing needs on the credit markets cultivated by his Spanish, Habsburg, and Burgundian forebears: Genoa, Augsburg, and Antwerp. Genoa's merchant bankers turned more and more to the western Mediterranean as rival Venice gained a dominant trading position in the eastern Mediterranean during the fifteenth century; they were active in the fruit trade centered at Málaga in Moorish Granada and had representatives at the North African terminal points for the trans-Saharan caravan routes that served as an outlet for West Africa's Gold Coast. Portugal's quest to reach the source of this mysterious gold opened new opportunities for the Genoese in Iberia,[24] as did the fact that the masterships (*maestrazgos*) of Castile's three military orders were annexed to the crown. The Consejo de la Hacienda did not have the personnel or the know-how for administering these lands and revenues, but the bankers did; bidding for the first three-year *maestrazgo* contract in Charles's reign was won by a Genoese-backed consortium.[25] But it was only with Andrea Doria's change of allegiance, and subsequent political changes in the city, that Genoa came to be an indispensable backer of Charles and his wars. For about fifty years following the events of 1528, the main business of Genoa was banking,[26] and the Habsburg dynasty would be Genoa's main customer.

Ansaldo Grimaldi (d. 1539), Genoa's leading banker, earned Charles's gratitude by agreeing in November 1528 to lend 100,000 scudi, a sum that was invaluable in preliminary preparations for the army the emperor wanted to form in Italy the next summer. At the same time, Charles's ambassador to Genoa, Figueroa, appointed after the republic had rejected Soria, could not call upon Grimaldi until he had first paid his respects to Andrea Doria. The two men were bitter rivals, both for influence within the city, and for recognition by the emperor in the form of honorable appointments for family members. Adamo Centurione, Doria's son-in-law and at times

---

[23] J. A. Goris, *Étude sur les colonies marchandes méridionales à Anvers, 1488–1577* (Louvain, 1925); James C. Boyajian, *Portuguese Bankers at the Court of Spain, 1626–1650* (New Brunswick, N.J., 1983); and Henry Kamen, *The Spanish Inquisition: A Historical Revision* (New Haven, Conn., 1997).

[24] Jacques Heers, *Gênes au XVe siècle* (Paris, 1961), 97–146, 473–496; William D. Phillips and Carla Rahn Phillips, *The Worlds of Christopher Columbus* (New York, 1992), 94.

[25] See note 42.

[26] Vito Vitale, *Breviario di storia di Genova* (2 vols., Genoa, 1955), I, 129–219; Rodolfo Savelli, *La repubblica oligarchica. Legislazione, istitutzione e ceti a Genova nel cinquecento* (Milan, 1981), 40–48, for an interesting critique (c. 1567) of Genoa's post-1528 economy, in which wealth is said to be wasted on usurious loans to foreign princes, rather than on developing the city's trades.

the deputy commander of his war fleet, represented the Doria circle in financial arrangements, including loans to the emperor. More than once during the two subsequent decades, Charles's agents in Genoa would try a delicate game of negotiating for loans from Adamo Centurione and Ansaldo Grimaldi at the same time, but without alienating one or the other.[27] Grimaldi, notoriously tight-fisted, was also clever enough to get good security for his loans in the form of *juros* issued by the treasury, a procedure discussed further in Chapter 14. To preserve his credit with those who participated in his loans to the emperor, Centurione depended more on personal contacts. For a war fleet that Doria led into the Adriatic in 1538 (see Chapter 8), Centurione and his brothers advanced the money to pay for sailing ships; when the 100,000 ducats from Spain that was earmarked for their repayment was spent in Sicily instead, Centurione went to Spain and extracted from Cobos a promise that he would get his money from a *servicio* now being discussed by the Cortes. When this money in turn was reassigned elsewhere, for a new loan with the Fuggers of Augsburg, Doria weighed in with the emperor, who sent Cobos instructions in no uncertain terms. This finally did the trick, although Cobos complained that the admiral's "insistence" caused him "more trouble than your majesty can imagine" to make sure that Centurione got his money.[28]

Augsburg and Nuremberg were the two German cities that prospered most from the central European silver- and copper-mining boom of the late fifteenth century, sparked by new technology as well as by new ore discoveries. While Nuremberg's merchants financed mostly small-scale mining operations in the nearby Harz Mountains and Erzgebirge, Augsburg firms like the Fugger and the Welser risked handsome loans to various princes of the Habsburg house (among them Emperor Maximilian I, Charles's grandfather) in return for temporary control of regalian rights to wealth from beneath the ground, including the right to purchase ore at slightly less than market prices. Pressing their advantage, the Fugger imposed a vertical monopoly on the mining economies of Tirol and Slovakia (part of Habsburg Hungary after 1527), providing capital for the new mining and smelting technology, while compelling hitherto independent small producers to accept the status of wage laborers.[29]

---

[27] Pacini, *La Genova dell' Andrea Doria nell'impero di Carlo V*, 65–67, 147–148, 344, 352, 364–365, 396–397.

[28] Ibid., 354, 368, 408–412; Charles to Cobos, 6 January 1540, Estado, 497, 166. The reference is to loan 150 in Carande Thobar, *Carlos V y sus banqueros*, III, 232.

[29] For an overview, John Munro, "Patterns of Trade, Money, and Credit," in Brady, Oberman, and Tracy, *Handbook of European History*, I, 147–196; for the copper industry, Hermann Kellenbenz, *Schwerpunkte der Kupferproduktion und des Kupferhandels in Europa, 1500–1650* (Cologne and Vienna, 1977).

In the context of Charles's campaign for election as Holy Roman Emperor in 1519, the Fugger and the Welser made the transition from lending against the Habsburg dynasty's Austrian mining rights to lending against its Castilian and Neapolitan revenues. The total required to persuade the empire's seven electoral princes to vote for the right candidate – France's Francis I was offering almost equally generous terms – was reckoned at 851,918 Rhine gulden (about 602,026 ducats), of which the Fugger provided 543,585, the Welser 143,383, and three Italian firms 55,000 each.[30] As noted in Chapter 3, the Welser got a good deal of their money back through the activities of Charles Leclerc in Naples, but the Fugger loan, originally assigned on the *servicio* that collapsed in the revolt of 1520–1521, was apparently not liquidated until the *maestrazgo* contract of 1523–1525.

By about 1500 Antwerp (Brabant) had passed Bruges (Flanders) as the leading financial center of the Low Countries; merchants from non-Hanseatic Nuremberg and Augsburg were welcome here, but not in Bruges, the chief western entrepôt for the Hanseatic League as well as the northern terminus for Italian galleys.[31] Stocks of Fugger-controlled ore and refined copper were hauled across the Carpathian Mountains to the Vistula, for shipment to the Baltic and thence to the Low Countries, with Antwerp as the final destination. When Portuguese merchants came to the Low Countries bearing spices from the Moluccas, and seeking the copper that fetched premium prices in Portuguese India, Antwerp became a world entrepôt.[32] With one interesting exception,[33] the merchant-bankers who supplied credit for Margaret of Austria and Mary of Hungary were the same men with whom Charles's agents in Antwerp did business. Erasmus Schetz (d. 1550), the city's premier merchant-banker, had married into a substantial interest in an important calamine mine in his native region of Aachen (calamine was essential in the refining of copper). Moving to Antwerp, he developed connections both with copper-mining interests in

---

[30] Pölnitz, *Anton Fugger*, I, 51–52, 380–381; Fernández Alvárez, *Carlos V, el César y el hombre*, 109: the two greediest electors were the count-palatine of the Rhine (139,000 Rhine gulden) and the prince-archbishop of Mainz (107,000).

[31] For loans to Duke Philip the Bold (d. 1404) by Dino Rappondi of Lucca, see A. van Nieuwenhuysen, *Les finances du Duc de Bourgogne, Philippe le Hardi (1386–1404)* (Brussels, 1984), 343–351.

[32] Raymond De Roover, *Money, Banking and Credit in Medieval Bruges* (Cambridge, 1948); Herman van der Wee, *The Growth of the Antwerp Market and the European Economy, 14th to 16th Centuries* (3 vols., The Hague, 1963); and for the German trading connection, Donald Harreld, "High Germans in the Low Countries: German Merchants and Their Trade in Sixteenth Century Antwerp," Ph.D. dissertation, University of Minnesota, 2000.

[33] During the 1540s Gasparo Ducci of Pistoia often served as Mary of Hungary's loan broker on the Antwerp exchange: see the references in Pölnitz, *Anton Fugger*, II-i and II-ii. But for Charles's suspicion of him, see Mary to Granvelle, 10 and 15 January 1544, HHSA-Belgien, PA 41; Charles to Philip, 27 November 1547, *Corpus Documental*, Letter CCCLXXVI, II, 558–559; and *Anton Fugger*, II-i, 795–796, n. 198.

central Germany and with Lisbon, where copper goods were in demand
not only for the Asian trade but also for the bronze arm bands (*manilhas*)
that figured in Iberia's West African slave trade. With his sons, Balthasar,
Gaspar, and Melchior, Schetz competed on all fronts with agents of the
Fugger in Antwerp: in the copper trade; in bidding for the monopoly contract for distribution of Portuguese spices; in contracting loans with Mary
of Hungary's government; and in contracting loans with the emperor's
factors in Antwerp.[34]

Table 5.1 shows the importance for the emperor's finances of the these
three financial centers, and of the banking houses mentioned by name.
Between 1521 and 1555, roughly 28 million ducats in loans were charged
to the treasury of Castile (the total figure is misleading, because many
loans carried forward the unpaid balances from previous loans). Of the
28 million, slightly more than 18 million (64.4%) was supplied by seven
firms. In order of importance, these were the Fugger and the Welser of
Augsburg; the Grimaldi, Spinola, and Gentile of Genoa; the Schetz of
Antwerp; and the Centurione of Genoa. It goes without saying that firms
providing this much credit were in a strong position to dictate the terms
of their loan contracts.

The Hunt for Pristine Revenues

For bankers lending to princes, the prime concern was the quality of the
promised assignation (in Spanish, *consignacion*). Lenders and their agents
made it a business to know which revenues were burdened by long-standing
charges, and which remained more or less at the ruler's disposal. When organizing the loan for Charles's election as emperor in 1519, the Fugger and
the Welser knew very well that the young emperor-elect could never find
850,000 Rhine gulden from the Habsburg family's Austrian lands. Charles's
grandfather Maximilian I, a spendthrift even for a prince, left behind debts
still estimated at 400,000 Rhine gulden (about 282,669 Spanish ducats) as
late as 1531, after many creditors had elected to be satisfied with part payment.[35] Charles was, of course, also the Holy Roman Emperor, but the
revenues of the imperial crown were not worth a banker's glance, owing
to the dissipation of imperial rights during the medieval centuries. For
this and subsequent loans contracted on German soil, the bankers looked
for repayment to Charles's other lands, principally to the three that are of
interest here.

---

[34] My essay on "Shipments to Germany by Erasmus Schetz and Other Antwerp Merchants during
the Period of the Hundredth Penny Tax, 1543–1545," still awaits publication.

[35] Charles to Wolfgang Pranter, one of his proctors for negotiations with Maximilian's creditors,
14 January 1531, Lanz, Letter 158, I, 421–422.

Table 5.1. *Lenders to Be Repaid by the Treasury of Castile, 1521–1555*

	Total Sum Loaned	Number of Loans	Average Loan	Percentage of Total
Augsburg				
Fugger	5,499,516	74	73,418	19.54
Welser	4,223,822	41	103,020	15.01
Others	491,490	12	49,957	1.74
SUBTOTAL	10,214,828	127	80,432	36.30
Genoa				
Centurione	1,085,637	32	32,926	3.86
Gentile	1,537,139	20	76,857	5.46
Grimaldi	2,379,301	60	39,655	8.46
Lomellini	470,171	22	21,371	1.67
de Negro	652,159	20	32,606	2.32
Spinola	2,111,424	76	27,782	7.50
Others	1,413,838	55	25,706	5.02
SUBTOTAL	9,649,790	285	33,859	34.29
Antwerp				
Germans	98,901	4	24,273	0.35
Italians	1,198,149	19	63,060	4.26
Schetz	1,285,758	10	128,576	4.57
Flemings	150,840	4	50,280	0.54
Spaniards	251,667	10	25,167	0.89
SUBTOTAL	2,985,315	46	64,898	10.61
Spain				
Spaniards	2,035,674	83	24,526	7.23
Italians	646,363	32	20,199	2.30
Officials	2,366,395	35	67,611	8.41
SUBTOTAL	5,048,432	150	33,656	17.94
All others	240,001	13	18,461	
				0.85
GRAND TOTALS	28,138,393	621	45,726	100

Source: Loan tables in Carande Thobar, *Carlos y sus banqueros.*

Some important differences in the revenue structure of the three realms are summarized in Table 5.2. As noted in Chapter 3, because "ordinary" income was the oldest component of the prince's revenue portfolio, it was also the most burdened by standing obligations. Subsidy income was more attractive for assignations, especially in the Low Countries, where subsidies brought in considerably more than the crown's ordinary revenues. Charles viewed his lands as a whole and saw no reason why the future revenues of one kingdom – including subsidies – should not support the urgent present needs of a distant realm. Essentially, he used bankers as

Table 5.2. *Revenue Structure of Charles V's lands*

	Castile[a]	Naples[b]	Core Provinces[c]
Population c. 1550	5,896,515	2,129,185	2,175,000
Income 1520s–1540s[d]			
Ordinary	1,023,515/1,159,923	785,150/1,539,420	74,816/102,729
Ordinary Subsidies	111,645/268,800	None[e]	161,746/375,970
Extraordinary Subsidies	44,444/125,867	60,671/201,381	252,987/255,968
All Subsidies	156,090/394,667	60,671/201,381	414,733/631,938
Other Income	298,462/726,572	———/108,694	31,361/———
Indies Treasure	38,667/282,005		
Maestrazgos	133,333/152,000		
Clerical *Subsidios*	58,795/166,667		
Cruzada	66,667/125,900		

[a] Carande Thobar, *Carlos V y sus banqueros*, I, 64 (est. of hearths 1541), II, 91 (*rentas ordinarias*), II, 536–537 (*servicios*), I, 240 (accepting Earl Hamilton's estimates of the king's share of Indies treasure), II, 378–425 (*maestrazgos*), II, 466–486 (*subsidios*, on which see also Table 6.1), and II, 435–464 (the *cruzada*).

[b] Coniglio, *Regno di Napoli*, 152 (hearths in 1553); Coniglio, *Consulte e bilanci del Viceregno di Napoli*, Document 38, Alonso Sanchez's revised statement of income (see Chapter 3) for 24 March–1 December 1529, subtracting from the income column the 676,033 Neapolian ducats in loans that Sanchez counts as income; Calabria, "State Finance in the Kingdom of Naples," 143 (chart XI, "Patrimonial Income for 1560–1600," 1560 receipts for the hearth tax or *focatico* and the *dogna di Foggia*, both counted here as ordinary income, and "other" income); D'Agostino, *Parlamento e societá nel regno di Napoli*, 217–282 for the *donativi* or extraordinary subsidies.

[c] Core provinces of the Low Countries: for population, 75% of the estimate for all of the Low Countries in 1550 by De Vries, "Population," in Brady, Oberman, and Tracy, *Handbook of European History*, I, 13; for domain income in the 1520s, Aud. 873, 1–21, estimating 60% as the total for the core provinces (as for the year 1535, Aud. 868, 62–88, and for "the 1540s," average domain income for the core provinces for the years 1536–1539, Aud. 868, 62–88, 115–119v); for other income as well as subsidy income in the 1520s, Aud. 867, 71–91, taking 75% of the subsidy totals as the amount for the core provinces (cf. Aud. 850, 33–42, a document dated October 1560: for a special subsidy, Flanders will be asked for 12/36 of the total, Brabant for 10/36, and Holland for 5/36), and apportioning ordinary and extraordinary subsidies as for Holland, cf. Tracy. "The Taxation System of Holland," 110–111); for subsidy income in the 1540s, Aud. 650, 406–449, summary of the subsidy income for these three provinces for the years 1540–1548.

[d] Annual averages, sums expressed in Spanish ducats.

[e] The *focatico* (see Chapter 3) originated as what would be called an ordinary subsidy in other realms, but I count it here as ordinary income, not a subsidy, because from the early sixteenth century parliamentary approval was no longer needed for its collection.

intermediaries to effect transfers of this kind. As Anthony Calabria has found for Naples, "between 1541 and 1559, loans for nearly 7,000,000 ducats [6,510,000 Spanish ducats] were assigned for payment on Naples, or sent from the Kingdom to support Imperial efforts in Italy, North Africa, and Northern Europe."[36] In the Low Countries, short-term loans charged

[36] Calabria, *The Cost of Empire*, 50. See also my Chapter 13.

against the central government amounted to 3,801,992 Carolus gulden (2,078,454 Spanish ducats) in 1554, and 5,377,421 gulden (2,939,702 ducats) in 1555; it should be noted however that, in contrast with Naples, most of this debt, if not all, was for money spent by the Netherlands government, not by the emperor.[37] But any transfers beyond the borders of sums voted by parliamentary bodies for the needs of their own realm caused political problems. In 1531 deputies from Amsterdam were outraged to be told that receipts from Holland's ordinary *bede* for the following year were already "gone," having been pledged to bankers who lent the emperor what he needed for his travels.[38] As the level of the *donativi* rose in Naples, so did the demands of the parliamentary committees that met with the viceroy that at least some of the money be kept back for the needs of the kingdom.[39] In Castile and Aragón too there was growing discontent over massive transfers of money to Italy, some of which had to come from the *servicios*.[40]

Protests of this kind did not prevent the emperor's officials from assigning repayment of loans on subsidies or bankers from accepting them.[41] But from a lender's perspective they made subsidies less desirable than some "other incomes," especially those reported for Castile in Table 5.2. These revenues did not depend on parliamentary consent, and they were too new to have accumulated a long train of standing obligations. At the start of Charles's reign, the so-called *maestrazgos* were the most important "other income." To carry on the struggle against Muslim Spain, reduced in the thirteenth century to the single kingdom of Granada in the south, medieval Castile had formed three military orders, similar to the Knights Templar and other warrior-monks of the Crusade era. With

---

[37] Tracy, *A Financial Revolution*, 3; using figures from a different source, Michel Baelde, "Financiële Politiek en Domaniale Evolutie in de Nederlanden onder Karel V en Filips II," *Tijdschrift voor Geschiedenis* LXXVI (1963): 14–33, gives a figure of 3,071,000 gulden for 1553. See Chapter 12.

[38] Tracy, "The Taxation System of Holland," 77 (for the transfers in question, Aud. 875, 15, 120,000 crowns [150,000 gulden] sent to Charles in 1531 were charged against the subsidies of 1531 and 1532); Charles to Ferdinand, 11 January 1530, *Familienkorrespondenz*, Letter 388, II, 559–561.

[39] Chapter 13.

[40] Charles to Margaret, 7 December 1522, Lanz, Letter 43, I, 75–76; Charles to Ferdinand, 8 September 1523, *Familienkorrespondenz*, Letter 46, I, 72–75; Margaret to Charles, 21 February 1524, Lanz, Letter 49, I, 91, and Adrien de Croy, Sieur de Beaurain, to Charles, 5 May 1524, Lanz, Letter 56, I, 134–138; Lope de Soria to Charles, 26 February 1525, *Corpus Documental*, Letter XXI, I, 96–98; Ferdinand to Charles, 28 October 1526, *Familienkorrespondenz*, Letter 250, I, 482–485, and Charles to Ferdinand, 23–30 November 1526, *Familienkorrespondenz*, Letter 252, I, 490; Charles to Ferdinand, 27 November 1527, *Familienkorrespondenz*, Letter 130 (separate numeration of letters starts for this volume), II, 148–152; Charles to Ferdinand, two letters of 19 April 1528, *Familienkorrespondenz*, Letters 174 and 175, II, 204–206, 208; and Charles to Ferdinand, 11 January 1530, *Familienkorrespondenz*, Letter 388, II, 559–561.

[41] Carande Thobar, *Carlos V y sus banqueros*, II, 108–110; Braudel, "Les emprunts de Charles V sur le place d'Anvers," in 190–201.

the conquest of Granada (1492), they ceased to have a purpose. Hence, as the grandmastership (*maestrazgo*) of each order became vacant (1487, 1494, 1499), members were persuaded to elect Queen Isabella as administrator of the order and its properties, including large flocks of sheep and tracts of land that collected handsome grazing fees from Castile's important sheepherders' guild. Early in his reign Charles V was recognized as "perpetual administrator" of the three orders by his erstwhile tutor, Pope Adrian VI (1521–1523). Using the leverage they had from their unpaid balance for the imperial-election loan, the Fugger set a pattern for other lenders by targeting these receipts: they pushed aside the Castilian financier (backed by the Grimaldi of Genoa), who had hitherto held the income-farming contract for administering the *maestrazgos*, and signed the first of many three-year contracts.[42]

Castile's two other sources of as yet unmortgaged income also attracted keen interest among the great firms. The first consisted of two special privileges granted by the papacy: the *cruzada*, dating from 1484, by which one could gain a plenary indulgence (full remission from the pains of purgatory) by contributing to the war against infidel Granada; and the *subsidio*, by which Castile's clergy was constrained to pay an annual tax to the crown, with the amount to be determined by negotiation.[43] The most novel source of income in Charles's reign depended on the treasure fleets, whose intermittent arrival from the New World was always an occasion for great joy at court. The flows of silver from the great mines of Potosí in the Viceroyalty of Peru and Zacatecas in Mexico were just beginning in the latter years of Charles's reign. Thus, as Table 5.2 indicates, the average annual value of the king's share of the treasure rose from about 39,000 ducats in the 1520s to 282,000 in the 1540s. More important, Charles also claimed the right to sequester the silver to which his subjects had title, in return for new *juros* charged against the treasury (money from sequestrations is not reflected in Table 5.2). Backed by the Council of Finance and by the House of Trade in Seville, Philip more than once conveyed to his father fears that such "taking" of private silver would ruin merchant credit in the kingdom. But Charles's demand for the cash he needed to keep his armies in the field was not to be gainsaid, and neither was the bankers' demand for having at least part payment for their loans in *oro y plata* from the New World.[44] The only question was whether Castile's political community, as represented not just by the Cortes but also by treasury officials, would continue to accept this diversion of national treasure to the needs of wars in other lands.

---

[42] Kellenbenz, *Die Fuggersche Maestrazgopacht (1525–1542)*, 2–6.
[43] Carande Thobar, *Carlos V y sus banqueros*, II, chaps. IX, X, and XI.
[44] Ibid., I, 232–244.

Defending the Interests of the Realm

Politically conscious subjects of all of Europe's principalities were united in their detestation of seeing local revenues squandered on foreign escapades; if parliamentary bodies were not in a position to prevent such transfers, the officials of the ruler's own treasury were capable of setting up roadblocks of their own. In each of the Habsburg lands, the small army of officials and tax farmers who collected revenue was overseen by a council of finance made up of senior bureaucrats and a few great nobles. Councils of this type, dating from the late thirteenth century, have been described as an early stage in the emergence of representative institutions: they understood themselves as acting in the interests of the realm, which were not necessarily identical to the interests of the prince.[45]

Hence it is not surprising that Charles's various councils of finance often refused to honor payment orders for debts that might more properly be charged to one of his other realms. The assignation that Charles gave an Italian banker on the Gravelines toll was "broken" in Flanders, just as the pensions for Germany's electoral princes he had assigned on other domain revenues in the Low Countries often went unpaid, other charges being deemed more important. When Charles ordered that 600 crowns in expenses for his ambassador to England be paid from Low Countries receipts, his aunt, Margaret of Austria, regent from 1517 to 1530, promised to "induce the gentlemen of your finances" to accept the unwonted charge; in other words, she could not or would not do so by fiat.[46] The fisc in Naples was guarded by the Sommaria. In 1526 Ferdinand signed over to the Fuggers a debt of 60,000 scudi, owed by Charles, for which he had not been able to make good on the assignation on the revenues of Naples he had been given. By 1528 the Fuggers too had collected nothing; worse still, it seems officials in Naples had sold bonds with 7,000 to 8,000 scudi in annual interest charges against the income in question.[47]

In some cases an assignation circulated from one council of finance to another while interest accumulated. In 1544 Mary of Hungary by Charles's authorization contracted in Antwerp a loan of 161,450 crowns, to be repaid in Castile. Both Philip and Francisco de los Cobos (d. 1547) assured the emperor that no assignation could be made for this debt save on revenues four or five years in the future, which would mean a "mountain" of interest.

[45] Ellen E. Kittell, *From Ad Hoc to Routine: A Case Study in Medieval Bureaucracy* (Philadelphia, 1991).
[46] Charles to Margaret, 4 May 1526, Lanz, Letter 87, I, 208; Charles to Count Palatine Frederick, 16 September 1531, Lanz, Letter 209, I, 533–534; Margaret to Charles, 5 April 1530, Lanz, Letter 132, II, 382.
[47] On the Sommaria, see Galasso, "Trends and Problems in Neapolitan History in the Age of Charles V," 24–30. Charles's instructions for Sanchez's mission to Ferdinand, 8 November 1528, *Familienkorrespondenz*, Letter 240, II, 323–324.

Charles then assigned part of the debt to his portion of a tax for a war aide recently voted by the imperial diet in Germany (see Chapter 9), but in vain, because the tax was only partly paid, and Charles had to fight with Ferdinand for what was available. For a time he believed that Sicily's revenues might cover the debt, or at least 50,000 crowns. But in the end, he induced Mary's creditors in Antwerp to accept payment in Castile at dates later than those originally contracted for. Aquiescing in what he could not prevent, Cobos still insisted that Mary's lenders drop their demand, unheard of in Castile, for "interest on interest" – that is, interest on unpaid interest as well as unpaid principal.[48]

This episode raises a point of fundamental importance for Habsburg finance: it was easier for Charles to apply Castile's revenues to the needs of other lands than to apply the revenues of other lands to Castile's needs. Between 1530 and 1532, for example, Ferdinand was the beneficiary of several such transfers. In July 1530 Charles wrote his wife Isabella from Germany, asking her to find a way of paying immediately the 50,000 ducats assigned to Ferdinand on the Cruzada income for 1530; she did so by contracting a loan with agents of the Fugger and the Welser. When arranging Ferdinand's election as King of the Romans (September 1530), he hoped the electoral princes would be satisfied with the 200,000 ducats he took from the carefully husbanded sum that France had paid for the ransom of the sons of Francis I according to the 1529 Treaty of Cambrai. But because they also demanded sums still owing them from his own election as emperor in 1519, he had to assign a further 300,000 ducats against what the Welser would be paying for the *maestrazgo* contract in 1533–1534. Meanwhile, Ferdinand himself was still owed 200,000 ducats as the dowry for his marriage to Anne of Hungary (1515), as determined by a settling of accounts between the two brothers. In 1524 the emperor assigned this sum to what Venice owed him according to a just-concluded treaty, but owing to continuing border conflicts with Habsburg Austria Venice found reasons for not paying. In 1531 Charles promised Ferdinand to assign this 200,000 (plus a further 35,000 ducats he owed) to the ordinary subsidies of the Low Countries provinces, but it seems he did not do so. In 1532 Charles wrote Mary that he was assigning 100,000 ducats from Ferdinand's dowry debt "to Spain rather than Venice." In fact, the debt was assigned first to what the Welser owed for the

---

[48] Philip to Charles, 28 September 1544, *Corpus Documental*, Letter CCXC, II, 283, and Cobos to Charles, 28 September 1544, *Corpus Documental*, Letter CCXCI, II, 285; Charles to Philip, 17 October and 30 November 1544, *Corpus Documental*, Letters CCXCII and CCXCV, II, 289, 294; Veltwijk to Charles, 11 December 1544, Lanz, Letter 529, II, 421; Charles to Philip, 15 January 1545, *Corpus Documental*, Letter CCCV, II, 328–329; Charles to Ferdinand, 24 January 1545, HHSA-Belgien, PA 5; Charles to Philip, 3 March 1545, *Corpus Doumental*, Letter CCCX, II, 349; Cobos to Mary, 23 May 1545, HHSA-Belgien, PA 42. The references are to loan no. 235 on Carande's list, *Carlos V y sus banqueros*, III, 330.

maestrazgo contract in 1536–1537, then to a loan that the duchess of Béjar allowed to run interest-free until she was issued a *juro* with the same face value.[49]

As noted earlier, the Italian wars were a veritable sinkhole for Castile's revenues, even before Charles himself sailed to Italy in 1529. In that year, one of his lieutenants was reported to be bringing 500,000 to 600,000 scudi (465,000 to 568,000 ducats) to Genoa, but the viceroy of Naples thought the army he was preparing for the emperor's arrival would cost twice as much. Most of this money went for garrisons, fortifications, and field armies in northern Italy.[50] Transfers from Castile to the Low Countries began in the 1530s and continued throughout Charles's reign. Mary of Hungary was sent 120,000 ducats for defense of the frontier against France (1535), and 50,000 for an army she raised in case of a French invasion (1537). In addition to the loan for 161,450 crowns already mentioned, Mary was authorized in 1544 to assign her debts for cartage during the recent campaigning season to the treasury of Castile, even if the assignation was not honored by Alonso de Baeca, the treasurer of Castile. During the Habsburg-Valois war that began in late 1551, impressive quantities of New World gold and silver were shipped from Spain, either for Mary's use in raising troops or to satisfy the demand of her lenders in Antwerp for part payment in specie. From 1552, according to a recent and insightful discussion, "Mary negotiated a seemingly inexhaustible string of loans and freely assigned their repayment to other states, particularly Spain."[51] Ironically, this stream of remittances from Castile did nothing to change the beliefs of many Netherlanders that their money was being siphoned off to other Habsburg dominions. As Erasmus of Rotterdam had put it some years earlier, "Taxation beyond measure is something everyone has to bear, but for us it is worse, because the money is carried off to Germany and Spain."[52]

Spaniards were no more generous than anyone else about seeing the treasure of their kingdoms pay for other people's wars, but they knew

---

[49] Charles to Isabella, 8, 31 July, and 6 December 1530, *Corpus Doumental*, Letters LXXVI, LXXXIV, and XCIV, I, 220, 234, 238; Charles to Ferdinand, *Familienkorrespondenz*, Letter 446a, III, 3–5; Mary to Ferdinand (with Wolram's citation of a nearly contemporaneous letter from Charles to Mary), *Familienkorrespondenz*, Letter 654, III, 601–602; Ferdinand to Mary, 12 August 1532, *Familienkorrespondenz*, Letter 657, III, 611–613, with Wolfram's note; Charles to Isabella, 2 September 1532, *Corpus Documental*, Letter CLIX, I, 393; and, on the Duchess of Béjar's loan, Charles to Isabella, 22 April 1532, *Corpus Documental*, Letter CXLI, I, 355 (Carande Thobar, loan no. 93, *Carlos V y sus banqueros,* III, 140).

[50] Lodewijk van Praet to Charles, 30 July 1529, Lanz, Letter 119, I, 321–322.

[51] Charles to Isabella, 13 December 1535, *Corpus Documental*, Letter CXXXII, I, 444–446; Charles to Mary, 19 August 1537, Lanz, Letter 691, II, 679–680; Tracy, "Herring Wars," 249–272 sources cited in n. 62, p. 267; Mary to Charles, 23 January 1544, Aud. 55, 43–44; Rodriguez-Salgado, *The Changing Face of Empire,* 54–62 (the quote, p. 59).

[52] Allen, *Opus Epistolarum D. Erasmi,* Letter 2177, lines 47–55, III, 194 (my translation).

better than Netherlanders which way the money was flowing. In 1536, when Charles ordered a shipment of Peruvian gold sent to Genoa by way of Barcelona, the Generalities (permanent parliamentary committees) of the kingdoms of Aragón and Valenica refused to permit the precious metal to exit their ports; Charles had to have it rerouted far to the south, by way of Cartagena in Castile. In the 1550s, when Mary of Hungary contracted with Antwerp bankers for loans to be repaid in Castile, Philip and his Council of Finance vigorously protested what a modern scholar calls "this unwarranted assault on the autonomy of the Spanish realms," but, in the end, to no avail.[53]

Castile became Charles's treasury of last resort not because Castilians wished it so, but because Castile had the revenues to which bankers preferred to have their loans assigned. Moreover, Charles was probably better able in Castile than his other realms to override opposition to the transfers of funds on which his campaigns depended. Part of his success in this respect was due to Cobos, a loyal servitor who had a unique ability to bypass inconvenient regulations and procedures.[54] Equally important, if impossible to quantify, was the fact that Charles had chosen to live in Castile, adopting its language and manners. A "natural prince" resident among his people had in the sixteenth century an authority that we who live in a more democratic and a more skeptical century find difficult to grasp. Finally, in the perilous years when Charles himself was on campaign, he had a weapon of last resort against all of the most solid arguments that Philip and his Council of Finance could muster about dangers to the solvency of the kingdom. No matter how difficult it was to find unpledged receipts in Castile, a dutiful son could not turn aside a father's solemn warning, sent from an encampment facing the enemy, that he risked losing "honor and reputation" for lack of a mere 300,000 or 400,000 ducats more.[55]

The argument of this book rests on the observation that by choosing on numerous occasions to risk his own person in defense of his honor and reputation, Charles greatly increased the cost of his wars, and hence the size of the loans needed from his bankers. This chapter may close with the observation that by inducing Philip to share responsibility for the dangers in which he had placed himself, Charles made sure that Castile, even more than his other lands, would be left to face the fiscal consequences of his military adventures.

[53] Charles to Isabella, 18 February 1536, *Corpus Documental*, Letter CXCI, I, 470: Rodriguez-Salgado, *Changing Face of Empire*, 59.

[54] See Cobos's instructions to Juan Vazquez de Molina (his nephew), telling him to ignore a memo from the auditors (*contadores*) objecting to a pension granted by Charles to one of his treasury officials: Cobos to Vazquez, 24 August 1541, Estado, 51, 78–80.

[55] See, e.g., Charles's letter to Philip from his camp at Landshut, 10 August 1546, *Corpus Documental*, Letter CCCXLIX, II, 491–492.

PART TWO

Impresario of War: Charles's Campaigns, 1529–1552

Charles and his inner circle had regular reports on the affairs of dozens of kingdoms and principalities in Europe and overseas, and occasional reports on many others. Tracing the interconnections among these separate histories would require a gargantuan effort of the mind, a simulcast on thirty or forty different channels of the historical imagination. This section of the book has a simpler purpose. From a fabric made up of many separate histories, it pulls out only those strands that help to explain why Charles chose to take command of his own armies for nine "enterprises" of war: the Italian campaign of 1529–1530 (Chapter 6), the Danube war flotilla of 1532 and the 1535 conquest of Tunis (Chapter 7), failures in Provence (1536) and at Algiers (Chapter 8), the "grand plan" to attack in the Rhineland and then in France (1543–1544; Chapter 9), the First Schmalkaldic War (1546–1547; Chapter 10), and the futile assault on Metz (Chapter 11).

In these cases "honor and reputation" required that Charles take personal command. As Charles wrote Isabella in April 1532, if the Grand Turk came against Austria "in person, at the head of a great force," he had resolved "to sally forth against him in my own person."[1] But Charles too went to war only "at the head of a great force" – all the preparations had to be more careful if the emperor himself were at risk. In 1536, for example, Antonio Leyva, imperial commander in Milan, was asked about the size of the artillery train for the upcoming invasion of Provence. If the emperor sent his army under a captain general, Leyva replied, forty pieces would suffice; if he went in person, seventy to eighty pieces would be required.[2]

This added margin of safety drove up the cost of war during Charles's reign. To measure the difference that the emperor's participation made, one must first make the assumption that it is possible to distinguish between

---

[1]   See Chapter 7, note 18.
[2]   Leyva to Charles, s.d., *Corpus Documental*, Letter CLXXXIII, I, 445–447.

Table II.1. *Warfare and Loans against the Treasury of Castile in Charles's Reign*

	Years of Peace	*Empresa* Years	Other War Years
1520s	231,107 (2)	813,017 (2)	300,169 (6)
1530s	468,112 (5)	771,434 (3)	890,314 (2)
1540s	351,029 (4)	1,132,346 (5)	346,030 (1)
1550s	1,505,362 (1)	2,985,992 (2)	1,115,017 (2)
TOTAL LOANS	5,712,251	15,003,272	6,157,108
TOTAL YEARS	12	13	11
ANNUAL AVERAGE	476,021	1,154,098	559,737

Notes: Sums are in Spanish ducats; number of years are given in parentheses. Figures are from loan tables in Carande Thobar, *Carlos y sus banqueros.*

years of peace and years of war in Charles's reign. If one considers the whole complex of Habsburg lands it may seem there were no years of peace at all; but the years in which there was no serious fighting that directly involved Castile, Naples, or the Low Countries may count here as years of peace. Second, to get a rough idea of the sums Charles borrowed for his personal campaigns, one may use the sums he borrowed each year against the treasury of Castile, as documented by Carande Thobar.[3] The relationship of annual borrowing to war expenses is not clear-cut, because new loans often carried forward unpaid sums from loans contracted during previous years of war. Also, Charles paid some of his campaign expenses from other sources, such as the huge sum King Francis I agreed to pay to ransom his two sons by the 1529 Treaty of Cambrai (see Chapter 7).[4] Nonetheless, the greater part of the money was borrowed in one way or another, and Castile was Charles's great reserve treasury.

Keeping these distinctions in mind, Table II.1 distinguishes between years of peace, years in which Charles undertook a military *empresa* or enterprise, and other years of war. What stands out is the amount Charles borrowed during the thirteen *empresa* years, roughly twice as much as during other war years, and two and a half times as much as during years of peace. The fact that this pattern does not hold for the 1530s points to a further distinction that deserves mention. Rather than mortgaging the receipts of Castile's treasury for his three campaigns against Islam (1532, 1535, and 1541; Chapters 7 and 8), Charles found money elsewhere. If these three years are excluded from the middle column of Table II.1, the cost, for Castile, of Charles's battles against France and against the German

---

[3] *Carlos V y sus banqueros.*

[4] Tables in Chapters 8 and 11 estimate the amount of money from different sources that Charles used in paying for his campaigns.

Protestants stands out all the more sharply. During years when these wars were fought Charles borrowed an average of 1,355,69 ducats, or 2.25 times as much as during war years when he did not take the field himself. In effect, he borrowed slightly more during ten years of personal campaigning against France and the Schmalkaldic League (13,556,960 ducats) than during the remaining twenty-five years of his reign included in the table (13,215,671 ducats). Having the emperor undertake in his own person an *empresa* of war cannot be called a foolish idea – for the "honor and reputation" of the dynasty was a pearl of great price – but it was truly an expensive idea.

In Chapters 6 through 11, this point is made by occasional comparisons with the cost for Charles of major imperial campaigns in which he did not participate: the sequence of events leading up to the great imperialist victory at Pavia (1524–1525; see Chapter 2), Andrea Doria's conquest of Coron in the Morea (1532), and the futile siege of Parma by a combined papal and imperial army (1550–1551).

It must also be borne in mind that wages for experienced soldiers rose steeply during the first half of the sixteenth century. According to information from Charles's correspondence and from the papers of the Council of State in the Low Countries, High German *Landsknechte* earned the equivalent of 2.73 Spanish ducats in 1506, and, between 1521 and 1531, 2.83 ducats. For the latter period, the cost per man rises to 3.53 ducats, if one takes into account added pay for the captain, sergeants, flag bearers, drummers, trumpeters, and provost (judicial officer) that filled out the ranks of each unit or "banner" of 400 men. According to Spanish accounts cited by René Quatrefages for 1536, the High Germans were paid 3 ducats a month, and the cost for officers raised the total to 1,315 ducats a month for a banner of 400, meaning an effective rates of 3.29 ducats per fighting man. By 1541 the effective rate had risen to 3.81 ducats per month; by late 1552 *Landsknechte* could expect the equivalent of 4.31 ducats for garrison duty during the winter months and 5.47 ducats for field service during the campaign season, not to mention a "joining-up fee" (*loopgelt*) and the "going-home" pay, usually a month's wages, that kept men being mustered out from causing grief to their erstwhile employer.[5]

For Spanish infantry the case is more complicated, because the men were paid at different rates. Pikemen were the backbone of an infantry company, the honorable men who braved the enemy face to face, but

---

[5] Aud. 867, 53 (1506); Ferdinand to Margaret, [December 1523], *Familienkorrespondenz*, Letter 47, I, 75–78; Charles to Ferdinand, 31 January 1528, *Familienkorrespondenz*, Letter 149, II, 178–179; Margaret to Ferdinand, 16 June 1529, *Familienkorrespondenz*, Letter 312, III, 434–437; Charles to Ferdinand, 5 October 1531, *Familienkorrespondenz*, Letter 553, IV, 367–369; Aud. 650, 529–531 and 141–148 (estimates for the campaign seasons of 1553 and 1558). Quatrefages, "L'organisation militaire de l'Espagne," 350–351. For further discussion, see Chapter 7, note 39.

they were paid less than those who carried firearms; again according to Quatrefages, in 1536 *arcabuceros* earned 3 scudi a month (3.73 ducats), and *escopeteros* (carrying an older form of arquebus) earned 3.25 scudi (3 ducats), whereas pikemen got only three scudi (2.8 ducats). Thus for a company of 279 men, including 81 *arcabuceros* and 21 *escopeteros*, monthly wages would have been 843 ducats, an average of 3.02 ducats. According to Charles's correspondence, Italian infantry were paid slightly more than Spaniards (3.27 and 3 ducats per month respectively in 1527). Low German and Walloon levies were less highly valued – 4.31 ducats in 1558, for example. Similarly, German heavy cavalry commanded significantly higher pay than the *compagnies d'ordonnance* on station in the Low Countries; in 1553, pay was 13.12 ducats per month for the former and between 5.78 and 6.17 per month for the latter. Light horse, often recruited in Italy, commanded an intermediate rate, 9.54 ducats in 1553 and 1558.[6]

One issue I cannot address from the sources I have used is attrition. Charles's armies were always depleted on the march, but this was especially so in certain campaigns; it is estimated that he lost half his men to disease or desertion during his 1536 invasion of Provence,[7] and there were many who melted away as the ground hardened during winter engagements (the Danube campaign of 1546, the assault on Metz in 1552). To compensate for my counting units on the imperial payroll as being at full strength through their term of engagement, I use what seems to me a low estimate for an aggregate of campaign expenses for which my sources give little specific information: officers' pay, victuals, and artillery and baggage trains (or, at sea, transport and troop ships). Keeping a draft horse for a month was estimated to cost 5.47 ducats a month in 1553, and, for a campaign during the French Religious Wars (1568), one modern scholar estimates the cost of the artillery train alone at about 4% of the total.[8] In 1529, Margaret of Austria's officials, reckoning the cost of sending to Italy the *Landsknechte* ordered by the emperor, estimated 12,500 "pays" per month for the men, including 2,500 (25%) for the combined expenses for officers' pay and the artillery train.[9] Margaret's correspondence does not mention victuals

---

[6] Quatrefages, "L'organisation militaire de l'Espagne," 331–336. Leyva to Charles, 14 July–7 August 1527, Lanz, Letter 100, I, 237–238; for wages of Low German and Walloon infantry, and of the various kinds of mounted troops in 1553 and 1558, Aud. 650, 141–148 and 529–531.

[7] Quatrefages, "L'organisation militaire de l'Espagne," 350.

[8] Aud. 650, 529–531; James B. Wood, *The King's Army: Warfare, Soldiers, and Society during the Wars of Religion in France, 1562–1576* (Cambridge, 1996), 284.

[9] Margaret to Ferdinand, 16 June 1529, *Familienkorrespondenz*, Letter 312, I, 434–437: the 10,000 *Landsknechte* Margaret is to send to Italy will require 12,500 *payes* per month, that is, one for each man, plus 2,500 for the cost of officers' pay, and of horses and carriages and men for the artillery train. Charles to Ferdinand, 5 October 1531, HHST-B, PA 5, Konvolut 1: the wages for eight banners of *Landsknechte* reckoned here at 500 men will be 4,320 *payes* per month, that is, 1 for

or the baggage train, which would surely add another 5% to 10%. But instead of counting 25% or 30% of troop wages for all of these additional costs, for the reason just mentioned, I use a figure of 20%. Also, where my sources give different numbers for units on the imperial payroll and one does not seem more credible than another, I choose the lower number.

To measure the outcomes of war against Charles's objectives, each of the chapters in this section looks first at the pertinent campaign or campaigns, as recounted in Charles's correspondence and by contemporary historians. Next comes an estimate of the forces under his command, based on the same sources, and of how much it will have cost to engage their services for the period in question; for each class of fighting men I assume the documented rate of pay nearest in date to the campaign. Finally, as a check on my estimates of cost, there is also, for each campaign, an estimate of the sums Charles had remitted to him, either from monies on hand or from bankers' loans. Ideally, one ought to deduct from the remittances for exchange fees as well as interest; for example, sending Carolus gulden of the Low Countries to Germany as Rhine gulden could cost as much as 16% of the principal. But I do so here only when I have precise information for current exchange rates.[10] Similarly, I deduct for loan interest only when it is clear that the bankers insisted on collecting interest before sending on the remittance.

---

each soldier, and 320 "payes-perdus" [8%] for the officers for each banner, including "captains, standard-bearers, sergeants, quartermasters, provosts and sheriffs [*escoutette*] and all other officers."

[10] Aud. 875, 15, from a summary of income and expenses for 1531: sending to Charles in Germany a sum of 120,000 crowns (150,000 Carolus gulden) taken from the ordinary subsidies of the Low Countries cost 19,140 gulden in exchange fees. Mary to Charles, first letter of 1 July 1543, Aud. 54, 141–143: the Portuguese king's factor in Antwerp wants to charge 12% for delivery of a sum of 150,000 gulden (half the dowry for Philip's wife Maria – see Chapter 9); this is reasonable, because if Charles borrowed the same amount, "you would be obliged to pay the exchange fee, which sometimes is more than 12%."

Chapter 6

Finding Uses for an Army: Charles in Italy, 1529–1530

In an autograph reflection on the choices open to him, just before news came of the victory at Pavia, Charles felt he had yet to gain the "reputation" that could only come, as Gattinara said, from "employing your person in affairs of state in a manner that can be judged for good or ill." Like the chancellor, he believed there was no better place than Italy for gaining reputation by exploits of war.[1] But he could not sail across the Mediterranean without leaving a member of the dynasty to govern Castile and Aragón; this was a good reason, he thought, for agreeing to the marriage to Infanta Isabella of Portugal, proposed by the parliaments of Castile and Portugal (in fact, the royal pair were married on 10 March 1526).[2] But there was another difficulty, as Charles explained to Ferdinand (June 1525): crossing a sea cruised by North African corsairs required an armada, for which he lacked funds.[3]

Doria's change of allegiance solved this second problem. In October 1528 Charles announced to Ferdinand and Mary that he would sail with Doria's galleys to Italy, not merely to be crowned as emperor, but "to put my own person at risk" by carrying the war across the Alps into France.[4] The loan contract with Ansaldo Grimaldi for nearly 200,000 scudi, needed to begin preparations for assembling an army in Italy, was

---

[1] Gattinara's memorandum on war and peace, dated Dunquerque, 30 July 1521, *Staatspapiere*, Document 1, here p. 4: "votre majesté doit sur toutes choses serrcher [*sic*] de acquerir reputacion," for he has hitherto not employed his person in affairs of state "dont l'on puisse arguer bien ou mal."

[2] For Charles's autograph reflection, Brandi, "Eigenhändige Aufzeichnungen Karls V aus dem Anfang des Jahres 1525," "Berichte," IX, 256–260.

[3] Charles to Ferdinand, June 1525, and 26 July 1526, *Familienkorrespondenz*, Letters 143, 216, I, 308, 408–411.

[4] Charles to Ferdinand, 9 October 1528, enclosing a copy of his agreement with Doria, *Familienkorrespondenz*, Letter 234, vol. I, 310; Charles's instructions for Willem van Montfoort for Margaret and Ferdinand, 8 October 1528, *Familienkorrespondenz*, Letter 232, vol. I, 295–308, here pp. 295–299: he will cross to Italy in December, to take the war into France, asking Margaret and Ferdinand to help

Figure 6.1. Titian, *La Emperatriz Doña Isabella*, Prado, Madrid

signed in November. Santa Cruz inserts into his chronicle a "speech of the emperor to his council," presumably of roughly the same date, "in which he disclosed that he had made up his mind to go to Italy." This public justification of his plans has a different emphasis. Charles is not going,

in every way they can, for "puisque nous y mectrons nostre personne, la chose touche tant à nostre honneur que ce nous seroit incroyable regret que riens y fust espargné."

he says, merely to be crowned emperor, for the pope has offered to send the crown to Spain. He is not going to take vengeance on his enemies, for vengeance belongs to God, as the king of France has learned. Rather, he is going in order to persuade the pope to call an ecumenical council of the church, "to uproot heresies and reform the church," for "I will deserve to be infamous in the centuries to come, and punished by the justice of God in the next world, if I do not do all that can be done and try all that can be tried to reform the church and destroy this accursed heresy."[5] Charles's determination to root out "the heresy of Luther," for which a council seemed a necessary first step, should not be taken lightly (see Chapter 10). But his concrete plans for this trip focused on the military dimension brushed aside in his speech to the council. In addition to Spanish infantry, there must be *Landsknechte*; but those recently led into Lombardy by the duke of Brunswick had broken up and returned to Germany, it seems for want of pay.[6] Hence the German regiments that Charles had wanted Ferdinand to mobilize for a strike into France from the east would have to be "diverted" to Italy. To pacify Italy, and "throw all our forces against France," Charles needed 10,000 *Landsknechte*, plus the 2,000 cavalry Margaret was to send from the Low Countries.[7]

Charles initially set his departure for December 1528 but did not actually sail until July 1529. In the meantime, there were objections from all sides to his ambitious plan. Charles's speech to the council also brushed aside financial problems: no prince should hold back from "heroic action" for want of money[8] – yet money had to be found. To assure his men their pay for some months in advance, Charles agreed to mortgage Castile's claims to Ternate, one of the fabled Spice Islands, to his brother-in-law, King

---

[5] For the loan, see note 56; Santa Cruz, *Crónica del Emperador*, II, 454–455.

[6] Charles's instructions for Montfoort's mission to Ferdinand, 31 January 1528, *Familienkorrespondenz*, Letter 149, II, 180–181 (Ferdinand has used the 100,000 ducats remitted by Charles to send Brunswick and his men to Italy); the prince of Orange (Philibert de Châlons) to Charles, from besieged Naples, 14 June 1528, Lanz, Letter 108, I, 271, expressing surprise that Charles's forces in Lombardy "are not marching" to the south; for Charles's orders to this effect, via Leyva in Milan, Charles to Ferdinand, 5 July 1528, Lanz, Letter 109, I, 275–276.

[7] Charles's instructions for Moqueron and Montfoort to Margaret and Ferdinand, 28 November 1528, *Familienkorrespondenz*, Letter 247, II, 335–345, here 335–340, 341–342. See also Charles to Ferdinand, 16 February 1529, *Familienkorrespondenz*, Letter 268, I, 370–372: because "the enemy" hopes to have the Turk descend [on Italy], Charles will need 10,000 to 12,000 German infantry in addition to the 2,000 horse from the Low Countries and the Rhineland.

[8] Santa Cruz, *Crónica del Emperador*, 456: there are indeed debts from his past wars, "mas al fin habeis de pensar que pues no me falteron dineros para entretener pocho años continuos de guerra, menos me faltara ahora para irme à coronar. Muy gran poquedad es de un Principe dejar de emprender algun acto heroico con pensar que le ha de faltar el dinero, porque para las cosas de honra han los Principes de arriscar las personas y empeñar las haciendas."

John III of Portugal, for 350,000 ducats; he would also forgo the dispatch of a planned Spanish armada to the Moluccas. As he later explained to Ferdinand, his embarkation was held up by Portugal's delay in getting to Barcelona the mule train carrying the money in gold coin.[9] The Council of Castile apparently objected to the fact that Spain's galleys were to go to Italy, along with Doria's. Alonso de Fonseca (d. 1534), archbishop of Toledo and president of the council, offered to pay for new galleys (so that Castile's fleet could remain on station against Barbary corsairs), but Charles politely declined.[10] In fact, the council's fears were well grounded; from his base in Algiers, Khair-ad-Din Barbarossa had good intelligence about the movements of Castile's war fleet and made his plans accordingly (see Chapter 7). From Brussels, Margaret and her council also urged Charles to postpone the expedition. Contacts with Louise of Savoy (d. 1531), the mother of Francis I and sister of her late husband, gave Margaret reason to hope for a treaty of peace; the emperor should await the outcome of these discussions, rather than trusting his person to the promises of financial support from supposed allies in Italy. But Charles had already decided that Margaret was too eager for peace: France's apparent reasonableness was only a ploy to forestall his great *empresa* in Italy.[11]

Finally, Charles was still technically at war with the Medici pope, Clement VII. This issue was resolved just before his departure. By the Treaty of Barcelona (16 July 1529), the pope renounced the League of Cognac, and renewed for Charles's benefit important fiscal privileges formerly enjoyed by the kings of Castile.[12] The emperor's key promise was to restore to Medici control the great city of Florence, which had proclaimed itself a republic in the aftermath of the Sack of Rome;[13] he would also work to gain recognition of the Papal State's claim to Parma and Piacenza, currently held by the duke of Ferrara.[14]

---

[9] Charles to Ferdinand, 16 February 1529, *Framilienkorrespondenz*, Letter 268l, I, 370–372, and 11 January 1530, *Familienkorrespondenz*, Letter 388, II, 556–557; Brandi, *Kaiser Karl V*, I, 397; Salinas to Ferdinand, 6 May 1529, in Antonio Rodriguez Villa, *El Emperador Carlos V y su Corte según las cartas de Don Martín de Salinas, embajador del Infante Don Fernando (1522–1539)* (Madrid, 1903), Letter 179, p. 431.

[10] Charles to Isabella, from Barcelona, 27 July 1529, in Gómara, *Crónica des los Barbarrojas*, appendix 25, 491–493.

[11] Margaret to Charles, with the support of seven named members of her council, 26 May 1529, Lanz, Letter 117, I, 300–308 (she added, however, that if Charles heard nothing further by 20 July, he was to assume the negotiations had failed); Charles's instructions for Montfoort's mission to Ferdinand, 3 April 1529, *Familienkorrespondenz*, Letter 279, II, 386–390.

[12] For the *cruzada* and the *subsidio*, see Chapter 5.

[13] For the most recent account of Florentine politics in this period, J. N. Stephens, *The Fall of The Florentine Republic* (Oxford, 1983).

[14] Brandi, *Kaiser Karl V*, I, 237–239.

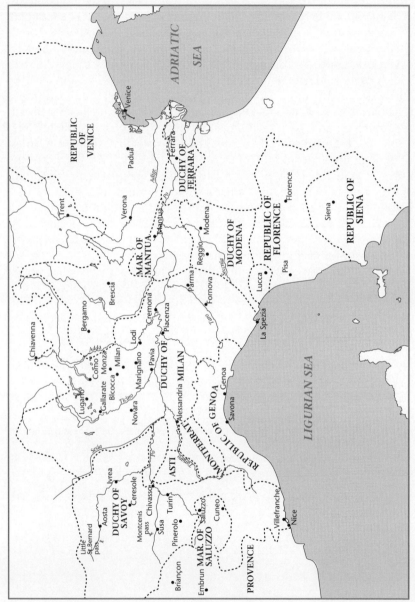

ADRIATIC
SEA

Venice

REPUBLIC
OF
VENICE

Padua

Ferrara

DUCHY OF
FERRARA

Florence

REPUBLIC
OF
SIENA

Siena

REPUBLIC OF
FLORENCE

Trent

Verona

Adige

Mantua

MAR. OF
MANTUA

Modena

DUCHY OF
MODENA

Pisa

Reggio

Secchia

Brescia

Parma

Taro

Fornova

Lucca

Bergamo

Cremona

Piacenza

La Spezia

LIGURIAN SEA

Chiavenna

Adda

Lodi

DUCHY OF

Como

Monza

Milan

Pavia

DUCHY OF MILAN

Genoa

Lugano

Bicocca

Marignano

Savona

Gallarate

Novara

Ticino

Alessandria

REPUBLIC OF GENOA

Sesia

Po

MONTFERRAT

Ivrea

Tanaro

ASTI

Aosta

Ceresole

Chivasso

Turin

DUCHY OF
SAVOY

Montcenis
pass

Susa

Pinerolo

MAR. OF
SALUZZO

Saluzzo

Cuneo

Villefranche

Nice

Little
St Bernard
pass

Briançon

Embrun

PROVENCE

Map 6.1. Northern Italy, with Alpine passes, 1530

Charles in Italy

Charles sailed at the end of July, arriving in Genoa on 12 August.[15] According to a contemporary Florentine historian, Benedetto Varchi (1511–1565),
Doria's galleys deployed in three squadrons, after the fashion of land armies:
the vanguard, the "battle," and the rear guard. The first ship to receive a
welcoming salvo from the harbor battery was a carrack built by Ansaldo
Grimaldi; *La Grimalda*, as it was called, "the largest and best ship made,"
had been bought by the city and given to the emperor as a gift.[16] In addition to the Spanish infantry and cavalry traveling in Charles's armada,
Margaret sent 2,000 cavalry from the Low Countries, and had cash remitted
to Ferdinand for the recruitment of *Landsknechte*.[17] Meanwhile, Orange
with a Neapolitan army of "12,000 to 13,000 good infantry, German and
Italian," was encamped before Perugia, which had thrown off its allegiance
to the Papal States.[18] Charles planned to keep under his command the forces
needed for a strike across the Alps into France, leaving Orange's army to
follow up on his commitments to the pope. But there was now no reason to
invade France. By 5 September Charles had a copy of the Treaty of Cambrai
(3 August 1529): Francis I promised to surrender all fortified places held by
his troops in Naples, and to pay 2 million French crowns (valued in Spain
at 1.2 million ducats) as a ransom for his two sons, held in Spain in consequence of their father's renunciation of the 1526 Treaty of Madrid. Meanwhile, a large Turkish army had been marching up the Danube. Charles
had also envisioned (or so he wrote to Ferdinand) the possibility of using
his army in northern Italy to relieve Turkish pressure on Vienna. Now that
France had concluded peace, Ferdinand urged Charles to advance toward
Verona and have Doria's galleys sail up the Adriatic, giving the Ottomans
cause to fear an attack in that quarter. But having heard from Ferdinand
shortly after reaching Italy that Vienna itself was not in danger, Charles
made no move toward the northeast. When he learned that the Austrian
capital was actually under siege, he wrote, there was little he could do.[19]

The emperor made his way slowly southeast, toward Bologna, where
he had chosen to be crowned emperor by Pope Clement VII, prior to

[15] Brandi, *Emperor Charles V*, 282–283.

[16] Lelio Arbib, ed., *Storia fiorentina di Benedetto Varchi* (3 vols., Florence, 1838–1841), II, 23–24.

[17] For an estimate of the size of Charles's army, see the "Sinews of War" section at the end of this
      chapter.

[18] Praet to Charles, from Rome, 30 July 1529, Lanz, Letter 119, I, 331–332, warning that Orange
      lacked the 55,500 ducats a month needed for his troops; Hook, *The Sack of Rome*, 258–261, notes
      that Cardinal Lorenzo Pucci of Florence, a Medici ally, advanced Orange the money he needed.

[19] Charles to Ferdinand, 8 July 1529, Ferdinand's instructions for Noguerol's mission to Charles, 18
      August 1529, Charles to Ferdinand, 5 September 1529, and Charles's instructions for Noguerol's
      mission back to Ferdinand, 23 September 1529: *Familienkorrespondenz*, Letters 322, 342, 348, and
      356, II, 449–450, 473–476, 484–489, and 499–509.

his departure for Germany. Against which of his or the pope's enemies in the peninsula should he direct his forces? Venice had yet to disgorge the Neapolitan towns it had seized; Charles also suspected the Venetians of coordinating their plans with the Ottomans, and he was well aware of Ferdinand's long-standing grievances against the Serene Republic.[20] The duke of Ferrara still held Parma and Piacenza against the pope. Perugia surrendered to Orange (12 September), but 3,000 Florentine troops defending Perugia were allowed to depart for Florence, which continued to defy its erstwhile Medici ruler.[21] Charles wrote Ferdinand he was considering a plan to join all his forces at Piacenza, where he would be in position to strike at Florence, Venice, or Ferrara; this would "add reputation to our plans, and give all of the above reason to come to terms quickly." Ferrante Gonzaga, younger brother of the duke of Mantua and commander of the army in Lombardy, was ordered to take Charles's *Landsknechte* and "harry" Venetian territory, while Orange with his Neapolitan army as well as troops supplied by the pope made preparations for an assault on Florence. Francesco Maria Sforza of Milan was another problem. Because the Italian powers firmly opposed direct Habsburg control of Milan, Francesco Maria was restored as duke after the imperialist victory at Pavia, but he then joined the League of Cognac, and now defied the emperor from strongholds his men controlled. As of 3 October Antonio Leyva and the Spanish army of Lombardy were besieging Francesco Maria in Pavia, but Charles chose not to join this operation, because he anticipated that Clement VII would insist on keeping the Sforza ruler in place, despite his disloyalty. Instead, Charles wrote Ferdinand, he would lead the remaining forces under his command to the northeast, to increase pressure on Venice. In fact he continued his progress southeast, toward Bologna, which he entered on 5 November.[22] Meanwhile, the Ottoman army's abandonment of its siege of Vienna (15 October) deprived Venice of

[20] Ferdinand's instructions for Salinas's mission to Charles, 2 April 1525, and Charles to Ferdinand, 5 September 1529, *Familienkorrespondenz*, Letters 136 and 348, I, 288, and II, 484–489; Salinas to Ferdinand, first letter of 24 September 1529, from Piacenza, *El Emperador Carlos V*, Letter 190, p. 442: Ferdinand's affairs will turn out well if Charles makes war on the Venetians, "por ser ellos los inventores de la venida del turco."

[21] Hook, *The Sack of Rome*, 258–261. Charles to Ferdinand, 5 September 1529, *Familienkorrespondenz*, Letter 348, II, 484–489: Charles says he told emissaries from Florence he was willing to mediate in their quarrel with the Medici, but "denièrement m'ont repondu que la communauté de Florence disoit avoir riens d'affaires audict sainct père," save to restore to the Medici family its Florentine properties. For the political climate in republican Florence that ruled out negotiations with the pope, see Stephens, *The Fall of the Florentine Republic*, 241–255.

[22] Charles to Ferdinand, 5 September 1529 (cited in note 21); Ferrante Gonzaga's instructions for Seigneur de Peloux's mission to Charles, 14 September 1529, Lanz, Letter 122, I, 330–332; Charles's instructions for Noguerol's mission to Ferdinand, 23 September 1529, and Charles to Ferdinand, 3 October 1529, *Familienkorrespondenz*, Letters 356 and 359, II, 499–509 and 511–513.

hopes that Charles might have to divert his forces elsewhere. In an agreement signed in Bologna (26 November), Venice gave up the towns it held
in Naples, and joined a league of Christian powers against the Ottomans.
Charles accepted demands by Venice and the pope that Francesco Sforza
remain as duke of Milan, in return for the surrender of two key citadels to
be held by Spanish infantry and a promised indemnity of 800,000 ducats.

Charles's coronation was postponed until 24 February 1530, while he
and Clement VII conducted negotiations lasting from December through
the end of March. The two men had apartments with a communicating
door in Bologna's Palazzo Pubblico, and what they discussed in private is
uncertain. Charles apparently received assurances concerning King Henry
VIII's petition to the pope for an annulment from Charles's aunt, Catherine
of Aragón;[23] Clement apparently received assurances that Charles would
not press for convening the ecumenical council of the church that the
pope so greatly feared.[24] Control of church wealth in Castile was high
on the emperor's agenda; in Bologna the pope confirmed the crown's
annexation of the properties of Castile's military orders (see Chapter 5) and
issued a papal brief directing that the *quarta* or 25% tax on clerical income
granted to Charles by the Treaty of Barcelona was to be paid forthwith,
notwithstanding protestations by the Spanish clergy. By dispatching a copy
of this brief to Valladolid, Charles enabled Isabella to offer anticipated
revenues of the *quarta* as security for a large loan contract[25] needed for the
wages of his troops in Italy.

Charles's long letter to Ferdinand (11 January 1530) gives the fullest
explanation of what he had hoped to accomplish by coming to Italy. It
seems he had to justify the Italian *empresa* to his brother, since "some"
were saying that the emperor was "worse off" for coming to Italy. He
came, he said, to pacify Italy, because "neither those instructed to make
peace or those instructed to make war [in the peninsula] have accomplished
their task"; to have himself crowned as emperor, so as to head off plans by
Lutheran princes in Germany to recognize someone other than Ferdinand
as King of the Romans; to make war on France; to make a demonstration
against the Turks, in aid of Ferdinand; and to make friends with the pope,
as was necessary for whoever wished to be the dominant power in Italy.
"I knew I could not accomplish all these things, but I also knew I could
accomplish some of them, God willing, and even should I lose much in

[23] Henry's petition (for an annulment that would allow him to marry Anne Boleyn) was revoked to
Rome when the papal legate charged with hearing the case in England abruptly adjourned the
proceedings (July 1529).

[24] No council was called until Trent (1545), during the pontificate of Paul III (1534–1549). For Charles's
role in removing obstacles to its convening, see Chapter 9.

[25] Charles to Isabella, c. January 1530, *Corpus Documental*, Letter LIII, I, 188–190; on the discussions
at Bologna, Brandi, *Emperor Charles V*, 282–288, and Fernández Alvárez, *Charles V*, 86–88.

the attempt, it would still be more honorable to have crossed the sea than to have remained in Spain." He cannot be "worse off" than he was before leaving Spain, for he had "all my Kingdom of Naples free and clear" of enemy occupation and thus better able to pay for its own defense. Besides, "I have twelve thousand Spaniards and nine thousand Germans in Italy, all paid through mid-April"; once Florence came to terms – Charles's last remaining problem in Italy – there would be other uses for these men.[26]

Subjugating Florence

In the same letter Charles relates that in Genoa he was told that the subjugation of Florence would not take "more than 15 or 20 days." Indeed, when Orange drew up his army of 12,000 to 15,000 men on the south bank of the Arno in October, both he and the pope expected the city to come to terms without a siege. But Charles did not understand the grim determination of the Florentines to maintain their ancient republican traditions any better than Clement VII did. The great walled city of some 70,000 souls was defended by 10,000 to 12,000 Italian mercenaries and 3,000 to 5,000 citizen volunteers. At the southeast corner of the enceinte, Florentine troops had occupied the summit of San Miniato, directly facing the imperial forces, and fortified it well, under the direction of Michaelangelo Buonarotti. On St. Martin's Eve (10 November), traditionally a festive night, Orange had his men plant siege ladders at various points along the wall, but Florentines were vigilant, and the assault was decisively repulsed. The next day Orange's men began work on a siege trench to encircle the smaller part of Florence, south of the Arno, while he set out for Bologna to ask pope and emperor for more men. Charles had been warned by Margaret not to "waste time amusing yourself in laying siege to cities," and business in Germany was indeed too pressing to allow him the luxury of seeking honor and reputation by taking charge of operations at Florence.[27] Instead, he ordered the transfer to Orange's command of some 8,000 men from his army in Lombardy; their job was to extend the siege trench around the main part of the city, north of the Arno.[28]

---

[26] On Charles to Ferdinand, 11 January 1530, *Familienkorrespondenz*, Letter 388, II, 549–564, based on a draft with marginal notes in Charles's hand, I agree with Brandi, *Emperor Charles V*, 283–286: "Feeling the need to justify himself to his brother, he wrote . . . a full and confidential letter."

[27] Margaret to Charles, 2 October 1529, Lanz, Letter 125, I, 341–347, here 344. For the honor and reputation gained by Henry VIII through his successful sieges of Tournai (1512) and Boulogne (1554), C. G. Cruikshank, *Army Royal: An Account of Henry VIII's Invasion of France* (Oxford, 1969), 134, and David J. B. Trim, "The Context of War and Violence in Sixteenth-Century English Society," *Journal of Early Modern History* 3 (1999): 246–247.

[28] Luigi Simeoni, *Le Signorie* (2 vols., Milan, 1950), II, 867–868; Cecil Roth, *The Last Florentine Republic* (London, 1925), 232, 243.

By the beginning of 1530 Orange was pinching off routes by which Florence could be supplied, but it was a slow process. In May 1530 García de Loaysa, Charles's one-time confessor and now his confidential agent in Rome, gave a sober assessment of what was at stake:

> It is certain that Florence cannot be stormed, but it can be starved into submission; this means the encirclement has to be tighter, which will take until the end of June. You must thus be prepared for further expenses, but I beseech your majesty not to desist even if the siege takes another four months, for victory will satisfy the demands of your estate, your honor, and your authority; and failure would mean a flood of problems.[29]

Loaysa's estimate of Florence's capacity for resistance was about right. Not until a relief force coming up the Arno from Pisa was ambushed and defeated (3 August 1530) did the republic agree to terms, including 80,000 ducats in dismissal pay for the besiegers. Within a few weeks, an assembly of the citizenry convened "in the ancient manner" shouted approval for a committee of Medici loyalists to decide how the city should be governed. Florence's proud days as a republic were over.[30]

Charles had arrived in Augsburg in June, for the imperial diet at which he negotiated with the electoral princes for Ferdinand's election as King of the Romans (January 1531), and approved a framework for theological discussions with Germany's newly formed "Protestant"[31] party. The success of his army at Florence complicated these discussions, for the free imperial cities of south Germany, many of which had turned to Protestantism, were not pleased to see a great republic bow to a prince's yoke. Moreover, because it was not Charles himself who had forced Florence to submit, he still lacked the "honor and reputation" that could only come from "employing [his] own person in matters of state that can be judged for good or ill." Yet Loaysa had also been correct in his strategic vision: it would have been far worse for "reputation" in the sense that mattered to Charles if a mere city-state had been able to defy his will. Having a large

---

[29] Loaysa to Charles, 13 May 1530, in *Correspondencia del Cardenal de Osma con Carlos V y su Secretario Don Francisco de los Cobos, Collecion de Documentos Ineditos para la Historia de España*, XIV (Madrid, 1849), 8.

[30] Simeoni, *Le Signorie*, II, 867–868, 1071–1072 (contemporaneous return to power in Siena of the Noveschi, a faction favorable to the imperialists); Francesco Guicciardini, *The History of Italy*, tr. Sidney Alexander (New York, 1969), 420–422, 426–432; Charles to Isabella, Innsbruck, 29 May 1530, *Corpus Documental*, Letter XXIV, I, 214.

[31] At the Diet of Speyer in 1529, a majority among the princes and cities voted to reinstate the recently suspended provisions of the Edict of Worms (1521), by which the teachings of Martin Luther were outlawed throughout the empire. In a formal protest, eight princes and fourteen cities declared they could not accept the decisions of the majority in a matter of conscience. This first demonstration of unity among leaders of the evangelical movement has given its name to the Protestant Reformation.

and properly paid army behind him had in fact "added reputation" to the emperor's plans to "pacify" Italy.

Sinews of War

The men under Charles's command in Italy included units that served regularly to guard Habsburg interests in Naples and Lombardy. According to an eight-month budget projection for Naples (24 March–1 December 1529), it seems that in a period when French and Venetian garrisons still occupied a number of strongholds, the kingdom carried on its payroll some 6,000 Spanish infantry, 5,400 Germans, and 4,400 Italians, at a cost of 50,480 scudi per month – not too much less that the 55,500 scudi per month Orange's army was said to cost in June 1529.[32] From the time Charles first sent troops from Spain to fight the French in Lombardy, there was also a separate Spanish military establishment in the north of the peninsula, though it seems to have depended for money on Naples and lacked a permanent base until Charles decided to hold Milan as an imperial fief, following the death of Francesco Maria Sforza (1535).[33] Between 1 April 1536 and 1 August 1537, it cost 340,000 scudi to maintain the army of Lombardy,[34] or 21,325 per month, meaning a garrison of about 7,000 men; the Lombardy garrison that Charles instructed Leyva to use in besieging Pavia (as noted earlier) was probably a bit smaller.

As needed, the Spanish-Italian backbone of Habsburg defenses in Italy was supplemented by German levies. One may take as an example the campaign that culminated in the battle of Pavia, from June 1524 through February 1525, with March as the going-home month. Using the smaller of the estimates given by two Spanish chroniclers,[35] it seems that Bourbon's march to Marseilles (June through September) was supported by 16,000

---

[32] Coniglio, *Consulte e bilanci del Viceregno di Napoli*, Document 38, budget projection by Treasurer Alonso Sanchez: 153,417 [Neapolitan] ducats (scudi) for the German infantry, 144,000 for Spanish infantry, and a total of 106,421 for various units of Italian infantry, some listed as for the protection of key towns. At the pay rates assumed in this chapter (3 ducats a month for Spanish and Italian infantry, 3.53 ducats for *Landsknechte*), and if we ignore the distinction between Spanish and Neapolitan ducats, this would mean 5,432 Germans, 6,000 Spaniards, and 4,434 Italians. For Orange's army in June 1529, see, note 18.

[33] In the year or so following Charles's departure for Germany, Loaysa believed that the depredations of the 5,000 Spaniards who remained in northern Italy after the siege of Florence were so terrible that if this army could not be paid, it would be better to "echarla en la mar" (throw them in the sea): to Charles, 25 August, 1, 20 October, 4 November 1530, 21 January and 24 October 1531 (the quote), *Correspondencia del Cardenal de Osma*, 69–70, 72–73, 85–86, 94–95, 96–98, 190–191, and 239–240.

[34] Chabod, *Lo stato e la vita religiosa a Milano nell'epoca di Carlo V*, in *Opere*, III, 109.

[35] Mexia, *Historia del Emperador*, 348–386; Santa Cruz, *Crónica del Emperador*, II, 82–100.

infantry,[36] 1,000 cavalry, and the seventeen galleys; Lannoy remained behind at Asti with (at a minimum) 2,000 Italians and about 1,000 heavy cavalry. Bourbon's army will have suffered attrition on its retreat across the Alps. But if Leyva had 5,000 *Landsknechte*, 1,000 Spaniards, and 300 heavy cavalry in Pavia, Lannoy and Pescara will not have had fewer men between them if they expected to hold both Lodi and Cremona. Alarcon brought 5,000 Spaniards and 700 heavy cavalry from Naples by the end of October, and the men sent by Ferdinand with Bourbon – 10,000 *Landsknechte*, plus some heavy cavalry – will have crossed the Alps by January. By this reckoning, the army that set down opposite the French camp on the Ticino would have had some 13,000 *Landsknechte*, 5,600 Spaniards, 3,000 Italians, 1,500 light horse, and 800 heavy cavalry,[37] not counting Leyva's men in Pavia. Wages for all these units, serving different periods, may be estimated at 785,872 Spanish ducats,[38] or 943,046, if one adds 20% for artillery, victuals, and officers' pay. This would be about the same as what it cost Charles to "pacify" Italy a few years later, not counting the siege of Florence.

According to Pedro de Mexia, the emperor set sail with 8,000 Spanish infantry, thirty galleys, and many sailing ships. "Letters from Genoa" (summarized by the Venetian diarist Marino Sanudo) describe an armada of twenty-eight galleys (Doria's twelve plus sixteen from Spain) and seventy sailing ships, said to carry 10,000 Spanish infantry and 1,000 cavalry. But for the infantry Mexia's lower figure is confirmed in Spanish accounts used by Quatrefages.[39] North of the Alps, Ferdinand, preoccupied by the Turkish threat to Vienna, had no money for the 10,000 *Landsknechte* Charles needed. Hence Margaret had to remit from the Low Countries enough money to pay recruitment costs as well as wages for the 10,000 German infantry as well as 2,000 Low Countries cavalry for

[36] This is Mexia's figure; he does not differentiate in terms of nationality. According to Santa Cruz, Bourbon had 7,000 Germans, 5,000 Spaniards, and 5,000 Italians.

[37] I follow the numbers given by Gianini, *Mirabello di Pavia*, 140, based on the account of a contemporary observer, dated 12 January 1525, but with one crucial difference: Gianini's source gives only 600 Spaniards, a figure that obviously does not include the 5,000 Spaniards brought from Naples by Alarcon, as reported in Ferdinand's letter to Charles of 1 November 1524 (cited in Chapter 2, note 18). Might it be that Gianini's source did not count men on the payroll of Naples as part of the imperial army?

[38] Using the same wage rates as in note 41: for June through September 1524, 84,720 for 6,000 *Landsknechte*, 144,000 for 12,000 Spanish and Italian infantry, 38,080 for heavy cavalry, and 22,032 for the galleys; for October through December, 105,900 for 10,000 *Landsknechte*, 63,000 for 7,000 Spaniards, and 17,940 for 1,300 heavy cavalry; and for January through March, 190,620 for 18,000 *Landsknechte*, 86,400 for 6,600 Spaniards and 3,000 Italians, 18,000 for 1,500 light horse, and 15,180 for 1,100 heavy cavalry.

[39] Mexia, *Historia del Emperador*, 522; Sanudo, *I Diarii*, ed. Federico Stefani, Guglielmo Berchet, and Niccolo Barozzi, vol. LI (Venice, 1898), 288; Quatrefages, "L'organisation militaire de l'Espagne," 437–438.

three months, at (respectively) 3.53 and 4.6 ducats per month.[40] Charles remained in Italy until his departure for Germany in May 1530. If he had all of these men on his payroll for ten months (August 1529–April 1530, with May as the going-home month), the cost would have been 657,900 ducats. One should add 20% for victuals, officers' pay, and the artillery and baggage trains, plus 125,000 ducats for the emperor's household expenses during a year of absence from Spain,[41] and 18,144 for the service of twenty-eight war galleys for July and August of 1529,[42] for a grand total of 932,624.

Charles's objectives in going to Italy depended on forging an alliance with the pope, which in turn depended on keeping his promise to subdue Florence. Clement VII will of course have helped to meet the expenses of the siege. In May 1530 Juan Antonio Mujetula, Loaysa's agent in dealings with Genoese bankers, reported to Charles that the pope could not find more than the 62,000 scudi he had promised, which was enough for one month's wages for the men on Orange's payroll, except for the 12,000 scudi for the light horse and other expenses.[43] Perhaps because he wished to highlight the valor of his native city in standing off so great a force, Benedetto Varchi puts the number of men under arms in Orange's camp at 40,000, not counting the many unpaid "adventurers" hoping for plunder.[44] According to a report from a Sienese observer at the beginning of February 1530, the number was closer to 30,000: 6,000 Spanish infantry, 8,000 Germans, 14,000 Italians, 2,000 light horse, and 800 heavy cavalry.[45] Monthly pay for units of this size would have been 99,920 Spanish ducats, or 106,914 scudi[46] – quite a bit higher than Mujetula's figure. But some men in Orange's camp were on the pope's payroll – 600 light horse and

---

[40] Charles to Ferdinand, 3 April 1529, and Margaret to Ferdinand, 16 June 1529, *Familienkorrespondenz*, Letters 280 and 309, II, 390–393, 434–437.

[41] I count nine months for 8,000 Spanish infantry at 3 ducats a month, nine months for 10,000 *Landsknechte* at 3.53 ducats a month (assuming that the money sent by Margaret took care of the months of June, July, and August), and nine months for 3,000 cavalry, assuming the same wage of 4.6 ducats a month for the 1,000 from Spain as well as the 2,000 from the Low Countries.

[42] At the rate of 324 ducats per galley per month, for the contingents of seamen and soldiers required in Portoundo's *asiento* for 1529, cited in Chapter 2, note 14.

[43] Mujetula (or Muxetula) to Charles, "sobre Florencia," 2 May 1530, in Roth, *The Last Florentine Republic*, appendix 9, 359–364. Mujetula is frequently praised for his services in Loaysa's letters to Charles.

[44] Roth, *The Last Florentine Republic*, 243; Varchi, *Storia fiorentina*, II, 123–127, 247–248.

[45] Cited by Roth, *The Last Florentine Republic*, 243, n. 68.

[46] That is, at the rates of 3 Spanish ducats per month for Spanish and Italian infantry, 3.53 ducats for the German *Landsknechte*, 4.6 ducats for heavy cavalry (if we assume Italian heavy cavalry were paid at he same rate as their Low Countries counterparts), and 4 ducats per month for the light horse (my estimate, based on the rate of 5 scudi or 4.67 ducats per month thirteen years later: Charles to Philip, 19 June 1543, *Corpus Documental*, Letter CCLXVIII, II, 132–133).

as many as 8,000 Italian infantry, at a combined monthly wage of 26,400 ducats; this would make Orange's monthly wage obligation fairly close to the 74,000 scudi (69,072 Spanish ducats) mentioned by Mujetula.[47] Thus the 30,000 reported by the Sienese observer seems a good figure for the number of men in Orange's camp during the siege.

If the siege has to be counted as part of Charles's Italian campaign, even if he did not participate, the allocation of its costs is complicated. How much did Clement VII contribute? In early July, Ferdinand's ambassador to the Curia reported that the pope complained of "having spent, until now, over 700,000 ducats on this necessary expedition against Florence, which he had hoped could be accomplished for only 80,000."[48] A sum this large would cover not just the wages of papal troops serving under Orange, but periodic support for units serving under Charles's banner, as noted earlier.[49] In addition, it is not easy to separate the costs of the army that helped Charles achieve his objectives in Italy from the ordinary military expenditures of the Kingdom of Naples. As is clear from the correspondence of Loaysa,[50] expenses relating to Spanish military operations in central and northern Italy were often charged to the treasury of Naples. For this discussion, I treat the siege as an imperial operation from the time that men previously under Charles's command began serving under Orange – let us say from January of 1530 through August, when Florence capitulated, or nine months in all, with September as the going-home month. If we use Mujetula's figure of 69,072 ducats per month (74,000 scudi), the wages for men in the siege army on the emperor's payroll would have been 621,648 ducats, or, with an added 20% for artillery and other expenses, 745,978 ducats. Some unknown portion of these costs will have been borne by the pope and by other allies.[51] Also, lest the 8,000 men who came from Lombardy be counted twice for the months of January through April, one should

[47] For troops on the pope's payroll, see Santa Cruz, *Crónica del Emperador*, III, 15. It should also be noted that Mujetula's letter of 2 May reports that Orange has been able to pay off and dismiss some of his men, as commanded by Charles, so as to have no more than were needed to maintain and tighten the siege.
[48] Letter of Andrea del Burgo to Ferdinand, 3 July 1530, cited by Ludwig Pastor, *History of the Popes*, tr. Ralph Francis Kerr, vol. X (St. Louis, 1912), 100, n. 4. Paolo Giovio, usually well informed, believed that in the end Clement VII paid out 1 million florins for the conquest of his native city: Zimmerman, *Paolo Giovio*, 126.
[49] Hook, *The Sack of Rome*, 259: Orange, encamped before Perugia, complained of inadequate funds to pay his troops; a Medici ally, Cardinal Lorenzo Pucci (d. 1531), "personally lent the money for the operations out of his own large fortune."
[50] Cited in note 29; see also the correspondence of Fernando Martín, abbot of Nájera: Enrique Pacheco y de Leyva, *La política española in Italia. Correspondencia de Don Fernando Martín, Abad de Nájera, con Carlos I*, vol. I (Madrid, 1919).
[51] Mujetula's letter of 2 May 1530 mentions a payment of 5,000 scudi from Siena, which now had a pro-imperial government (Simeoni, *Le Signorie*, II, 1071–1072).

subtract about 100,000 ducats.[52] It seems reasonable to think that Charles and his government in Naples will have been responsible for 300,000 to 400,000 ducats. This would bring total expenses for the Italian campaign to around 1,250,000 or 1,350,000 ducats.

* * *

During the 1520s, war in Italy strained the resources of both Castile and Naples, even without the added worry of ensuring the emperor's personal security. From Charles's correspondence, one can document remittances for Italy of 1,696,533 ducats between 1522 and 1528: 135,333 ducats in 1522, 121,200 in 1523, 300,000 in 1524, 100,000 in 1525, 180,000 in 1526, 400,000 in 1527, and 460,000 in 1528. It was surely an understatement when Charles wrote to Ferdinand from Italy in 1530, "you cannot believe, good brother, how much they detest in Spain everything I have spent in this realm of Italy."[53] The accounts of Girolamo de Francesco, paymaster for Spain's armies in the rest of the peninsula as well as in Naples, show 12,753,860 scudi (11,904,452 Spanish ducats) in payments for the period between 28 October 1525 and 30 November 1529,[54] a figure that seems hardly to be believed.

Deferring for the moment a consideration of the Neapolitan revenues that supported Orange's army at Florence, one can identify four sources of income for Charles's campaign in Lombardy. First was the 350,000 ducats in gold for which the emperor agreed to pawn Spain's claims in the Moluccas (Spice Islands) to his brother-in-law, John III.[55] Because Charles delayed his departure until the money arrived, it seems likely he took it all with him in Doria's galleys.

Second, Carande Thobar identifies three loans (nos. 76, 77, 80) contracted with Genoese bankers in November and December 1529 for remittances to Genoa for the emperor's campaign in Italy, marked as due in

---

[52] If the men who came from Lombardy included 4,000 of the Germans and 4,000 of the Spaniards whose wages for January through April have already been counted as part of the expenses of Charles's army, the total would be 104,480 ducats.

[53] Charles to Margaret, 7 December 1522, Lanz, Letter 43, I, 75–76; Charles to Ferdinand, 8 September 1523, *Familienkorrespondenz*, Letter 46, I, 72–75; Margaret to Charles, 16 January 1524, Lanz, Letter 49, I, 91, and Adrien de Croy, Sieur de Beaurain, to Charles, 5 May 1524, Lanz, Letter 56, I, 134–138; Lope de Soria to Charles, 26 February 1525, *Corpus Documental*, Letter XXI, I, 96–98; Ferdinand to Charles, 28 October 1526, *Familienkorrespondenz*, Letter 250, I, 482–485, and Charles to Ferdinand, 23–30 November 1526, *Familienkorrespondenz*, Letter 252, I, 490; Charles to Ferdinand, 27 November 1527, *Familienkorrespondenz*, Letter 130 (separate numeration of letters starts with this volume), II, 148–152; Charles to Ferdinand, two letters of 19 April 1528, *Familienkorrespondenz*, Letters 174 and 175, II, 204–206, 208; and Charles to Ferdinand, 11 January 1530, *Familienkorrespondenz*, Letter 388, III, 559–561.

[54] Coniglio, *Il regno di Napoli al tempo di Carlo V*, 113–114, 243–245.

[55] See note 9.

Genoa: 50,000 ducats from Giovanni Battista de Usodemar; 145,600 from Francesco Lomellini, with his Spanish partner Rodrigo de Dueñas; and 186,668 from Ansaldo Grimaldi, subsequently reduced to 154,668.

A fourth loan of 107,334 (no. 79) was assigned for payment on Naples, but since 32,000 ducats of the assignation could not be found there, Grimaldi was allowed to reduce by this amount the sum he was obliged to deliver in Genoa by the terms of his other loan. Deducting the 7% that was current for exchanges from Spanish ducats to scudi in Italy, plus another 7% for the first year's interest,[56] these loans made the equivalent of 301,230 ducats available to Charles in Genoa; by the time the loans were retired, the treasury of Castile paid out 76,123 ducats in interest, or 25.3% of the sum actually delivered.[57] Rates like this explain why the emperor preferred, if possible, to accept the risks of a sea voyage, bringing specie from Spain to Italy in galley fleets.[58]

In June 1529 Margaret of Austria reported she was sending the 348,000 Carolus gulden (190,706 ducats) for recruitment fees as well as for three months' wages for the 10,000 Landsknechte and the 2,000 Low Countries cavalry. Because Ferdinand refers in their correspondence of this period to "the 400,000 pounds granted by the estates," it is clear that the money "sent" by Margaret was advanced by bankers in Antwerp against the receipts of the "coronation subsidy" approved by the several provincial states in the spring of 1529, payable over a term of six years (1529–1534).[59] Margaret's officials dealt on this occasion with Antwerp agents of the Augsburg firms of Welser, Fugger, and Herwart. Subtracting (one may assume) about 52,000 gulden or 13% for exchange fees, the bankers contracted to remit 348,000 Carolus gulden to Germany in Rhine gulden, in stages corresponding to the timing of mobilization and the route the Landsknechte would take to cross the Alps: 20,000 gulden in Augsburg in June (presumably for the colonels and their captains), plus 41,000 at the end of July, a total of 106,000 at Kempten, Füssen, and Innsbruck, and a further 43,000 for the cavalry coming from the Low Countries. The Low Countries money would thus get the troops as far as Italy, leaving it to Charles to find money to keep them there. Meanwhile, Margaret's government took out a separate loan for 125,000 Holland pounds, at the high rate of 21%, to retire part of its debt to the Augsburg firms; 21% for a single year was cheaper than what it would have cost to pay annual interest

[56] Santa Cruz, Crónica del Emperador, III, 11–12, speaks of Charles giving his Italian bankers 14% in "interest" for the transfer to Italy at this time of 100,000 ducats.
[57] Carande Thobar, Carlos V y sus banqueros, III, 80, 136.
[58] E.g., Charles to Isabella, 8 September 1536, Corpus Documental, Letter CCXIV, I, 528.
[59] See note 40; Ferdinand to Margaret, 3 June 1529, Familienkorrespondenz, Letter 304, II, 420–421; Tracy, "The Taxation System of Holland," 111.

on the loan until the last installment of the coronation subsidy on which it was assigned would be collected (1534).[60]

The fourth major infusion of funds into Charles's Italian campaign depended on one of the most complicated fiscal negotiations of his reign. In December 1529 the three officials whom Charles had left in charge of finances in Castile proposed a loan of unprecedented proportions from as yet unnamed bankers. The lenders would be asked to provide 500,000 ducats at the fairs of Medina del Campo during 1530, another 500,000 in 1531, 300,000 in 1532, and 200,000 in 1533. Repayment was to be assigned as follows: 650,000 ducats on the *cruzada* for the years 1530–1532, 600,000 on the clerical *subsidio* for the same period, and 200,000 from as yet unnamed buyers of life *juros*. Agents of the Fugger and Welser in Spain signed the contract on 18 February 1530.[61] Charles ratified the agreement in Bologna on 20 March 1530, but already in January he was counting on the money it would provide. He wrote Isabella that the loan "for 1,200,000 ducats" could be assigned on the income from the *quarta* (the elevated clerical *subsidio*) and the *cruzada*, both of which were contingent on his current discussions with Clement VII. The queen was to take special care that the bankers deliver the sums contracted for in 1530 "at the times and places appointed, so as to provide the 400,000 ducats to be sent according to my memorandum."[62] In other words, Charles expected Isabella or her officials to arrange the remittance of 400,000 ducats to Italy, based on the 500,000 the German bankers were to pay out in Spain that year. In fact, he may not have gotten more than about 200,000, because agents of the Fugger and Welser in Spain insisted on withholding the equivalent of 286,010 Rhine gulden (202,115 ducats) in recognition of what the firms were owed for loans provided for the expenses of Germany's imperial government between 1524 and 1529.[63] In the end the German firms did not pay out anything like 1.5 million ducats. The total was reduced by 280,000 ducats, because no assignations could be found for that amount, and by 260,000, which the Fugger and Welser credited to their own ledgers in payment of other unsettled debts from previous years, as well as by the previously mentioned 202,115 for unpaid loans in Germany. Total interest paid by the treasury of Castile was 148,800 ducats, meaning 12.4% on the 1,200,000 contracted for, or 19.6% on the approximately 750,000 in usable funds the bankers actually delivered.[64]

[60] Pölnitz, *Anton Fugger*, I, 161–162.

[61] Carande Thobar, *Carlos V y sus banqueros*, III, 86–93, 138.

[62] Charles to Isabella, January 1530, *Corpus Documental*, Letter LIII, I, 188–190. From his knowledge of Castilian fiscal records, Carande-Thobar assumed that the intent of this gigantic operation was to cleanse the ledgers of old debts the Hacienda could not pay.

[63] Pölnitz, *Anton Fugger*, I, 512–513.

[64] Carande Thobar, *Carlos V y sus banqueros*, III, 138–140; nos. 81, 81–1.

From these four sources Charles seems to have had the equivalent of about 1,041,936 ducats[65] at his disposal for expenses in Italy, not counting what he got from the Kingdom of Naples. Naples was expected to provide Charles's share of the cost for Orange's army, but Loaysa's letters show how hard it was to get money from the Kingdom. On 7 June 1530 he reported sending Mujetula to Naples in quest of a suitable assignation for a proposed loan of 50,000 scudi. On 25 August he indicated that the 50,000 "has to come from the compositions" or fines by which Neapolitan barons who had rebelled against the crown during Lautrec's invasion were to buy pardon. This was evidently not a good way to raise money quickly, for as of 1 October "there have been three compositions thus far, but we will need to have eight," for unpaid men from the army of Florence were wreaking havoc in Siena and elsewhere, so that "by not paying the army one loses one's soul, and gains infamy."[66]

For the fiscal year beginning 1 September 1530, treasury officials in Naples projected income of 283,897 scudi, as against 382,663 in expenses and 858,052 in bankers' loans and old debts.[67] In other words, any money that came to Orange had to be supplied not from current revenues, but from bankers willing to extend still more credit on the future revenues in Naples. One can be sure that a good portion of the 1,194,117 scudi charged against the treasury in 1530 for *cambi*, that is, for payments that bankers made on the treasury's behalf outside the Kingdom, will have been spent on the siege of Florence.[68] Two likely assignations may be mentioned: payments by the new purchasers of baronial lands confiscated after the rebellion of 1528,[69] and the parliamentary subsidy or *donativo* of 1531. Charles ordered in July 1530 that a Parlamento be summoned and asked for a subsidy, but not until August 1531 did the assembly grant 600,000 scudi, payable over four years. According to a comment by a high official in Naples, the money went to pay for debts relating to Orange's army at Florence.[70] It seems that the process by which bankers were willing to advance the money all at once discounted the value of a *donativo* by about 40%,[71] which means that about 360,000 scudi (336,000 ducats) could have been available from this one

---

[65] I.e., 350,000 from the sale of the Moluccas, 301,230 from the Genoese bankers, 190,706 sent from the Low Countries, and about 200,000 of the 400,000 he wanted from the 500,000 the Fugger and Welser were to provide in Spain in 1530.

[66] Loaysa to Charles, 7 June, 25 August, and 1 October 1530, in *Correspondencia del Cardenal de Osma*, 14–15, 72–73, 85–86.

[67] Coniglio, *Consulte e bilanci del Vicereyno di Napoli*, Document 40, 417–453.

[68] Coniglio, *Il regno di Napoli*, 243–245.

[69] For a list of confiscated properties and their estimated values, see Pedio, *Napoli e Spagna*, 274–289.

[70] Ibid., 297. The official was Gregorio Rosso, *Eletto* of the *Seggio del Populo* in the capital. For this subsidy, and for the administrative hierarchy of the kingdom, see Chapter 13.

[71] On this point, too, see Chapter 13.

source to pay off Orange's men – or rather to pay the bankers who had paid their arrears. A transfer of this magnitude from the *donativo* – not counting other assignations in Naples – would mean that, in all, Charles employed remittances well in excess of 1,400,000 ducats for the pacification of Italy.

* * *

Whatever the cost in hard cash was, the actual cost was even greater. Mortgaging a claim in the Moluccas meant a lost opportunity for Castile's overseas traders. The treasuries of Naples and the Low Countries had to pay dearly for the privilege of having bankers "anticipate" subsidy revenues due over a period of years. In Castile, interest charges for the Genoese and German loans – 56,000 and 148,800 ducats – added to an overall deficit that was climbing at least as fast as new sources of revenue (like the *quarta* approved by Pope Clement VII) flowed into the treasury.

Was all of this money, with its hidden costs, sufficient to exorcise the demon of political instability (see Chapter 2) and establish in Italy an order favorable to Habsburg authority? If one broadens the question to include all the sums spent on the Italian wars by Charles's governments between roughly 1525 and 1530, the answer is yes. The subjugation of Florence to Medici rule, followed a few years later by the accession of a strong prince,[72] added to an arc of pro-Habsburg states across northern Italy, shielding Naples. To be sure, opponents of the Habsburgs, backed by France, could still mount important challenges in the final years of Charles's reign (see Chapter 11), but Spanish power was not again to be expelled from Milan or Genoa, or seriously threatened in Naples. Through the chaotic conditions described in Loaysa's letters of 1530–1531, one can already glimpse the outlines of a military system in which at last 3,000 to 4,000 Spanish infantry were kept on station in each of three key areas: Lombardy, Naples, and Sicily.[73] When Charles launched his attack on Tunis in 1535, he brought 9,000 new recruits from Spain, to replace veterans from the garrisons in Sicily and Naples who embarked on his troop transports (see Chapter 7). Thus it was Charles who created the Pax Hispanica in Italy that underpinned the grandeur of Spain under Philip II, with a network of garrisons that could serve as a rapid-reaction force for conflicts elsewhere in Europe or the Mediterranean.[74]

---

[72] Cosimo de Medici (d. 1573), who ruled as duke of Florence from 1537, and as grand duke of Tuscany, including Siena.

[73] Referring to a decision taken at a council of war held at Mantua (presumably as Charles was en route north from Bologna), Loaysa supports taking 2,000 men from the army of Lombardy to be stationed in Sicily, and 2,000 in Naples; he would add 500 men to each *banda*: to Charles, 13 May, 25 August 1530, *Correspondencia del Cardenal de Osma*, 8–9, 69–70.

[74] Parker, *The Grand Strategy of Philip II*, 84.

Chapter 7

Crusades in Austria and the Mediterranean, 1532–1535

Sixteenth-century Europeans still lived in the era of the Crusades.[1] Despite a growing flow of trade goods and merchants across the religious frontier, the long boundary between Christendom and Islamdom – through southern Russia, the Balkans, and the Mediterranean – was at every point a zone of war. In Germany, Ferdinand and the imperial princes expected Charles, as Holy Roman Emperor, to defend the empire's southeastern frontier, Habsburg Austria, against the advance of Ottoman power up the Danube basin. In Castile and Aragón, subjects expected their king to halt the depredations of "Barbary" corsairs.[2] According to one Spanish chronicler, more Christian captives were taken in Spain during the first 40 years of the sixteenth century than during the previous 800 years; and no meeting of the Cortes of either kingdom passed without a discussion of needed countermeasures. According to another, Khair-ad-Din Barbarossa (c. 1466–1546) alone took 10,000 Christian slaves along the coastline between Barcelona and Granada over a period of ten years. Christian merchantmen in the western Mediterranean had to sail in convoy, but this precaution was not enough for seven Genoese grain ships taken by corsairs off Sardinia. Whether aligned with France or with Spain, Genoa was aggressive in launching counterattacks; on these expeditions, Andrea Doria, who had his own war fleet, often served as the republic's commander as well.[3]

---

[1] Setton broke down the idea that the Crusades ended with the fall of Acre (1297) with his monumental *The Papacy and the Levant, 1204–1571*. It must be noted, however, that the author's few mentions of the subject show an almost palpable dislike for the Habsburgs and their Crusade projects.

[2] Understood by contemporaries as extending from Cape Bojador on Morocco's Atlantic coast as far east as Tripoli: Godfrey Fisher, *Barbary Legend: War, Trade, and Piracy in North Africa, 415–1830* (Oxford, 1957), 17–40.

[3] Gómara, *Crónica de los Barbarrojas*, 334, 362, 385; Santa Cruz, *Crónica del Emperador*, II, 162.

Christians taken as slaves in the Danube basin were equally to be pitied and (as anti-Habsburg observers pointed out) were far more numerous.[4] But unlike Ferdinand, Charles did not have in this region tax-paying subjects whose lamentations had to be taken seriously. Moreover, there was no one at Ferdinand's court he trusted as he trusted his own advisers, educated, for the most part, in the school of Burgundian politics. Finally, Austria's revenues were small by comparison with those of Charles's western and southern lands, and none of his bankers, not even the Augsburg firms, had in southeast Europe a network of correspondents that could support military operations on an imperial scale. Conscious of his responsibilities as emperor to defend Christian Europe,[5] Charles was also a realist. As far as possible, he confined his wars against the infidels to the Mediterranean.

Mediterranean warfare meant raids alongshore by oared galleys landing soldiers to burn, loot, and take captives for Muslim or Christian slave markets. The conflict between Christian Spain and Portugal and the kingdoms of the Barbary Coast was mainly a campaign of reciprocal plunder.[6] Portugal opened the North African phase of the Christian Reconquista of Iberia by taking Ceuta (1415). Spain's greatest early success came in 1509 when, in a venture financed by private investors, the Aragonese admiral Pedro de Navarro captured the port of Oran with a force of 8,000 infantry and 3,000 cavalry, brought from Spain by eighty sailing vessels accompanied by ten galleys. The king of Tunis, alarmed by Spanish advances, invited in a Turkish merchant-corsair known as Baba Oruç or (to Europeans) "Barbarossa" (d. 1518),[7] who ejected the Spaniards from Algiers (1516) and made it his base of operations.

In May 1519 Charles V ordered the viceroy of Sicily, Hugo de Moncada, to bring the galleys of Naples to join those of Genoa in action against thirty-two Moorish vessels operating off Sardinia under the command of Oruç's brother and successor, Khair-ad-Din Barbarossa. The shipwreck of Moncada's fleet opened the way for Khair-ad-Din's galleys to raid the

---

[4] For an anti-Habsburg view of a recent Ottoman campaign into Hungary, Jan Łaski to Erasmus, 25 August 1533, in Allen, *Opus Epistolarum D. Erasmi*, Letter 2862, lines 61–71, vol. X, 295: "I pass over the thousands of men who either perished or were carried off into perpetual slavery. It is certain that the sultan, to whom every tenth captive is given, received 7,000 for his portion" (my translation). Until his patron's death in 1540, Łaski's elder brother Hieronim (see note 23) was in the service of Janos Szapolyai, Ferdinand's Ottoman-backed rival for the crown of Hungary. The Łaski brothers were not alone in the belief that Turkish attacks in this region were a response to Habsburg ambition.

[5] E.g., note 18.

[6] John Guilmartin, *Gunpowder and Galleys: Changing Technology in Mediterranean Warfare at Sea in the Sixteenth Century* (Cambridge, 1974); Andrew Hess, *Forgotten Frontier* (Chicago, 1978).

[7] For this derivation of the name, rather than from the reddish beards sported by both brothers, see William Spencer, *Algiers in the Age of Corsairs* (Norman, Okla., 1976), 19.

coast of Aragón, landing as they pleased to pillage and take captives. In response, officials in the Kingdom of Valencia (a dependency of the crown of Aragón) had to arm the local population; Charles will have remembered that the Valencians, once armed, joined in a general rebellion (see Chapter 14) that shook the foundations of Habsburg rule in Iberia.[8] Four years later Moncada received instructions to attack Khair-ad-Din's base, taking with him veterans from Spain's garrisons in Sicily and at Oran. Landing his men and supplies, Moncada occupied the heights above Algiers and prepared for an assault. But the *maestre del campo* of the infantry refused to attack until Spain's ally, the king of Tlemcen, had arrived with his forces, claiming authorization from the emperor to act as he did. Furious, Moncada ordered all his men back on board their ships, just in time for a violent storm, "which that night destroyed twenty-six great ships and many small ones" (23 August 1523).[9]

Spain's next naval calamity was linked to Charles's Italian campaign, because Rodrigo de Portoundo, commander of Castile's war fleet, had accompanied the emperor to Italy with his eight galleys. Knowing there were no galleys or *fustas*[10] to defend Spain's east coast, Barbarossa in Algiers sent one of his captains, known to Europeans as Cachiadiabolo, to lie in wait for merchant shipping off Cártagena. Warned from France that Portoundo had left Genoa to seek him out, Cachiadiabolo agreed to take on board the Moorish tenants[11] of the Count of Oliva and sailed away, only to be blown off course to Formentera, southernmost of the Balearic Islands. Learning that Portoundo was coming, he landed his Moorish passengers, "with the crossbows at which they are very adept." Portoundo mistook the enemy *fustas* for friendly vessels, and by the time he could draw up in battle order, his fleet was caught in a crossfire between Cachiadiabolo and the crossbows on land; Portoundo was killed, and seven of his eight galleys were taken as prizes to Algiers (25 October 1529).[12]

According to Alonso de Fonseca (d. 1534), archbishop of Toledo and president of the Council of State, the loss of Portoundo's fleet did more than

---

[8] The rebellion in Aragón known as the Germanía coincided with a separate and more dangerous revolt in Castile: Stephen Haliczer, *The Comuneros of Castile: The Forging of a Revolution, 1475–1521* (Madison, Wis., 1981).

[9] Gómara, *Crónica de los Barbarrojas*, 380–382.

[10] Unlike the biremes and triremes of ancient times, which had banks of rowers seated one above the other, many galleys of the sixteenth century had three oarsmen on the same angled bench, pulling against oars fitted to closely spaced tholes; the smaller *fustas* had two oarsmen on a bench. See Robert Gardner, ed., *The Age of the Galley: Mediterranean Oared Vessels since Pre-Classical Times* (London, 1995), chap. 10, "The Naval Architecture and Oar Systems of Medieval and Later Galleys," 142–162.

[11] Fear of revolt by Aragón's large Morisco population is a recurring theme in the emperor's correspondence during his periods of absence from Spain.

[12] Gómara, *Crónica de las Barbarrojas*, 395–399.

Figure 7.1. Anonymous, *Andrea Doria with a Cat*, Palazzo Doria, Genoa.

endanger Spain's outposts in North Africa: "Unless this disaster is reversed, we will lose the commerce of the Mediterranean from Gibraltar to the east." The only remedy was a new Castilian fleet of at least twenty galleys "sailing with a great armada to hunt out Barbarossa in his own house [Algiers], for money spent solely for defense will otherwise be wasted." Isabella wrote to Charles in the same vein, expecting that he would mobilize an armada in the spring to go against Barbarossa, said to have eleven galleys and thirty *fustas*.[13] Charles told Isabella not to employ for his needs in Italy a financial expedient then under discussion: "Let us see what may be needed for the armada and other matters that cannot be put off."[14] When Charles wrote Ferdinand that troops seconded to Orange could have other uses if Florence came to terms quickly, he was thinking of Algiers.

From Innsbruck, en route to Augsburg, Charles informed Isabella he could not now take charge of the *empresa* at sea. Instead, he turned to his new ally, Andrea Doria. With his fifteen galleys and thirteen French galleys placed at Charles's disposal by the terms of the Treaty of Cambrai, Doria found Barbarossa with a small fleet near Algiers, forcing him to take refuge in the citadel at Cherchell. Doria took eight vessels as prizes, but lost several hundred of the men he landed when an ill-disciplined plundering party was set upon by Cherchell's defenders. In July Charles ordered Castile's new galley fleet, under Admiral Alvaro de Bazán, to join Doria's in Sicily, but the combined armada managed to capture only a few more ships. Fonseca believed that even if Barbarossa's fleet had been more dramatically reduced in size, Spain's Barbary fortresses were still at risk; "from such cares" Charles would be delivered only by taking Algiers itself.[15]

Meanwhile, at the Diet of Augsburg, leaders of the evangelical or Protestant party were pleasantly surprised by the flexibility shown in private discussions by some of Charles's Spanish advisers.[16] But amicable discussions did not allay their fears of a preemptive strike by the empire's Catholic princes, or by the Habsburgs. Led by Elector John of Saxony

[13] Fonseca to Charles, 15 November 1529, *Corpus Documental*, Letter XLV, I, 173–175, and Isabella to Charles, 16 November 1529, *Corpus Documental*, Documenal, Letter XLVI, I, 176–178. Fonseca's insistence on attacking Barbarossa "in his own house" bears out the argument by Guilmartin, *Gunpowder and Galleys*, chap. 1, that modern strategic notions of sea power or control of the sea did not have to await the Anglo-Dutch Wars of the seventeenth century.

[14] Charles to Isabella, January 1530, *Corpus Documental*, Letter LIII, I, 188–190.

[15] Charles to Isabella, 7, 29 May, and 8 July 1530, *Corpus Documental*, Letters LXXI, LXXIV, and LXXVI, I, 209–211, 214–215, and 219; Fonseca to Charles, 15 September 1530, *Corpus Documental*, Letter LXXXV, I, 234–235; and the reports from Genoa and Sicily summarized in Sanudo, *I Diarii*, vol. LIII, 286–287, 296, 325, 443, and 539–540.

[16] Vinzenz Pfnur, *Einig in der Rechtfertigungslehre?* (Munich, 1970).

(r. 1525–1532) and Landgrave Phillip of Hesse (r. 1518–1567), evangelical territories and cities agreed at Schmalkalden (December 1530) to form an alliance. Signatories presented the Schmalkaldic League as purely defensive, but Charles and Ferdinand saw it as an active threat to their authority, especially when Saxony and Hesse refused to recognize Ferdinand's election (January 1531) as King of the Romans. Yet the Habsburg brothers needed the cooperation of leading Protestant princes in order to coax from the imperial diet the subsidies that would put troops in the field the next time Sultan Suleyman sent his armies up the Danube basin. Thus Ferdinand undertook further discussions with Saxony and Hesse, while Charles traveled to Brussels to reorganize the government in the Netherlands, with his sister Mary of Hungary as regent. Writing from Brussels (October 1531), Charles asked Isabella to have her council draw up a budget for the armada that, "please God," he would lead against Algiers the following year.[17]

The Vienna Campaign

By April 1532 Charles had information that a huge Turkish army, led by the sultan himself, was marching up the Danube; there were also reports that "one hundred galleys and as many *fustas*" were being fitted out at Istanbul, with orders to sail by 15 May for an assault on Naples or Sicily. Strategists on both sides understood that a seaborne attack could prevent the enemy from concentrating his resources for a land campaign. Charles explained to Isabella (6 April 1532) that "in light of the duty I have to defend the faith and the Christian religion," if the Grand Turk should indeed be coming against him "in person," he had resolved "to sally forth against him in my own person, with everything I can find to resist him." This language implies a campaign in defense of Vienna, but Charles was apparently thinking also of the possibility that Suleyman might not come against him in person; in the same letter he explained that the armada "for my passage and the *empresa* against Algiers" would have to be accompanied by ships carrying at least 25,000 infantry, according to Doria's calculations.[18]

Even if Charles intended to sail against Algiers, he could not have left Germany during negotiations at the Diet of Regensburg (17 April–27 July). The diet's Protestant estates suspected that the troops the emperor was requesting would be used for Ferdinand's private war against Janos Szapolyai,

[17] Charles to Isabella, 18 October and 25 November 1531, *Corpus Documental*, Letters CXXII and CXXVI, I, 313–314 and 328–329; Brandi, *Emperor Charles V*, 292–324.
[18] Charles to Isabella, second of two letters dated 6 April 1532, *Corpus Documental*, Letter CXXXVIII, I, 349–351.

his Turkish-backed rival for the crown of Hungary. Once assured by detailed reports that the sultan's host was indeed marching up the Danube,
the estates voted a "Turk tax," but they refused Charles's request to increase
the level of their customary contributions, and they stipulated that imperial troops were not to be employed beyond the borders of the empire – in
other words, not in Hungary. In all, the estates agreed to raise 38,000 infantry, 6,000 heavy cavalry, and 6,000 light horse, all to join with Charles's
and Ferdinand's forces in Regensburg, on the Danube, by 15 August.
According to a letter of Ferdinand's to Mary (22 June 1532), Charles for
his part agreed to mobilize 12,000 *Landsknechte*, 10,000 Spanish and 10,000
Italian infantry, 4,000 heavy cavalry, 2,000 light horse, and 3,000 to 4,000
"pioneers" for digging trenches. Backed by grants from the estates of the
various Austrian duchies and the Kingdom of Bohemia, Ferdinand himself was to have 42,000 infantry, 6,000 heavy cavalry, 2,000 light horse,
and 10,000 boatmen for service on the Danube war flotilla. Pope Clement
VII sent Cardinal Ippolito d'Este (accompanied by the historian Paolo
Giovio) with money for the 10,000 Hungarian and Croatian hussars he
had promised to engage.[19]
   Well before the allied flotilla embarked at Regensburg for its voyage
down the Danube (3 September), Suleyman turned aside from his march
toward Vienna to besiege the small castle of Güns (Köszeg) in Habsburg-
held western Hungary (roughly equivalent to modern Slovakia), not far
from the Austrian border. The fortress, commanded by a Croatian captain,
Nicholas Jurišić, was well supplied with artillery; Jurišić 's 738 men held out
for three weeks (7 August–28 August) against an army thought to include
86,000 infantry (including 12,000 of the Janissary elite), 20,000 cavalry,
and 30,000 lightly armed skirmishers (*Alkindschi*), equivalent to the unpaid
"adventurers" of European armies. In the end the sultan settled for a form
of surrender in which Jurišić acknowledged Turkish supremacy but kept
possession of the castle. In a letter to Charles seen by Giovio, Suleyman
explained that Güns was able to defy him because he had brought in his
train only field artillery, not the heavy cannon needed for a siege. At this
point Suleyman turned his army back toward Istanbul, making a detour
through the Austrian duchy of Styria (south of Vienna) to ravage enemy
country. It may be that Suleyman chose not to offer battle when he learned

---

[19] *Deutsche Reichstagsakten, Jüngere Reihe,* vol. X:1, *Der Reichstag in Regensburg . . . 1532,* ed. Rosemarie
    Aulinger (Göttingen, 1992), 167–175. The numbers for Charles's obligations are those given in
    Ferdinand to Mary of Hungary, second letter of 22 June 1532, *Familienkorrespondenz,* Letter 645,
    III, 580–582; as Wolfram notes, slightly different numbers are given in Charles to Isabella, 11 June
    1532, *Corpus Documental,* Letter CXLIII, I, 361–362, and in Granvelle to Mary of Hungary, 11 June
    1532, cited by Wolfram from HHSA-B, PA 6.

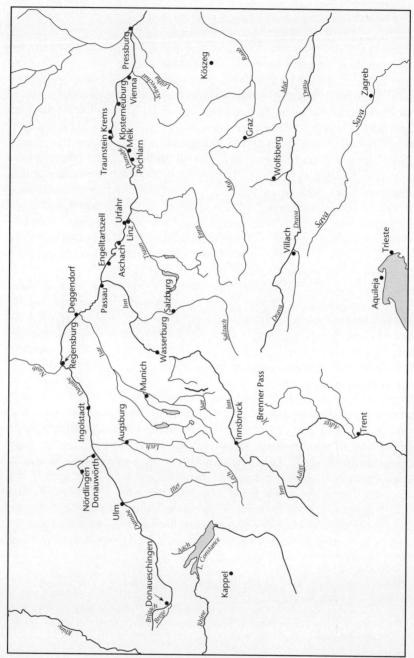

Map 7.1. The Danube campaign of 1532

that the combined allied force would be somewhat larger than his own. As he neared Vienna, Charles will have heard that one of Ferdinand's commanders defeated the Turkish skirmishers in Styria (9 September). He apparently contemplated breaking off his own participation in the campaign at once, because Adrien de Croy, one of the inner circle, wrote from Vienna urging that the emperor's "honor" required him at least to come as far as Vienna and hold a council of war before taking any resolution. From just outside Vienna, Charles wrote the empress that the next objective might be the relief of the Hungarian Danube metropolis of Esztergom (Gran), then besieged by Szapolyai with forces lent by his Ottoman protector. But hopes for a massive thrust in this direction were frustrated by the refusal of imperial troops to cross the Hungarian frontier, as per the diet's instructions. Charles entered Vienna on 23 September and departed again on 4 October, heading south across the Alps. He mustered out his German troops, took the Spaniards with him, and left Ferdinand "8,000 Italians paid for a month and a half" to help in further campaigning in Hungary, leading to the relief of Estzergom.[20]

The Coron Campaign

Meanwhile, Charles had issued instructions for the armada sailing under Doria's command. The new viceroy of Naples, Pedro de Toledo (1532–1553), was to have his Italian colonels recruit Italian infantry, while veterans from Spain's garrisons in Sicily were to await embarkation at Messina. Doria sailed into Messina with twenty-seven galleys, including the sixteen of his galleys that were now on the emperor's payroll; with Doria's other six galleys, coming from Naples, plus vessels from the Papal States, the Knights of Malta, and Monaco, there were thirty-eight or thirty-nine galleys in all. They sailed from Messina on 18 August, with some forty sailing ships from Genoa and Spain; the flagship for the vessels under sail was *La Grimalda* of Genoa, the carrack that led Charles's fleet into harbor three years earlier.[21] The plan was simply to look for and defeat the Turkish war fleet, and do damage in Ottoman Greece. By 21 September, Charles (near Vienna) had received Doria's report of how he encountered and drove off an enemy fleet of similar size near the southeasternmost promontory of Morea (the Peloponnesus). The promontory had two strongholds, Modon on the

[20] *Deutsche Reichstagsakten, Jüngere Reihe*, X:1, 172–175; Zimmerman, *Paolo Giovio*, 124; Siegfried Fiedler, *Kriegswesen und Kriegsführung im Zeitalter der Landsknechte* (Koblenz, 1985), 211–213; Anthony Bridge, *Suleiman the Magnificent, Scourge of Heaven* (New York, 1983), 123–124; Adrien de Croy, lord of Roeulx, to Charles, 14 September 1532, Lanz, Letter 300, II, 14–15; Charles to Isabella, 21 September 1532, *Corpus Documental*, Letter CLXII, I, 398–402.
[21] Santa Cruz, *Crónica del Emperador*, III, 143–146; Francisco de Laiglesia y Auser, *Estudios Historicos (1515–1555)* (Madrid, 1908), 106–110.

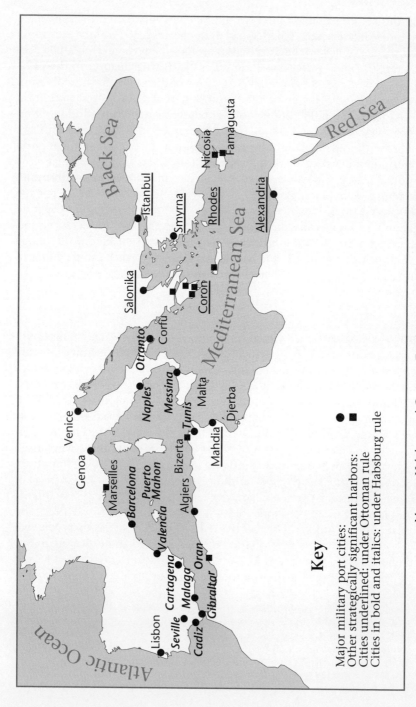

Map 7.2. Habsburg and Ottoman Empires at war in the Mediterranean

Atlantic Ocean

Black Sea

Red Sea

Mediterranean Sea

Istanbul
Smyrna
Salonika
Rhodes
Nicosia
Famagusta
Alexandria
Coron
Corfu
Otranto
Venice
Naples
Messina
Malta
Djerba
Genoa
Marseilles
Barcelona
Puerto Mahon
Valencia
Cartagena
Malaga
Cadiz
Seville
Lisbon
Gibraltar
Oran
Algiers
Bizerta
Tunis
Mahdia

Key

Major military port cities:
Other strategically significant harbors:
Cities underlined: under Ottoman rule
Cities in bold and italics: under Habsburg rule

western and Coron on the eastern shore. Charles's best analyst of events in the Ionian Sea was Fernando Castriota, marquess of Atripalda and governor of the Neapolitan province of Otranto; as a descendant of the fifteenth-century Albanian commander, Scanderbeg, Atripalda had a network of informants in Albania and Morea. It fell to him to explain to the emperor that while Modon's city walls were strong, its castle was "weak, almost like a house that has been leveled." Conversely, Coron's city defenses were "very weak, but they say the castle is in good condition and very strong." The few thousand troops Doria landed on the promontory would do better at holding a castle against attack than a city. Hence the council of war on Doria's galley decided to have 2,500 infantry occupy Coron, not Modon. Some recommended pursuing the Turkish fleet, but Doria chose to sail north to Patras, at the entrance to the Gulf of Corinth, where he dismantled two other castles.[22]

The seizure of Coron, temporary though it proved to be, won prestige for Charles, because any conquest in Greece was an affront to the sultan.[23] Upon his arrival in Italy, from the Vienna campaign, Charles was assured by Doria that Coron was secure for the moment. As usual, however, Charles was reluctant to depend entirely on one adviser; he asked Pedro de Toledo to verify Doria's assessment.[24] Before returning to Spain, the emperor tarried for further discussions with Clement VII (Bologna, December 1532–February 1533). He managed to wrest from the pope a promise to convene a much-needed ecumenical council of the Church, but it was a promise in which Charles reposed little confidence.[25] Back in Spain, he ordered Doria to organize a fleet for the relief of Coron, now beset by sea and land. Coron was in fact saved this time, but only because the troops

[22] Charles to Francisco Quiñones, father general of the Franciscans, 11 July 1532, and to Isabella, 22 July and 21 September 1532, *Corpus Documental*, Letters CL, CLII, and CLXII, I, 370–371, 374, 400; Sanuto, *I Diarii*, LVI, 980–981, 988, 1006–1007, 1019–1025, and LVII, 29–31; Santa Cruz, *Crónica el Emperador*, III, 143–146; for Atripalda's role in the Habsburg intelligence network, J Morial, *El Virrey de Napoles*, T 99–111; and for excerpts from Atripalda's reports to the new Viceroy of Naples, Pedro de Toledo, and to Charles himself, Laiglesia y Auser, *Estudios Historicos*, appendices, 488–492.

[23] See "La relacion que hiza Laschi [Hieronim Łaski, a Polish diplomat formerly in the service of Janos Szapolyai, recently sent by Ferdinand on a mission to the Sultan] de las cosas del Turco quando vino con el rey de Romanos [Ferdinand] a Gante [Ghent]," March 1540, Estado 638, Document 6, paragraphs 3 and 4: the sultan was "gravely offended" by Doria's conquest of Castilnuovo in 1538 (see Chapter 8).

[24] Charles to Ferdinand, 26 October 1532, Lanz, Letter 304, II, 18; Toledo to Charles, 5 November 1532, in Laiglesia, *Estudios Historicos*, 491–492. For the developing enmity between Doria and Toledo, see Chapter 13.

[25] Charles's ostensible and secret instructions for Lambert de Briarde, the former telling him simply to accompany the papal nuncio on his mission to Ferdinand, the latter bidding him to watch closely for any deviation from the stated purpose of his mission, which was to announce the convening of a council, with Briarde's report to Charles in July 1533: *Staatspapiere*, Document 23, 102–110.

sent to besiege it were recalled to join in the sultan's march against Shi'ite Persia. In Genoa, Doria had great difficulty raising money to carry out Charles's orders. The relief fleet for Coron arrived late, after the Turkish army had withdrawn, with fresh men to replace a garrison disenchanted by lack of pay. Originally from the Sicily garrison, these men were now added to Spain's payroll in Lombardy; Doria and Adamo Centurione raised loans for their monthly wages, secured by shipments of grain from Sicily, but when the viceroy of Sicily failed to carry out his orders to ship the grain, the admiral had to carry the burden himself, because no one would lend further on assurances from Sicily. Early in 1534 the sultan again sent a large force overland against Coron, backed by galleys to prevent the landing of a relief force. Habsburg officials made no response, and the Coron garrison accepted honorable terms of surrender (1 April 1534). Meanwhile, the sultan had commissioned thirty new galleys, in addition to the forty that had returned from the encounter with Doria in 1532. He had also summoned Khair-ad-Din Barbarossa from Algiers and commissioned him as Kapudan Pasha (admiral of the sea).[26]

Cornelis de Schepper, a Flemish humanist-diplomat who was also an expert on naval warfare, was then in Istanbul as Ferdinand's envoy to the Porte.[27] He sent Doria an ominous report, evidently based on personal observation as well as on information gleaned from Christian captives serving as oarsmen in the Turkish fleet. Barbarossa sailed from Istanbul on 28 May 1534 with fifty-two galleys expecting to find more at Gallipoli;[28] he may at one time have had over eighty galleys but had to leave some poorly armed vessels behind, so that he now had about seventy. Each galley carried between 100 and 120 fighting men, including some adventurers serving without pay. There were 2,233 Christian slaves on board, plus many Christian Serbs and Bulgarians also chained to their oars. To keep up the wages for his paid men, Barbarossa carried the equivalent of 50,000 ducats in gold coin, 40,000 in precious stones, and 300 bolts of cloth of gold. The only encouraging note was that his cannon, one mounted on the prow of each galley, fired stone balls, not iron shot.[29]

[26] Morial, El Virrey de Napoles, 111–135; Pacini, La Genova dell'Andrea Doria nell'impero di Carlo V, 340–343.

[27] On Schepper's mission to the Porte, see Finlay, "Prophecy and Politics in Istanbul: Charles V, Sultan Süleyman, and the Habsburg Embassy of 1533/1534," 1–31. On his role in naval affairs in the Low Countries, see Tracy, "Herring Wars" 249–272.

[28] Possibly galleys that had returned from the successful siege of Coron.

[29] "Memoria de la orden que tiene la armada de Barbarossa, 1534," in Gómara, Crónica del Emperador, appendix 37, 521–523. The character of this document is evident from the last paragraph: let [Jean d'] Andelot remember to tell Prince Doria to ask any Flemish or German prisoners [from Barbarossa's fleet] who may fall into his hands if they had had dealings with "Cornelius, the ambassador of Ferdinand," for they will have been "induced by the said Cornelius" to try and escape.

The Tunis Campaign

Charles's published correspondence is curiously free of any hint of plans to meet Barbarossa's assault. He was forewarned of French collaboration with the Turkish fleet. When Clement VII met with Francis I at Marseilles (October–November 1533) to solemnize the marriage of his niece, Catherine de Medici, with the king's second son, Henry, duke of Orléans, Francis told the pope he would not only "not oppose" but would even "favor" a Turkish attack on Christendom, so as to recover from the emperor what was rightfully his [Milan]. This message the pope was meant to pass on, and did. Hence Charles instructed Doria and his galleys to remain on station at Genoa, to guard against action by the French in concert with Barbarossa. On the Adriatic coast of Naples, a target of Turkish raids since the 1480s, Viceroy Pedro de Toledo evacuated civilians from vulnerable points and found money "under the ground" to strengthen garrisons and fortifications. Barbarossa apparently knew of the enemy's dispositions. Bypassing the Adriatic coast, he took his seventy galleys and thirteen *fustas* through the Straits of Messina, to strike at the undefended western coast of the kingdom. At Fondi, north of Gaeta, he took a large number of captives, terrifying the population. For added injury, he returned to Naples to burn the six galleys Toledo had under construction. He then continued south to his real objective, Tunis, where he ousted Charles's ally, the unpopular Mulay Hassan, and claimed the city for the sultan. Tunis was now a javelin aimed at Habsburg Sicily, barely a hundred miles east-by-northeast across the water.[30]

As Charles wrote Lope de Soria, Fondi required a response. Naples was to build as many galleys as possible, while Spain increased its fleet to twenty galleys, as part of a "grand armada" to "attack the enemy and chase him from the seas of Christendom." Charles refused to be distracted by events in Germany, where troops of the Schmalkaldic League, paid by France, invaded and occupied the duchy of Württemberg, hitherto under Habsburg administration. Neither was he dissuaded from his determination to lead the expedition himself when Juan Pardo de Tavera (d. 1545), Fonseca's successor as archbishop of Toledo and president of the Council of State, expressed strong reservations about a course of action that might leave Castile in the hands of Charles's eight-year-old son, the future Philip II. In February 1535 Martín de Salinas, Ferdinand's representative at Charles's court, believed that Italy, not Tunis, was the real target for the armada then under preparation. But in a circular letter to vassals of the crown of Castile (1 March 1535), as he crossed into Aragón en route to Barcelona,

---

[30] Knecht, *Renaissance Warrior and Patron*, 299–302; Morial, *El Virrey de Napoles*, 132–135, 162–169; Fisher, *Barbary Legend*, 312–314.

Charles explained that Barbarossa's attack on Naples the previous year was
the sultan's revenge for the loss of prestige he suffered in 1532, when "we
forced him and his army to retreat" from Austria and Hungary, and Doria
scored successes in Greece. Now was the time for a counterstroke. The
new pope, Paul III (r. 1534–1549), sent a messenger to Barcelona urging
that the emperor turn Christendom's great fleet against Istanbul itself, but
Charles followed Doria's advice in declining: it was too dangerous to venture into the eastern Mediterranean while leaving a foe like Barbarossa at
one's back. Tunis, not Istanbul, was the objective.[31]

Doria brought his galleys to Barcelona, while Alvaro de Bazán read-
ied Castile's galleys at Málaga, where other officials loaded victuals on
supply ships. Many Low Countries caravels were either requisitioned in
northern Spain's Atlantic ports, or sent from Antwerp, along with con-
victed Anabaptists and other "prisoners and vagrants," for enforced service
as oarsmen on the galleys.[32] In Malaga, these and other ships embarked
newly recruited Spanish infantry and a good number of cavalry, many of the
latter recruited and paid by Charles's vassals. On or shortly before 28 May
the *caballeros* (knights) who were embarking with the emperor had been
ordered to assemble at dawn at a certain point outside Barcelona, where
Charles held muster for 1,000 mounted men. They accompanied him into
the city, following a great colored banner featuring a crucifix and Charles's
device, *Plus Ultra*. When a further 400 knights were mustered, there were
not enough transport ships to carry them all; four galleys had to be stripped
of their oar banks, each to carry seventy horsemen and their mounts. On
30 May Charles boarded the specially commissioned imperial quadrireme,
with four rowers to a bench instead of the three common for war galleys.
Doria's sixteen galleys sailed in his wake, followed by a long train of floating
fortresses, troop ships, and supply ships of various kinds, including some

[31] See the autograph memorandum of Tavera, speaking in the name of the council, presenting
objections to what Charles had announced as his final decision to lead a campaign against Tunis:
Fritz Walser, ed., "Fünf Spanische Denkschriften an den Kaiser," in "Berichte," VI, 133–143. Salinas
to Ferdinand and to the secretary Castillejo, both on 21 February 1535, Rodriguez Villa, *El Emperador
Carlos V*, Letters 270, 271, pp. 631, 633 (Salinas also explained he would not be accompanying the
emperor, because of his mortal terror of sea voyages). Charles to the vassals of the crown of Castile,
1 March 1535, *Corpus Documental*, Letter CLXVIII, I, 409. That Charles and Ferdinand had "driven
off" the Turks in 1532 was the official version of events. See, Etrobius, *Commentarium seu potius
Diarium Expeditionis Tuniceae*, sig. A8, and Charles to Soria, 10 May 1535, *Corpus Documental*, Letter
CLXXIII, I, 424–425. The idea of an assault on Istanbul is also promoted in Soria's letters to
Charles: *Calendar of Letters, Despatches and State Papers, Relating to Negotiations between England and
Spain*, vol. 5:1, ed. Pascual de Gayangos (London, 1886, Kraus Reprint 1969), letters of 21 May
and 9 August 1535, pp. 460, 526.
[32] The sending of prisoners for the galleys is discussed in the correspondence of the Council of
Holland with officials of the central government in Brussels, e.g., Gerrit, lord of Assendelft, to
the count of Hoogstraten (*Stadtholder* of Holland), 15 April 1535, Aud., 1529, pp. 107–108. For the
Anabaptist movement in Holland at this time, see Tracy, *Holland under Habsburg Rule*, 160–170.

built to carry horses. On 12 June Spain's fleet made rendezvous off Caligari (Sardinia) with the fleets of Italy, including galleys provided by Pope Paul III, the Knights of Malta, and the Republic of Genoa, as well as those of Naples and Sicily, and troop ships carrying the German and Italian infantry as well as Spanish veterans from garrisons in Naples and Sicily (it seems that the new recruits from Spain took their places on garrison duty).[33] At a given signal on 14 June, oarsmen propelled the imperial quadrireme along a water lane dividing the massed fleet, with trumpet blasts and volleys of cheers.[34] The grand *empresa* was at last under sail.

"Before dawn" the next day, Charles's galleys (always out front of the slower-sailing vessels) weighed anchor off the west bank of the channel leading to Tunis, near the ruins of ancient Carthage. Charles and his council of war decided that the strongly defended fortress on the peninsula of Goletta, three miles down the fifteen-mile channel, had to be taken before advancing to Tunis. During the next month Italian regiments entrenched opposite the fortress extended their lines to take in strategic heights and fought off repeated sallies from Turkish troops on Goletta, many of whom had sailed with Barbarossa's fleet the year before. During these actions the emperor more than once "advanced with lance in hand" (according to Santa Cruz), "putting himself in the same danger as a poor common soldier." Meanwhile, Mulay Hassan, the ruler whom Barbarossa had ousted, came to Charles's tent, seeking restoration. He "kissed [the emperor's] hands and feet" in token of submission, but failed to rally local potentates he claimed would support him. At last, at the direction of two Italian military engineers, the cannon were properly placed for a bombardment (*batería*) from three different points. While these imperial guns hammered Goletta "for six or seven hours without interruption," they were echoed from the sea by two great ships built to carry more artillery on their upper decks, the largest of Portugal's galleons and the carrack of the Knights of Malta. Meanwhile, three squadrons of eight galleys each executed a naval version of firing-by-ranks, advancing and retiring by turns to fire from their prow guns the iron shot that had some chance of damaging Goletta's

---

[33] Santa Cruz, *Crónica del Emperador*, III, 255, 264, and Gómara, *Crónica de los Barbarrojas*, 414: 9,000 Spanish infantry were embarked at Málaga, but the Spaniards brought to Caligari on Italian ships, and those who fought at Goletta and Tunis, are described as "old soldiers." But Giovio, *Historiarum*, in *Opera*, IV, 313, mentions that Leyva in Milan had strict orders from Charles not to let any of the Lombard-garrison veterans embark for Tunis; in this quarter, there was thought to be too great a danger of a French invasion. For the muster of the cavalry at Barcelona, see Salinas to Ferdinand, 28 May 1535, Rodríguez Villa, *El Emperador Carlos V*, Letter 278, pp. 652–653.

[34] Etrobius, *Commentarium, Expeditionis Tuniceae*, A2v–B6v. In the preface, "Joannes Berotus Valence-nas" explains that he has seen the work through the press at the request of his late friend "Etrobius," who had translated his own French text into Latin. The text Bérot translated was actually written by one of Charles's secretaries, Antoine Perrenin. See also Charles to Soria, from Caligari, 12 June 1535, *Corpus Documental*, Letter CLXXIV, I, 425–427.

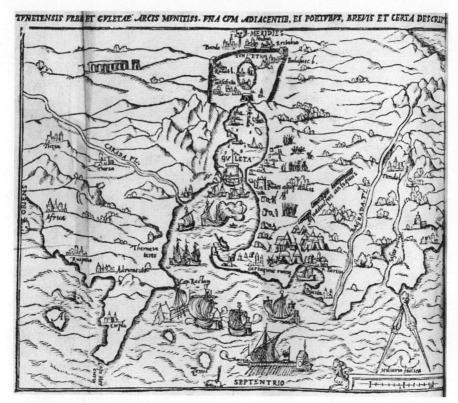

Figure 7.2. *Siege of Goletta*, in the 1555 Antwerp edition of *Historiarum sui Temporis* by Paolo Giovio, University of Minnesota Library.

curtain wall. Although the effect was not what Charles had hoped, the fortress was stormed and quickly taken, with a loss to the enemy of some 2,000 men, and sixty galleys and *fustas* based at Goletta. In the ensuing council of war, some favored leaving a force to occupy Goletta and sailing home,[35] but the weight of opinion was for advancing to Tunis.[36]

While Doria's galleys and some of the German troops remained behind to guard Goletta, each man among the rest of the infantry carried provisions for three or four days. But Barbarossa had already fled Tunis at the news of Goletta's fall; when he returned to retrieve treasure from the

[35] Spanish occupation of Peñon, an island fortress opposite Algiers (retaken by Barbarossa in 1529) would have been a precedent for this strategy.

[36] Etrobius, *Commentarium Expeditionis Tuniceae*, C6–E5v; Santa Cruz, *Crónica del Emperador*, III, 255–270; Charles to Hannart, 23, 24, and 28 June 1535, Lanz, Letter 406, II, 188–192; Charles to Soria, 29 June, 30 June, 14 July 1535, *Corpus Documental*, Letters CLXXV, CLXXVI, CLXXVIII, I, 427–432, 432–433, 434–435.

citadel, Christian captives, fearing they would be slaughtered before the emperor's entry, found weapons to drive him off again. Reports reaching Genoa claimed that Tunis had not been "plundered," because the gracious emperor promised his men three months' pay instead. In fact, "because the gates of the city were not opened to us," Charles gave his men permission to sack the city.[37] Thus as "eighteen to twenty thousand" Christian captives were released, thousands of Tunisian civilians were cut down in their homes and shops; Spanish troops broke into mosques and stripped sacred texts of their gold leaf, "for such is that nation's thirst for gold." They also rounded up as many "Moors" as they could in the surrounding countryside, selling some 10,000 on the slave market of Tunis. There was talk among Charles's advisers of moving on to Algiers, but since many of the men were suffering from dysentery, the council of war decided to sail for Naples, where Charles took the occasion to visit his southern kingdom for the first and only time. While Mulay Hassan reclaimed his position in Tunis (redeeming many of those the Christians had sold into slavery), Antonio Doria with ten galleys and Bernardino de Mendoza with 1,000 Spaniards remained behind to defend Goletta.[38]

Sinews of War[39]

How many men did Charles actually raise for the Danube campaign? From information given by Giovio (who accompanied the imperial camp) and

[37] *Keyserlicher Majestät Eroberung des Königreiches Thunis* (Nuremberg, August 1535), copy in the James Ford Bell Library, University of Minnesota. On the usages of war, including the circumstances in which armies would be given permission to sack besieged cities, see Simon Pepper, "Siege Law, Siege Ritual, and the Symbolism of Walled Cities in Renaissance Europe," in James D. Tracy, ed., *City Walls: The Urban Enceinte in Global Perspective* (Cambridge, 2000), 573–604.

[38] Etrobius, *Commentarium Expeditionis Tuniceae*, E7–G6 (the French-speaking author does not have kind words for the emperor's Spanish and German contingents); Charles to Soria from Tunis, 25 July 1535, *Corpus Documental*, Letter CLXXX, I, 438–440; Charles to Mary, 23 July 1535, Lanz, Letter 409, II, 196–199 (Lanz identifies this letter as meant for publication, because copies are found in many archives); Charles to Soria, from Goletta, 16 August 1535, *Corpus Documental*, Letter CLXXXI, I, 441–444.

[39] The two most reliable figures I have for the wages of *Landsknechte* come from Low Countries budget summaries for 1530 and 1553 (Part II, note 5, and Chapter 11, note 19), indicating for those years monthly wages equivalent to 3.53 and 5.67 ducats. This suggests an annual additive (not compound) increase of .097%. If we assume wage increases at this rate, the monthly wages for *Landsknechte* would be 3.724 ducats in 1532 and 4.015 in 1535; rounding off the small fraction, I assume 3.7 ducats a month in 1532 and 4 ducats a month in 1535. Assuming a similar rate of increase, I estimate wages for Spanish and Italian infantry at 3.2 ducats a month in 1532 and 3.4 in 1535, as opposed to 3 in 1529–1530. I also assume for 1532 and 1535 4 ducats a month for light horse (as opposed to the 5 scudi or 4.67 ducats mentioned in Charles to Philip, 19 June 1543, *Corpus Documental*, Letter CCLVIII, II, 132–133); and 5 ducats per month for German heavy cavalry (a bit higher than the 4.6 ducats a month for Low Countries cavalry in 1529).

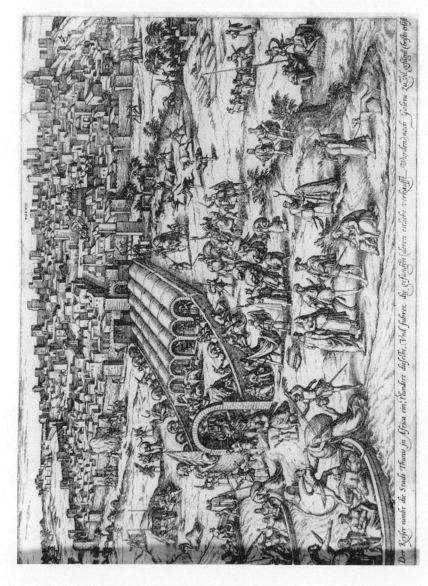

Figure 7.3. *Tunis Captured*, in the 1555 edition of *Kurze Verzeichnis wie Keyser Carolus der V in Africa...*, Herzog August Bibliothek Wolfenbüttel.

Santa Cruz, it seems that the emperor's portion of the army that mustered at Regensburg included 12,000 *Landsknechte*, 6,200 Spanish veterans from Italy, more Spaniards from Spain, heavy cavalry from the Low Countries, 10,000 Italian infantry, and 1,200 light horse.[40] If one assumes that the heavy cavalry from the Low Countries – the *compagnies d'ordonnance* – came in the same strength as in 1529 (2,000 men), and that Charles had perhaps 2,000 Germany heavy cavalry[41] as well, plus 2,000 or so infantry from Spain itself, the emperor will have come close to meeting his commitments to the diet, as described in Ferdinand's letter to Mary of 22 June.[42] In other words, he will have had 12,000 *Landsknechte*, 8,200 Spanish infantry, 10,000 Italians, 2,000 heavy cavalry from the Low Countries and 2,000 from Germany, and 1,200 light horse. It seems that pay for these men began in August and that Charles's troops were paid through the first half of November.[43] Three and a half months' pay for the units listed will have amounted to 443,240 ducats,[44] to which one should add 20% for pioneers, victuals, officers' pay, and artillery, for a grand total of 531,888.

During these same months, Charles's realms also had to shoulder most of the cost for Doria's armada. According to Santa Cruz, Doria's ships carried 7,000 Italian mercenaries and 1,500 Spanish veterans from garrisons in Sicily. Of the thirty-eight or thirty-nine galleys, nine were paid for by the pope, and still others by the Knights of Malta, and the Grimaldi principality of Monaco. Thus Charles had on his account Doria's standing fleet of sixteen galleys, paid by Castile's treasury;[45] the six others commanded by Doria's nephew; and a few from Naples and Sicily – let us say twenty-five in all. He will also have been responsible for most of the thirty-six "ships and carracks" from Spain that carried men and supplies; I have no figures for ship-hire and crew's wages in Spain,[46] but costs will have been small by

---

[40] Giovio, *Historiarum*, in *Opera*, IV, 210, 227 (for Giovio's activities in Charles's camp, see Zimmerman, *Paolo Giovio*, 122–126); Santa Cruz, *Crónica del Emperador*, III, 136. Santa Cruz is less reliable, because he gives much larger total numbers for the imperial host (170,000 infantry and 70,000 cavalry, as opposed to Giovio's 90,000 and 30,000), and because he has his hero, Charles, advance to Vienna by way of Günz.

[41] I make this assumption partly because of Giovio's figure of 30,000 cavalry for all the host.

[42] Cited in note 19.

[43] See Wolfram's notes to the same letter: Ferdinand to Mary, second letter of 22 June 1532, *Familienkorrespondenz*, Letter 645, III, 581–582, as modified by Charles to Isabella, 21 September 1532, *Corpus Documental*, Letter CLXII, I, 398–401.

[44] All for three and a half months: for 18,200 Spaniards and Italians at 3.2 ducats, 203,840; for 12,000 *Landsknechte* at 3.7 ducats, 155,400; for 2,000 German heavy cavalry at 5 ducats, 35,000; for 2,000 Low Countries heavy cavalry at 4.6 ducats, 32,200; and for 1,200 light horse at 4 ducats, 16,800.

[45] E.g., Charles to Isabella, 30 September 1530 and 10 March 1531, *Corpus Documental*, Letters LXXXVI and CI, I, 240, 275–276.

[46] Gemeentearchief, Amsterdam, "Stadsrekening" for 1532, 51v: the costs for two caravels hired by the city between 11 March and 8 April were only five pounds sixteen schillings in Flemish pounds,

comparison to those for a galley and its complement of ninety or so oars-men. At 500 ducats per month per galley, four months' pay (July through October) for twenty-five galleys would be 50,000 ducats.[47] Four months' wages for 8,500 Spanish and Italian infantry would be 108,800 ducats, meaning a total cost for the expedition of about 192,960 ducats, counting an added 20% for victuals, transport ships, and officers' pay.[48] In sum, Charles would have needed around 724,848 ducats for military expenses between July and October 1532, plus a further 125,000 for his household while ab-sent from Spain, or 849,848 in all. This estimate does not include a further loan for 100,000 ducats provided by Ansaldo Grimaldi (March 1533), some of which was needed for ship-hire fees still owed to captains of the sailing ships that were now to accompany Charles on his voyage back to Spain.[49]

There was no prospect for getting any of this money from Castile's revenues. Isabella had summoned the Cortes at Charles's request, but the deputies granted a rather meager 240,000 ducats over the next three years, so that in view of existing debts and obligations there was nothing to spare for the emperor. The *maestrazgos*, the *cruzada*, and the clerical sub-sidy were already pledged for repayment of the huge loan contracts of recent years, and this was also a lean period for imports of specie from the new world. When Bartholomaeus Welser agreed (April 1532) to provide 100,000 scudi (93,334 ducats), payable in Genoa or Milan, he insisted on doling out the money in four installments, each to be released only when the Augsburg banker had written notice from agents in Castile that the pre-vious installment had been repaid, with interest. As Carande Thobar notes, Welser was in effect reloaning the same small sum four times.[50] Because of its timing, the Welser loan was probably meant for current expenses in Italy and Germany, not for the upcoming "enterprises" in Austria and the Ionian Sea.

To pay for this year's fighting, Charles had to break into the treasure that accrued to him from the great victory won by his generals at Pavia (1525).

or 34.8 Carolus gulden (19.07 Spanish ducats). One must bear in mind that Holland skippers were notorious for carrying small crews, and that wages will have been higher during the prime sailing season.

[47] Charles to Isabella, 21 April 1530 and 10 March 1531, *Corpus Documental*, Letters LXVII and CI, I, 205–207, 275–276: Doria receives 15,000 ducats every two months for his fifteen galleys, meaning 500 ducats per month per galley; Charles to Isabella, 22 July 1532, *Corpus Documental*, Letter CLII, I, 374: Charles is pleased "the thirty-six ships and carracks" have sailed from Barcelona to join at Messina with Doria's galleys plus "the pope's nine and Monaco's"; he does not mention those of the Knights of Malta (four?), or say how many Monaco had (two?). Charles to Isabella, 8 July 1530, *Corpus Documental*, Letter LXXVI, I, 219): Doria has twenty-nine galleys under his command.

[48] I am assuming that the cost of transport ships for a naval campaign was roughly equivalent to the cost of the artillery and baggage trains for a land campaign.

[49] Pacini, *La Genova dell'Andrea Doria nell'impero di Carlo V*, 328.

[50] Carande Thobar, *Carlos V y sus banqueros*, III, 111–119.

The 1529 Treaty of Cambrai pledged 2 million ecus d'or (approximately 1.2 million ducats) to ransom the two sons of King Francis I, held in captivity in lieu of their father. Once this money was delivered, Charles ordered it guarded by Alvaro de Lugo, keeper of the royal treasure in the castle of La Mota, in the merchant-fair city of Medina del Campo. In the course of negotiations leading to Ferdinand's recognition as King of the Romans, the emperor had to take 200,000 ducats from La Mota to help meet his obligations to Germany's electoral princes. The rest he instructed Isabella not to touch, "for I consider it the foundation of peace," that is, a guarantee against future French aggression. But in April 1532 he ordered that 500,000 ducats be transferred "secretly" to safekeeping in Barcelona, "for if the Turk comes against me this year, I will go against him in person." He assured Isabella the money could be returned to La Mota if it were not needed, and he was not pleased that his wife withheld 70,000 of the 500,000 for emergency use within the kingdom. The delivery of the 430,000 ducats, brought by Doria in his galleys from Barcelona in June, explains why Charles was able to pay in advance, through the first half of November, the men he mustered at Regensburg in August. But by the time Doria sailed, the emperor already needed more money. The sum remaining at La Mota was now only about 400,000 ducats, because Welser agents at Medina del Campo had taken 108,000 ducats in interest and principal payments for the previously mentioned loan. This 400,000 Charles wanted brought to Cartagena, thence to be carried to Italy by Alvaro de Bazán, commander of the Castilian galley fleet on station to guard against Barbary corsairs. Instead the money was sent to Barcelona, where it to be taken on board by Bazán.

For reasons unknown to me, the sum was now only 300,000, but to it were added the 70,000 that Isabella had held back, plus a 60,000 ducat "gift" from the duchess of Medina-Sidonia and her brother-in-law, Juan Alonso de Guzmán. In any case, Bazán and his galleys were ordered to remain for a time at Barcelona, because Isabella and her council were unwilling to denude the coast of protection by Bazán's galleys during the sailing season.[51] Hence the second 430,000 ducats did not reach Genoa until late September, just as Charles was about to return from Vienna. But because the money was needed urgently, Genoa's bankers had to step into the breach. The emperor's loan broker, Tomasso Fornari, had little luck at first, even against the promise of the specie coming on Bazán's galleys, but

[51] Charles to Alvaro de Lugo, 6 April 1532, *Corpus Documental*, Letter CXXXVI, I, 345–346; Charles to Isabella, 6 April 1532, a second letter of 6 April, 22 April, 11 June, 11 July, 9, 26 August, 2 September 1532, *Corpus Documental*, Letters CXXXVII, CXXXVIII, CXLI, CXLIII, CXLVII, CLIII, CLVII, and CLXI, I, 347, 350–351, 355–356, 361–362, 366–367, 376–377, 388–389, and 395–396; Charles to Tavera, 11 October 1532, *Corpus Documental*, Letter CLXIV, I, 403.

eventually, and on their own terms, Adamo Centurione and his partners promised loans of 120,000 ducats, and Ansaldo Grimaldi 150,000.[52] Thus for the land and sea crusades of this year, with subtractions for interest on the loans just mentioned, Charles will have had something less than the 860,000 ducats from two shipments of 430,000 each, representing what was left of the treasure at La Mota, plus the duchess of Medina Sidonia's gift.

* * *

Information about the men and ships on the assault on Tunis can be gleaned from five sources: Charles's letter of 12 June from Caligari to Lope de Soria, his ambassador in Genoa; the "Diary" of one of Charles's secretaries, Antoine Perrenin, translated into Latin by one Jean Bérot, who took the penname of Johannes Etrobius;[53] and the accounts of Giovio, Gómara, and Santa Cruz.[54] Santa Cruz gives the most detail, but he was also writing at the farthest remove from the events in question, some fifteen or sixteen years later. Both Charles and Etrobius say there were seventy-four or seventy-five galleys in all, not counting *fustas*, or the sailing vessels, said to number as many as 300. By putting the various comments together, one can make out that the emperor and his realms were responsible for about fifty of the galleys: the sixteen of Doria's that were on Castile's pay-roll, fifteen from Spain, commanded by Bazán, twelve from Naples, and six from Sicily. Pope Paul III paid for three papal galleys, three more out-fitted at Genoa, and the five or six of Doria's that were commanded by his nephew Antonio. The Republic of Genoa sent nine galleys, and the barons of Naples (including Viceroy Pedro de Toledo in his own name) fitted out seven more. The Knights of Malta sent four or five galleys, the carrack used in bombarding Goletta, and 800 knights, or men-at-arms. Charles's brother-in-law, John III, had no galley fleet, but he did send 2,000 infantry and twenty-two ships of the line, including (according to Charles) "ten to twelve galleons well provided with artillery," including the great carrack used in the bombardment of Goletta. Doria's plan for an assault on Algiers in 1532 – calling for 25,000 infantry[55] – seems to have remained the guide-line for this amphibious campaign. Gómara says there were 26,000 infantry

[52] Pacini, *La Genova dell'Andrea Doria nell'impero di Carlo V*, 330–333. The Centurione loan was later reduced to 50,000.

[53] Charles to Soria, 12 June 1535, *Corpus Documental*, Letter CLXXIV, I, 425–427; Etrobius, *Commntarium Expeditionis Tuniceae.*

[54] Giovio, *Historiarum*, in *Opera*, IV, 312–315; Gómara, *Crónica de los Barbarrojas*, 414; Santa Cruz, *Crónica del Emperador*, III, 255–269. Pacini, *La Genova dell'Andrea Doria nell'impero di Carlo V*, 350, mentions in December 1534 Doria was having three new galleys built at Genoa and Pope Paul III three more, all to go on Charles's payroll.

[55] See note 18.

in all. Taking the smaller numbers where other authors differ on the size of national contingents yields the following totals: 8,000 Spaniards, veterans from Naples and Sicily, commanded by the marquess of Vasto; 8,000 Italians, commanded by Ferrante Gonzaga; and 8,000 *Landsknechte*, led across the Alps by Maximilian von Eberstein and embarked at La Spezia in Genoese territory. One can get to Gómara's estimate of 26,000 by adding in the 2,000 infantry paid by Portugal.[56] Charles was also responsible for 800 light horse and (one would think) at least 1,000 of the heavy cavalry.[57]

For the months of June through September, with October as the going-home month, wages would have been 432,000 ducats for the 24,000 infantry on the emperor's payroll, and 39,000 for the cavalry.[58] The cost for fifty galleys for five months would have been 125,000, bringing the total to 596,000. Adding 20% for victuals, officers' pay, and the 300 transport ships, plus 125,000 ducats for the emperor's household expenses for the year, the overall cost of the Tunis campaign may be estimated at 840,200 ducats. This does not count the cost of building new ships for the expedition, including the emperor's quadrireme. Because expenses for the galleys fitted out at Barcelona came to 118,226 ducats,[59] it seems reasonable to double this figure. Thus total costs for the Tunis campaign would come to 1,076,652 ducats.

The Tunis enterprise was possible only because Francisco de Pizarro's conquest of Peru restocked the emperor's treasure chamber at La Mota. When Pizarro and his men seized the last Inca emperor, Atahualpa (whom they later killed, 26 July 1533), they found themselves masters of wealth beyond belief. Gabriel de Espinosa, a companion of Pizarro's, traveled posthaste to Panama to send Charles an account of these happy events, later printed in German and Italian translations: the *conquistadores* took possession of 1,356,539 pesos of gold (approximately 1,591,897 ducats), and 51,610 marks of silver. This estimate was confirmed by the governor of Peru, who reported that some 2 million ducats worth of gold and silver had been registered in his office after the conquest. To many Spaniards such a windfall seemed the gift of God, to aid the emperor, as Espinosa put it, "in the

---

[56] Santa Cruz may also be counting in the 2,000 paid by Portugal when he gives the number of Spanish infantry as 10,000, not 8,000 (Giovio's figure). Pacini, *La Genova dell'Andrea Doria nell'impero di Carlo V*, 351, gives a smaller number (7,000) for the Germans who embarked at La Spezia. He also mentions 3,900 Italian infantry embarking there; others presumably came from Naples.

[57] Etrobius says 6,000 heavy cavalry were embarked at Málaga, "many" recruited and paid by Charles's vassals. Giovio says there were 700 heavy cavalry, Santa Cruz 1,500. In this case, the smaller estimate seems a bit too small.

[58] For 8,000 *Landsknechte* at 4 ducats a month (see note 39) for five months, 160,000; for 16,000 Spaniards and Italians at an estimated 3.4 ducats a month, 272,000; for 800 light horse at 4 ducats a month, 16,000; and for 1,000 heavy cavalry at 4.6 ducats, 23,000.

[59] Carande Thobar, *Carlos V y sus banqueros*, III, 155–175.

holy enterprise of war against the Turk, Luther, and other enemies of the faith." As treasureships brought the gold and silver from Panama to Seville – the first arrived in December 1533 – Charles's royal "fifth" would have amounted to approximately 400,000 ducats, minus a 1% share he had promised Cobos. But for the plans Charles was forming as 1534 drew to a close, a fifth was not enough. Already in December 1534 he ordered that at least 60,000 ducats' worth of treasure registered to the names of private parties be "sequestered" for his use, with the owners to be compensated by *juros* carrying an interest rate of 3%.[60]

On 4 March 1535 he decreed a second and much larger sequestration for 800,000 ducats, to be levied proportionally on all persons receiving shipments of more than 400 pesos (480 ducats) in gold and silver. To justify this intrusion on the rights of merchants and investors, Charles appealed to the sentiments expressed by Espinosa: "The cause of the sequestration is the dire need for fitting out armadas to resist the Grand Turk and his captains." It took time for the Seville mint to turn gold and silver bars and Inca objets d'art into coin of the realm, and it seems that part of a large loan contracted with the Fugger (February 1535) was meant to bridge the gap: 100,000 ducats of the 800,000 sequestration was allocated for part payment of this loan. Another 450,000 ducats went to the royal secretary Juan de Enciso, a confidant of Cobos who remained behind in Valladolid as Cobos accompanied Charles to Barcelona. Some of the money that passed through Enciso's hands was no doubt spent within the borders of Castile, but more was spent for mustering troops and fitting out ships at the main points of embarkation, in Barcelona (Aragón) and in the Italian realms: between February and July 1535 the treasury authorized exports of specie beyond the borders of Castile totaling 1,031,267 ducats. The only portion of the money coming from the sequestration that can be identified as spent for purposes other than Tunis was a sum of 120,000 ducats used to repay bankers who remitted a like sum to Antwerp, to ease Mary of Hungary's fears about what the French might do while Charles was occupied with Barbarossa. With the 400,000-ducat royal fifth, the 100,000-ducat Fugger loan, and the 450,000 that went through Enciso's hands, Charles had at least 950,000 for the Tunis enterprise, and perhaps as much as 1,140,000. By the time he rode into Tunis as its conqueror (August 1535), there was probably nothing left of the approximately 1,260,000 ducats that had come to him from the far-off treasure house of Atahualpa.[61]

[60] Ibid.
[61] Ibid.; Pölnitz, *Anton Fugger*, I, 328–329, thinks the 600,000 ducats loan contracted with the Fugger (number 106 in Carande Thobar's series) was "probably" destined for the campaign against Tunis, but Carande's discussion of the loan contract – with all but 100,000 assigned for repayment on other incomes – suggests otherwise.

* * *

Charles did not burden the future incomes of his realms for the two crusades of 1532, but he did in 1535. If interest for the 3% *juros* by which owners of the 860,000 ducats in private treasure were compensated added only
about 25,800 ducats to the annual charges against Castile's *rentas ordinarias*,
it was by seemingly gradual increments like this that these revenues would
come to be fully pledged by the end of Charles's reign. But might it not
be said that Atahualpa's treasure, seen by Spaniards as a gift of divine provi-
dence, had given the emperor a great victory over the infidel, and a fitting
riposte to Barbarossa's 1534 campaign? The answer is less clear than it may
seem, because Barbarossa himself escaped from Tunis. He took twelve galleys into the harbor at Bona (Anaba) and sailed out again, despite the fact
that fifteen galleys under Doria's nephew Juanetin and Adamo Centurione
lay in wait for him at the entrance to the harbor. He had eleven galleys
more at Algiers, whence he sailed in force into Spanish waters, landing
near Mahon on Minorca, then a town of some 400 households. According
to Gómara's account, he first defeated and killed the garrison from the
fortress at Ciudadela that had come out against him, then talked his way
into Mahon itself under a flag of truce; once inside the walls, he had no
difficulty killing those who resisted, and taking away some 1,800 men,
women, and children to the slave market of Algiers. For the people of
Minorca, it was as if the battle at Tunis had taken place on another planet.
By December, Barbarossa and his warships were again in Istanbul, awaiting
new orders from the sultan. Charles had won a victory, not a war.[62]

---

[62] Gómara, *Crónica de los Barbarrojas*, 418–423; Charles to Isabella, 13 December 1535, *Corpus
Documental*, Letter CLXXXII, I, 444–446.

Chapter 8

Failures in Provence and at Prevesa and Algiers, 1536–1541

Charles hoped to profit from the *reputacion* gained from his success at Tunis by pressing the campaign against Algiers. From Naples, he instructed the empress to make sure that Alvaro de Bazán's galleys were ready to sail again 1 March, carrying the required complement of eighty-three men (including twenty-three sailors), "seeing that Barbarossa's galleys carry at least 130 men." Yet he also kept an eye on France. Francis had assured Charles that those who supported in his name the Schmalkaldic League's conquest of Württemberg in 1534 were acting beyond their mandate. But Charles knew better, and his chief agent in Germany sent evidence of France's continuing efforts to build an alliance with the empire's Lutheran princes. During the summer of 1535 the French were known to be mustering six of the provincial "legions" of 6,000 men Francis I had created and were thought to be providing the sultan and Barbarossa with information about Charles's armada.[1] Then (1 November 1535) the death without heirs of Francesco Maria Sforza reopened the troublesome question of Milan. As part of a proposed comprehensive peace plan, Francis now demanded Milan for his second son, Henry, duke of Orléans. Charles indicated he could offer Milan to the king's third son, the duke of Angoulême, but not to the second son; Orléans was too close to the French throne (in fact, he became heir apparent when his older brother died in 1536), and he would also have a claim to Florence by right of his wife, Catherine de Medici. Meanwhile, Francis gathered his new army near Lyons and threatened retaliation against his uncle, Duke Charles III of Savoy-Piedmont, for unsettled claims on behalf of his late mother, Louise of Savoy. French troops and their Swiss allies quickly overran Savoy, advancing as far as Turin, capital of Piedmont

---

[1] Johan van Weeze, exiled archbishop of Lund, to Charles, 1 August, 3 November, 12 November 1534, and 8 April 1535, Lanz, *Letters* 375, 386, 390, and 400, II, 107–108, 135–136, 144–145, and 165–167; Charles to Soria, 10 May 1535, *Corpus Documental*, Letter CLXXIII, I, 424; Knecht, *Renaissance Warrior and Patron*, 350–352.

(February 1536). Francis insisted the emperor had no grounds for offense, because there had been no infringement on the boundaries of Piedmont's neighbor, the Habsburg duchy of Milan. Yet Savoy was not only an ally but the emperor's brother-in-law – their wives were both daughters of Portugal's John III. In Naples, Charles meditated a response to this affront.[2]

Provence

On 1 February 1536, even before the French actually invaded Savoy, Charles from Naples sent the empress instructions for a concentration of forces that could be directed against Algiers if Francis I chose peace, or against France itself if he chose war. The 10,000 German *Landsknechte* thought by planners to be needed for the Algiers *empresa* would soon be in Lombardy, ready for either eventuality. Similarly, Isabella was to have the twenty-five galleys now in Spanish harbors sail for Genoa as soon as possible, carrying 3,000 Spanish infantry with their wages paid for a month after embarkation.[3]

By the time Charles left the city of Naples in March, he had decided on an invasion across the Alps. On his journey to Rome he was accompanied by a guard of 700 heavy cavalry and a "legion" of Spanish veterans from Naples, many of whom were recognized by Romans as complicit in the infamous Sack of 1527.[4] He paused a few days to meet with Pope Paul III and with the ambassadors of Venice and other Italian powers. In a prepared speech before the papal consistory (18 April) he rejected the charge that it was he who ruptured the peace of Christendom and prevented a united offensive against the Turk: Francis I was the culprit, because he had troops on the march before Charles began recruiting, and his invasion of Savoy (an imperial if not a Habsburg territory) was a direct violation of the 1529 Peace of Cambrai. Paul III conveyed the gratifying news that the consistory had endorsed his decision to convene a council of the church within the next year, but the pope was not to be budged from a studied neutrality between France and the Habsburgs.[5] Charles moved on to Florence, where

[2] Brandi, *Emperor Charles V*, 368–370; Knecht, *Renaissance Warrior and Patron*, 329–333.

[3] Charles to Mary, 28 January 1536, Lanz, Letter 626, II, 656; Charles to Isabella, 1 February 1536, to Alvaro de Bazán, 1 February 1536, and to Isabella, 20 February 1536, *Corpus Documental*, Letters CLXXXVII, CLXXXVIII, and CXCII, I, 459–463, 464–465, and 473–476.

[4] Giovio, *Historiarum*, in *Opera*, IV, 351.

[5] Charles recounts his speech in a letter to Hannart, his ambassador in France, 17–18 April 1536, Lanz, Letter 428, II, 223–226. Cf. Francis I's response, as cited by Knecht, *Renaissance Warrior and Patron*, 333: "I cannot understand how the emperor can claim that in making war on the duke [of Savoy] I contravene any treaty against him, for nothing belonging to the empire has been touched by my troops; on the contrary, both the generals and captains of my army have received instructions not to attempt anything against the emperor's territory." On the council, see Charles to Isabella, 18 April 1536, *Corpus Documental*, Letter CXCVII, I, 488–491.

he was feted in grand style by Duke Alessandro de Medici (d. 1537), the bridegroom of his natural daughter, Margaret of Parma.[6]

Meanwhile, with 2,000 Spaniards from the Milan garrison and 15,000 *Landsknechte*, Leyva had set out from Milan (2 May) on a campaign to roll back French advances in Piedmont.[7] Passing through Asti, he forced the submission of Fossano (24 June 1536),[8] farther up the Tanaro River, then struck northwest to begin a siege of Turin. When Charles himself arrived in Asti, bringing Italian infantry recruited in the area around Florence, it was time for a council of war. According to Giovio, who got his information on this campaign from the marquess of Vasto,[9] Ferrante Gonzaga and Vasto himself argued for applying the whole imperial army to the reconquest of Turin, an action that might break France's hold on the Italian side of the Julian Alps. Leyva wanted to send the army into France to do as much damage as possible; Doria for his part believed that his war fleet, combined with Spain's, could support an invasion of Provence more effectively than Moncada and Portoundo had done for Bourbon in 1524. Charles decided on the latter option, says Giovio, because he knew that his diplomats had persuaded the Swiss to remain neutral in this campaign – effectively depriving Francis I of a field army – and because it seemed not much would come of Mary of Hungary's efforts to send a large army into northern France from the Low Countries.[10] With a force of perhaps 10,000 men[11]

---

[6] Following his assassination on 7 January 1537, Alessandro was succeeded in Florence by a cousin from another branch of the family, Cosimo I, later Grand Duke of Tuscany. Margaret (1522–1586), the daughter of Johanna van der Gheenst, with whom Charles had a liaison in Brussels, takes her familiar name from her second marriage, to the natural son of Pope Paul III, Ottavio Farnese, duke of Parma. Their son, Alexander of Parma, would later be Spain's most successful commander in the early decades of the Dutch Revolt.

[7] Charles to Isabella, 18 May 1536, *Corpus Documental*, Letter CCIV, I, 503–504.

[8] Giuseppe de Leva, *Storia Documentata di Carlo V, in Correlazione all'Italia* (5 vols., Venice, 1863–1894), III, 168.

[9] Giovio, *Historiarum*, in *Opera*, IV, 356, "sicut a Vasto accepimus." Cf. Zimmerman, *Paolo Giovio*, 87–88, 149: as bishop of Salerno, during the French siege of Naples (1527–1528), Giovio spent his time on the island of Ischia, as part of the circle of the *chatelaine*, Costanza d'Avalos, who was then raising her brother's orphaned children, including Alfonso d'Avalos, the future marquess of Vasto. In December 1536, when Giovio was in Lombardy working on his *Histories*, "to Giovio's relief and pleasure, Alfonso d'Avalos became military governor of Milan, and he went to celebrate the Christmas holidays with him."

[10] The force that did eventually cross the French frontier (commanded by Count Henry of Nassau) became bogged down in an ultimately futile siege of Peronne: see Charles to Mary, 8 September 1536, Lanz, Letter 444, II, 259: in a passage underlined in the copy used by Lanz, which means it was probably in cipher in the original, Charles tells Mary that he understands that her "progress" was held up by the inability of "those of your finances" to procure funds, and that she and her councillors have done the best the could in trying to persuade the provincial states to approve a war subsidy.

[11] Santa Cruz, *Crónica del Emperador*, III, 398–399, my only source for this point, says that the force left at Turin included 4,500 Italian infantry under Giovanni Jacopo de Medici, marquess of Marignano; 900 lances (= 4,500 heavy cavalry) and some light horse, with artillery and munitions; and 15,000

remaining behind to keep the French garrison in Turin occupied, the various units in the imperial army, including *Landsknechte* recalled from the siege of Turin, began to break camp on 13 July. While the Spanish and Italian infantry and the artillery train descended the Ligurian Alps to embark on Doria's armada, the emperor and the rest of the army marched around to the north of Genoa, descending into the plain of Provence through the Col de Tende (25 July). Doria had in the meantime offloaded the artillery at Antibes, and the infantry he landed forced the submission of Grasse. When the whole army joined at Fréjus, it was a grand sight; as Vasto later told Giovio, "the emperor had never had such a large and well-equipped army in camp for war against another Christian power."[12]

Marching due west from Fréjus, the imperialists forced the surrender of Brignolles and, between Marseilles and Arles, set up camp at Aix-en-Provence, undefended. Only now did Charles and his commanders begin to appreciate the defensive measures put in place by Anne de Montmorency, constable of France. Montmorency had deliberately left Aix-en-Provence unprotected, because it could not support the 6,000 men he calculated were required to hold it. While units of the imperial army were assembling across the Alps, he had strengthened the fortifications of Marseilles and Arles, and of towns or castles guarding fords across the Rhône River. In areas where he knew the imperial army might pass, he forced peasants to migrate with their belongings into fortified centers, and dismantled every grain mill in sight. Finally, he concentrated his troops in a superbly constructed military camp at Avignon, bristling with artillery. Hence Charles bided his time at Aix, increasingly "inglorious" in the sight of his men, as Giovio says. The emperor himself went to inspect the defenses of Marseilles while Vasto did the same at Arles as Albanian light horse scouted the Rhône fords, but no one brought back encouraging news. Meanwhile, his men had bread to eat only because the Spaniards and Italians were able to fashion makeshift mills; the Germans, lacking beer, were getting sick on new wine made from young grapes. In getting supplies to the army (including beer) Doria's galleys were not as helpful as

Landsknechte under a German colonel he calls Castelalto (Hohenberg?). But his number for the *Landsknechte* at Turin is surely a mistake. Giovio, *Historiarum*, in *Opera*, IV, 356, says the army that crossed into Provence included "50 banners" of Germans, with each banner "somewhat less than 500 men." Santa Cruz gives a comparable figure for the army of Provence, 24,000 Germans. While it is true that Giovio does not mention "Castelalto" or his regiment in recounting the action in Provence, Santa Cruz was evidently thinking of the 15,000 *Landsknechte* Leyva had taken with him on setting out from Milan on 2 May (note 7). A force of 24,000 or 25,000 *Landsknechte* would have been larger than any yet mustered by Charles; that there were as many as 40,000 all told (eighty to 100 banners) is highly improbable.

12 Charles to Isabella, 18 April and 18 May 1536, *Corpus Documental*, Letters CXCVII and CCIV, I, 488–490, 503–504; Andelot to Ferdinand, 30–31 March 1536; Roland von Hemste to Charles, 7 April 1536, Lanz, Letters 422 and 423, II, 216–217, 218–219; and Giovio, *Historiarum*, in *Opera*, IV, 340–345, 351–357.

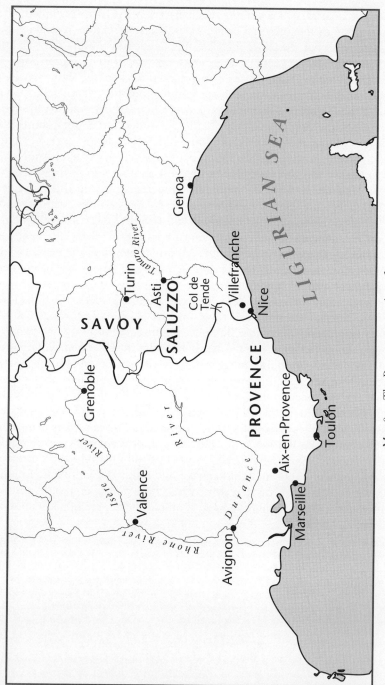

Map 8.1. The Provence campaign of 1536

Charles had hoped: bad weather prevented anchoring his ships at the point closest to Aix, and "brigands" made it necessary for each supply train to have a large escort. By 11 September Charles had decided to withdraw. His Lombard army had made some progress in Piedmont, and an attack on Genoa by pro-French exiles had been repulsed. But as the French soldier-diarist Blaise de Montluc put it, the emperor himself retired from France "with shame and loss."[13]

Another Maritime Crusade?

In October, some weeks before Charles took ship in Genoa for his return to Spain, the emperor's council of war was pessimistic: "Conscience bids us advise you of the great inconvenience of continuing this war" against France. Francis I would surely demand Milan for Angoulême, now his second son, and no prudent man could contradict the emperor if he insisted that giving the king Milan would merely enable him to cause more trouble. Yet Charles's lands were exhausted by war, and peace if it were possible could have many dividends, including a united Christian campaign against the Turks.[14] Back in Castile, a dispirited Charles seemed for some months less interested in European affairs than in conversations (possibly about The New World) with his chief geographer (*cosmografo mayor*) and later chronicler, Alonso de Santa Cruz.[15] Meanwhile, Francis I, in a solemn appearance before the Parlement of Paris, denounced Charles for his unilateral violations of the Treaty of Cambrai and reasserted France's ancient claim to the county of Flanders. Preoccupied with negotiations for subsidies from the Cortes of his Spanish realms, Charles left it to Mary to manage the war along the Low Countries frontier, and also to open diplomatic discussions, using their sister Eleanor (Francis's wife) as an intermediary. On the northern front, the ten-month armistice signed at Bomy (30 June 1537) followed a military stalemate, just as indecisive fighting in Piedmont led to the truce of Monzon (November 1537). Emissaries traveling back and forth between Paris and Monzon (meeting place of the Cortes of Aragón)

---

[13] Knecht, *Renaissance Warrior and Patron*, 334–338; Charles to Cifuentes (his ambassador in Rome), 31 August–5 September 1536, *Corpus Documental*, Letter CCXIII, I, 521–524; Charles to Henry of Nassau, 14 September 1536, Lanz, Letter 442, II, 248–252; Blaise Monluc, *The Habsburg-Valois Wars*, ed. Ian Roy (modernizing a 1674 translation of the *Commentaires*) (Hamden, Conn., 1972), 71.

[14] Memorandum of Charles's council (no names given), dated October 1536, Lanz, Letter 446, II, 263–267. For Brandi's comments, *Kaiser Karl V*, I, 327–328, and *Emperor Charles V*, 381–382. Wedgwood's "the sum of their arguments was gaseous and feeble" is a bit stronger than Brandi's "Wie das ganze Gutachten etwas Mattes hat."

[15] Cited by Fernández Alvárez, *Charles V*, 109–110. For Charles's concern about French intentions in the Indies (including the voyages of Jacques Cartier, 1534–1536), Charles to Mary, 27 April 1537, Lanz, Letter 670, II, 673: a plan for two armadas, one against Brittany, the other to defend the Indies.

raised the possibility of a face-to-face meeting between the sovereigns to seal a lasting agreement.

Meanwhile, the idea of a combined attack against the Turks was gaining ground in Italy, especially because Barbarossa's raid against Corfu (summer 1537), Venice's island fortress in the Aegean, had convinced the Serene Republic to break off its long-standing entente with the Sublime Porte. The announcement of a Holy League against the Ottomans (8 February 1538), involving Venice and the pope as well as the Habsburg brothers, put pressure on Francis to agree to the joint meeting at Nice (then in Genoese territory) proposed by Paul III. Shuttling between Charles and Francis, who did not see each other, the pope persuaded both to sign off on a ten-year truce (18 June 1538), leaving Milan and other issues unresolved. But Eleanor invited her brother to meet with her husband, and Charles enthusiastically accepted. Charles greeted Francis on board his imperial quadrireme at Aigues-Mortes (14 July) and went on land the next day to accept the king's hospitality. Leaving subordinates to work out the details, the two sovereigns agreed in general terms to a dual marriage, with Charles's son Philip to wed one of Francis's daughters, and Angoulême to wed a daughter or niece of Charles, with Milan as her dowry. Both monarchs were to combat heresy in their lands, and Francis pledged to join in a grand crusade against Christendom's Muslim foes.[16]

Anticipating a happy conclusion to his negotiations with France, Charles was already envisioning the grandest *empresa* of all. Next year, he had told ambassadors to his court convened for a special meeting (24 May 1538), he would lead an armada of 60,000 men and 200 ships (including 100 large caravels from the Low Countries) against Istanbul itself. But Barbarossa did not wait for Christian powers to mobilize their full strength. In June 1538, with ninety galleys and fifty smaller galiots, he sailed past the Gulf of Corinth, aiming for Corfu. Venice sent fifty-five galleys to defend the island, joined on June 17 by twenty-seven papal galleys. Neither side took decisive action, because if Babarossa landed on Corfu the men and cannon needed for an assault on the fortress, his own galleys would be vulnerable to attack by a smaller but better armed Christian fleet. When Doria arrived with forty-nine Genoese and Spanish galleys in early September (later than was agreed), the Christians had a numerical edge. But Barbarossa had retreated inside the Gulf of Prevesa, whose narrow entrance was covered from both sides by well-entrenched Ottoman artillery. There followed a period of futile negotiations; Barbarossa professed a willingness to change sides if given Tunis, but Doria had instructions to offer him anything but

[16] Knecht, *Renaissance Warrior and Patron*, 338–340; Brandi, *Emperor Charles V*, 384–390.

Tunis. The Christians then landed a sizable force but failed in three days of fighting to take the castle of Prevesa, guarding the north side of the entrance to the gulf. The Christian galleys now retreated, and as they broke formation while withdrawing, Barbarossa sallied forth to attack. Even though he did not do much damage, his escape from this indecisive engagement was a victory for Barbarossa; Venice's commanders were angry at Doria for not reforming to sail in pursuit of the smaller Turkish fleet.[17]

As in 1532, Doria instead turned north, to the Gulf of Valona, at the narrowest point of the Adriatic, where he left 3,500 Spaniards under *maestre de campo* Luis de Sarmiento to hold Castilnuovo. This fortress would have been a more strategic foothold in Ottoman Greece than Coron was, had it been held. The next summer, while Barbarossa blockaded Castilnuovo from the sea with the entire Ottoman fleet – 130 oared warships and 200 sail – Bazan Pasha encircled it from the landward side with 70,000 infantry and 10,000 skirmishers. Following Sarmiento's refusal of an honorable surrender, the battle lasted some five weeks, until the besiegers broke into a nearly flattened citadel on 6 August; few of the Spaniards were left alive, but according to Santa Cruz the victors lost 12,000 paid fighting men and 9,000 skirmishers.[18]

Charles had his mind not on Prevesa or Castilnuovo but on next year's campaign. In July 1538 he sent Mary two letters, one with instructions on requisitioning Low Countries caravels, the other, in cipher, revealing that he himself would command the great enterprise against Constantinople. Mary in response wrote what Brandi calls a magnificent letter, enclosing a memorandum setting forth her views in greater detail. The second of Charles's letters she had not dared to reveal, lest her council "despair" of the emperor's coming in person to address the urgent problems of his native country. Even if Charles were victorious, what would a single victory mean in this unending war? What if the Turks withdrew, refusing to offer battle? Where would the money come from, now that all Charles's lands were already at the point of exhaustion? And could he count on the acquiescence of Francis I, who still coveted Milan, or of supposed allies like

[17] Brandi, *Emperor Charles V*, 412–417; Guilmartin, *Gunpowder and Galleys*, 16–56. Some have thought it likely that Doria had similar contacts with the Porte, in light of the fact that the Ottomans neglected during Suleyman's reign to possess themselves of the weakly defended island of Chios, a key Genoese commercial outpost. But Guilmartin believes that the geography of the strait and Barbarossa's tactics are sufficient to account for Doria's decisions at Prevesa, without recourse to ulterior motives. When the news of Prevesa arrived in Spain, Salinas counted it as a victory for Doria, setting aside the sniping of the Venetians: to Castillejo, 26 November 1538, Rodríguez Villa, *El Emperador Carlos V*, Letter 374, p. 893.

[18] Santa Cruz, *Crónica del Emperador*, II, 529–530; III, 29–35.

the Venetians, "who are a republic, and thus inconstant in their policies, looking out only for their own interest"? And how would he answer to God for what might happen to his wife and children, and to the Christian religion, in the event of his defeat?[19]

Charles was not deterred. He renewed his orders for Mary to prepare the dispatch to Spain of a large fleet of Low Countries "hulks" (caravels). As he explained to her a few months later, he could "do no less," because the pope and Venice had pledged to meet in full their commitments "for the Levant." Because the destination of an expedition like this had to be kept secret, the preparations visible to observers occasioned anxiety. In Toledo, where Charles was meeting with the Cortes of Castile, Martín de Salinas knew of remittances to Doria and Vasto, and to Flanders for "munitions," and he presumably knew the purpose of these preparations. But in England, Henry VIII repeatedly inquired of Charles's ambassador why merchant ships were being fitted out with cannon in the Low Countries if Spain was their destination – was not Spain itself well supplied with munitions? In the province of Holland, where many of the ships being requisitioned had their home ports, his majesty's faithful servitor, the president of the council of Holland, thought that England, rather than Spain, might be the real objective, but he added that such matters were "beyond my understanding, just like theology." Holland's fleet of requisitioned merchant ships fitted out for war did indeed sail in March 1539, only to be recalled in April. Mary sent word to Charles that Francis I had let it be known that he could not stand idly by if the emperor were to strengthen his position by a successful campaign against the sultan.[20] This was not after all to be the year of the grand *empresa*.

---

[19] Mary to Charles, 10 August 1538, Lanz, Letter 459, II, 289, with *Staatspapiere*, Document LIV, dated August 1538, pp. 263–268. Brandi, *Emperor Charles V*, 412–414: "Style and orthography both betray [the memorandum in question] as her personal work."

[20] Charles's instructions for Bossu's mission to Mary, September 1538, Lanz, Letter 709, II, 685; Charles to Mary, 5 December 1538, Aud. 52, 225–238; Salinas to Castillejo, from Toledo, 26 November 1538, Rodríguez Villa, *El Emperador Carlos V*, Letter 375, p. 896 (I take it that his reference to the "eclipse" that now darkens the skies is literal, not metaphorical); Eustache Chapuys (Charles's ambassador in England) to Charles, 9 January 1539, Lanz, Letter 465, II, 304 (cf. Knecht, *Renaissance Warrior and Patron*, 388). Mary and her council, instructions for the mission of Bossu and Meester Vincent Corneliszoon to Lord Gerrit van Assendelft and his colleagues on the Council of Holland, 6 November 1538, Aud. 1533, 77–80, calling for a fleet of seventy ships from Holland and ten from Zeeland to be ready to sail for Gibraltar by mid-December for a certain *"emprinse"* of his majesty. Assendelft to the *Stadtholder* of Holland, Antoine de Lalaing, count of Hoogstraten, 15 December 1538 (Aud. 1527, 82–83), 1 January (Aud. 1528, 245–246), 28 January (Aud. 1532, 48–50), 12 February (Aud. 1532, 236–237), and 9 March 1539 (Aud. 1531, 1–2). On the sailing of Holland's ships and their recall, Dirk Wouters (sheriff of Texel) to Assendelft, 21 March 1539, and [Hoogstraten?] to Mary of Hungary, 17 April 1539 (Aud. 1528, 1–2). Fernández Alvárez, *Charles V*, 113.

The Problem of Ghent

Soon Charles was mourning the loss of his wife Isabella, who died (1 May 1539) of complications following the birth of a child who predeceased her. He was not to marry again. But matters of state, including the problem that Mary and her council "despaired" of solving without the emperor's presence, left little time for grieving. In 1537 Ghent, the largest city in Flanders, had balked at paying its share of a war subsidy, claiming not to be bound by majority rule – that is, the affirmative votes of the other three "members" of Flanders.[21] While Mary worked for a negotiated settlement, local politicians, appealing to the hatred of taxation that was especially strong among the craft guilds, pushed Ghent into open rebellion, seeking help from France (albeit in vain) against its Habsburg overlord. Knowing that Charles had to tend to his affairs in the Low Countries, Francis I invited him to travel through France as a welcome visitor, so as to avoid the perils of a sea voyage. Charles accepted, and was royally feted in one town after another as he made his way from Bayonne to St. Quentin (27 November 1539–20 January 1540). Only the lingering issue of Milan obstructed amity between the monarchs. Charles wanted Francis's younger son to marry one of his own daughters, with the Netherlands as her dowry, but Francis insisted on a marriage with one of Ferdinand's daughters, with Milan as her dowry. Ominously, when neither side changed its position, discussions eventually broke off (June 1540).[22]

In February, the appearance before its gates of 2,000 Spaniards of the emperor's guard, plus 3,000 Germans recruited for the occasion, led Ghent to surrender. More than fifty burghers were placed under arrest, and sixteen were beheaded for treason. Charles pardoned the citizenry as a whole only after hundreds of them came to kneel before the emperor, loudly crying "Mercy!" Having ordered the carefully guarded original copies of the city's precious privileges brought before him, Charles temporarily annulled all of them; some he never restored – in particular, the privilege of the craft guilds to provide from their ranks one of the "members" or colleges of magistrates whose approval was required for taxation. He also required Ghent to pay for construction within its walls of a new fortress, to be garrisoned by the emperor's men. A member of Charles's entourage writing to Spain described his retribution on Ghent as "so severe and of

---

[21] The Four Members were the cities of Bruges, Ghent, and Ypres, and a federation of small towns and castleries known as the Franc of Bruges. They represented what might be called the third estate in Flanders, save that neither the nobles nor the clergy had any formal representation in Flanders. See Chapter 12.

[22] Brandi, *Emperor Charles V*, 417–420; N. Maddens, "De opstandige houding van Gent tijdens de regeering van Keizer Karel," *Appeltjes uit het Meetjesland* 28 (1977): 203–229; Knecht, *Renaissance Warrior and Patron*, 389–394.

such authority in these lands that one has not seen its like even in Constantinople." This comparison with the Grand Turk offers an interesting sidelight into the thought-world of Charles's advisers. Giovio believed the treatment of Ghent to be a calculated act of severity, meant to cow Charles's other dominions, all groaning under heavy taxation.[23] One must be skeptical about whether the real burden of taxation was heavier than it was under Charles's predecessors. But it seems the punishment of Ghent did indeed have an effect – salutary from Charles's perspective – on the willingness of Low Countries towns and provinces to cooperate with the government's fiscal demands (see Chapter 12).

Theological Compromise?

Charles spent the balance of 1540 "visiting" the Low Countries provinces and catching up with news from Germany. The previous year, Ferdinand had sponsored negotiations at Frankfurt between leading princes of the Schmalkaldic League and representatives of the two Habsburg brothers, with a papal legate looking on. The resulting Frankfurt Agreement (19 April 1539) gave the league security guarantees sufficient to clear the way for agreement on a diet that would consider the Turkish military threat (to be held at Worms in May) and a second diet, set for Nuremberg in August, to resume the discussions of a possible theological compromise, broken off after the 1530 Diet of Augsburg. The results of these assemblies were disappointing, but Ferdinand came to Ghent (February 1540) to urge upon Charles the urgency of continuing efforts to find a settlement. At the same time, the pope's nephew and legate to Brussels, Cardinal Alessandro Farnese, was warning the emperor against open-ended discussions with Protestant heretics. Even though renewed discussions among the German estates at Hagenau (June 1540) were again fruitless, Charles accepted Ferdinand's view of the matter. He named Granvelle his representative to the next diet, set for Worms in November, with "full powers" to conclude an agreement on his behalf. Working behind the scenes, Granvelle enlisted men of irenic temper for a secret colloquy, to work out contentious issues in private, removed from the argus-eyed scrutiny of theologians on both sides who feared compromising essential doctrines.[24] As discussions moved on to

---

[23] Pedro Giron, *Crónica del Emperador Carlos V* (Madrid, 1964), 346–355; Charles to Tavera, 31 May 1540, *Corpus Documental*, Letter CCXXXVIII, II, 66; Zimmerman, *Paolo Giovio*, 171. Burghers of Ghent still commemorate the day when their forebears were made to walk barefoot, with nooses around their necks, to implore the emperor's pardon: see the picture in Burke, "Presenting and Re-Presenting Charles V," 475.

[24] Granvelle picked four theologians personally interested in compromise: Martin Bucer, the leading Protestant preacher of Strasbourg; Wolfgang Capito, a preacher at the court of Landgrave Philip of Hesse (currently estranged from other leaders of the Schmalkaldic League because of a recently

another diet at Regensburg, Charles reported to Ferdinand that Granvelle and his carefully chosen committee had made progress; he enclosed the Latin text of a hard-won consensus on the doctrine of original sin.[25]

Both Charles and the papal legate, Cardinal Gasparo Contarini of Venice, were in Regensburg well before the opening of the next and final diet of the series, Charles to ease the fears of Protestant princes, Contarini to stiffen the resolve of Catholics. Granvelle's committee, now with the formal approval of the diet, continued its work. When the conferees struck agreement on the crucial issue of justification, Regensburg's magistrates had the church bells rung in celebration. But other issues proved intractable.[26] The final parting of the ways came when Contarini insisted that Catholic conferees retain the term "transsubstantiation" (to which Protestants vehemently objected) as a proper way of describing how bread and wine are transformed into the body and blood of Christ in the sacrament of the Eucharist. Charles summoned the legate to his quarters (15 May), demanding to know if peace among Christians must really be held hostage to a single word. Contarini stood firm: it had been so also in the ancient church, torn apart over the vital assertion in the Nicene Creed (325) that God the Son is "consubstantial" with God the Father.[27] Although there was not to be a grand compromise, Charles stayed on in Regensburg in order to salvage something from the months of negotiation. The best he could get was an agreement (29 July) whereby the Protestant estates accepted assurances about their freedom to interpret as they wished language on which the Catholic estates had insisted. If nothing else, Charles would not have to worry about a possible religious war in Germany while he tended to other affairs.[28]

---

disclosed bigamous marriage); the Louvain theologian Geraard Veltwijk, a protégé of Granvelle; and Johann Gropper of Cologne, who had befriended Bucer during public colloquies sponsored by peace-minded German princes. Using articles drafted by Gropper, the four men agreed by 31 December on a text covering key disputed points. At Regensburg, Granvelle had a revised version of this text presented to the full committee (including two who could only suspect whence it had come, Philip Melanchthon and Johann Eck) as the "basis for discussion" decreed by the emperor.

25 Peter Matheson, *Cardinal Contarini at Regensburg* (Oxford, 1972), 10–35; Cornelis de Schepper to Granvelle, Brussels, 26 October 1540, relaying Charles's instructions, in Brandi, "Aus den Kubinettsakten des Kaisers," "Berichte," XIX, Document IV, 229–238; Charles to Ferdinand, 3 January 1541, Estado 638, 209 (for the Latin text of the article on original sin, folio 206), and a very similar if not identical letter, Charles to Ferdinand, 22 January 1541, HHSA-B, 4 (alt 5).

26 With regard to the infallibility of the doctrinal decrees of ecumenical councils of the church, Catholics could not imagine a church that did not have authority to interpret scripture, while Protestants could not imagine one that did.

27 Matheson, *Contarini at Regensburg*, 97–135; Charles to Tavera, 7 May 1541, Estado 638, 81, enclosing a copy of the articles agreed to on original sin and on faith and works, "que son dos puntes de las mas principales."

28 Matheson, *Contarini at Regensburg*, 136–170.

Algiers

For both Charles and Ferdinand, the discussions at Regensburg were a means to achieve unity among Christian powers for the larger struggle against the Turk.[29] For Ferdinand, the field of struggle lay to the east, where the recent death of his rival for the Hungarian throne, Janos Szapolyai, presented new opportunities. With the help of influential former supporters of Szapolyai, he hoped to gain control of the royal city of Buda, held by Szapolyai's widow for her infant son. Charles had no interest in a forward policy in Hungry – in fact, he got Ferdinand to promise to rely on diplomacy in dealing with the Ottomans. But the King of the Romans was not without resources of his own. The troops he sent in the fall of 1540 succeeded in taking the merchant town of Pest, on the opposite bank of the Danube, but in renewed fighting the next year they failed through sheer incompetence to break through Buda's defenses. As Charles left Regensburg in August 1541, it was known that Sultan Suleyman was leading an army into Hungary to exact vengeance. But as Charles admitted to Mary, he lacked the resources to mobilize a force fit to meet his adversary. In Genoa, he learned the Turks had taken both Pest and Buda – a disaster comparable with the debacle at Mohács in 1526; the Ottomans would henceforth rule central Hungary for over 150 years. But the emperor resisted entreaties from Doria and Pope Paul III to take the troops he was mobilizing back across the Alps to Hungary. His mind was fixed on Algiers.[30]

Charles had spent much of his time in Regensburg corresponding with officials in Spain and Italy about the coming naval campaign.[31] His thinking seems to have been shaped by a long communication from Doria, delivered orally by Francisco Duarte, who arrived in Regensburg on or about 1 March. Having sifted information from Venice and Ragusa (Dubrovnik) as well as from freed Spanish captives recently returned from Istanbul, Doria expected a great Turkish armada to sail from the Dardanelles that summer, perhaps 150 galleys. Pedro de Toledo, viceroy of Naples, should be encouraged to relocate civilians from undefended points along the

[29] Some Christian rulers (like Poland's King Zygmunt I, d. 1548) saw a difference between the interests of Christendom and Habsburg interests in Hungary, where Janos Szapolyai's claim to the crown was backed (against Ferdinand) by the Ottomans: Zygmunt Wojciechowski, *Zygmunt Stary (1506–1548)* (Warsaw, 1979), especially chaps. 2, 5, 8, 12, 13, and 15.

[30] Géza Perjés, *The Fall of the Medieval Kingdom of Hungary: Mohács 1526–Buda 1541*, tr. Márió D. Fenyö, *War and Society in Central Europe*, vol. XXVI (Boulder, Colo., 1989), 155–167; Fichtner, *Ferdinand I of Austria*, 118–128; Charles to Tavera, 4 February 1541, Estado 638, 66; Charles's instructions for Praet's mission to Mary, Innsbruck, 6 August 1541, "Berichte," IX, Document VII, 241–250 (discussed by Brandi, *Emperor Charles V*, 454); Giovio, *Historiarum*, in *Opera*, V, 65. Villegagnon, *Caroli V Imperatoris Expeditio*, Aii, for Charles's meeting with Paul III.

[31] E.g., Charles to Tavera, 4, 25 February 1541, Estado 638, 66, 72–73.

Adriatic coast and concentrate them in well-fortified towns like Otranto and Brindisi. Similarly, key points in Sicily could be strengthened by the transfer of Spanish troops from garrison duty in North Africa, where they were less needed. Provided that these defensive precautions were taken, Doria proposed that Christian naval forces take the offensive. The fifty to sixty galleys of Charles and his allies in Italy (including Doria's) should rendezvous at Messina or perhaps Brindisi, ready to sail "wherever they can do the most good for your majesty's service." Similarly, because recent losses suffered by Barbarossa diminished the threat to the Iberian coast, the galley fleet now commanded by Bernardino de Mendóza should take up station in Catalonia, to go wherever Charles saw the need.[32]

If the fleet was to rendezvous at Messina or especially Brindisi, Doria can only have been thinking of a campaign in the eastern Mediterranean, as in 1532 and 1538. As is evident also from his just-mentioned recommendation that Charles give priority to Hungary in 1541, the Genoese admiral believed that Christian forces ought to strike at the Grand Turk on his home ground, one way or another; this had been the consistent aim of Europe's fourteenth- and fifteenth-century crusades. But for those primarily concerned with the defense of Spain, Sicily, and Naples, this traditional strategy failed to reckon with the fact that Turkish naval power, under Barbarossa's command, was now on the rise in the western Mediterranean as well. In fact, Doria's long message to Charles makes clear that he understood the concerns of his peers in the complicated administrative hierarchy of the Habsburg Mediterranean. Because the best defense is a good offense, Doria asked Charles's permission to pick twenty-five or thirty-five of the best galleys, to sail to the Dardanelles at the beginning of April and "block the channels so the armada of the Turk cannot accomplish what he thinks it will."[33] So as not to have things tied up in endless objections, he also suggested short-cutting official procedures. The 3,000 Spanish infantry based in Monastir (North Africa) should be transferred to Sicily "without the need for further memoranda [*consultas*] on this subject." Ferrante Gonzaga, viceroy of Sicily (1537–1547), should be instructed to have large quantities of biscuit ready at Messina and Palermo for the needs of the armada, "without the need for sending again to consult with your majesty." Similarly, Pedro de Toledo should have

---

[32] Duarte's long oral report is transcribed in Estado 638, 78ff. See especially paragraphs 1–5, 7, 9, 13, 20, 27, and 28.

[33] Ibid., paragraph 13: "las galeras de vuestra magestad [i.e., those in Italy] de necesidad han de andare este verano por Pulla [Apulia], y podria ser que conveniesse pasar con ellas la vuelta de Levante." Doria also asked Charles's permission to pick twenty-five or thirty galleys, "las mejor en horden y mas legeras," and sail at the beginning of April "hasta la canal de Constantinopla," in order to "dilatar y estorvar que el armada del Turco no haga los efetos que piensa hazer." In its naval wars against the Ottomans, Venice had on occasion blocked the Dardanelles in this way.

biscuit in Otranto and Brindisi; "he will say that he is not bound to provide the said biscuit, but you should command him in such a way that he does it."[34]

On 3 March, citing Doria's advice, Charles sent Tavera and the Council of Castile instructions to have Castile's galleys ready to sail "wherever they can do the most good." But two months later (7 May), in an apparent concession to the concerns of Tavera and his colleagues, he wrote that he was having Martín Alonso de los Ríos, a loyal Castilian, "find out more" about what Doria had proposed through Duarte. On 31 May he wrote to Tavera that Algiers would be the target of the enterprise and that he himself would command; the combined fleet would sail not from Messina or Brindisi, but from Naples. The departure date was fixed for September, "the best time of year" for an attack of this kind. Only now was a copy of "the *paracer* of Prince Doria" sent to Tavera, carried by the same Martín Alonso de los Ríos. The same day Charles sent a copy of this letter and its enclosures with a message in cipher to the trusted Cobos: even though he doubted not that the archbishop of Toledo would loyally carry out his instructions, "I cannot fail to charge you in particular" to see that he did so.[35]

Charles does not say why September was "the best time of year," and there were those among his commanders, Doria included, who thought that such a plan risked disaster in a Mediterranean known for its fierce autumn storms. Because the protracted negotiations at Regensburg kept the emperor in Germany longer than expected, Doria wrote in July urging that the whole expedition be put off until the following year. But Charles did not accept the admiral's warnings, either now, or in Genoa in September. Why had he chosen so late a date to sail? John Guilmartin has worked out a plausible answer to this question. For expeditions during the sailing season, the attackers needed extra men and artillery to defend against a possible relief fleet sent by the sultan; in September, they need only bring the men and armaments required for an assault on their target.[36] In fact,

[34] Ibid., paragraphs 5, 9, and 13. For ill will between Doria (who in Naples was the prince of Melfi) and Pedro de Toledo, see Morial, *El Virrey de Napoles*, 102–105, and Chapter 13.

[35] Charles to Tavera, 3 March, 7 and 31 May 1541, Estado 638, 77, 81, 95–96; Charles to Cobos, 31 May 1541, Estado 638, 93–94.

[36] Pacini, *La Genova dell'Andrea Doria nell'impero di Carlo V*, 427; Guilmartin, *Gunpowder and Galleys*, 77–78. A precedent for this strategy may be seen in Doria's assault on Monastir in the late summer of 1539, as described by Santa Cruz, *Crónica del Emperador*, IV, 70–76: with fifty-one galleys (the combined fleets of Naples and Sicily as well as Doria's), forty-five sailing ships, and twenty-five companies of infantry (perhaps 7,500 men), Doria sailed from Messina in September, captured Monastir, and helped Charles's ally, Mulay Hassan, king of Tunis, take two other cities. The *proveedor general de la flota* on this expedition was Francisco Duarte, who brought Doria's long oral message to the emperor in March 1541.

Charles seems to have been determined to repeat his success at Tunis, but at a lower cost, because he would be carrying fewer soldiers. He also intended to spare the treasury of Castile as much as possible. In the same letter of 31 May, he assured Tavera that the expense of this *empresa* would mainly be borne by Naples and Sicily.

In June or July Charles's staff in Regensburg calculated the sums that would be needed for the *Landsknechte* the emperor planned to take with him, and the Italians to be recruited south of the Alps.[37] Ferrante Gonzaga, viceroy of Sicily, was to mobilize at Naples the galleys of Sicily and Naples, plus troop and supply ships for men from Spanish garrisons. Castile's galleys, commanded by Bernardino de Mendóza, were to escort the troop and supply ships arriving at Cártagena (from northern Spain and from the Low Countries). Embarkation was complicated by a rush of gentlemen volunteers paying their own way, like Hernán Cortés, the conqueror of Mexico. The number of ships involved would match or exceed totals for the Tunis expedition, but the total number of infantry they carried was noticeably smaller, apparently (as noted) because there was no need for men to defend against a counterattack from the sea. This decision as to timing reduced the cost of the enterprise, but, in a Mediterranean known for severe autumn storms, it also left a dangerously narrow margin for delay.

On 15 June Charles wrote Tavera that all elements of the armada must be ready for an 8 September sailing date. On 5 July, having consulted with Doria on a report from Venice that the Turkish war fleet would be larger than expected, Charles announced to Tavera that rather than massing the fleet at Naples, as was originally planned, he would sail west from Genoa and launch the *empresa* from Spanish waters. In effect, Charles would be shielding Spain while preparing for his attack on Algiers. This meant that Mendóza should bring Castile's galleys to join the emperor not at Naples but at Genoa. But Mendóza never got to Genoa. Charles's letter of 5 July crossed with one from Tavera reporting that consideration of emperor's "honor" required the council to send Castile's galleys to North Africa; a ship carrying long-overdue wages for the garrison at Oran had been taken by the enemy, and the recent mutiny of an unpaid garrison at Bona (Anaba) showed that such matters could not be taken lightly. Cobos kept Charles informed of the Castilian galley fleet's movements, and in early August sent assurances that Mendóza would be at Genoa without fail by the end of the month.

But the collecting of troop and supply ships at Málaga was not going well. Sailing vessels were slow to arrive from northern Spain and the Low Countries; as at Barcelona in 1535, more ships were needed than had been planned for, owing to the influx of Spanish gentlemen and their retainers,

---

[37] "Lo que es menester aqui en Alemana antes de la partida," Estado 638, 98.

all clamoring for the honor of accompanying the emperor on his *empresa*. Preparation of biscuit was stalled by a shortage of flour. Sicily's government had not released for export to Spain the quantities of grain that were promised; even in time of war Charles could not override what his officials perceived as the vital interests of the lands entrusted to them. Meanwhile, famine in Málaga's hinterland forced a shift to Cártagena as the port of muster. These difficulties seem to have been real enough, but the council also had to defend itself against a charge of foot dragging: we [the council] have not attempted to dissuade your majesty from this *empresa*, Tavera wrote on 24 August, but have merely pointed out difficulties due to lack of time, lack of support from the Italian realms, and lack of ships. Mendóza and his galleys made it as far as La Palma in Majorca, possibly en route to Genoa, but were recalled to Cártagena, apparently because it was considered dangerous to send out a fleet of sail unprotected by the swifter galleys.[38]

Having finally departed from Regensburg in early August, Charles of necessity followed the longer eastern route to Italy, through Austrian lands to the Brenner Pass to Trent; western passes were held by Swiss Protestants, or by the French occupying Savoy. This meant that he and the *Landsknechte* he brought with him had to march across the breadth of Lombardy to reach Genoa. En route, he detoured for a few days to meet with Pope Paul III, in a vain effort to persuade the pontiff that the Council of the Church he planned should be convened on German soil. By the time he got to Genoa, Doria's opinion that the season was now too far advanced to launch the great *empresa* was seconded by others with experience of the sea. But as Charles notes in his memoirs, the money already spent would have been wasted if he did not go forward, trusting in God's help. With "thirty-six long ships" (galleys, including Doria's) Charles sailed from the Genoese port of La Spezia on 27 September and reached La Palma by way of Corsica and Sardinia, with a few days more delay because of an attack of the gout. Ferrante Gonzaga with more galleys – enough to make 50 in

[38] Charles to Tavera,15 June 1541, 5 July 1541, Estado 638, 109–110, 123–124; Tavera to Charles, 6 July 1541, Estado 51, 31–33; on the mutiny at Bona, Charles to Tavera, 7 May 1541, Estado, 638, 81; on Bernardino de Mendoza's voyage to North Africa, Cobos to Vazquez, 9, 24 August 1541, Estado 51, 142, 78–80, and Tavera to Charles, 24 August 1541, Estado 51, 40–43 (this is also the letter in which Tavera defends the council against the charge of foot dragging, referring to Charles's letter of 1 August). On problems at Málaga and Cártagena, Cobos to Charles, 30 July, 9 August 1541, Estado 51, 130, 142, the *proveedores* of the fleet at Malaga to Charles, 21 August 1541, and Tavera to Charles, 16 October 1541, Estado 51, 221, 135–141 (p. 12). Tavera's letter of 24 August also says that still more ships will be needed, since Mendoza's galleys will not accompany the fleet as it sails from Cártagena. Vazquez to Cobos, Palma de Mallorca, 15 October, reports on the movement of Charles's fleet since his sailing from La Spezia, and notes that Mendoza with his galleys was at Palma but has returned to Cártagena: *Calendar of Letters, Despatches and State Papers, Relating to Negotiations between Spain and England*, 6:1, 371–374.

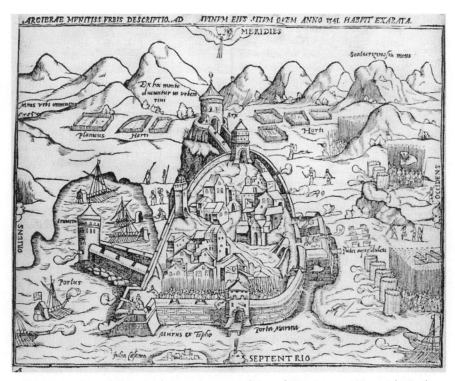

Figure 8.1. *Siege of Algiers*, in the 1555 Antwerp edition of *Historiarum sui Temporis* by Paolo Giovio, University of Minnesota Library

all – and about 140 troop and supply ships was already anchored off La Palma. But Bernardino de Mendóza was nowhere to be seen. After a few days, a galley got through with the message that Mendóza, with the combined Spanish fleet, had been at Ibiza for ten days, trying in vain to make headway for Mallorca against contrary winds. Charles sent word that Castile's fleet should make directly for Algiers. On 20 October Mendóza's galleys, with approximately 100 troop and supply ships in their train, joined the rest of the armada offshore from Algiers.[39] For the better part of two days, storms prevented the offloading of men and supplies.

[39] Charles to Tavera, 5 July 1541, Estado 638, 123–124; Charles's instructions for Praet's mission to Mary, 6 August 1541, "Berichte," XIX, Document VII; Tavera to Charles, 21 September 1541, Estado 51, 133; Villegagnon, *Caroli V Imperatoris Expeditio*, Aiii–Aiv: I follow Villegagnon in saying that Charles sailed with thirty-six galleys (Santa Cruz gives the same number), and that Gonzaga had another fourteen or so galleys plus 140 troop and freight ships, but not in his statements that the emperor sailed from Porto Venere, and that Spain's fleet went on to Africa on its own (Spain's authorities would not likely take such a step without orders from Charles); Charles to Diego Hurtado de Mendóza, 2 November 1541, *Corpus Documental*, Letter CCLXI, I, 71–75.

Late on 22 October, the infantry began landing at the point about seven miles east of Algiers chosen by Doria. The next day the men were building three camps "according to nations," with the Italians closest to shore and the Spaniards occupying the lower slopes of a ridge of hills dominating the shore line. During the day the Spaniards drove off tribesmen showering them with arrows, and occupied the heights within sight of the city, while the Italians repelled a fierce attack on a stone bridge connecting the sites chosen for the Italian and German encampments. All was now ready for offloading the artillery and supplies that would permit bombardment of the city to begin. But that night there arose a storm of uncommon ferocity, known in later centuries to local people as "the wind of Charles." During the next day (24 October) ships were either broken to pieces as they rode in the water, or broke their anchor cables and were dashed against the rocks; the "Numidians" (as Villegagnon calls them) cut down many soldiers and seamen trying to save themselves in the water. When it was over, 140 sailing ships and 15 galleys were lost, and with them much of the artillery and much of the biscuit. As the diminished force moved further east to another point chosen by Doria, Charles ordered that the horses be slaughtered to feed his men. Some in the council of war (among them Hernán Cortés) argued that Algiers, with its small garrison, could still be taken, but Charles gave heed this time to the voice of prudence and ordered a withdrawal.[40] This was to be the emperor's last crusade.

Sinews of War

To judge from information provided by Charles's correspondence,[41] Giovio,[42] and Santa Cruz,[43] the army that he assembled to invade France

---

[40] Giovio, *Historiarum*, in *Opera*, V, 77–82; Villegagnon, *Caroli V Imperatoris Expeditio*, Bii-verso; Charles to Hurtado de Mendóza, 2 November 1541, cited in note 39, Ernle Bradford, *The Sultan's Admiral: The Life of Barbarossa* (New York, 1968), 188–189 ("Charles's wind").

[41] Charles to Isabella, 18 April 1536, *Corpus Documental*, Letter CXCVII, I, 489–490: for the campaign in Provence, he has taken with him on the march north an unnamed number of Spaniards (presumably the Naples garrisons), 3,000 Italian light horse, and 6,000 to 7,000 Italian infantry, and he can raise 5,000 to 6,000 more around Florence, the best recruiting ground in Italy. Leyva at Milan has 2,000 Spaniards plus "10,000 good Germans," 4,000 more are on the way, and he has sent orders to raise as many as 25,000 more; he also expects 3,000 heavy cavalry from Germany and the Low Countries.

[42] *Historiarum*, in *Opera*, IV, 356–357: Doria loaded the Italian troops under the prince of Salerno (number not given) on the galleys at Savona; by land came the heavy cavalry, under Maximiliaan van Buren, count of IJsselstein; the light horse, led by Ferrante Gonzaga; the Italian and Spanish heavy cavalry, led by Fernando Alvárez de Toledo, third duke of Alba; 8,000 Spaniards, and fifty banners of German infantry. Giovio says the banners of Germany infantry had fewer than 500 men, but on the basis of other sources in the same period I count them as 400 men each.

[43] *Crónica del Emperador*, III, 387–398: in Provence, Charles had 24,000 German infantry, 10,000 Spaniards, 15,500 Italians, 2,450 light horse, and 2,300 lances of heavy cavalry – 100 Burgundian, 900 German, and 600 Spanish. Quatrefages, "L'organisation militaire de l'Espagne," 437–438, confirms

was indeed, as Vasto told Giovio, the largest he had yet brought together, even without counting the men left behind to keep the Turin garrison busy as part of the emperor's campaign. In Provence, Charles had at least 20,000 *Landsknechte* and 8,000 Spaniards, as well as 15,500 Italians, perhaps 5,000 of whom were unpaid "adventurers,"[44] plus 2,450 light horse, and 2,300 "lances" or 11,500 heavy cavalry – 500 Burgundian, 8,000 German, and 3,000 Spanish and Italian. This number of heavy cavalry, unusually large for Charles's armies, were no doubt required as part of a plan to ravage enemy country as far and wide as possible,[45] but they served little purpose as things turned out, because Montmorency's defenses hemmed them in a part of France, bounded by the Rhône and the Saône, that was already devastated by his scorched-earth policy. For a campaign of five months, if we assume that the men were recruited in June and dismissed in October, wages for these troops would have amounted to 1,054,000 Spanish ducats.[46] Adding in 20% for victuals, officers' pay, and the artillery and baggage trains (210, 800), pay for fifty galleys[47] for five months (125,000), and Charles's house-hold expenses for a year (125,000), this ill-planned and futile campaign will have cost the emperor and his realms something like 1,514,800 ducats.

Between 7 May and 5 August, Charles ordered further sequestrations of Indies gold and silver totaling 304,000 ducats. The clamor of merchants who had been promised there would be no more sequestrations – not stilled by Isabella's claim that the money was needed for debts from the Crusade against Tunis as well as for the war with France – was loud enough to prevent Charles from expecting to obtain more by this means. In any case the 304,000 ducats was only part of the money sent in specie to Italy for this campaign: on 19 May Rodrigo Valenzuela arrived in Genoa with 3,000 Spanish infantry and 408,500 scudi (381,253 ducats). Meanwhile, the emperor's men in Genoa had to resort to the usual desperate measures

Santa Cruz', figure of 10,000 Spanish infantry, but I use Giovio's lower numbers, for the Germans also.

[44] Giovio (*Historiarum* in *Opera*, IV, 356) says Charles's Spanish infantry was outnumbered by the Italians, "qui praeter descriptos conductosque stipendio, voluntariam et liberam praedae spe militiam sequebantur." Santa Cruz's list of the 15,500 Italians (*Crónica del Emperador*, III 399) looks like a roster of the army of Naples, save for the first entry: Colonel Fabricio Maramaldo with 10,000 men. In 1527 Maramaldo's company of 2,000 volunteers was notorious for its part in the Sack of Rome; to Pope Calement VII's displeasure, the company participated also in the siege of Florence: Guicciardini, *History of Italy*, 426, 429. I assume half of Maramaldo's men in Provence were unpaid "adventurers."

[45] See note 10.

[46] According to the formula I am using for estimating the wages of *Landsknechte*, the rate for 1536 would be 4.1 ducats per month, meaning a cost of 410,000 for 20,000 men for five months. For other units I use the same figures as in Chapter 7 for the 1535 Tunis campaign. Thus 18,500 Spanish and Italian infantry for five months at 3.4 ducats a month would be 314,500; 2,450 light horse at 4 ducats a month would be 49,000; 8,000 German heavy cavalry at 5 ducats a month would be 200,000; and 3,500 Spanish and Low Countries cavalry at 4.6 ducats would be 80,500.

[47] This is Santa Cruz's figure.

to keep troops on the payroll; Doria at one time put up the family silver as security for a short-term loan, while Figueroa had to find 8,000
ducats "among friends." Once Valenzuela's fleet had arrived, negotiations
with Genoa's great bankers were a bit easier. After meeting personally
with Charles at Sarzana, outside Genoa, Adamo Centurione and Ansaldo
Grimaldi signed *asientos* for 100,000 and 200,000 scudi respectively. For
added security, however, both men demanded *juros* at 6.25% interest, with
a capital value equal to the face value of their loans, plus interest – that
is, 144,000 ducats for Centurione (22%), and 230,000 ducats for Grimaldi
(23%). Grimaldi had permission to market his *juro* as of 1 January 1537 if his
loan had not been repaid, with interest, as of the previous October. He also
forced Tomasso Fornari to promise on the emperor's behalf that Charles
would not contract *asientos* with any other banker for two months.[48] This
clause, in fact, restricted Charles's ability to borrow, but in the end, between 12 April and 5 September 1536, he and his officials contracted nine
loans (including the two just mentioned) totaling 915,198 ducats.

Finally, because many of the Spanish and Italian fighting men in his camp
were on the payroll of Naples, one may assume the kingdom made a substantial contribution to the Provence campaign. While in Naples, Charles
convened a Parlamento that agreed to a *donativo* of unprecedented size:
1 million scudi or Neapolitan ducats, to be collected over a period of five
years. By "anticipating" a parliamentary grant of this kind through bankers'
loans, the treasury could have as much as 60% of the face value available
for *cambi* or transfers outside the kingdom.[49] Because Charles asked for
the money to retire the kingdom's old debts as well as for his coming war
against France, it seems reasonable to think that roughly half of the available money went for each of the two purposes, meaning about 300,000
scudi (280,000 ducats) for Provence. In all, he will have had something like
1,576,000 ducats available for the war against France: the 381,000 ducats
brought by Valenzuela, including money from the 300,000 ducats in sequestrations, charged to Castile's long-term debt; about 915,000 in bankers'
loans, charged to Castile's high-interest short-term debt; and 280,000 from
Naples. Already in April he was asking Isabella to send 300,000 or 400,000
in specie to meet his anticipated engagements to lenders, but the 300,000
did not arrive until September; in the end, several of these war loans could
not be repaid by Castile's treasury until 1541 or 1542.[50]

* * *

[48] Pacini, *La Genova dell'Andrea Doria nell'impero di Carlo V*, 358–370.

[49] For details of this and other *donativi*, see Chapter 13.

[50] Carande Thobar, *Carlos V y sus banqueros*, III, 175–179, and loans 112–121, III, 226–228; Charles
to Isabella, 18 April 1536 (asking for the money to be spent in connection with his negotiations
with the Genoese banker, Ansaldo Grimaldi, see nos. 115–117 in the Carande Thobar series), and
8 September 1536, *Corpus Documental*, Letters CXCVII and CCXIV, I, 486–487, 528, and Charles
to Nassau, 14 September 1536, Lanz, Letter 442, II, 248–252.

The size of the force Charles took to Algiers can be estimated from a planning document prepared for the emperor while still at Regensburg,[51] and from the accounts of Giovio, Villegagnon,[52] and Santa Cruz. The planning document does not mention infantry from Spain, and the 3,000 men who arrived with Valenzuela in May (as noted earlier) may have been meant as replacements for veterans from the Italian garrisons embarking for Algiers. According to Santa Cruz, twelve companies of Spaniards came from Naples, seven from Sicily, and nine from the garrison at Bona (Anaba), transferred for this purpose to Sicily to embark with the others; if one assumes 250 men per company, this would mean 7,000 Spaniards, which is the number Villegagnon gives, though he is not aware that some of the men came from Bona, as well as Naples and Sicily. The planning document envisions that the emperor will recruit 6,000 German infantry and 6,000 Italians, and according to Santa Cruz this was the number of men that embarked with Charles at La Spezia, plus another twelve banners of *Landsknechte* (4,800 men). This would mean 23,800 infantry in all, but Giovio says there were 20,000 and Villegagnon too gives a slightly smaller number: 22,000, including the 7,000 Spaniards, 7,000 Germans, an unstated number of Italians, and 3,000 adventurers, or as he calls them "volunteers who accompanied the emperor *honoris causa*." For Charles's payroll, I will assume 7,000 Spaniards, 7,000 Germans, and 6,000 Italians. As for the cavalry, Santa Cruz has 800 Spaniards and 500 Germans; Villegagnon, 700 Spaniards, 400 Italians, and 130 Knights of Rhodes (including himself). In fact, it seems likely that the three infantry battalions were each supported by cavalry of the same nation; I will count as being on Charles's payroll 400 Spaniards (the rest being gentleman volunteers), 500 Germans, and 400 Italians.[53]

This would be a smaller force than he took to Tunis (26,000 infantry, 1,000 cavalry, and 800 light horse),[54] supporting the idea that Charles hoped to keep expenses down for the Algiers campaign. The letter from Regensburg (31 May 1541) in which he gave the go-ahead assumes the *empresa* could be launched for about 400,000 ducats.[55] This estimate was

[51] Estado 638, 98, "Lo que es menester aqui in Alemana, antes de la partida."

[52] For Villegagnon's long and interesting career, see Robert Dauber, *A Knight of Malta in Brazil: Ambassador and Admiral Commander Fra François de Villegagnon, 1510–1571* (Malta, 1995).

[53] Santa Cruz, *Crónica del Emperador*, IV, 113–115; Villegagnon, *Caroli V Imperatoris Expeditio*, bi; Giovio, *Historiarum*, in *Opera*, V, 72. Because Giovio says there were only 20,000 infantry in all, I assume that the 4,000 new Spanish infantry that Charles ordered the duke of Alba to recruit (according to Santa Cruz) was meant not for the Algiers campaign, but to replace veterans from Italian garrisons, as in 1535 (see Chapter 7). Another parallel to the Tunis campaign is that Charles took Spanish veterans from garrisons in Naples and Sicily but not Lombardy.

[54] See Chapter 7.

[55] Charles to Cobos, 31 May 1541, Estado 638, 93–94; Carande Thobar, *Carlos V y sus banqueros*, III, 218.

not terribly far off, despite the fact that the anonymous author of the just-mentioned planning document used unrealistically low figures in estimating wage costs.[56] For four months, the costs for the infantry and cavalry units mentioned here, plus sixty-one galleys[57] – the number given by Villegagnon, counting fifteen from Spain – would have been 478,000.[58] Adding 20% for victuals, officers' pay, and troop and transport ships would bring the total to 573,600 ducats.[59] But owing to the fact that the sailing date was postponed until the second half of October, it became a five-month expedition, meaning that the cost would have been more like 717,000 ducats, or, with the 125,000 ducats for Charles's household, 842,000 ducats.

Financial planning for this expedition began in late 1540: from an *asiento* for 156,000 scudi signed in December 1540, 50,000 (46,685 ducats) was to be reserved for initial expenses of the Algiers campaign.[60] Raising the rest of the money was problematic. The Council of Castile, where key men like Tavera no longer saw conquering another North African outpost as the best way to defend the kingdom, was not likely to scour the account books for all possible sources of funds. Charles could not count on his bankers either, because too many loans contracted in the years 1536–1538 were still running at interest, unpaid. To find interest and principal to satisfy Adamo Centurione's loan for 100,000 scudi (November 1538), Cobos spent six months persuading Lady Ana de la Cerda to buy a cluster of *maestrazgo* villages the crown was authorized to sell. In the months when preparations for the Algiers expedition were under way, Charles charged but four other

---

[56] Estado, 638, 98, "Lo que es menester acqui en Alemana antes de la partida." For example, the author estimates the cost for 6,000 German infantry for three months "counting the victuals one will give them" at 35,000 scudi (*escudos*); assuming that victuals equal 10% of the wages, this would mean a monthly wage of only 1.77 scudi or 1.65 ducats per month.

[57] Villegagnon says there were sixty-five galleys in all, including fifteen that came from Spain, but I assume that four were galleys of the Knights of Malta, not on Charles's payroll.

[58] Using the same formula (Chapter 7, note 39), 128,800 for 7,000 *Landsknechte* at an estimated 4.6 ducats per month; 197,600 for 13,000 Spaniards and Italians at an estimated 3.8 ducats a month; 17,600 for 800 Spanish and Italian cavalry at an estimated 5.5 ducats per month; 12,000 for 500 German cavalry at an estimated 6 ducats a month; and 122,000 for the galleys.

[59] Tavera to Charles, 24 March 1541, Estado, 51, 5–7: he has agreed with the viceroy of Sicily (Ferrante Gonzaga) concerning the shipment of 15,000 *salmas* of wheat to Andulasia, as Charles requested; Tavera to Charles, 29 July 1541, Estado, 51, 34–35: the viceroy has sent only 10,000 *salmas*, so Tavera has sent money to the *corregidor* of Cártagena to buy what he can, even at the high prices now prevailing in Andalusia; Charles to Tavera, 1 August 1541, Estado, 638, 138–139: the viceroy has sent all he can, owing to a dearth in Sicily this year. Cf. Philip to Charles, 18 February 1546, *Corpus Documental*, Letter CCCLXI, II, 449–450: Philip has sent to Sicily a *cambio* for "60,000 florins of 11 *sueldos*, 4 *dineros*" for the delivery to Valencia in forty days of 10,000 *salmas* of wheat and 2,000 of barley.

[60] Pacini, *La Genova dell'Andrea Doria nell'impero di Carlo V*, 427.

loans to the treasury of Castile, all with the Fugger, for a total of only 110,609 ducats.[61]

Hence Charles stressed in his May 1541 letters to Spain that Castile itself would be spared as much as possible; as Cobos and Tavera could see from the enclosed memoranda, the Italian realms most directly threatened by Barbarossa would pay more. Charles's advisers budgeted for 202,000 of the needed 400,000 ducats from Naples and 30,000 from Sicily, with only 152,000 to come from Spain. He was fortunate in guessing that his viceroys would be able to extract from the parliaments of the two hard-pressed Italian realms monies earmarked for this expedition. In Naples, Pedro de Toledo won approval (July 1541) for a large *donativo* of 730,000 scudi over the next three years. Discounting this grant by 40%, for the reasons noted earlier, the kingdom's treasurers (or rather their bankers) could have provided Charles with as much as 438,000 scudi, or 408,829 ducats. In fact, Toledo contracted for a loan of 230,000 scudi in July; in September he brought to Charles in Genoa a further 109,000 scudi in cash and a letter of exchange for 90,909. Because Toledo assured Charles there was nothing more to be gotten from the *donativo* of Naples, the emperor canceled an *asiento* contract he had signed just prior to Toledo's arrival.[62] In Sicily, at about the same time, the Parlamento endorsed a special grant of 100,000 scudi for the emperor's African campaign, meaning (by the same reasoning) a disposable sum perhaps equal to 56,000 Spanish ducats.[63] From these sources – bankers' loans secured by the treasury of Castile (157,294 ducats), the Naples *donativo* (401,406 ducats), and Sicily (56,000 ducats) – Charles will have gotten about 615,000 ducats. One way or another, Castile had to supply the 225,000 ducats or so he still needed, perhaps by using money earmarked for other purposes, thus taking the kingdom a bit deeper into debt. But the support from Naples and Sicily is noteworthy, because historians of Charles's wars seem to have neglected it. Had it not been for the *donativi* of his southern Italian realms, Charles could never have launched his ill-fated *empresa* against Algiers.

* * *

Table 8.1 gives a rough idea of how Charles paid for the campaigns discussed in Chapters 6, 7, and 8. The royal share of the Peruvian treasure is

---

[61] Cobos to Charles, 24 March, 26 June, and 5 November 1541, Estado 51; the loan contracted with Adamo Centurione of Genoa is no. 150 in the series: Carande Thobar, *Carlos V y sus banqueros*, III, 232–236.

[62] Pacini, *La Genova dell'Andrea Doria nell'impero di Carlo V*, 429–432.

[63] Sicily's deputies underlined their claims about the island's penury by refusing to grant the viceroy his usual annual gift of 50,000 scudi. D'Agostino, *Parlamento e societa nel regno di Napoli*, 272–274; Giovanni Evangelista Blasi e Gambacorta, *Storia cronologica de' Vicerè . . . di Sicilia*, introd. Illuminato Peri (5 vols., Palermo, 1974–1975), II, 79–80.

Table 8.1. *Sources of Funds (in Spanish ducats) for Charles's Campaigns, 1529–1541*

	Windfalls	Naples/ Sicily	Low Countries	Castile's Long-Term Debt	Castile's Short-Term Debt	Totals
1529/30	350,000	500,000?	190,706		501,230	1,541,396
1532	860,000					860,000
1535	400,000			740,000		1,140,000
1536		300,000		300,000	915,198	1,515,198
1541		457,406			157,294+?	614,700+?
TOTALS	1,610,000	1,257,406	190,706	1,040,000	1,573,722	5,671,294
	(28.4%)	(22.4.3%)	(3.4%)	(18.3%)	(27.7%)	(100%)

counted as a "windfall," while sequestrations of private treasure are counted as added to Castile's long-term debt. What is striking about these figures is that Charles got less than a third of what he needed (27.7%) from short-term, high-interest bankers' loans. He was fortunate in the "windfalls" that came his way during these years, and for his later campaigns he would be even more fortunate. But owing to the rising costs of war during his reign, the windfalls of later years would count for less in the overall picture. As Chapters 9–11 show, Charles made up the difference by being increasingly reckless in burdening his adopted kingdom with both long- and short-term debt.

Chapter 9

Charles's Grand Plan, 1543–1544

Charles's loss of prestige at Algiers meant opportunity for his enemies. In Germany, the Lutheran Duke Moritz of Saxony took advantage of the provisions of the recent Recess of Regensburg to secularize one bishopric adjoining his lands and, in another, to prevent a duly elected Catholic prelate from taking possession. The Rhineland duchy of Guelders, a French ally in earlier campaigns, had been incorporated into the Habsburg Netherlands in 1536.[1] But the territorial estates had voted in 1538 to transfer sovereignty over their land to Duke William IV of Cleves, who was quickly befriended by France; Maarten van Rossum, a Guelders marshal who led punishing raids into the Low Countries in earlier wars, boasted of what his men could do with French gold in their pockets. In November 1541 Cleves, with Guelders, sought admission to the Schmalkaldic League. At the Diet of Speyer (February 1542), even the Count Palatine and his brother, hitherto allies of the emperor, seemed to speak with a French accent. The Landgrave of Hesse, partially estranged from his Schmalkaldic partners,[2] did Charles a service by blocking a French alliance with the league; but he also joined in the large Schmalkaldic force that invaded and occupied the lands of a Catholic prince, Duke Henry of Brunswick. The bellicose Henry had been more of an embarrassment than a useful ally to Charles, but Mary in Brussels was alarmed by the prospect of a solid block of Schmalkaldic territories running from Hesse through Brunswick and Cleves-Guelders to the Low Countries border.[3] In November 1541

---

[1] Struick, *Gelre en Habsburg, 1492–1528*: Guelders was conquered by Burgundy's Duke Charles the Bold, but regained its independence while Maximilian I ruled in the Netherlands and was, from that time forward, a determined foe of the Habsburg-Burgundian state.

[2] Though married to a sister of Duke Moritz of Saxony, he contracted a bigamous union with one of his wife's ladies-in-waiting, which he had hoped to keep secret, but was forced in 1541 to acknowledge publicly.

[3] Charles to Mary, 6 August 1541, "Berichte," XIX, Document VII, 241–250, promising to recover Guelders from Cleves once he has dealt with Algiers; Naves to Charles, 12 November 1541,

King Christian III of Denmark signed a treaty with France that presaged a breakdown in negotiations for a settlement of issues still outstanding from the Netherlands–Denmark war of 1534–1536.[4]

Francis I had a *casus belli* any time he chose to use it, owing to the murder by Spanish troops in Lombardy (July 1541) of his two envoys to Sultan Suleyman, Antonio Rincon, a Spaniard, and Cesare Fregoso, of the Genoese family loyal to France. The marquess of Vasto, Spain's governor in Milan, alleged that his men had set upon the travelers without realizing their identity, but the king and his officials indignantly rejected this claim.[5] Any time needed, French bases in Piedmont and the alliance with Cleves-Guelders provided jumping-off points for simultaneous invasions of Milan and the Low Countries. In January 1542 French troops occupied the fortified town of Stenay on the Moselle, the southern gateway to strategic Luxemburg. In March 1542 the envoy sent to the Porte to replace the murdered Rincon returned with promises of a Turkish offensive on land and sea coordinated with actions by the French. En route back to Istanbul some weeks later, the same ambassador paused in Rome to let the cat out of the bag, with a remark no doubt intended for transmission to the Habsburgs.[6] By the time Francis I formally declared war on Charles and his lands (12 July 1542), preparations were underway for an offensive

and Naves to Granvelle, 25 February 1542, Lanz, Letters 480 and 484, II, 330–333, 339–340; on Brunswick, Charles to Ferdinand, 5 March 1542, HHSA-B, PA 4, and Mary to Charles, 2 July 1542, HHST-B, PA 33, Konvolut 1; and on Hesse's role in blocking French advances to the league, report by Cornelis de Schepper, 28 October 1542, *Staatspapiere*, Document LXIV, 337–338. For the earlier history of the conflict over Guelders, see Struik, *Gelre en Habsburg, 1492–1528*.

[4] Knecht, *Renaissance Warrior and Patron*, 396; Brandi, *Emperor Charles V*, 471; Charles to Mary, 26 January 1542, 14 March 1542, Mary to Charles, 23 March and 12 May 1542, Aud. 53, 32v, 94v, 105v–106, and 156v. Christian III is referred to as "duke of Holstein," because Charles still maintained that the rightful queen was his niece Dorothea (daughter of Charles's sister Isabella and Denmark's exiled king, Christian II), on whose behalf he embroiled the Netherlands in the so-called Counts' War among claimants to the throne (1534–1536).

[5] Message from Doria to Charles via Francisco Duarte, c 1 March 1541, reporting on Antonio's Rincon's journey from the Porte back to the French court: Estado 638, 78, paragraph 23; undated memorandum on "Los razones por las quales no se puede tener por rompido la tregua" (i.e., the 1538 Truce of Nice) because of the murder of Rincon and Cesare Fregoso: Estado 638, 97; Abbot of St. Vincent to Charles, 3 August 1541, Lanz, Letter 438, II, 324–326, on incredulity at the French court; see also the indirect indication of Charles's sense of guilt over the murders cited by Fernández Alvárez apropos of Charles to Tavera, 26 July 1542, *Corpus Documental*, Letter CCXLIV, II, 78–79.

[6] Brandi, *Emperor Charles V*, 472; Knecht, *Renaissance Warrior and Patron*, 479; Charles to Ferdinand, 10 May 1542 – Poul[a]in [de la Garde] told Pope Paul III that his master "ne vouloit perdre ny ses amys ny la conjoncture qui s'offert, baillant ouvertement a entendre la venue dudit Turcq, et aussy il [Francis I] renvoye ledit Poulain et ung autre personage avecq luy d'envers ledit Turcq" – HHSA-B, PA 4.

on three fronts. While the Dauphin (the future King Henry II) led a huge force[7] toward the Pyrenees frontier and French troops mobilized in Piedmont, two other French armies were preparing to strike across the Low Countries border, as was Maarten van Rossum, coming from the Rhineland.[8]

Charles knew that France was recruiting troops in Germany (February 1542), despite the Diet of Speyer's attempt to prohibit citizens of the empire from enrolling in the service of foreign princes. Mary had information about French troops massing in northern France and in the duchy of Lorraine (an imperial territory) in May, and by early June she knew of a French emissary who had brought a large amount of cash to Guelders. Despite Charles's desire that she not give Francis a pretext for war by violating the no-recruitment clause of the Recess of Speyer, Mary "secretly" raised troops for the Luxemburg frontier in May, and by late June she had 25,000 infantry and 3,000 cavalry ready for action.[9] Meanwhile, Charles gave Leyva in Milan permission to raise troops in Germany (despite the Recess of Speyer), and he prepared "to put my own person at risk" against the great army that was expected to march against Perpignan, possibly to be supported from the sea by Barbarossa's galleys. The army the Dauphin was leading toward Perpignan kept him in Spain, even if he fantasized about joining in the expedition to Hungary by which Ferdinand hoped to reverse gains made by Sultan Suleyman during the campaign season of 1541.[10] But while the duke of Alba raised fresh troops for Perpignan and supervised works on the city's fortifications, Charles had seasoned veterans transferred from Sicily and even from Lombardy, where fighting on the Piedmont frontier was indecisive. Perpignan was thus made strong enough to resist a month-long siege by the Dauphin's army. Even after the Dauphin's withdrawal from Perpignan (August 1542) Charles was

[7] Estimated by Santa Cruz, *Crónica del Emperador*, IV, 167–171, to include 24,000 German infantry, 18,000 Gascons (many of these may have been "adventurers," as on previous campaigns), 8,000 French, 7,000 Italians, 2,000 Swiss, and 5,000 cavalry; Francis I kept 20,000 men with him at Narbonne for his guard and sent the rest on to Perpignan under the Dauphin.
[8] Knecht, *Renaissance Warrior and Patron*, 478–480.
[9] Mary to Charles, 23 February 1542, Aud. 53, 73 (her negotiations with the provincial states for a subsidy to be levied in case war should come); Charles to Mary, second of two letters dated 14 March 1542, HHSA-B, PA 33, Konvolut 4 (Mary has asked permission to raise 2,000 High Germans to guard Luxemburg's frontier, but she should do nothing to give Francis I the occasion to break the peace); and Mary to Ferdinand, 29 May 1542, HHSA-B, PA 42, Konvolut 1 (Francis himself is in Lorraine, within one or two days' march of Luxemburg, hence despite the terms of the Recess of Speyer she has "secretly" levied 400 cavalry for the Luxemburg frontier); and Mary to Ferdinand, 25 June 1542, HHSA-B, PA 42, Konvolut 1, apologizing for raising troops in Germany, and reporting on the number of men now in her pay.
[10] Brandi, *Emperor Charles V*, 475; Baumgartner, *Henry II*, 35–36.

sufficiently concerned about danger on this front that he sent Mary a *cambio* for 50,000 ducats to embark ten banners of her High German mercenaries (4,000 men) for Spain.[11]

The most serious problem developed in the Low Countries, where Charles had earlier rejected Mary's request to levy troops in Germany – lest by violating the Recess of Speyer she afford Francis a pretext for war.[12] In July, Mary reported that one French army with 15,000 infantry and 6,000 cavalry had crossed from Lorraine into Luxemburg, while another with 10,000 infantry and 400 horse invaded Artois, and Maarten van Rossum pushed into Brabant with 12,000 infantry, 2,500 cavalry, and "much artillery." Van Rossum defeated a smaller force under the prince of Orange,[13] but most of Orange's men found shelter within the walls of Antwerp, stoutly defended by its burghers. Rossum had no better luck against Louvain, where university students stood in arms with burghers on the walls. Turning southeast to Luxemburg, he joined one of the two French armies in forcing the submission of the citadel of Yvoy. The capital city, Luxemburg, surrendered two weeks later. Luxemburg was the least populous and the least developed of Charles's Low Countries lands, but its importance lay in its location; as Mary noted to Charles, an enemy holding Luxemburg would cut off the Netherlands from its sources of military manpower in Germany.[14]

As Mary also reminded him, when he left the Netherlands in 1540, Charles had promised her that in the event of war with France, he would come to her aid if she withstood the initial attack; indeed, it was the common talk among his subjects in the Netherlands that "if they sustained the first shock of combat, you would not fail to succor them with all your

[11] Mary to Charles, 6 July 1542, and Charles to Mary, 3 November 1542, HHSA-B, PA 33, Konvolut 1 and Konvolut 3. Santa Cruz, *Crónica del Emperador*, IV, 171, says there were 2,500 Spanish infantry in Perpignan when the French army set down before the city, and 2,700 more who got in during the course of a forty-day siege. Naves to Granvelle, 25 February 1542, Lanz, Letter 484, II, 340; Mary to Ferdinand, 29 May and 7 June 1542, both in HHSA-B, PA 42, Konvolut 1; Charles's instructions for his commissioners to the Diet of Nuremberg, 29 June 1542, Lanz, Letter 488, II, 347–348, and to Tavera, 26 July 1542, *Corpus Documental*, Letter CCXLIV, II, 78–79.

[12] Charles to Mary, second of two letters dated 14 March 1542, both in HHST-B, PA 33, Konvolut 4.

[13] By the death of Philibert de Châlons in the siege of Florence (Chapter 6), his title as prince of Orange passed to his sister's husband, Henry of Nassau, head of the Netherlands branch of the Nassau family, by whose death the title passed to his son Reynier van Nassau, who served in the Habsburg campaigns of 1542–1544; by his death at the siege of Saint-Dizier (August 1544) the title passed to a young member of the elder, German branch of the Nassau family, William of Nassau, future leader of the Dutch Revolt.

[14] Mary's instructions for Falaix to Charles, 28 August 1542, revising figures given in Mary to Charles, 20 July 1542, both in HHST-B, PA 33, Konvolut 1; Brandi, *Emperor Charles V*, 466–480; Mary to Charles, 23 April 1543, Aud. 54, 60–62v.

resources."[15] Mary now proceeded to live up to her part of the bargain. By September she had "eighty banners" under arms, or about 32,000 infantry, including some 12,000 men previously in the service of the Landgrave of Hesse, and 3,000 native cavalry, the *compagnies d'ordonnance*. In Luxemburg her troops recaptured all but one of the strongholds that had fallen to the French. Her defense of the country was highly praised by Praet, a member of Charles's inner circle, who noted among other things that Mary's order to remove within fortified towns all bridges across the river Aa had slowed Maarten van Rossum's movements after his failure at Antwerp, giving Louvain and other cities time to ready their defenses.[16] The campaign season was not over yet, and by the end of November Mary calculated that her war expenses had been 1.5 million Carolus gulden (around 820,012 Spanish ducats). Two extraordinary subsidies granted by the provincial states (one in case of war, the other after the war had begun) were already gone, as was the 300,000 gulden she had borrowed "in my own name" on the Antwerp exchange. She had no money at all for expected expenses of 100,000 gulden per month during the winter for the garrisons of key towns and citadels. She had, of course, summoned the states to ask for a still larger subsidy, but negotiations were difficult, and in January 1543 Mary urged that Charles's presence was the only hope, for she feared "losing a province" before the subsidy agreements that would prompt the bankers to lend money were in place.[17]

The Rhineland Campaign

Charles was already making preparations for an extensive campaign, first in the Rhineland, then against France. Portugal's John III once again came to his aid, this time with a 300,000-ducat dowry for the marriage of his daughter Maria Manuela to the emperor's son Philip; half was sent in cash to Castile, the other half remitted "by exchange" to Antwerp. Mary was authorized to draw on the latter sum for the 3,000 Spanish infantry Charles sent by ship to be ready for his arrival in the Low Countries (Mary preferred that he not bring Spaniards, because they were harder than Germans to send home once the fighting was done, but Charles had come to depend on his Spanish fighting men). On 6 May 1543, about to

---

[15] Mary to Charles, 18 September and 28 November 1542, Aud. 53, 288–292, 342v–343: in the second letter, the common people are described as saying that when you left "leur avez promis que en souffrant le premier socq vous ne defauldries les secourrir de toute votre puissance."

[16] Mary to Ferdinand, 29 May 1542, HHSA-B, PA 42, Konvolut 1; Mary to Charles, 17 and 18 September 1542, HHSA-B, PA 33, Konvolut 1, and Aud. 53, 288–292; Praet to Charles, 24 September 1542, Lanz, Letter 498, II, 364–367.

[17] Mary to Charles, 17 September 1542, HHSA-B, PA 33, Konvolut 1; 24 September 1542, Aud. 53, 299v; 28 November 1542, Aud. 53, 340; and 4 January 1543, Aud. 54, 8–9v.

embark for Genoa from Palamos, he penned the "secret instruction" to Philip cited in Chapter 1, in which Brandi believes Charles poured out his heart. He was undertaking this journey against his will "for honor and reputation, for if our vassals [i.e., the duke of Cleves] will not serve us, we cannot sustain the charge of governing."[18]

In Genoa, Charles made no secret of his plans for a campaign across the Alps, as in a conversation with the historian, Paolo Giovio: "You had better hurry up and write what I have already done, Giovio, because this war is going to give you a new and great labor."[19] Traveling (as usual) from Genoa to Cremona to have a safe passage across the Alps, the emperor paused for yet another meeting with Pope Paul III, at Busseto, near Cremona. The aged pontiff wanted Milan for his grandson, Ottavio Farnese, the second husband of Charles's natural daughter, Margaret of Parma; he offered 500,000 ducats, and was even willing to consider the 2 million ducats mentioned by Charles as a proper price. Much as he needed money, however, the emperor was persuaded by his advisers that Milan was too strategic a territory to give up. Accompanied by his Spanish and Italian troops, with Ferrante Gonzaga as their commander, Charles moved on to Germany, where he met at Speyer the regiments of *Landsknechte* recruited according to his instructions. By 17 August he was in Bonn, the residence of Cologne's prince-archbishops. With an army behind him, he compelled Prince-Archbishop Hermann von Wied to dismiss the two Protestant preachers he had called in to reform his lands.[20]

The first objective of this campaign was Düren in nearby Cleves. The duke had thought to protect his town's curtain wall against bombardment by surrounding it with an earthen rampart of equal height – a quick and cheap version of the new "bastion trace" fortifications developed by Italian military engineers, using low earthen ramparts to absorb cannon fire.[21] But the imperial artillery train proved its mettle: "forty heavy cannon firing without interruption almost the whole day" made breaches in the rampart and wall (25 August). After a three-hour battle in the breach, according to Santa Cruz, veteran Spanish and Italian troops finally prevailed, though not without heavy casualties. During this action Charles, watching from a height, refused to consider the withdrawal recommended by one of his

---

[18] Mary to Charles, 1 July 1543, Aud. 54, 141–143; Philip to Charles, 7 August 1543, *Corpus Documental*, Letter CCLIX, II, 140; and Charles to Philip, secret instruction of 6 May 1543, *Corpus Documental*, Letter CCLII, II, 105; for the passage quoted more extensively, see Chapter 1, with the comments of Brandi, *Emperor Charles V*, 488–494.

[19] Zimmerman, *Paolo Giovio*, 184–185.

[20] Brandi, *Emperor Charles V*, 501–503; Zimmerman, *Paolo Giovio*, 185; Charles to Philip, from Cremona, 19 June 1543, *Corpus Documental*, Letter CCLVIII, II, 126–129.

[21] See the literature cited in the introduction to J Tracy, *City Walls*, 12–14.

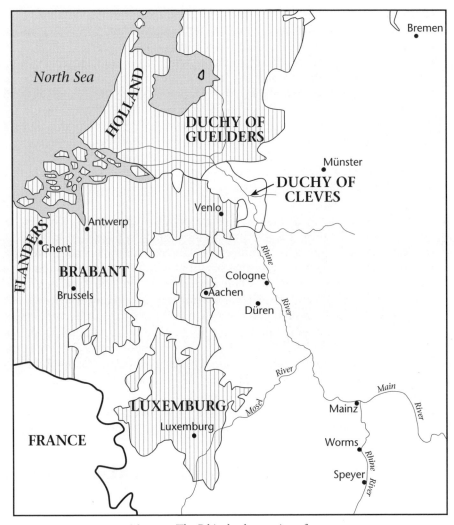

Map 9.1. The Rhineland campaign of 1543

commanders: "Those are Spaniards in the breach" was all he would say.[22]
Angered by the loss of their comrades, the victors slaughtered left and
right and fired the town, including its church; Charles looked on with
satisfaction, intending for Düren to be an example to other cities held by
Cleves. At this point according to Santa Cruz, the prince of Orange made

---

[22] *Crónica del Emperador*, IV, 241. On this point the patriotic Santa Cruz might best be taken with a
grain of salt.

his juncture with Charles, with more German infantry, and the cavalry of the *compagnies d'ordonnance*. Crossing into neighboring Guelders, the combined army forced the submission of Roermond (2 September), and was digging in before Venlo when Duke William IV came to Charles's camp. In keeping with protocol, he first paid his respects to the imperial field commander, the duke of Alba, in his tent; this gave Charles's servants time to spread brocade on the "throne" in his tent or "palace," so the duke could kneel before the emperor and make his submission with due ceremony. Wisely, Charles offered his disobedient "vassal" generous terms: William kept his ancestral duchy of Cleves, but had to renounce his claim to Guelders, his Protestant convictions, and a recently acquired French bride. Only now did the Spaniards sent by ship to the Low Countries reach the emperor's camp.[23]

Charles now set off for Hainaut, where he attended a meeting of the States General at Mons, possibly hoping for money to pay off his troops (see Chapter 12). Just now, however, one French army again invaded Luxemburg, retaking Yvoy and the city of Luxemburg, while Francis I himself led a second force into Hainaut, where he occupied and began fortifying the city of Landrecies. Charles marched toward Landrecies with all of his forces, even though it was feared that the arrival of French reinforcements meant he would be facing a larger army. The emperor made his confession on 28 October; this was when, in response to Mary's plea that he not risk his own person, he assured her that "I will not do anything you would not do if you were in my place." After two days of skirmishing between armies encamped on either side of the Sambre, near the border citadel of Cateau-Cambrésis, Charles and his council decided to withdraw rather than attempt to dislodge the French from Landrecies. But after another day of fighting it was Francis who pulled back. French troops still held key sites in Luxemburg, but their withdrawal from Hainaut allowed Charles's captains to seize Cateau-Cambrésis, a key border stronghold hitherto held by the pro-French prince-bishop of Cambrai.[24]

[23] Both Giovio and Santa Cruz have Orange and his army join Charles at Düren: *Historiarum*, in *Opera*, V, 155–158, and *Crónica del Emperador*, IV, 241 (for details of the duke's submission, IV, 250). But Giovio does not mention the Spaniards under the command of Pedro de Guzmán (see note 32), who joined the combined army shortly after the duke of Cleves had surrendered (Santa Cruz, IV, 254). I follow Santa Cruz in having Orange and his army join Charles just after the siege of Düren. According to Zimmerman, *Paolo Giovio*, 190, Giovio relied for his account of this campaign on a letter sent him by Francesco Franchini of Cosenza, a secretary of Charles's son-in-law, Ottavio Farnese.

[24] Brandi, *Emperor Charles V*, 504–506; Mary to Charles 29 October 1543, and Charles to Mary, 30 October (the quote) and 4 November 1543, Lanz, Letters 513, 514, and 518, II, 404–405, 408; Charles to Philip, Cambrai, 15 November 1543, describing the fighting near Cateau-Cambrésis, *Corpus Documental*, Letter CCLXV, II, 179–181; on the nature of Charles's claims to Cateau-Cambrésis

In the Mediterranean, Barbarossa with 110 galleys had been attacking at will at points in Sicily and Calabria; as feared, he effected a juncture with French galleys off Marseilles in July. The combined fleets reconquered for France the port of Nice, recently occupied by Andrea Doria. Barbarossa now threatened to return to Istanbul if not given the means to refit his fleet, so Francis I ordered the port of Toulon placed at his disposal for the fall and winter months, as citizens were evacuated to make room for a new population of 30,000 soldiers and oarsmen, with their servants and Christian slaves. The sight of Turkish power ensconced in a Christian harbor inspired fear along the Spanish coast, leading Philip and the council of Castile to concentrate troops along Aragón's Mediterranean frontier with France, even if there was no way to pay for them save by "gold and silver" from the Indies fleet. But Spain's needs were not to be the first priority; for example, it was decided that fortifying the port of Rosas was not worth the 60,000 ducats it would cost, after 200,000 had been spent to refortify Perpignan, the major city of the border region.[25] Charles made it clear that Castile's resources were to be at the service of his plans for an invasion of France the following year.

The Campaign in France

Already on 27 October 1543, prior to the last fighting of the current campaign season, Charles informed Philip that he intended to lead "a great army from here [the Low Countries]" the next spring into northern France, "where the land is flat and provisions are abundant," and "sustain it for four or five months." Because "we cannot defend all our lands at once," it made sense to press the enemy from this side, forcing him to concentrate his forces in the north, which would mean the Franco-Turkish armada, by itself, could not do a great deal of damage. Meanwhile, Charles's diplomats arranged an alliance with Henry VIII of England, who was to bring 37,000 infantry and 7,000 cavalry across the Channel, to be joined by 2,000 *Landsknechte* and 2,000 cavalry Charles would provide. By 22 February 1544 the emperor's military planners had worked out the numbers needed for his own army. To build up his contingent of the prized Spanish infantry, Charles had already instructed Philip to send 5,000 men by sea to the Low Countries, negating the governor of Milan's request

and on sums spent to refortify the citadel (40,000 gulden by Charles's government, 100,000 by the inhabitants of the rural environs of Cambrai, known as the Cambrésis), autograph letter of Lodewijk van Schoer to Granvelle, 29 May 1545, and Granvelle's reply of 25 June 1545, HHSA-B, PA 42, Konvolut 5.

[25] Knecht, *Renaissance Warrior and Patron*, 487–489; Philip to Charles, 7 August 1543, 4 February 1544, *Corpus Documental*, Letters CCLIX, CCLXVII, II, 141–143, 193–195, 191, 197–198.

for more Spaniards in light of an expected French invasion across the Alps.[26]

Help for Charles now appeared on the horizon from an unexpected source. Ongoing discussions about religious peace in Germany reached an impasse in 1543, owing to rising distrust between the two sides and to skillful intervention by the representatives of Francis I. But at the Diet of Speyer (February–June 1544), Charles was able to profit from Protestant indignation about the Most Christian King's open alliance with the Ottomans. For his part, Charles agreed to a recess (bitterly protested by the papal legate) in which he personally warranted that no subject of the empire would be attacked for the sake of religion. In return the diet agreed to raise a sum large enough to support 24,000 infantry and 4,000 cavalry for six months, for service both against the French and against the Turks.[27]

While waiting in Speyer for the troops raised by the diet to muster, Charles sent out orders for the assembly of his own forces, including Spanish infantry, other *Landsknechte*, cavalry from Spain and the Low Countries as well as Germany, a sizable artillery train, more than 1,000 *pionniers* to dig trenches, and seventy riverboats carried on wagons. He sent a small force under Ferrante Gonzaga to block a French move to resupply the capital city of Luxemburg. This operation "succeeded so well" (as Charles puts it in his memoirs) that the city surrendered; as the emperor sent more men, Gonzaga quickly regained the rest of the province for the Habsburgs and continued up the Moselle valley as far as Metz, a free city of the Holy Roman Empire. Here Gonzaga and his men then crossed the Moselle and marched along the right bank of the Marne to Saint-Dizier, where they began digging in for a siege (8 July). Meanwhile, Charles had left Speyer and, taking some weeks to collect all his forces at Metz, joined Gonzaga before Saint-Dizier. There was no news of Henry VIII's movements in France, although the agreement between the two monarchs called for both to advance on Paris. Saint-Dizier was well fortified and well defended by its garrison. On 20 July, Charles wrote Mary that he could not advance beyond Saint-Dizier because of a shortage of victuals and of *pionniers* – some had run away. At the same time, because all the remittances he had requested from Spain still left him no money to pay his troops beyond 25 September,

---

[26] Charles to Philip, 27 October 1543, 22 February 1544, *Corpus Documental*, Letters CCLXII, CCLXX, II, 171, 212–213; on the 5,000 Spaniards, Philip to Charles, 4 February 1544, Charles to Philip, 14 February 1544, and the second of two letters dated 6 July 1544 (Charles has heard the 5,000 have landed at Calais [then part of Flanders] and are on the march), *Corpus Documental*, Letters CCLXVII, CCLXVIII, and CCLXXIX, II, 193, 206–207, 230.

[27] Charles to Philip, 27 October 1543, *Corpus Documental*, Letter CCLXII, II, 170–172; Brandi, *Emperor Charles V*, 504–514; Horst Rabe, *Reichsbund und Interim. Die Verfassungs- und Religionspolitik Karls V und der Reichstag von Augsburg, 1547/1548* (Cologne and Vienna, 1971), 41–43.

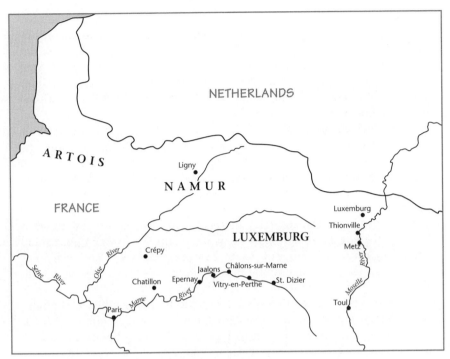

Map 9.2. Charles's invasion of northern France, 1544

he would have to "accomplish something" within a month and then pay his men their going-home wage, in order to "avoid disorder."[28]

When Saint-Dizier's garrison finally made its honorable surrender (17 August), the emperor held a council of war. According to Santa Cruz, both Gonzaga and Granvelle recommended withdrawal: it was late in the season, the next obvious target (Jalons, on the opposite or left bank of the Marne, where a large French force kept watch) would not be easily taken, and the army might have to abandon its precious artillery if withdrawal were postponed until the autumn rains came. Charles insisted on pushing past Jalons on to Châlons-sur-Marne on the right bank; the army came even with Châlons on 30 August, but this was not the emperor's real objective. Again according to Santa Cruz, Charles convened his colonels and *maestres de campo* to explain that he intended to march on Paris; he could

---

[28] Brandi, *Emperor Charles V*, 514–517; Knecht, *Renaissance Warrior and Patron*, 490–493; Charles's *Memorias*, paragraphs 49–54, in Morel-Fatio, *L'historiographie de Charles-Quint*, pp. 80–85; Charles to Philip, second and third of three letters dated from Metz, 6 July 1544, *Corpus Documental*, Letters CCLXXIX, CCLXXX, II, 235–236, 240–243; Charles to Mary, 20 July 1544, "Berichte," XIX, Document VI, 250–259.

not do so without their help, because they were short of food, and they would have to accept his "royal word" that the camp would not be broken up until each of the men had been paid his last farthing. Charles took this risk because, as he had explained to Mary the previous month, "the goal of this army has always been to penetrate into the heart of this kingdom and force the enemy to see reason." By now he knew that Henry VIII was using his army not to advance on Paris but to besiege Boulogne, an important city near Calais, England's foothold in France. As Granvelle reported to Mary, it was also understood that none of the nearby towns of any importance could be taken without a long siege, and that the emperor's men were now eager to go home. Yet Charles persisted. He marched his army past the well-fortified Châlons and, hoping to draw the French into battle, got his men across the Marne on an old wooden bridge, only to discover that another branch of the river (narrower but deeper) still lay between him and the enemy. According to Charles's memoirs, his men just missed getting to the stone bridge at Epernay before the French could fortify it.[29]

Charles's insistence on pushing closer to Paris, though fraught with peril, seems to have paid dividends in the ongoing negotiations that were now taken more seriously on both sides. As Granvelle and his French counterparts worked out the details of an agreement, Granvelle's son, the bishop of Arras, brought an ultimatum to Henry VIII's camp before Boulogne: the king must either march on Paris at once, or Charles would claim the freedom to negotiate a separate peace. In fact, Charles consented to the terms of the Treaty of Crépy before Arras returned with the news that Boulogne had fallen to the English (14 September) and that Henry's army would march no further. Charles and Francis agreed that each side was to restore any conquests made since the Truce of Nice (1538); for a lasting peace, Francis's younger son was to marry either Charles's daughter (with the Low Countries as her dowry), or a daughter of Ferdinand (with Milan as her dowry), the choice being left to Charles (several months later, he decided it would be Milan). The publication of this treaty left imperial partisans wondering what Charles had gained from bringing an army within striking distance of Paris. The chaplain-historian Bernabé Busto, thinking the emperor may have been influenced by the pro-French sentiment common among his Low Countries advisers, made bold to ask him, in Brussels, why he had accepted the terms of Crépy; Charles said he had done so because he needed a free hand to deal with affairs in Germany. Busto remained skeptical, but Charles's answer to the question is the one modern historians give. According to the text of the separate secret Treaty of Crépy, not published until the twentieth century, Francis I promised

[29] Santa Cruz, *Crónica del Emperador*, IV, 401–406; Charles's *Memorias*, 80–85, and Charles to Mary, 20 July 1544, cited in note 28; Granvelle to Mary, 18 August 1544, HHSA-B, PA 5, Konvolut 4.

to abandon his opposition to the convening of an ecumenical council of the church; indeed, he would send France's bishops to whichever of three locations named by Charles would be designated by the pope. He promised further to provide military assistance to Charles in the event that France's erstwhile allies, the German Protestant estates, proved unwilling to return peacefully to the Catholic fold.[30] Charles had indeed gotten the freedom he needed to press for an end to Germany's dissensions, either by peaceful means, should Protestants agree to submit disputed issues to the adjudication of a council, or if not, as was more likely, by force of arms.[31]

Sinews of War

For his march against Cleves-Guelders, Charles brought across the Alps a "guard" of 4,000 Spaniards, 4,000 Italians, and 600 light horse. Before leaving Spain, he had sent letters to Germany, authorizing recruitment of up to 16,000 *Landsknechte* and 4,000 German heavy cavalry, to meet him at Speyer. Putting together the accounts of Giovio and Santa Cruz, and taking the smaller numbers for estimates of troop strength, it seems that on 17 August Charles and his guard joined forces in Speyer with 14,000 *Landsknechte* and 4,000 cavalry. By analogy with the First Schmalkaldic War, when Charles assumed responsibility for the Netherlands army led by the count of Buren (see Chapter 10), the 12,000 infantry and the 2,000 Low Countries cavalry commanded in this campaign by Reynier van Nassau, the prince of Orange, must also have been on Charles's payroll, at least from the time they joined him at Düren in August. The 2,700 Spaniards sent by ship to Bruges, as Charles had ordered, did not join the imperial camp until September.[32] If we assume that the guard and the 2,700 Spaniards

---

[30] Brandi, *Emperor Charles V*, 517–522; Knecht, *Renaissance Warrior and Patron*, 493–494; Charles to Philip, 20 September 1544, *Corpus Documental*, Letter CCLXXVIII, II, 278–279; cf. Charles to Vega (his ambassador in Rome), January 1543, *Staatspapiere*, Document LXVI, 352–54, in response to Cardinal Farnese's proposal to Granvelle (if Charles were to agree to a truce with France, the pope might convene a council during the truce): we know for certain that Francis and his council decided some time ago that a council of the church is not in France's interest. Loos-Corswaren, *Bernabé Busto, Geschichte des Schmalkaldischen Krieges*, I, xvii, citing from the portion of Busto's history of Charles's wars during the 1540s that remains unpublished. Santa Cruz, *Crónica del Emperador*, IV, 406, is puzzled by the fact that the army suddenly turned north on September 9, away from its march along the Marne, but thinks it may have had to do with the peace negotiations.

[31] Brandi, *Emperor Charles V*, 517–522; Rabe, *Reichsbund und Interim*, 16–18; Heinz Schilling, "Veni, Vidi, Vixit Deus – Karl V zwischen Religionskrieg und Religionsfrieden," *Archiv für Reformationsgeschichte* 89 (1998): 144–166, here 148–150.

[32] Charles to Philip, from Cremona, 19 June 1543, *Corpus Documental*, Letter CCLVIII, II, 126–131. Giovio, *Historiarum*, in *Opera*, V, 155; Santa Cruz, *Crónica del Emperador*, IV, 241–249. Santa Cruz says Charles was joined in Speyer by as many as 18,000 men, Giovio that he was joined in Bonn

were on Charles's account for seven months (May through October, plus November as the going-home month), the 14,000 *Landsknechte* and the 4,000 cavalry for five months, and the 12,000 (Low German) infantry and the 2,000 Low Countries cavalry for three months, the cost for these units, at prevailing wages, may be estimated at 960,414 ducats.[33] Adding 20% for victuals, officers' pay, and the baggage and artillery trains would bring the total to 1,152,497, or 1,327,497 with the 175,000 for Charles's household.

For the invasion of France in 1544, Charles's military planners envisioned a force of 16,000 High Germans, 10,000 Low Germans, 9,000 Spaniards, and 7,000 heavy cavalry. Charles also had a detachment of Spaniards sent to Flanders by ship, and he also undertook to pay for 2,000 *Landsknechte* and 2,000 cavalry to join Henry VIII's army on invasion.[34] Giovio and Santa Cruz again give roughly the same figures for the combined army: 16,000 *Landsknechte*, 10,000 Low Germans[35] and 2,000 Low Countries cavalry under Orange's command, 7,000 Spaniards plus the 3,000 sent by ship from

(this seems unlikely) by 14,000 German infantry and 4,000 cavalry. Mary was reluctant to release the Netherlands cavalry (the *compagnies d'ordonnance*) that Charles wanted (see Mary to Charles, first letter of 1 July 1543, Aud. 54), but, according to both Giovio and Santa Cruz, Reynier van Nassau (d. 1544) joined Charles with 12,000 infantry and 2,000 horse from the Low Countries. Giovio's and Santa Cruz's numbers differ slightly from those projected in Charles's instructions for Boussu's mission to Mary, 13 June 1543, Aud. 54, as well as in the 19 June letter to Philip cited earlier. Only Santa Cruz knows about the 3,000 Spaniards under the command of *maestro del campo* Pedro de Guzmán, on whom see also Mary to Charles, 16 June 1543, Aud. 54 (Guzmán has arrived but has no money to pay his men), and by the hand of Lodewijk van Schoer, second letter dated 1 July 1543, Aud. 54 (the men can be paid from the 150,000 ducats Portugal's factor in Antwerp will provide [half of the dowry for Prince Philip's bride], if Charles pays 12% interest), and Philip to Charles, 7 August 1543, *Corpus Documental*, Letter CCLIX, II, 140 (Guzmán's 2,700 men [*sic*] arrived in Bruges by 17 July and are on the march).

[33] According to the way of estimating described in Chapter 7, note 39, the monthly wage for *Landsknechte* in 1543 would be 4.8 ducats, meaning a cost of 336,000 for 14,000 men for five months. I estimate 4 ducats a month for the Spanish infantry (up from the estimate of 3.4 used for 1535), meaning a cost of 299,600 ducats for 10,700 men for seven months; 130,000 for the 4,000 German cavalry for five months (at 6.5 ducats per man); and 19,614 for the 600 light horse for seven months (for the rate of 4.67 ducats per month mentioned in 1543, Charles to Philip, 19 June 1543, *Corpus Documental*, Letter CCLVIII, II, 132–133). For the Low Countries cavalry I assume the 5.2 ducats per month (thus 31,200 for 2,000 men for three months), and for the infantry (I take them to be Low Germans rather than High German *Landsknechte*) the same 4 ducats per month as for the Spaniards (thus 144,000 for 12,000 men for three months).

[34] Charles to Philip, 27 October 1543, 22 February 1544, *Corpus Documental*, Letters CCLXII and CCLXX, II, 171 and 212–213. On the 5,000 Spaniards, Philip to Charles, 4 February 1544, Charles to Philip, 14 February 1544, and the second of two letters dated 6 July 1544 (Charles has news that the 5,000 Spaniards have landed at Calais [then part of Flanders] and are on the march), *Corpus Documental*, Letters CCLXVII, CCLXVIII, and CCLXXIX, II, 193, 206–207, and 231–232. Because Santa Cruz speaks of 3,000 Spaniards joining Charles's army in September, it seems that some were assigned other duties.

[35] Said by Santa Cruz, (*Crónica del Emperador*, IV, 395,) to have been recruited in Holland and Guelders.

Spain, and a further 5,000 cavalry, of whom (according to Santa Cruz) 3,000 were German heavy cavalry. Brandi accepts Giovio's estimates, save that he gives different figures for the cavalry: 4,000 were German and 3,000 Italian – perhaps the light horse Charles normally recruited in Italy. Brandi also mentions that the expedition included 1,400 *pionniers* (diggers of trenches), sixty-three cannon drawn by 3,500 horses, 200 supply wagons with eight horses each, and (for making bridges if needed) seventy riverboats carried on wagons, with their crews.[36] But neither Brandi nor the two contemporary authors mention the 2,000 *Landsknechte* and 2,000 cavalry to be paid by Charles while fighting under Henry VIII's banner. All told, it seems Charles was responsible for 18,000 *Landsknechte*, 10,000 Spanish infantry, 10,000 Low German infantry, 5,000 German heavy cavalry, 2,000 Low Countries cavalry, and 2,000 Italian cavalry, which I take to have been light horse. The cost of all these units for five months (June through September, with October as the going-home month) would have been approximately 1,116,500 ducats,[37] or 1,339,800 with the usual 20% additions, and 1,514,800 counting the 175,000 for Charles's household.[38]

* * *

Charles's total costs for the two years of campaigning will thus have been something like 2,842,297 ducats. In both years he was again able to meet part of his expenses from what may be called windfalls, including the Portuguese dowry mentioned earlier, for the Infanta Maria's marriage to the future Philip II. With subtraction for interest charges for the first half of the 300,000 ducats, and exchange fees for the second, Charles will have had about 262,500 in cash.[39] Mary was able to use the second

[36] Giovio, *Historiarum*, in *Opera*, V, 210–211: Charles had "four legions of Germans drawn from the best cohorts [banners]," meaning, it seems, four units of ten banners, or 4,000 men (for the concept of regiments of ten banners, see Chapter 11, note 47); Santa Cruz, *Crónica del Emperador*, IV, 395–397; as was true also for the 1543 campaign, Santa Cruz knows about the Spaniards coming by ship (he puts their number at 3,000), but Giovio does not. Brandi, *Emperor Charles V*, 515. Kohler, *Karl V*, 287, accepts Brandi's estimates.

[37] A cost of 441,000 for 18,000 *Landsknechte* at 4.9 ducats a month for five months; 205,000 for 10,000 Spaniards at 4.1 ducats; another 205,000 for 10,000 Low Germans at the same rate; 165,000 for the 5,000 German heavy cavalry at 6.6 ducats; 53,000 for the 2,000 Low Countries cavalry at 5.3 ducats; and 47,500 for 2,000 Italian [light] horse at 4.75 ducats.

[38] Charles to Philip, 14 February 1544, *Corpus Documental*, Letter CCLXVIII, II, 206–207. Giovio, *Historiarum*, in *Opera*, V, 210–211, says Charles had "four legions of Germans from the best cohorts [four regiments of ten banners each would be 16,000 men]," as well as 7,000 Spaniards and cavalry from Germany and the Low Countries.

[39] Mary to Charles, second letter of 1 July 1543, Aud. 54, 141–143: if he is to pay out the first installment by August, Portugal's factor in Antwerp demands "the 12% it would cost him to raise this amount," which is less than the fee that would be charged to "change" or remit the money from Spain or Portugal.

half of the dowry, payable in Antwerp, for the 2,700 Spaniards.[40] In Italy Charles collected 150,000 scudi from Florence's Duke Cosimo I de Medici (r. 1537–1571) for the return of two citadels that had been occupied by Spanish troops since the surrender of the republican government in 1530, but it seems this money was earmarked for the marquess del Vasto and his garrisons in Lombardy.[41] In August, just as he was assembling his army, Charles received the happy news that the Indies treasure fleet commanded by Martín Alonso de los Ríos had arrived safely at Seville, with gold and silver valued at 542,000 ducats, meaning a royal share of 108,400. Young Philip, well taught by officials of the Consejo de la Hacienda, wrote his father that what was available from this treasure would have to be used for repairing the defenses of Calabria (ravaged by Barbarossa) and other urgent needs; for the *cambio* that Charles wanted other assignations would have to be found. Cobos was more cooperative, indicating that after the necessary subtractions he detailed, 300,000 ducats of this money (implying a sequestration in the amount of 191,600) would be remitted to Flanders, as the emperor had wanted.[42] Finally, the Parlamento of Naples voted in 1543 a *donativo* that may have yielded the emperor about 84,000 in Spanish ducats.[43]

For the French campaign Charles got help from another quarter when the Diet of Speyer (June 1544) agreed to support 24,000 infantry and 4,000 cavalry for six months, both for Charles's war against France and for standing guard against a possible Ottoman attack.[44] If this money had been raised at once and placed at Charles's disposal, he would have had the equivalent of about 650,000 ducats. But the imperial aide was also intended for Ferdinand's war against the Turks, not just Charles's war against France, and the imperial estates were notoriously remiss in meeting their quotas. It seems unwise to presume that Charles could have gotten his hands on anything more than the approximately 113,000 ducats that had been raised for the aide as of December 1544.[45] One should add a further

[40] Henry Kamen, *Philip of Spain* (New Haven, Conn., 1997), 8, 12; Mary to Charles, second letter of 1 July 1543, Aud. 54; Cobos to Charles, 7 August 1543, *Corpus Documental*, Letter CCLX, II, 154–155.

[41] Zimmerman, *Paolo Giovio*, 184–185; Charles to Philip, 19 June 1543, *Corpus Documental*, II, 130.

[42] Philip to Charles, 7 August 1543, and Cobos to Charles, also 7 August 1543, *Corpus Documental*, Letters CCLIX and CCLX, II, 135–136, 152–153; Carande Thobar, *Carlos y sus banqueros*, III, 248–252, seems to assume that Philip's opposition to a sequestration carried the day, but the correspondence seems to indicate otherwise.

[43] See Chapter 13.

[44] Paul Heidrich, *Karl V und die deutsche Protestanten am Vorabend des Schmalkaldischen Krieges, Frankfurter Historische Forschungen*, vols. 5 and 6 (Frankfurt, 1911).

[45] Charles to Philip, 17 October 1544, *Corpus Documental*, Letter CCXCII, II, 289, Charles hopes to get from the imperial aide some of the money needed to repay Mary's *cambio* of 171,450 ducats; Veltwyck to Charles, 11 December 1544, Lanz, Letter 529, II, 421, the imperial aide has brought in

168,000 ducats from another *donativo* granted by the Parlamento of Naples in 1544.[46]

From these sources, Charles will have gotten about 646,500 ducats in 1543 and no more than 281,000 in 1544. For the rest — some 1,914,797 according to the cost estimates given previously — Charles depended on short-term credit. But these were not good years to go knocking at the bankers' doors. The debacle at Algiers did not inspire confidence among lenders who (as noted in the preceding chapter) were already reluctant to lend during the months when ships for the great *empresa* were outfitted. In late November 1541, Tavera, having consulted with members of the Consejo de la Hacienda, had painted a grim picture for Cobos: merchants said to have cash on hand had none and, even if they had it, would not lend the crown a *maravedí* (1/375 of a ducat), not even on the promise of reimbursement from Indies gold and silver.[47] The only sizable loan contracts during 1542 were for 100,000 and 80,000 ducats in April and May, both payable by the Fugger in Germany.[48] Because Ferdinand and the German princes complained about Charles's lack of support for the campaign in Hungary,[49] one must assume the Fugger bank did not make these sums available for his benefit. More likely, the money was used by Mary in her recruitment of troops; she also received a second *cambio* for 50,000 ducats to meet her own military expenses.[50]

Hence instead of facing the enemy at Perpignan in the summer of 1542, Charles occupied himself in negotiations with the Cortes of Castile and

about 160,000 Rhine gulden (about 113,000 ducats) to date, and the archbishop of Salzburg will not pay his assigned portion, though he has money; Charles to Ferdinand, 15 January 1545, HHSA-B, PA 5, Konvolut 1, Charles has assigned on what is still due from the imperial aide the payments due to wagoneers from the last war, and for a detachment of Spaniards being sent to Hungary at his expense; and Charles to Ferdinand, 29 September 1545, HHST-B, PA 5, Konvolut 1, asking Ferdinand to release to his agent, Wolf Haller, money from the remnants of the aide, else it will be "impossible to satisfy" the Spaniards sent to Hungary and other expenses assigned on this money.

[46] See Chapter 13.

[47] Tavera to Cobos, 24 November 1541, Estado 51, 57–58.

[48] Carande Thobar, *Carlos V y sus banqueros*, III, 236–237 (nos. 169 and 170 in the series of loans), also 195, 243; the money was payable (in Germany) at the rate of 84 Kreutzer per ducat. The fact that the interest charges for loan no. 169 (100,000 ducats at 13% per annum) amounted to 57,712 confirms that it was not actually repaid until 1546.

[49] Fichtner, *Ferdinand I*, 129–135.

[50] Charles to Mary, 3 November 1542, cited note 11; Pölnitz, *Anton Fugger*, II, 244, cites (from *Letters and Papers, Foreign and Domestic, of the Reign of Henry VIII*, ed. J. S. Brewer [reprinted, 21 vols., Vaduz, 1965] 17, 534) a report from William Paget to Henry VIII, dated at Lyon, 31 July 1542, that Mary had contracted for a loan of 250,000 crowns from the Fugger just before the war began, and had since received 600,000 ducats from Spain. In fact, as Pölnitz notes elsewhere (II, 243, 575–576), Mary used Gasparo Ducci of Pistoia and Erasmus Schetz of Antwerp, rivals of the Fugger, as her loan brokers during this war (cf. Mary to Granvelle, 10 January 1544, HHSA-PA 41, Konvolut 1). That either Mary or Charles could have borrowed as much as 600,000 ducats in one loan during the first seven months of 1542 may be doubted.

Aragón for a renewal of the annual *servicios* in both kingdoms. Discussions with the Cortes of Aragón at Monzon lasted from June through August 1542, and the 71,111 ducats per year the deputies granted will not have allowed much for Charles's plans, once the costs for defense of the Pyrenees frontier and the coastline were subtracted. But Castile's much larger *servicio* was granted more quickly (see Chapter 14), and gave Charles room for maneuver, albeit not in the sense of providing security for new loans. Of the two loans for 1542 mentioned earlier, the first could not be repaid until collection began for Castile's ordinary *servicio* for the years 1546–1548, approved by the Cortes of Valladolid in February 1544. But Charles had no hopes of borrowing for the campaigns he had in mind until at least some of the unpaid loans from previous years were given assignations in which the bankers had confidence; this was what the *servicio* of Castile approved in 1542 accomplished.[51]

For loans for the current war, Charles's officials in Castile had to identify future revenues that bankers knew and trusted. Matching the references in Charles's correspondence to *cambios* by which he had money remitted with Carande Thobar's series of loans is not easy, because in some cases money from different sources was bunched together for remittance to Germany or Flanders. Once Charles departed from Spain (May 1543), he received four transfers of funds for the balance of 1543, not counting the previously mentioned 262,500 ducats for the Infanta Maria's dowry: (1) 165,000 ducats payable to Francisco Duarte as treasurer of Charles's forces in Germany, according to the terms of a larger loan contracted in Alcala (March 1543) by Rodrigo de Dueñas and agents of the Welser;[52] (2) 60,000 ducats also payable to Duarte, representing a loan negotiated by Granvelle in Augsburg in March 1543;[53] (3) a large *cambio* to Flanders for 420,000 ducats, which seems to have included the 300,000 taken (as Cobos promised) from the treasure fleet of Martín Alonso de los Ríos;[54] and (4) 210,000 ducats remitted to Antwerp by the Welser firm and Rodrigo de Dueñas as part of a much larger loan (August 1543).[55]

In other words, for 1543 Charles had some 1,201,300 ducats at his disposal: 370,900 in windfalls (the royal share of Martín Alonso's treasure plus the Infanta's dowry), 84,000 from Naples, 191,400 charged against Castile's long-term debt (*juros*) for the owners of sequestered treasure),

[51] Carande Thobar, *Carlos V y sus banqueros*, II, 536–537, III, 254; Brandi, *Emperor Charles V*, 473–476.
[52] Carande Thobar, *Carlos V y sus banqueros*, loan no. 189, and III, 244. The total transaction was for 150,000 scudi and 165,000 ducats, or 306,000 ducats in all.
[53] Ibid., loan no. 190, and III, 244–245.
[54] Cobos to Charles, 7 August 1543, cited note 42, and Carande Thobar, *Carlos V y sus banqueros*, III, 249.
[55] Carande Thobar, *Carlos V y sus banqueros*, III, 248, loan no. 201; a further 520,000 ducats was payable in cash or in merchandise within Spain.

and 555,000 in bankers' loans charged against other revenues in Castile. Charles also mentions a loan for 200,000 scudi (186,668 ducats) that he took out "here" (in Flanders) and assigned for repayment on the "gold and silver" of Martín Alonso's treasure fleet, despite the fact that Cobos had told him that what remained of the treasure was set aside for other purposes.[56] But because this loan does not appear in Carande Thobar's series, it must have been either refused in Castile, or rolled over into one of the transactions for the next year.

For the "great army" he planned to lead into France in 1544, Charles wrote Philip in November 1543 that Spain would have to furnish a *cambio* for 400,000 ducats, to go with some 300,000 he expected from subsidies granted or to be granted by Naples and Sicily. As the campaign season drew nearer, Charles decided he needed 500,000 from Spain; this money reached him in the form of *cambios* for 276,000, 200,000, and 33,500 ducats, representing two large loans contracted with the Fugger and one small loan from Rodrigo de Dueñas.[57] Between May and September, the Fugger and the Welser provided additional loans totaling 281,604, with the money payable in Germany or Flanders and repayable in Castile.[58] One should count also as spent on the war in France the 227,706 ducats sequestered from treasure ships arriving in November 1544; it was necessary to give disappointed owners of private treasure *juros* at 5% to 7% interest, instead of the usual 3%.[59] Charles thus got 1,018,810 ducats from Castile in 1544: 791,104 in bankers' loans, plus the 227,706 in sequestrations, charged against the kingdom's long-term debt. He also had some benefit from the grant from the imperial estates, estimated above at 113,000 ducats, and about 168,000 ducats from the *donativo* in Naples, and perhaps 60,000 from a *donativo* in Sicily, for a grand total of 1,359,810 in remittances for 1544.[60] For both years together, the remittances to the emperor that I can document came to 2,561,110 ducats, leaving him still a few hundred thousand ducats short of what he needed, according to the estimates previously given.

[56] Charles to Philip, 27 October 1543, *Corpus Documental*, II, 170. Cf. loan no. 207 in Carande Thobar's series (also *Carlos V y sus banqueros*, III, 253), a contract signed with agents of the Fugger in Brussels (December 1543), according to which the bankers were to pay out 176,000 ducats in Carolus gulden in Antwerp between January and April 1544, and a further 80,000 ducats in Rhine gulden in Speyer. Interest was 13% per annum, and the loan was assigned for repayment on the *cruzada*, clerical *subsidios*, and *remesas de las Indias*.

[57] Instructions to the Consejo de la Hacienda, with extracts from Charles's letters to Philip during November 1543, *Corpus Documental*, Letter CCLXIII, II, 173–174; Philip to Charles, 4 February 1544, *Corpus Documental*, Letter CCLXVII, II, 189–192; Charles to Philip, 14 February 1544, *Corpus Documental*, Letter CCLXVIII, II, 206–207; Carande Thobar, *Carlos V y sus banqueros*, III, 252–254.

[58] Carande Thobar, *Carlos V y sus banqueros*, loan nos. 229, 230, 231, and 236, also III, 253–259.

[59] Ibid., III, 269–273.

[60] See note 46; Blasi, *Storia de Vicere di Sicilia*, II, 85–86, mentions a Sicilian *donativo* of 100,000 scudi for the war in France.

The short-term campaign loans of these years – 555,000 ducats in 1543 and 791,104 in 1544 – have to be put in perspective. Between 1520 and 1542, the treasury of Castile contracted for short-term loans totaling 10,816,772 ducats, or an average of 470,293 ducats per year, including the 254,268 ducats borrowed during 1542. In 1543 and 1544 the treasury contracted for a total of 3,167,079 ducats in loans (1,583,539 ducats per year), or about 1.7 times as much as the largest amount for any previous two-year period. Of this amount, the thirty-one loans for 20,000 ducats or less, totaling 245,191 (average 7,907) may be treated as having to do with payments that had to be made even in peacetime (e.g., for garrison wages in Italy). But twenty-four large loans totaling 2,921,878 ducats (average 121,745) reflect overall expenses of the war against France and its allies. What is of most interest here is the portion of this sum – about 1,216,684 ducats, or 41.6% of the money borrowed – that was taken by Charles for his own campaigns.[61]

In September 1544, the Consejo de la Hacienda sent a report detailing how the greater part of the kingdom's disposable revenues for the years 1543–1548 had already been spent and for what purposes.[62] In preparing this report, the auditors did not count ordinary *servicio* income for the years 1543–1545 as available income, because the money was already spent, even if some of it was not yet collected. For the *rentas ordinarias* they reported only the amount expected to be left over after subtraction for *juro* interest. For incomes related to the church – the *maestrazgos*, the *cruzada*, and the clerical *subsidio* – they give estimates of gross receipts as well as of what remained after deductions for standing charges; my summary (Table 9.1) gives only the latter.

The auditors' tally of 1,871,367 ducats spent on *cambios* for the emperor suggests that my estimates for transfers to Charles were not large enough.[63] Charles will not have received the full 1,870,000 or so, because bankers sometimes deducted from their remittances (instead of charging the treasury) the 12% or more for exchange fees involved in moving funds from one country to another.[64]

The consequences of all this borrowing against future revenues may be gauged in two ways. First, all but the half of the Infanta's dowry that was transferred immediately to Antwerp involved interest payments:

---

[61] Carande Thobar, *Carlos V y sus banqueros*, III, 124–141 (loans for 1520–1532), 226–239 (loans for 1533–1542), and 321–351 (loans for 1543–1551). The previous highs for a two-year period were 1,851,604 in 1536–1537, and 1,734,863 in 1530–1531.

[62] "Relacion de la Hacienda," *Corpus Documental*, Letter CCLXXXV, II, 262–265.

[63] Especially since the first of the transfers for 1543 (the two loans for 165,000 and 60,000 ducats, payable in Germany) may have been assigned on the ordinary *servicios* for 1544 or 1545, and hence not counted in the Hacienda's memorandum of September 1544.

[64] See note 39.

Table 9.1. *Castile Revenues, 1543–1548, and* Cambios *for Charles Remitted, 1543–1544*

	Rentas	Servicios Ordinarias	Servicios Extraordinarias	Maestrazos	Cruzada	Subsidios	Oro y Plata
1543				74,100			
1544			266,667	74,100	100,000	(166,667)	573,500
1545	150,000		133,333	74,100	(148,000)	(166,667)	19,620
1546	150,000	266,667		74,100	(148,000)	(166,666)	
1547	150,000	266,667			(148,000)		
1548	150,000	266,667					
Spent on cambios	200,000		463,334	(70,613)	397,720	439,700	300,000
Other expenses			470,000	(70,613)	143,390	54,450	293,120
Left	400,000	266,667		156,113	18,690	0	0

Notes: Total listed revenues: 3,731,520; total for *cambios* 1543–1544: 1,871,367 (50.1% of total); total for other expenses: 1,031,573 (27.6% of total); total not yet spent as of September 1544: 841,470 (22.5% of total).
Source: "Relacion de la Hacienda," *Corpus Documental,* Letter CCLXXXV, II, 262–265.

3% to 7% in long-term *juro* interest to compensate the owners of sequestered Indies treasure, and 13% per annum for short-term bankers' loans, some of which could not be repaid for three years. Second, remittances to the emperor ate up just over half of all the disposable revenues surveyed in the September 1544 memorandum, some of which extended as far as 1548. After subtraction of about 27.6% for various other expenses, there was only about 22.5% left over for all of the government's unbudgeted needs over the next four years. In light of the fact that the 1544 estimate does not give figures for several kinds of income,[65] it might seem the future was not so grim. But if one takes into account that this government routinely had shortfalls of more than half a million ducats even in years of peace, it becomes clear that Charles's determination to "take" future revenues for immediate military needs portended disaster. The fiscal health of the kingdom had surely never been more endangered, as one may see from the initial refusal of Charles's demand (October 1544) that Spain take on still more debt (not listed here) to meet some of Mary's obligations in defending her Netherlands provinces.[66] What is truly remarkable is that in 1545, as officials in Castile were just beginning to appreciate how high the mountain of debt had risen, Charles was already laying plans for another great offensive.

[65] Extraordinary *servicios* for 1546–1549, *maestrazgos* for 1547–1548, the *cruzada* for 1548, and *subsidios* for 1547–1548.

[66] Charles to Philip, 17 October 1544, 30 November and 13 January 1545, *Corpus Documental,* Letters CCXCII, CCXCV, and CCCV, II, 289, 294, 328–329.

Chapter 10

The First Schmalkaldic War, 1546–1547

In the judgment of the Council of Trent's most distinguished historian, it was the Peace of Crépy that "removed the greatest obstacle" to the council's convening. Because the council was known to be ardently desired by the emperor, as a possible means of resolving Germany's dissensions, it would have been seen as a political instrument, lacking in religious legitimacy, had not France's king allowed his bishops to attend. But Germany's Protestant estates, suspicious of any synod of Catholic bishops, had made it clear they would not even consider sending representatives except to a "free" council, held on German soil, and thus not dominated by the papacy. Hence Charles in his discussions with Pope Paul III insisted on having the council meet in an imperial city (if not necessarily a German one); of the three such sites Charles proposed to the pope, and to Francis I at Crépy, the pope chose Trent, an imperial city on the Italian slope of the Alps. But the pope insisted on having his legate preside, which made it easier for German evangelicals to ignore the proceedings altogether. The bishops for their part showed little interest in conciliating Protestants. Instead of turning first to the question of how to reform the Catholic Church, they voted to take up doctrine. During the council's first session (December 1545–March 1547), Catholic responses on crucial points – like justification by faith and the sole authority of scripture – were formulated in ways that emphasized sharp differences between the doctrines of the Reformers and with what was henceforth to be Catholic teaching.[1] Thus if Charles by his victory in France had made it possible for the council to convene, he could not bend its will to serve his hopes for a peaceful reestablishment of religious unity in Germany.

---

[1] Hubert Jedin, *A History of the Council of Trent*, tr. Dom Ernest Graf (2 vols., St. Louis, 1957–1961), I, 501–504 (the quote); for the first session, vol. II.

Preparations for War

During the months following the Treaty of Crépy, Charles gave no sign he intended to make war on the Schmalkaldic League. An attack of the gout delayed until May 1545 his departure from the Low Countries for the Diet of Worms and yet another discussion of the terms on which Germany's estates might agree to raise an army against the Turks. In Castile, Philip promised to raise a good sum of money "for resistance to the Turk, or, in case he does not come [in person], for subjugation of those who have strayed [*desviados*]," meaning Germany's Protestants.[2] Brandi and Kohler both locate the emperor's decision for war in his conversations at Worms with the papal legate, Cardinal Alessandro Farnese, a nephew of Pope Paul III. Farnese had brought with him from Rome (and deposited at Augsburg) a sum of 100,000 scudi, to be used for war against the Ottomans. While Farnese returned to Rome for further instructions, Charles explained to Mary (2 June 1545) that the Turkish threat was less serious than had been thought and that the cardinal had not previously understood how unreasonable the Protestants were: they not only had no interest in sending representatives to Trent but demanded that Charles and Ferdinand give personal guarantees against any hostile action taken by the council. Mary's reaction was predictable. Even if it were true that the Protestants could not be reduced to obedience by peaceful means, one ought to consider "whether one can reduce them to obedience by force," and "whether it were not better for the good of Christendom to leave them as they are until it pleases God to dispose otherwise." Recalling wars of a hundred years earlier, when the Hussite armies of Bohemia stood off Emperor Sigismund (d. 1451), she wondered whether one could defeat the Schmalkaldic League in a single campaigning season. And could Charles truly rely on the continuing goodwill of France, or on the promises of the pope? Finally, Charles would have to depend on *Landsknechte*, "dangerous" men who were themselves infected with sectarian opinions: "I know not whether God wishes to reduce those who have strayed [*les desvoyez*] to obedience by men whose lives are so execrable."[3]

But Charles had already sent one of his Netherlands councillors, Viglius van Aytta, to explore an alliance with Duke William IV of Bavaria (d. 1550). Because Bavaria had long-standing territorial disputes with neighboring

---

[2] Charles to Philip, 13 January, 17 February 1545, and Philip to Charles, 25 March 1545, *Corpus Documental*, Letters CCCV, CCCVII, CCCXIII, II, 325–326, 337–338, 356.

[3] Brandi, *Emperor Charles V*, 525–528; Köhler, *Karl V*, 296, thinks Farnese was surprised by Charles's eagerness for war. Charles to Mary, 2 June 1545, HHSA-B, PA 42, Konvolut 2 (Charles to Philip, 2 August 1545, *Corpus Documental*, Letter CCCXXV, II, 402–403, offers the same rationale for a war against the Protestants); Mary to Granvelle, 1 July 1545, HHSA-B, PA 41, Konvolut 1.

Austria, it was considered a friendly neutral by the Schmalkaldic League; but it was also Germany's leading Catholic power. By early July, Farnese had returned with new instructions from Rome: for a war against the Protestants, the pope offered Charles 200,000 scudi (counting the 100,000 on deposit in Augsburg), in addition to 12,000 Italian infantry, paid for six months[4]. He also promised a grant of half the ecclesiastical incomes of all of Charles's realms for one year, and the right to sell lordships owned by monasteries, if he provided suitable incomes to replace them. Jean d'Andelot, a member of the inner circle, set out at once for Italy, ostensibly to visit Charles's daughter, Margaret of Parma (who was about to give birth), in fact to seek clarification from the Curia as to what rights the emperor would have over ecclesiastical property. But as Granvelle reported to Mary, it was also decided that "the season was too far advanced to make a great effort this year," especially as leaders of the Schmalkaldic League, fearful of attack, were already standing to arms.[5]

As a precondition for action in Germany, Charles had to have assurances of peace on the Ottoman front. Ferdinand and his forces had in recent years suffered major reverses, including the loss of Buda and Pest (1541) and of Esztergom (Gran, 1543), giving the Turks a direct control of central Hungary that was not to be shaken for more than 150 years. The alternative to further war was for Ferdinand to arrange a truce. But Charles and his advisers did not trust the King of the Romans to get things right; in their view, he had sent to the Sublime Porte an ambassador hobbled by "excessively humble" instructions.[6] Ferdinand agreed to having one of the emperor's councillors represent him at Istanbul. Cornelis de Schepper, who had represented Ferdinand to the Porte in 1533–1534,[7] was busy on other matters; hence Charles sent Geraard Veltwyck, a Granvelle protégé who had been one of the participants in the Regensburg Colloquy of 1541. In his new capacity as the emperor's ally, Francis I offered to have his ambassador at the Porte smooth the way for a Habsburg-Ottoman settlement. Charles gave Veltwyck ostensible instructions (to be shown to the French ambassador, whom he was to meet in Venice) endorsing the

---

4   Busto, *Geschichte des Schmalkaldischen Krieges*, 43, stresses this point: in addition to the 12,000 Italian infantry and 600 light horse, "para ayuda a pagar los alemanes [the pope] dio CC mill escudos." In fact, it seems the money was used for the pay of Spanish veterans from Naples coming by way of Venice (see note 58).

5   Charles's instructions for Viglius's mission to Duke William, June 1545, *Staatspapiere*, Document LXXIII, 394–397; Granvelle to Mary, 5 July 1545, HHSA-B, PA 41, Konvolut 4.

6   Granvelle to Mary, 19 March 1544, Charles to Granvelle, 26 March 1545 (responding to the latter's letters of 17 and 19 March 1545), HHSA-B, PA 41, Konvolut 4 (the first letter) and Konvolut 2; Veltwyck to Charles, from Istanbul, 12 July and 10 November 1545, Lanz, Letters 541 and 547, II, 456–459, 469–470.

7   See Chapter 7, note 29; it was Schepper who sent Doria a detailed report on Barbarossa's 1534 war fleet.

idea of cooperation, but his secret instructions were to find out, if possible, what his colleague's secret instructions were – what was France really up to? Veltwyck believed it was the French who had "tricked" Ferdinand into thinking that he would have to accept the humiliation of paying a tribute to the sultan. In the end, however, after more than a year of further discussions, the June 1547 Truce of Edirne (Adrianople) gave Ferdinand a five-year respite from war, in return for an annual tribute of 30,000 ducats. France was by now seeking another offensive alliance with the Porte, but the truce suited Suleyman's plans, because he was determined to lead a campaign against his foe to the east, the Safavid Shah of Iran.[8]

France was another source of concern, certainly in the view of Mary of Hungary and her advisers. Mary persuaded her brother to return to the Low Countries (September 1545) in hopes of concluding a peace between the kings of France and England, to forestall further fighting along her southern frontier. While in Brussels Charles learned of the death of Francis I's younger son, which in effect nullified the Peace of Crépy. France might now be expected to renew the war, because it was well known that Charles would never consent to have the dauphin (soon to be King Henry II) inherit Milan. At a meeting of the emperor's council on 24 September, as described by the duke of Alba, Lodewijk van Schoer, the president of Mary's Council of State, argued for seeking an alliance with England against France, putting the plans for a German campaign on hold; Alba favored following through on Charles's agreement with the pope to make war on the Schmalkaldic League. Meanwhile, negotiations between France and England dragged on; Henry VIII did not want to surrender Boulogne – he had conquered it fair and square – but he finally surrendered it for a payment of 2 million French crowns (June 1546). Mary continued to warn against the possibility of an attack from France, and on his return to Germany early in 1546, with Mary accompanying her brother as far as Maastricht, Charles promised her that in his efforts to pacify Germany he would "do everything possible to avoid the use of force." But in a letter to Philip he discounted the danger from France, calculating that both Francis I and his treasury were too exhausted to sustain another war.[9]

[8]   Veltwyck to Charles, 10 November 1545, cited in note 6; Lord Kinross, *The Ottoman Centuries* (New York, 1977), 233–235; Fichtner, *Ferdinand I*, 133–134.

[9]   Knecht, *Renaissance Warrior and Patron*, 494, 501–503; Charles to Mary, 25 July and 6 August 1545, both in HHSA-B, PA 42, Konvolut 2; Charles's instructions for Schepper's mission to Henry VIII, August 1545, HHSA-B, PA 42, Konvolut 5; Alba to Cobos, 4 October 1545, *Corpus Documental*, Letter CCCXXXII, II, 426; Mary to Granvelle (in the hand of Schoer), 10 January 1546, HHSA-B, PA 41, Konvolut 2; Charles to Mary, 9 June 1546 (recalling their conversation at Maastricht, "évitant jusques à l'extreme la voye de force"), Lanz, Letter 551, II, 486–487. Charles to Philip, 17 March 1546, *Corpus Documental*, Letter CCCXLIII, II, 453–454; Mary to Granvelle, 15 December 1546, HHSA-B, PA 41, Konvolut 1.

In Maastricht (February 1546), Charles was greeted by a delegation
of leading princes of the Schmalkaldic League, including Elector John
Frederick of Saxony (r. 1532–1556) and Landgrave Philip of Hesse, who
expressed concern about the rumored tenor of his recent negotiations
with papal emissaries and asked him not to bring troops into Germany.
The emperor replied that he had no plans for sending an envoy to Rome
and that his guests could see for themselves that his military escort or guard
was no larger than usual. But in an autograph memorandum of a few weeks
earlier, apparently intended for Ferdinand, Charles outlined his goals for
the forthcoming Diet of Regensburg: to make sure of his support among
the empire's Catholic princes, while "assuring [the Protestants] that I have
not made any treaty with his holiness." Ferdinand was delayed in coming,
but Charles wrote him from Regensburg (18 April 1546) that he would
not decide anything "until I have consulted with you expressly and in
detail." This note of indecision may have been intended for Mary's ears –
as Charles no doubt knew, Ferdinand and Mary regularly kept each other
informed of their efforts to influence his thinking[10] – but it may also have
been genuine.

  Busto presents a debate in Charles's council in which Granvelle argued
for the negative: there are no winners in a civil war, it would be dangerous
for the emperor to put himself in the hands of "Germans fighting against
Germans," and Germany's many fortified towns would take a long time to
subdue. Charles's Dominican confessor, Pedro de Soto, presented the case
for war: Germany is indeed populous and warlike, but "changeable as the
waves," an ill-disciplined people that "knows not what community is";[11] as
for their many fortified towns, "walls are an invention of weak and cowardly
men," as the ancient Spartans well knew.[12] Having weighed the opinions,
Charles declared that he had decided for war, and the council turned to
the question of how to achieve victory.[13] By 8 May Philip in Spain knew
about "the decision your majesty has taken to make this *empresa* against

---

[10] Charles to Philip, from Luxemburg, 17 March 1546, *Corpus Documental*, Letter CCCXLIII, II,
457–458; memo in Charles's hand, dated at Utrecht 30 January 1546, HHSA-B, PA 5, Konvolut 1;
for Charles's letter of the same tenor to Philip, dated 16 February 1546, Brandi, *Kaiser Karl V*, I,
465, and the citations given in II, 365; Charles to Ferdinand, from Regensburg, 18 April 1546,
HHST-B, PA 5, Konvolut 1. Mary and Ferdinand became well acquainted during the years between
her husband's death at Mohács (1526) and the beginning of her regency in the Netherlands (1531),
when she lived part of the time in Vienna. For examples of confidential exchanges between them,
Mary to Ferdinand, 30 September 1531, and Ferdinand to Mary, 15 November 1531, and 12 March
1532, *Familienkorrespondenz*, Letters 546, 586, and 629, III, 279–280, 378, 530.

[11] "No sabeys que cosa es comunidad."

[12] Soto was probably alluding here to Plato's *Laws*, bk. VI, 778B–E.

[13] Busto, *Geschichte des Schmalkalkdischen Krieges*, 28–35. For Soto's ardent advocacy of the treaty with
Paul III and the war against the Protestants, resisted by Charles for much of 1545, see Brandi,
Emperor Charles V, 536–538.

the Protestants."[14] The secret treaty of alliance with William of Bavaria, now concluded, was signed by both Charles and Ferdinand on 2 June, and by 9 June Charles was ready to communicate his decision to Mary: he and Ferdinand and the duke of Bavaria were agreed that the *conjuncture* was opportune, first, because the leading Schmalkaldic princes had lost credit because of war taxes that have "eaten their subjects to the bone" and, second, because the terms offered by Paul III promised a painless way to finance the campaign.[15]

Leaders of the Protestant estates at Regensburg glimpsed the mailed fist beneath the emperor's soothing words; when they asked him directly what purpose was to be served by the troops he was rumored to be raising, he answered that it was his duty to take up arms against the disobedient.[16] As the league's council decreed a mobilization for war, some member states took their own initiatives. According to a report from Bremen, the city's burgomasters were given authority to levy a 1% tax on property values to raise troops, for the citizens would rather give their life and blood than live under the pope. As Granvelle had said, Charles would in fact have had great difficulty subduing all of the centers of Lutheran militance in Germany. But his plan was to strike at the league's two preeminent leaders, John Frederick of Saxony and Philip of Hesse, in the hope that other princes and cities would then submit voluntarily. Hence in his official justifications for going to war, as in a letter to the Swiss Confederation, Charles stressed that his intention was to punish rebels, not, as the Schmalkaldeners claimed, "to wipe out God's Word with the sword." Ferdinand wanted to include Duke Christoph of Württemberg and the imperial cities of Augsburg and Ulm among those to be targeted, but Charles believed that having "punished" Saxony and Hesse "we will easily have our way with the rest." At Charles's direction, Ferdinand worked out the details of a secret alliance with John Frederick's cousin, Duke Moritz of Saxony; though himself a member of the Schmalkaldic League, Moritz agreed to attack Elector John Frederick's lands, in return for territorial concessions and vague promises about exchanging his ducal estate for the more prestigious electoral title.[17]

---

[14] Philip to Charles, 8 May 1546, *Corpus Documental*, Letter CCCCXLV, II, 470.

[15] On the agreement with Bavaria, Charles to Philip, 20 May 1546, *Corpus Documental*, Letter CCCXLVI, II, 471–472, and the text of the treaty, dated 2 June 1546, Lanz, Letter 623, II, 648–652; Charles to Mary, 9 June 1546, Lanz, Letter 551, II, 486–487.

[16] Brandi, *Emperor Charles V*, 543–549; some thought his target was the prince-archbishop of Cologne, who had refused to give up plans for a Protestant Reformation in his lands and had recently applied for membership in the Schmalkaldic League.

[17] Jan van der Vichte of Amsterdam to Cornelis de Schepper, 18 July 1546, *Staatspapiere*, Document LXXV, 402–406; Charles's instructions for Jean Mouchet's mission to Switzerland, 15 June 1546, with his letter to the Swiss Confederation, 1 August 1546, Lanz, Letters 553 and 561, II, 504, 512–514; Charles to Philip, 10 August 1546, *Corpus Documental*, Letter CCCLXIX, II, 489–491;

The Danube Campaign

Charles's plans called for blending armies coming from the west and south with regiments of *Landsknechte* raised by the colonels he kept on his payroll in Germany. From the Low Countries, Maximiliaan van Egmont, count of Buren, was to lead a large force of infantry as well as cavalry, paid for by raising a loan on Charles's rights to sell ecclesiastical property there. From Italy, Charles expected 2,000 Spaniards Philip was to send to Genoa on Doria's galleys; Spanish veterans from garrisons in Lombardy and Naples; and the Italian infantry and light horse promised by the pope.[18] Because the Schmalkaldeners were able to mobilize their all-German army more quickly, the crucial question was how soon help from Italy could reach the emperor and the *Landsknechte* who had joined him in Regensburg. North of Lake Como, troops coming from Spanish Milan had a choice of two routes. One ran east through the Val Tellina toward the valley of the Adige/Etsch River, leading to the Brenner Pass and Innsbruck; from here one could follow the Inn River northeast until it flowed out of the mountains near Rosenheim in Bavaria. The other and shorter route ran northeast through the Engadin (upper Inn) valley, following the river from its source; once in Tyrol, men on this track could save time again by turning north from the Inn (about forty miles west of Innsbruck) to cross a series of mountain shoulders, the last of which was the so-called Ehrenberger Narrows (Ehrenberger Klause), running between high peaks on the left and the Plan See on the right. Here the government of Habsburg Tyrol had built a fortress, commonly known from its Italian name, La Chiusa. Just beyond lay Füssen on the Lech River, leading toward Augsburg.[19]

Sebastian Schertlin von Burtenbach, the Schmalkaldic commander, knew his Alpine geography. Instead of attempting to attack Charles within the fortified city of Regensburg, he took the men who had first rallied to his banner – citizen militias from Augsburg and Ulm[20] – and marched up the valley of the Lech, past Füssen, to occupy La Chiusa at the Ehrenberger Narrows. Charles had to fall back to the south with most of his men, in order to shield the alternate route along the Inn; this retreat he judged

Charles to Ferdinand, 17 August 1546, HHSA-B, PA 5, Konvolut 1. On negotiations with Moritz of Saxony, see Rabe, *Reichsbund und Interim*, 68–70.

[18] Charles to Mary, 9 June 1546, Lanz, Letter 551, II, 489–491; Philip to Charles, 18 May and 3 July 1546, and Charles to Philip, 31 July and 10 August 1546, *Corpus Documental*, Letters CCCXLV, CCCXLVII, CCCLXVIII, and CCCLXIX, II, 470–471, 476, 481–483, 489–491.

[19] This shorter route also required having permission to cross the territory of the Graubünden (Grisons or Gray Leagues), a federation allied to but distinct from the Swiss Confederation.

[20] This detail from Avila, *Commentariorum de Bello Germanico*, 8v.

Map 10.1. The First Schmalkaldic War, 1546–1547

necessary, "even though some raised scruples in respect to the emperor's *reputacion*." Papal and Spanish troops reached the emperor's position near Landshut on 13 August, and Charles now set up camp near Ingolstadt to await Buren, as well as the German infantry and cavalry coming with him from the Rhine region. On 31 August the Schmalkaldic army, probably

Figure 10.1. *The Ingolstadt Cannonade*, in the 1550 Antwerp edition of *Commentariorum de Bello Germanico* by Luis de Ávila, University of Minnesota Library.

somewhat larger at this stage,[21] trained their artillery on the imperial camp.

In the accounts of two men who were there, Bernabé Busto and Luis de Ávila y Zuñiga, this was a bombardment like no other they had seen. For nine hours, says Busto, the ground shook as in an earthquake, "as if the hellish furies, the true authors of this pestilent invention, had sallied forth from their abyss of darkness." Avila notes that one ball fell at the emperor's feet, while another killed the man standing next to his commander in chief, the duke of Alba. Yet all during the bombardment Charles stood near his imperial standard (easily recognizable to enemy gunners) "as if made of marble," in Busto's words, and "by his example the other commanders did the same." As was the custom in this early age of artillery, soldiers who had withstood a bombardment collected the spent cannon balls, not just as a measure of their valor but also to be used again; on this occasion, after a second day of shelling, 1,700 cannon balls were piled up in the tent of Charles's master of artillery. Two weeks later (15 September), Buren's army and the additional German units joined Charles's new camp at Neuburg on the Danube.[22]

Charles now had an army large enough to seek battle, if the foe could be compelled to fight. In a council of war at Neuburg, his "colonels, *maestres de campo*, and other captains" discussed their next move. A strike at Augsburg was ruled out, lest the Schmalkaldeners, encamped near Donauwörth, get there first and force a long siege. Instead, it was agreed to make camp near Nördlingen, to cut off supplies coming to the enemy from Württemberg, and thus to force him to come out for a fight. According to Ávila and Busto, this decision was based on a collection of "maps of Germany and each of its provinces, painted" for the emperor before he came to Speyer (1545), and showing "the location of towns as well as the distances between them, and rivers and mountains." In the new camp, cold and disease took a toll; most of the pope's Italians left before the end of October, and in December Charles ordered Buren to withdraw towards the Rhine.[23]

---

[21] Busto, *Geschichte des Schmalkaldischen Krieges*, 61, says that at this time Schertlin had 70,000 infantry and 10,000 cavalry, or about twice as many men as Charles. This estimate is based on "a list I have containing the names and the quotas for the apportionment they [members of the league] made among themselves, indicating how much each prince and territory was to contribute in money and men." German princes and territories may have been more conscientious about their obligations as members of the league than about their obligations as estates of the empire (see Chapter 9, note 45), but Busto makes no allowance for the practical difficulties involved in raising men and money.

[22] Busto, *Geschichte des Schmalkaldischen Krieges*, 76–103; Avila, *Commentarium de Bello Germanico*, 30–31; Santa Cruz, *Crónica del Emperador*, V, 507–516 (the 1,700 cannon balls).

[23] Ávila, *Commentariorum de Bello Germanico*, 48; Busto, *Geschichte des Schmalkaldischen Krieges*, 111–112, 134, 147. While Ávila's translator speaks of a single *tabula* representing all of Germany, Busto speaks of *cartas y pinturas* for the separate provinces as well as a general map of the whole country. The description of what is shown on the map(s) – distances between the towns and so forth – is one point at which the language of the two authors is very close.

Nonetheless, Charles came out ahead in the Danube campaign, because of money.[24] To be sure, not even the emperor, with all his resources, could hold an army together indefinitely. He risked losing "religion, honor, and *reputacion*" (as he wrote Philip on 10 August) if he could not "sustain the camp" at least until the end of October; conversely, he could "accomplish something useful" with God's help and another 300,000 to 400,000 ducats – which Philip and his council were left to find as best they could. But the Schmalkaldeners were in a worse fix. By late October the Landgrave of Hesse was offering to negotiate; on 21 November, having used the last of his funds to give his men their going-home wage, he withdrew to Marburg. South German members of the Schmalkaldic League – the Count Palatine, the duke of Württemberg, and the free cities of Augsburg, Ulm, Frankfurt, and Strasbourg – opened discussions for the best terms they could get. Some in Charles's council urged making a winter camp rather than fighting on through the snows. Instead, he kept a good number of Spaniards and *Landsknechte* on his payroll, with some of the latter doing garrison duty in Augsburg and Frankfurt. The only army holding the field against him, that of John Frederick of Saxony, returned to the north (December 1546) to deal with the fact that Moritz of Saxony had invaded his cousin's lands, according to plan.[25]

The Campaign in Saxony

The fighting in Saxony did not go well. John Frederick repaid the compliment by laying siege to Moritz's chief towns, Leipzig and Dresden. Ferdinand was to have joined in Moritz's Saxon campaign with forces from Bohemia, but Lutheran and Hussite opinions were strong among the nobles and town deputies making up the estates, and they refused to credit the official Habsburg explanation for the war; rather, they gave ear to emissaries from John Frederick, who insisted that Charles and Ferdinand were out to eradicate the evangelical religion.[26] Ferdinand

[24] Brandi, *Emperor Charles V*, 549–562 (p. 555: "Charles had one advantage: his staying power was greater than that of the Schmalkaldic League").

[25] Charles to Philip, 10 August 1546, Philip to Charles, 27 September 1546, and Charles to Philip, 24 October 1546, *Corpus Documental*, Letters CCCXLIX, CCCLIV, and CCCLV, II, 489–492, 501–503, 508–510; Charles to Ferdinand, 4 December 1546 and 17 January 1547, HHSA-B, PA 5, Konvolut 1, and Konvolut 2.

[26] In fact, Charles considered issuing a general order for all subjects of the empire to return to the ancient faith, for it was widely believed he had fought the war for the sake of religion, and it was possible that "ordonnant avec ceste chaleur et chastisant les precheurs tous se y accomoderint." The alternative, favored by Charles, was to stay with the original plan of "punishing rebels," and consolidate the gains made thus far: Charles to Ferdinand, 9 January 1547, Lanz, Letter 566, II, 525–526.

made matters worse by ordering one of the opposition leaders decapitated, whereupon he himself was for a time immobilized by grief owing to the death in childbirth of his beloved wife, Anne Jagellio. Although John Frederick could not sustain the siege of Leipzig or Dresden, he maintained a strong position along the Elbe, not far from the borders of rebellious Bohemia.[27]

Thus in January 1547 Ferdinand sent urgent appeals for help from Charles. He wanted the emperor's cavalry, plus a third of his Spaniards.[28] Loath to divide his remaining forces, Charles recruited more troops and sent to Ferdinand's aid ten banners of infantry and 800 horse, commanded by a Protestant ally who was also a notorious robber-baron, Margrave Albrecht-Alcibiades of Brandenburg. The emperor himself would not venture into hostile country unless assured that imperial and allied forces would have superior numbers. How many men did Ferdinand have? Charles sent one of his Italian commanders to find out. News that Albrecht-Alcibiades had been intercepted and routed by John Frederick (2 March) – Charles blamed the defeat on a night of partying[29] – lent urgency to Ferdinand's continuing calls for help. Ferdinand now reported that he did not know how many infantry he would have, and that it seemed likely that Saxon forces would outnumber even the combined imperial army (in fact, the opposite was true). Nonetheless, Charles decided to march to Saxony, although his advance was delayed by an attack of gout.[30]

As planned, he joined forces with Moritz and Ferdinand at Eger, a Catholic town on the left bank of the Elbe, during the second week of April. They defeated a Saxon force near Meissen and proceeded downstream on the left bank, only to learn that John Frederick, having partially destroyed the bridge at Meissen, had crossed to the right bank. Disheartened by this news, Charles was about to turn back to Meissen when scouts reported there was a ford not far ahead, near Mühlberg. Although the Elbe was said to be chest-high at this point, and the opposite bank well defended by the enemy, Charles gave the order to press ahead. Arriving

[27] Fichtner, *Ferdinand I*, 151–156; Rudolf Kötzschke and Hellmut Kretzschmar, *Sächsische Geschichte* (Frankfurt am Main, 1965), 199–200.

[28] Busto says Charles had already sent *mastre del campo* Alvaro de Sande and his *tercio*, along with the marquess of Marignano and his *colonelia* of *Landsknechte* (4,000 men?): *Geschichte des Schmalkaldischen Krieges*, 160.

[29] According to Busto, *Geschichte des Schmalkaldischen Krieges*, 162, Albrecht-Alcibiades lodged in Rochlitz, where he "spent days and nights dancing"; knowing that John Frederick and his army were nearby, a lady of the town, married but not of good repute, and connected to the Landgrave of Hesse's sister, signaled to Albrecht that the time was opportune for a nocturnal visit. Ávila, *Commentariorum de Bello Germanico*, 99v–100, tells much the same story.

[30] Charles to Ferdinand, 17 January, 29 February, 10, 21, 26 March, and 2 April 1547, all in HHSA-B, PA 5, Konvolut 2; Charles to Ferdinand, 2, 19 February, and 10 March 1547, and Charles to Mary, 11 March 1547, Lanz, Letters 567, 572, 574 and 575, II, 530–531, 539–542, 545–547.

Figure 10.2. *Spaniards Wading the Elbe at Mühlberg*, in the 1550 Antwerp edition of *Commentariorum de Bello Germanico* by Luis de Ávila, University of Minnesota Library.

at the ford on 24 April, he positioned a few pieces of artillery and 1,000 Spanish *arcabuceros* to open fire on Saxon troops across the river, in hopes of breaking their line. At this point, according to Charles's description of the day's events to Mary, a small number of intrepid Spaniards (Busto gives eleven names) waded through chest-deep water, in the teeth of enemy arquebus fire, to seize enemy bridge-boats before the Saxons could scuttle them. Charles crossed on horseback at the ford, declining an offer to be carried across on the pikestaffs of his men, "as is done for the Po in Lombardy." Once the boats were lashed together the Spanish infantry and the imperial and allied cavalry were across within an hour. Shortly after nightfall the pursuers found where the remnant of the Saxon force had taken up positions in a wood, with their *arquebusiers* "like sleeves" on either side of the pikemen and crossbowmen. Discerning this disposition of the enemy, the duke of Alba divided his cavalry in squadrons to charge the *arquebusiers* and break their resistance. The battle was fierce but brief; John Frederick surrendered his sword. Brought to Charles, he was told that his fate would be decided according to the emperor's interests and his own deserts. Wittenberg opened its gates to Charles a few days later. With

John Frederick in captivity, Moritz was formally recognized as elector of Saxony and took up residence in Wittenberg.[31]

Philip of Hesse proved amenable to negotiation, through the mediation of Moritz (his son-in-law) and Elector Joachim of Brandenburg. Philip promised to pay an indemnity of 150,000 Rhine gulden (about 106,000 ducats), and to have all of Hesse's castles but one razed to the ground; on 19 June he knelt before Charles to offer his surrender, on the proviso that he not be punished in his person, or subjected to perpetual imprisonment. Charles ordered the Landgrave held in captivity until the indemnity was paid and the castles torn down. The two electors felt betrayed by this harsh treatment of their peer and kinsman, but owing to the fact that terms ruled out only a "perpetual" imprisonment, they had no grounds for complaint – at least not in the opinion of the emperor and his advisers. As Granvelle's son, the bishop of Arras, wrote rather smugly to Mary, Charles's *reputación* was enhanced by this humiliation of Hesse even more than by his victory over Saxony.[32]

The Augsburg Interim

In Protestant cities that had submitted to him, Charles mandated that Catholic mass once again be celebrated in some churches, notably in those belonging to the bishop, in episcopal cities like Augsburg and Strasbourg. (This reestablishment of the rights of Catholic minorities would turn out to be the only enduring change brought about by Charles's victory.) But it was now more doubtful than ever that the Council of Trent might be a venue for a general religious settlement: in March 1547, Paul III prorogued the council and ordered that it reconvene in Bologna, in the Papal States, where no Protestant delegates could possibly be expected to come. Charles was furious. His Spanish bishops refused to budge from Trent, and the reopened deliberations were stalled altogether when Charles's ambassadors proclaimed (January 1548) that, notwithstanding attacks on the church provoked by the pope, the emperor would take the church under his protection.[33]

The Habsburg brothers would thus have to settle Germany's quarrels on their own authority. Charles had considered the idea of simply requiring all

[31] Busto, *Geschichte des Schmalkaldischen Krieges*, 178–191; Ávila, *Commentariorum de Bello Germanico*, 107–109; Brandi, *Emperor Charles V*, 567–570; Charles to Mary, 25 April 1547, Lanz, Letter 583, II, 561–562.

[32] Charles to Ferdinand, 15 and 23 June 1547, both in HHSA-B, PA 5, Konvolut 2; Arras to Mary, 20, 21 June, and 11 July 1547, Lanz, Letters 591, 592, and 595, II, 585–586, 587–588, 599–600.

[33] Paul III ignored the emperor's wish to have a prelate of his choice take a turn at presiding over the council, and Charles refused to give the pope a veto over any religious concessions he might make to Germany's Protestants: Jedin, *History of the Council of Trent*, II, 403–413.

Figure 10.3. Titian, *Charles V as the Victor at Mühlberg*, Prado, Madrid.

subjects of the empire to conform to the old religion, in the hope that "if we punish the preachers everyone else will go along." But the tenor of this letter to Ferdinand (9 January 1547) indicates that he preferred "governing the empire according to its ancient customs, for it is important to rule each land according to the usages to which it is long accustomed." This meant convening a diet, to "make a confederation with the states of Germany against the rebels"; after all, the aims of "this enterprise" *(emprinse)* were to bring Saxony to reason, to punish Hesse, and to form a league. Ferdinand and his advisers proposed summoning the diet at once, but Charles declined to do so before "extirpating and defeating all the rebels [meaning Saxony and Hesse], to have the authority and *reputación* required for celebrating the said diet." Victory did indeed bring *reputación*, as may be seen from the portrait for which Titian was summoned from Venice to Augsburg in the spring of 1548, showing Charles as the victor at Mühlberg. Charles had invited select princes and cities to join him and Ferdinand in Augsburg in June, to discuss forming a league, but few of those in attendance showed any enthusiasm for the idea. Protestant cities saw a new league as an instrument of Catholic power, while the Catholic duke of Bavaria remembered the erstwhile Swabian League, cited by Charles as a precedent, as an instrument not of imperial unity but of Habsburg power.[34]

When the diet convened in September, also in Augsburg, the emperor's opening "proposition"[35] couched the issue of religious differences only in the most general terms, but these generalities were quite sufficient to spark furious debate. The diet's two colleges *(curiae)* – the seven electoral princes and the lesser princes of the empire – each had one vote. Deputies from the free cities, with no formal vote, could only hope to have their views incorporated in the responses *(vota)* to the emperor's proposition by one or another college. On this occasion, the college of imperial princes (in which prince-bishops and prince-abbots formed a majority) quickly endorsed the wisdom of the emperor's views. But the electoral princes could agree on nothing: over against the prince-archbishops of Cologne, Mainz, and Trier, the three secular electors, Saxony (a title now held by Moritz), Brandenburg, and the Palatinate, spoke for the empire's Protestant cities and territories. In the absence of consensus, the diet appointed a committee to craft a formula for religious peace. The committee's proposals (March 1548) included a compromise statement on the doctrine of justification by faith, similar to the one adopted by the conferees at Regensburg in 1541. They also allowed for marriage of the clergy, and for the laity to receive in communion the consecrated wine as well as the consecrated bread. In all other respects, Catholic beliefs and ceremonies were to be preserved, as well as episcopal governance of the church. This was the settlement, henceforth known as the Augsburg Interim, that Charles proclaimed (15 May 1548) as

---

[34] Rabe, *Reichsbund und Interim*, 118–176, 195–239, 407–449: the only concrete result of Charles's hopes for a league was an agreement by the Diet of Augsburg (May 1548) that the estates would make an annual contribution of 128,000 Rhine gulden to the imperial treasury. Charles to Ferdinand, 9 January and 2 February 1547, Lanz, Letters 566 and 567, II, 525–526, 530–531; Charles to Ferdinand, 19 February 1547, HHSA-B, PA 5, Konvolut 2.

[35] A formal statement of what the prince who convened the meeting wished the assembly to do, a usage common also in the Netherlands, Castile, and Naples (see Part III).

rules to govern the religious life of Germany until such time as a council of the church should provide a definitive solution.[36]

The Interim was the best Charles could do, even with the *reputación* of victory behind him, but it did not end Germany's religious divisions. To be sure, the Lutheran doctrine to which so many in Germany gave their allegiance insisted on the duty of obedience to rulers; it was thus unlikely to encourage a generalized rebellion against the lawful head of the empire. But in north Germany, important Lutheran towns fought off armed attempts to subdue them. This was notably true of Bremen and of Magdeburg, where theologians (refugees from Wittenberg) worked out the idea that under the imperial constitution it was the duty of imperial princes and imperial cities to resist the tyranny of the emperor. In south German cities that had submitted to Charles, preachers and their congregations were loath to return to Catholic ceremonies; in some towns, as in Ulm, pastors complied with the Interim only after being jailed for a time by a city government fearful of provoking the emperor's wrath. Moritz of Saxony, the emperor's key ally among Protestant princes, refused to accept the Interim. Philip Melanchthon and other theologians who had chosen to remain at Wittenberg (a university now under Moritz's control) drafted a modified version for use in Electoral Saxony, but even this compromise was rejected by the territorial estates.[37] Moritz of Saxony did prove willing to act as the emperor's deputy in dealing forcefully with Magdeburg and other pockets of resistance. But as the next chapter shows, Charles failed to reckon with the fact that Moritz was, like himself, a man of many agendas.[38]

Sinews of War

Barnabé Busto was a court chaplain who had enjoyed access to Charles since his appointment as imperial historian in 1545.[39] Luis de Ávila y Zuñiga was an old soldier who claimed to have fought in all the emperor's campaigns.[40] Both offer more detailed estimates of troop strength for this campaign than Charles's letters do. Busto believed he could give exact numbers for Charles's army at its greatest strength, after the arrival of Buren and the Germany cavalry in mid-September 1546: "I can give the particulars of the quantity of the emperor's army, because I looked at the

[36] Rabe, *Reichsbund und Interim*, 195–239, 407–449.

[37] Oliver K. Olson, "Theology of Revolution: Magdeburg 1550–1551," *Sixteenth Century Journal* 3 (1972): 56–79.

[38] Heinrich Lutz, *Christianitas Afflicta. Europa, das Reich und die päpstliche Politik im Niedergang der Hegemonie Kaiser Karls V (1552–1556)* (Göttingen, 1964), 63–64.

[39] Chapter 9, note 30.

[40] *Commentariorum de Bello Germanico*, 19v: "Omnibus bellis interfui." He lists all the campaigns discussed here save the failure at Algiers.

books of the paymasters and accountants;[41] this may seem idle curiosity, but I did not want to break faith with my readers, so they will credit me when I say there were not a thousand men more or less than what I report."[42] Both historians say there were about 8,000 Spaniards: the *tercio* of Hungary, under *maestre de campo* Alvaro de Sande (about 2,400 men);[43] about 3,000 redoubtable veterans who crossed the Alps, under *maestre de campo* Diego de Arze;[44] and the *tercio* of Naples (2,500 men) under *maestre de campo* Alonso Vivas, not the equal of the other two *tercios*, says Busto, because the men had grown "lazy" on garrison duty. There were also, in the army brought by Buren, another 800 Spaniards who had been fighting under Henry VIII's banner in France, no doubt in keeping with Charles's treaty with Henry of February 1544.[45] As ordered by the emperor,[46] there were also 16,000 High German *Landsknechte*, divided into regiments commanded by four of the colonels he kept on his payroll: Giovanni Baptista de Medici, marquess of Marignano, who was also master of artillery; Aliprando Madruzzo, brother of Cristoforo Madruzzo, the bishop of Trent; Georg von Regensburg; and Bernhard von Schaumburg.[47] Finally, there were also 10,000 Italian infantry commanded by the pope's grandson, Ottavio Farnese, and 10,000 "Low Germans" commanded by Buren,[48] making 44,000 infantry in all. The 7,000 cavalry were likewise of diverse composition: 3,000 German men-at-arms led by Archduke Maximilian,

[41] Busto's estimates for Charles's army would thus be more reliable than his estimates for the Schmalkaldic army, based on quotas for troops to be raised by leaque members (note 21).

[42] *Geschichte des Schmalkaldischen Krieges*, 44. Avila seems to have consulted the paybooks too: see note 45.

[43] These were the men Charles had sent to Hungary to assist Ferdinand in 1545, hoping to have them paid from remnants of the aide consented by the imperial diet in 1544 (Chapter 9, note 45).

[44] For these men, see Charles to Philip, 31 July 1546, *Corpus Documental*, Letter CCCXLVIII, II, 482–483: the "men from Hungary" have already arrived, and the "seven banners from Lombardy" will cross the Alps with the 2,000 men coming from Spain. The Spanish banner or company was evidently quite a bit smaller than the German banner of 400 men. Busto (*Geschichte des Schmalkaldischen Krieges*, 72) says of these 3,000 men that "they were all so skilled and experienced that each man could have been a captain."

[45] Busto, *Geschichte des Schmalkaldischen Krieges*, 44, 54, 72, 73, 103, and Ávila, *Commentariorum de Bello Germanico*, 7v, 18v. Avila does not mention the men from Lombardy, nor does he have any criticisms of the men from Naples. For the treaty of February 1544, see Chapter 9, note 26.

[46] Philip to Charles, 18 May 1546; Charles to Philip, 31 July and 10 August 1546, *Corpus Documental*, Letters CCCXLV, CCCXLVIII, and CCCXLIX, II, 470–471, 481–483, 489–491.

[47] Busto, *Geschichte des Schmalkaldischen Krieges*, 44–46; Ávila, *Commentarium de Bello Germanico*, 18v. Both writers also mention additional *Landsknechte* recruited by a bastard son of Duke William of Bavaria; Ávila says there were ten banners, or 4,000 men. It is not clear whether they formed a separate regiment or filled in the others, but I follow Ávila in estimating only 16,000 *Landsknechte* in all: "Quamquam pro librariorum ratione 20,000 numerus in tabulas militares referratur" (even though a figure of 20,000 men was entered in the books of the accounting clerks).

[48] Busto, *Geschichte des Schmalkaldischen Krieges*, 44, 62, 103.

Ferdinand's eldest son, Johann von Brandenburg, grand master of the Teutonic Knights, and his brother, Marquess Albrecht-Alcbiades of Brandenburg; 2,000 Low Countries heavy cavalry under Buren's command; the 600 Italian light horse serving, like Farnese's infantry, on the pope's payroll; and another 400 light horse not further described.[49] Charles planned to make several smaller units into what he called a company: the 100 men-at-arms he had with him (part of his guard?), 100 men from the Low Countries *compagnies d'ordonnance* and 200 mounted *arquebusiers* that Mary was sending with Buren, and 300 men-at-arms from Naples.[50]

Different units on the emperor's payroll served different lengths of time. Buren's 10,000 Low German infantry and 2,000 cavalry had to be mustered in August in order to reach Charles's camp by mid-September, and they went home in December (five months). According to Busto, Charles still had about 8,000 Spaniards at the time of the battle of Mühlberg (April 1547; because fighting continued into May, I count June as the going-home month). The *tercios* joined him at various times, but since those coming from farther away had to be mustered some time before their arrival in Germany, it seems reasonable to count all of them as serving for twelve months (July 1546–June 1547). Of the four regiments of *Landsknechte*, three joined Charles's camp during the course of July, but Schaumburg's men came only in September. Busto's account makes it seem that these units were kept up to strength until Mühlberg, because he represents Charles as marching into Saxony with about 6,000 Spaniards and 10,000 to 12,000 High Germans; the smaller figure for the *Landsknechte* is given also in Charles's correspondence.[51] These numbers do not include the 2,000 Spaniards and the regiment of *Landsknechte* previously sent to the aid of Ferdinand.[52] The emperor will thus have been responsible for 12,000 High Germans for six months (July through December), and 4,000 for four months (September through December). It seems he had about 2,000 fewer men from January on, but kept them on the payroll through June. Two thousand of the German heavy cavalry were scattered or captured when Albrecht-Alcibiades was defeated by John Frederick in early March (meaning they will have served for seven months), but at Mühlberg, again according to Busto, Charles still had some 2,000 cavalry, including 1,000 German men-at-arms, the 300 from Naples, and some light horse;

---

[49] Ibid., 44, 46, 62, 76, 103. In addition to these men (6,000 in all), Busto mentions 300 mounted "archers," the mounted men of Charles's guard, and 200 "courtiers" attending on the emperor. For the cavalry, I follow Busto rather than Ávila, *Commentariorum de Bello Germanico*, 19–19v, whose listing of units and commanders is less complete.

[50] Charles to Mary, 9 June 1546, Lanz, Letter 551, II, 489–490.

[51] Charles to Ferdinand, 17 January 1547, HHSA-B, PA 5, Konvolut 2.

[52] Busto, *Geschichte der Schmalkaldischen Krieges*, 160–163.

if dismissed in June, these men will have served ten months. The costs for all these units at the stated lengths of service may be estimated at 2,025,363 ducats.[53] One must also count 46,400 for a month's wages for the 10,000 or so newly recruited *Landsknechte* captured or scattered when Albrecht-Alcibiades was defeated,[54] and 386,000 ducats for another army that fought for Charles's cause in northern Germany. This force, 7,400 Low Germans and 1,400 horse recently released from the service of the Count Palatine, was enrolled under the emperor's banner in July 1546 by one of his Low Countries commanders, Josse van Cruningen; they presumably served under Cruningen until he fell in an unsuccessful siege of Bremen (30 March 1547).[55] To the combined figure of 2,457,763 ducats one must add 20% for victuals, officers' pay, and the artillery and baggage trains, and 175,000 for the emperor's household expenses, yielding a total cost for this war of 3,124,316 ducats.

* * *

Against this massive need for money the "windfalls" of 1546–1547 were meager. Cargoes on the treasure fleets of 1545 and 1546 were disappointingly small; Philip had 150,000 in specie, possibly representing the royal share from both fleets, taken from Seville "secretly," owing to the shortage of specie in the realm, for shipment to Genoa in September 1546.[56] In Charles's mind the money for his war against German heretics was to come from the wealth of the church. In private conversations with the emperor

53 For the *Landsknechte* (at an estimated 5.18 ducats per month, as explained in Chapter 7, note 39), 372,960 for the 12,000 men serving from July through December 1546, 82,880 for Schaumburg's regiment, and 435,120 for the 14,000 who continued serving through June 1547, or 890,860 in all. For the 8,800 Spaniards serving at an estimated 4.5 ducats a month, I count 475,200. For Buren's 10,000 Low German infantry and 2,000 cavalry for five months, I use the combined value of loans 259, 260, 261, 261bis, and 264 in Carande Thobar's series, that is, 370,403. For 2,000 German heavy cavalry in Charles's service for seven months, at an estimated 9.1 ducats, 127,400, and for 1,500 for ten months, 136,500; and for 500 light horse for ten months, at an estimated 5 ducats, 25,000.
54 Busto, *Geschichte des Schmalkaldischen Krieges*, 158.
55 Report of Jan van Vichte of Amsterdam to Cornelis de Schepper, covering the period 1–18 July 1546, *Staatspapiere*, LXXV, 404–406; Brandi, *Emperor Charles V*, 570–571. Elector Frederick of the Palatinate may have been hoping to assert the claim of Denmark of his wife Dorothea, Charles's niece, despite Charles's recognition of Christian III as king of Denmark in the 1544 Treaty of Speyer. He was also negotiating at this time to join the Schmalkaldic League, but negotiations broke down (Brandi, 540). Cruningen's force is obliquely mentioned in Busto, *Geschichte des Schmalkaldischen Krieges*, 158: Charles has two of his colonels raise twenty banners of infantry and some cavalry to attack the cities of "East Frisia" (Bemen?) and reduce them to obedience. I estimate four ducats a month for the infantry (thus 288,00 for ten months) and seven ducats a month for the cavalry (98,000).
56 Philip to Charles, 27 September 1546, *Corpus Documental*, Letter CCCLIV, II, 501–503; Carande Thobar, *Carlos V y sus banqueros*, III, 268–274.

at the Diet of Worms (May through June 1545), Cardinal Alessandro
Farnese promised on behalf of Pope Paul III a grant of 500,000 ducats on
church property in Spain, plus an equivalent sum in the form of a renewal
of the *subsidio* or tax on clerical income. As these negotiations were
finalized at the Diet of Regensburg (June 1546), the pope also undertook
to provide 100,000 scudi in cash, in addition to the 100,000 scudi already
on deposit with bankers in Augsburg, and to raise and maintain for six
months 12,000 Italian infantry and 500 light horse. In attempting to
persuade a skeptical Mary of Hungary that his plans for this war were
well made, Charles stressed the 200,000 scudi promised by the pope, plus
the 800,000 to 1 million more from rights given him by the pope to tax
clerical income in Spain and the Low Countries, and to sell monastic
properties.[57] The pope's 200,000 scudi (186,668 ducats) did indeed help
to oil Charles's war machine; in late June 1546, the Fugger firm's agent in
Rome received instructions that the second 100,000 as well as the 100,000
on deposit in Augsburg were both to be remitted to Venice,[58] presumably
for the pay of Spanish troops coming by way of the Adige valley and
the Brenner Pass. But the promise of money from church wealth proved
disappointing, especially in the Low Countries. Mary was to pay the
wages of Buren's infantry and cavalry (at least for the march to join Charles
in south Germany) by raising a loan on Charles's rights to sell ecclesiastical
lordships, recently granted by the pope. Because no banker would advance
money against this new and uncertain income, Philip had to send Mary a
letter patent authorizing her to charge the needed sum to the treasury of
Castile.[59]

Once he had managed to outlast the main armies of the Schmalkaldic
League, Charles also reaped a substantial windfall in the form of indemnities
from the Protestant towns of south Germany that submitted to him in
January and February 1547: 100,000 Rhine gulden each from Nördlingen,
Schwäbisch Hall, Dinkelsbühl, and Rothenburg-ob-der-Tauber, 200,000
from the duchy of Württemberg, and from large and wealthy Ulm. Charles
demanded a further 200,000 from Augsburg, Germany's banking center,
but because city fathers had already burdened their treasury in preparing
for a possible siege by the emperor, he settled for 150,000; the agreement
was the more attractive to Charles because Augsburg promptly paid the

[57] Brandi, *Emperor Charles V*, 527–529, 544–545; Charles to Mary, 9 June 1546, Letter 551, II, 487–488.
The statement by Pölnitz (*Anton Fugger*, III, 177) that Charles hoped for "800,000 ducats in papal
subsidies" is a misreading of this letter.

[58] Pölnitz, *Anton Fugger*, III, 190. Cf. Charles to Philip, 10 August 1546, *Corpus Documental*, Letter
CCCLXIX, II, 489–491, the army (*tercio*?) of Naples disembarked "in the sea of Venice" on 25 July
1546.

[59] Charles to Mary, 9 June 1546, Lanz, Letter 551, II, 489–491; Philip to Charles, 3 July 1546, *Corpus
Documental*, Letter CCCXLVII, II, 476.

full sum in cash, thanks to a 100,000 gulden loan to his native city by Anton Fugger. Landgrave Philip of Hesse also promised 150,000 gulden as part of his submission (June 1547). If all of these sums were in fact paid – not every city or prince had an Anton Fugger ready to hand – Charles will have collected the equivalent of about 777,340 ducats. It is possible these payments financed the campaign along the Elbe, including the subsidy for Duke Moritz of Saxony. More likely, as with the Landgrave's 150,000 gulden, money received in this way went to settle accounts and pay the going-home wage of troops no longer needed.[60]

Counting the money from the pope and the German princes and towns and the 150,000 in Indies treasure, Charles had about 1,114,008 of the 3,124,316 ducats he will have needed for the 1546–1547 campaign according to the previous estimate. Naples was again helpful but less so than usual: Charles may have had the use of about 123,000 Spanish ducats from the *donativo* of 1546.[61] The balance had to come in the form of short-term loans, charged against a treasury of Castile still struggling to meet its debts from the past two wars. According to Carande Thobar's figures, between 18 May 1546 and 5 July 1547 the treasury contracted for 1,939,992 ducats in loans. Subtracting in both cases loans provided by Spanish bankers and payable in Spain itself – monies that will mainly have been used for the defense of Castile and Aragon – we may estimate that Charles borrowed 1,563,431 of the 1,939,992 ducats for use outside Iberia between May 1546 and July 1547.

During the campaigns against Cleves and France, the treasury of Castile had been able to assign huge loans on future revenues. With the Welser and their Castilian partner, Rodrigo de Dueñas, there were contracts for 306,000, 730,000, and 170,000 ducats; the Fugger signed on for loans of 266,539, 200,000, and 112,500 ducats, while the Grimaldi of Genoa agreed to provide 158,667 ducats.[62] It was also possible to remit vast sums at Charles's command, notably the *cambios* for 466,500 ducats delivered into the emperor's hands in Brussels (1544) by Martín Alonso de los Ríos, commander of the Indies treasure fleet of 1543, whose gold and silver backed a large part of this transaction. During the First Schmalkaldic War, however, all but one of the loans in excess of 100,000 ducats involved a rollover of unpaid debts from previous transactions. Bankers in Antwerp would not lend money for Buren's army, even after Philip backed Mary's promises with a letter patent "signed by my hand," until they got agreement that at least part of their money would be repaid in Antwerp rather than

[60] Pölnitz, *Anton Fugger*, III, 326, 353, 362–366, 393–397, 414–415, 426, 451–452; the bishop of Arras (Granvelle's son) to Mary, 11 July 1547, Lanz, Letter 595, II, 600.
[61] See Chapter 13.
[62] Carande Thobar, *Carlos V y sus banqueros*, loan nos. 189, 201, 218, 207, 213, 229, and 224.

Spain. Mary protested (in vain) that a twofold *cambio* – sending money from Flanders to Germany for Buren's troops, and from Spain to Flanders for repayment – could reduce the value of that part of the loan by as much as 40%. The real worth of the various loans for Buren's men, with a face value equivalent to 370,403 ducats, was probably reduced by exchange fees to no more than 280,000.[63] Also in Antwerp, Italian and German financiers provided large sums to liquidate the controversial transaction in which Mary of Hungary had been authorized by Charles to charge some of her war debts to Castile (October 1544).[64] In Genoa, the loyal Centurione clan stepped in to take over loans from colleagues evidently not willing to bet on the emperor's solvency.[65]

The Fugger still provided an impressive sum – 499,162 ducats, including a loan for 140,000 ducats at the start of hostilities (May 1546) – but even they had provided more in 1543–1544 (785,653 ducats). The Welser loaned only 121,114, as opposed to 554,556 in 1543–1544.[66] Political circumstances in Germany help to explain the bankers' diminished enthusiasm for lending to the imperial house; the Catholic Fugger and Welser were under great pressure from Protestant Augsburg to open their purses to Charles's Schmalkaldic foes, not to the emperor himself.[67] Also, money was tight during these months in Antwerp and in south Germany.[68] Yet the bankers' knowledge that their loans were being assigned to revenues three years or more into the future was surely a major part of Charles's borrowing problem. In May 1547 the Welser agreed to provide 34,557 in new credits only when treasury agents in Castile had secured repayment of 168,443 ducats in old debts, partly by a transfer of the *maestrazgo* properties. In September 1547 the Fugger initially agreed to lend 208,000 scudi (200,387 ducats), but after certain arrears were cleared, Charles had to settle for 78,000 ducats in new funds – a sum that could not be repaid until it was rolled over in another transaction in 1552.[69]

In July 1548 Charles received a report from the Consejo de la Hacienda on the 3,315,000 ducats in debt still outstanding; counting exchange fees and interest running for several years, the auditors calculated that some of these loans would have netted the emperor only half of what it would cost to service and repay them. This overhang of debt hampered Charles's plans

[63] Philip to Charles, 3 July 1546, *Corpus Documental*, Letter CCCXLVII, II, 476; Carande Thobar, *Carlos V y sus banqueros*, III, 288–300, and (for Buren's men, as indicated in note 53) loans 259, 260, 261, 261bis, and 264 in the series; Pölnitz, *Anton Fugger*, III, 257.
[64] Carande Thobar, *Carlos V y sus banqueros*, loans 235, 238, 262, 263, and 281.
[65] Ibid., loans 266, 267, 270, 271.
[66] Ibid., loans 256, 258, 265, 282, 284, and 286 (Fugger loans), and 257, 285, and 287 (Welser).
[67] Pölnitz, *Anton Fugger*, III, 169, 178, 205, 222, 225.
[68] Ibid., 16, 280.
[69] Carande Thobar, *Carlos V y sus banqueros*, loans 287, 291, 293, and 371, also III, 304–306, 365.

for a political and religious settlement in Germany, which required keeping garrisons in cities that had submitted to him, and concluding negotiations with territories and towns that still held out. To be sure, these negotiations produced further indemnities that covered some of the costs; for example, Francisco de Eraso, the secretary who handled negotiations with lenders, sought to have the 150,000 Rhine gulden (about 106,000 ducats) provided by two Nuremberg bankers assigned on the indemnity agreed to by the duke of Pomerania.[70]

Some loans and obligations Charles tried to assign on Naples and Sicily, but not always successfully. The expenses of Philip's progress through the lands he would one day inherit (October 1548–May 1551), reckoned at 200,000 scudi per year, had to be borne entirely by Castile, because the Viceroys of the two southern realms convinced Charles there was no room in their budgets for the shares originally assigned to them.[71] During Philip's absence Charles entrusted Castile and Aragón to his daughter Maria and her new husband, Archduke Maximilian of Austria, Ferdinand's eldest son. In January 1549 he wrote Maria and Maximilian that he owed various bankers 600,000 scudi from his "recent military expedition"[72] in Germany for which Mary of Hungary had given her personal obligation, and from which she asked to be relieved; because one loan for 180,000 was due on 15 May, he ordered that the money be remitted to Antwerp in advance of that date. This request was a shock to the Consejo de la Hacienda: "We were assured your majesty would not be commanding any further remittance [cambio] for this year." In fact, the auditors reported, there were already over 1 million ducats in required expenses for 1549, as against a mere 132,000 ducats of revenue not yet assigned. Charles had suggested that the 180,000 scudi might be raised by selling juros or properties belonging to the three military orders (maestrazgos). The council scotched both ideas: no juros could be sold because there was nothing left of the rentas ordinarias on which these annuities were assigned,[73] and the treasury was counting on the one sale of order properties in prospect to pay the annual wages

<hr />

[70] Charles to Philip, second letter of 8 July 1548, Corpus Documental, Letter 397, II, 640–643; Pölnitz, Anton Fugger, IV, 143. These loans will not have been assigned on Spain: neither of the two bankers – Jobst Teztel and Gabriel Nützel – is mentioned in Carande Thobar.

[71] Charles to Maria and Maximilian, 9 October 1549 and 15 March 1550, Corpus Documental, Letters CDXLIX and CDLXIII, III, 159–160, 196. It is also possible that a loan by Anton Fugger for 150,000 scudi, to be repaid in Naples, had to be reassigned on Castile as 150,000 ducats, in effect adding a half year's interest as part of the principal: compare Pölnitz, Anton Fugger, III, 576, with loan no. 298bis in Carande Thobar, Carlos V y sus banqueros.

[72] The expression is jornada passada, which can mean either a journey or a military expedition; because Charles says much of this debt has already been "prolonged once" (i.e., extended beyond the usual one-year contract), it seems he is referring to debts contracted during the First Schmalkaldic War.

[73] According to Carande Thobar, Carlos V y sus banqueros, II, 91, the rentas ordinarias yielded 470,615 ducats in 1550; of this total, 291,032 went for interest on juros, and 117,910 for other standing

of troops guarding Spain's frontiers. In the end, it seems Charles got his 180,000 scudi from a sale of urban magistracies and notarial licenses.[74] Both Charles and his officials sought to lessen the burden on Castile. Only 147,370 ducats in new loans were charged to the treasury in 1549, and for 1550 Charles promised to find "here" (in the Low Countries) the 175,000 ducats for his household. Yet these measures did nothing to reduce the Schmalkaldic War debt still outstanding. In January 1550 Charles instructed Maria and Maximilian to bargain as best they could for an extension of unpaid loans, and to assign for their repayment all moneys received from fines and confiscations, including the portion previously assigned to the guilty party's hometown; he allowed himself the comfort of believing that in this way the debt might be paid off in "four or five years."[75]

charges on these revenues, leaving 167,792; these balances sometimes served as assignations for loans (see Table 8.1).

[74] Charles to Maria and Maximilian, 25 January 1549, Consejo de la Hacienda to Charles, 19 February 1549, and Charles to Maria and Maximilian, 26 March and 4 May 1549, *Corpus Documental*, Letters CDXVI, CDXXVII, CDXXXVII, and CDLII, III, 69, 92–94, 110–111, 119–121. See Chapter 14 for the political implications of the creation of surplus magistracies.

[75] Charles to Maria and Maximilian, 25 January and 29 April 1550, *Corpus Documental*, Letters CDLVI and CDLXVI, III, 173–174, 203; Carande Thobar, *Carlos V y sus banqueros*, loans 303–307.

Chapter 11

The Second Schmalkaldic War and the Assault on Metz, 1552

The financial exhaustion of Charles's realms mandated an interlude of peace. In the Low Countries, subsidies granted by the provincial states fell to a fraction of levels reached during the emperor's campaigns against Cleves and France.[1] As for Castile, Charles accepted Philip's assurances that he had "mortgaged" all of the kingdom's disposable revenues, and the bankers knew better than anyone that Castile's well was running dry. Asked in September 1547 to advance 208,000 ducats, the loyal Anton Fugger provided only 78,000, because his agents or factors in Spain could not certify that the conditions of repayment he demanded had been met.[2] As of July 1548, the Antwerp financiers who had provided most of the money Mary used for Buren's army two years earlier were still not satisfied by the terms of repayment Philip had offered. To save money, Charles dismissed most of the "guard" he maintained in Germany, and took up residence in the Netherlands (September 1548–July 1550).[3]

For the time being, Charles's enemies lacked either the will or the resources for an effective combination against him. Henry II of France (r. 1547–1559) had scores to settle, and anti-Habsburg exiles from Naples as well as Medici Florence had an honored place at his court. But the treasure that Francis I had left in the Louvre was mostly owed to the bankers of Lyons, and the kingdom was exhausted from four years of war against Charles and against Henry VIII (1542–1546). Sultan Suleyman, on

---

[1] Tracy, "The Taxation System of Holland," table I, p. 108: annual averages of total sums consented by the States of Holland were 276,920 gulden for the years 1542–1545, and 112,154 gulden (40% of the previous total) for 1546–1551.

[2] Charles to Philip, 8 July 1548; Charles to Philip, 18 January, 11 February 1548, and 16 September 1547, *Corpus Documental*, Letters CCCXCVII, CCCLXXIX, CCCLXXX, and CCCLXXI, II, 640–643, 572, 595–596, 547.

[3] Philip to Charles, 23 July 1547, Charles to Philip, 27 November 1547, and 8 July 1548, *Corpus Documental*, Letters CCCLXVI, CCCLXXVI, CCCXCVII, II, 536, 558–559, 640–642; Charles to Philip, from Speyer, 2 September 1548, *Corpus Documental*, Letter CCCXCIX. II, 660–661.

campaign against Persia in 1548, had no reason to break the five-year Truce of Edirne (Adrianople, June 1547). Charles had enemies among Germany's Lutheran princes – like Margrave Hans of Brandenburg-Küstrin, a former ally whom the emperor had expelled from the Diet of Augsburg for refusing to accept the Interim – but no one of the stature of John Frederick of Saxony or Philip of Hesse, both still held captive. Italy seemed secure, because pro-Habsburg states stretched in a great arc from Mantua (home of the Gonzaga) through Milan, Genoa, and Tuscany, ruled by Grand Duke Cosimo I de Medici, son-in-law of Charles's Viceroy of Naples, Pedro de Toledo.

Yet it was in Italy that a crack opened in the dynasty's defenses. As part of an offensive alliance with Pope Leo X in 1521, Charles promised the pope that Parma would be detached from the duchy of Milan and incorporated into the Papal States, along with neighboring Piacenza, which happened also to be an imperial fief. This arrangement, disrupted in subsequent wars, was reconfirmed as part of the 1530 Treaty of Barcelona, Charles's settlement with Pope Clement VII. In Milan, ruled after 1535 as an imperial fief, by a governor appointed by Charles, there was more than a bit of grumbling about the fact that Parma and Piacenza represented significant losses to a territory now expected to sustain the costs of a permanent Spanish military establishment. Nonetheless, by agreement in 1545 with Pope Paul III, Charles recognized the pope's son, Pier Luigi Farnese, as duke of both Parma and Piacenza.[4]

But in Ferrante Gonzaga, erstwhile viceroy of Sicily (1535–1546), Charles now had as governor of Milan a man who took an emphatic view of imperial authority. All across northern Italy, partisans of the empire were shaken by the attempted coup in Genoa led by young Gian Luigi Fieschi (2 January 1547). Some, like Andrea Doria, took comfort in the fact that the commoners of Genoa failed to rally to their cause as the plotters had hoped. Others, like Gonzaga, believed the coup had failed only because Fieschi, in seizing Doria's galleys in the harbor, fell overboard in his heavy armor and drowned. Gonzaga insisted that Genoa could be made secure for the empire only by having a new castle within its walls, with a Spanish garrison. Charles himself leaned toward this view, but, moved also by Doria's strenuous objections to the idea, on behalf of Genoese liberty, he endorsed the admiral's plan for further changes in the republic's governing ordinances.[5] In the case of Piacenza, however, Ferrante Gonzaga, an enemy

[4]   Chabod, *Lo stato e la vita religiosa a Milano nell' epoca di Carlo V*, in *Opere*, III, 79–85. Baumgartner, *Henri II*, 70–71, 85; Rodriguez-Salgado, *The Changing Face of Empire*, 41–42. Henry remembered with bitterness his years of captivity in Spain in his father's stead; he was also the Dauphin (married to Catherine de Medici) to whom Charles would not relinquish Milan.

[5]   Pacini, *La Genova dell'Andrea Doria nell'impero di Carlo V*, 610–636.

of the Farnese, was able to do things his way: he arranged the assassination of Pier Luigi (September 1547). This inspired in the aged pope a desire for vengeance. He entered into discussions with French agents in Rome about a French offensive into Italy in the spring of 1548; but Venice, considered a necessary partner, refused to cooperate. Henry II would have to await a better opportunity.[6]

Meanwhile, Charles was occupying himself with plans to secure the future of his son Philip. While Archduke Maximilian and the emperor's oldest daughter Maria were given charge of Castile and Aragón, Philip embarked on a long tour of the other lands that would fall to him, starting with Milan. Sailing from Barcelona on 2 November 1548, the taciturn Philip endured six months of elaborate receptions in the major centers of north Italy, south Germany, and the Rhineland before crossing into Netherlands territory (Luxemburg, March 1549). From 12 July until 26 October Charles accompanied his son on a tour of the seventeen provinces, in each of which Philip was acclaimed as heir in the customary fashion, after having sworn to uphold the privileges of the territory. But Charles had greater ambitions for Philip. At the beginning of 1550 he broached to Ferdinand a new order of succession for the Holy Roman Empire: Ferdinand would still succeed Charles, as had long been agreed between the brothers, but he would be followed not by his own son Maximilian, but by Philip, who would then be succeeded by Maximilian. Despite Mary's support Charles could not win his brother to this plan. Taking Philip with him, he journeyed to Augsburg (where a diet was to be held) to settle the matter in face-to-face discussions, held in the palatial mansion of Anton Fugger. Ferdinand remained unyielding. Summoned by Charles to mediate, Mary had no better luck and returned to Brussels. Maximilian, recalled from Spain, avoided contact with his cousin Philip. At Charles's request Mary journeyed a second time to Augsburg, spending long hours poring over the details of a prospective agreement with the bishop of Arras, who was now Charles's chief adviser (his father, Granvelle, had died some months earlier). Not until March 1551 did Ferdinand accept a version of Charles's plan, in which the electoral princes were to be asked (once Ferdinand had become emperor) to acclaim Philip as King of the Romans and, at the same time, to recognize Maximilian as his successor. In fact, Philip was never to reign as emperor, but these torturous family discussions had an important consequence. By forcing an agreement down his brother's throat, Charles created common ground between the King of the Romans and the empire's electoral princes. Long familiar with the affable Maximilian, the latter had no wish to be ruled by a foreigner who spoke only Spanish; they also recognized Charles's dream of a quasi-hereditary monarchy as a

[6] See note 4.

threat to their status as electors. Ferdinand would henceforth have scope for a more independent line in the affairs of the empire.[7]

Possibilities for another grand anti-Habsburg coalition were just now crystallizing. In northern Italy, Ottavio Farnese viewed the accession of Pope Julius III (r. 1550–1555) with the anxiety always felt by near kinsmen of the previous pope. In keeping with promises made at the time of his election, Pope Julius recognized Ottavio Farnese, son of the murdered Pier Luigi, as duke of Parma (February 1550), expecting that Charles would do the same for Piacenza. But Ferrante Gonzaga persuaded Charles to claim Piacenza for himself as an imperial fief. This led Ottavio Farnese to open negotiations with Henry II. In the spring of 1551, an army of Italian exiles based in Mirandola, controlled by the Farnese, invaded and ravaged papal territory around Bologna; in response, papal troops had begun a siege of Parma, with Ferrante Gonzaga as overall commander. Determined to support a pope who was more friendly to imperial interests than any of his predecessors had been, and not willing to allow France a foothold in Italy, Charles in June 1551 promised a papal emissary to provide up to 200,000 scudi for the support of papal troops, in return for further promises about his access to church revenue in Spain. At the same time, as he wrote Mary, he ordered a levy of *Landsknechte* and 1,500 cavalry to join in the siege of Parma, intending to keep them there as long as seven months. In the end, however, Charles wasted a considerable sum. Parma held out against its besiegers, and Julius III, alarmed by Henry II's threat to convene a national council of his own to remedy the ills of the church, signed a truce in which he accepted Ottavio Farnese's position in Parma, and declared his neutrality in the struggle between France and the Habsburgs (6 May 1552).[8]

Henry II was now looking for new allies. Following the death of Khair-ad-Din Barbarossa (1546), one of his protégés, Turgut Reis, succeeded him both as *kapudan pasha* of the Ottoman fleet and as the terror of Christian shipping in the western Mediterranean. When Andrea Doria and Bernardino de Mendóza combined their galley fleets for a successful

---

[7] Kamen, *Philip of Spain*, 36–47; Fichtner, *Ferdinand I*, 165–176; Brandi, *Emperor Charles V*, 592–600; Rodriguez-Salgado, *The Changing Face of Empire*, 33–40: "Charles was fortunate to have such a patient and moderate brother."

[8] Ludwig Pastor, *Geschichte der Päpste* (16 vols., Freiburg im Breisgau, 1891–1933), VI, 70–73, 97–104; Simeoni, *Le Signorie*, II, 928–930 (Ottavio was not helped by the fact that he was married to Charles's illegitimate daughter, since Margaret of Parma hated her husband); Charles to Mary, 13 June 1551, *Corpus Documental*, Letter CCCCXCV, III, 295–298; Lutz, *Christianitas Afflicta*, 48–57; Rodriguez-Salgado, *The Changing Face of Empire*, 51–52 (Milan's finances), 58 (the Netherlands); Carande Thobar, *Carlos V y sus banqueros*, III, 310, 348, loans 343 for 100,000 ducats) and 344–377, July 1551, totaling 165,000 scudi; Charles to Philip, June 1552, *Corpus Documental*, Letter DXXXVI, III, 428–433, with Carande Thobar, III, 350, 370–371.

attack on Turgut's North African bases (Monastir and Mahdia, September 1550), Sultan Suleyman had reason to complain that Charles had broken the Truce of Adrianople. He also objected to the fact that Austrian diplomats had persuaded Janos Szapolyai's widow to yield to Ferdinand (July 1551) her young son's claim to Transylvania, the hitherto independent eastern third of the old kingdom of Hungary. Hence Gabriel d'Aramon, Henry II's representative at the Porte, won Suleyman's consent to a combined Franco-Turkish attack by land and sea the following spring. Returning to France by ship, Aramon paused to watch approvingly as Turgut's forces completed a successful assault on Tripoli (September 1551), hitherto held by the Knights of Malta. As in 1544, public knowledge of this collaboration between France and the Ottomans worked at cross-purposes to French diplomacy among German Protestants. Henry requested that Suleyman send his fleet out early and delay his attack on Hungary, but the sultan did the opposite: his army set off for Transylvania in the spring of 1552, but the war fleet did not sail until late summer.[9]

The Second Schmalkaldic War

In Germany, Margrave Hans von Brandenburg-Küstrin and other princely foes of the Interim had organized a league among themselves to oppose the efforts of Moritz of Saxony (as authorized by the 1550 Diet of Augsburg) to force the submission of Magdeburg and other cities holding out against the imperial settlement. In this they were not successful, because Moritz and the troops the diet had paid for eventually forced Magdeburg to yield (November 1551). But Margrave Hans had detected that Moritz himself was not in his heart of hearts a protagonist of Habsburg and Catholic power. Indeed, as one scholar has put it, the prince, whose betrayal of his fellow Schmalkaldeners had contributed so significantly to Charles's victory in 1547, was placed in an awkward position by the emergence of a viable Lutheran opposition. His safest move was to do as he now did, putting himself at the head of the conspirators while continuing to conduct himself as an ally of the emperor. In October 1551 Jean de Bresse, bishop of Bayonne, represented Henry II in secret discussions with Moritz and his new confederates in a hunting lodge at Lochau, not far from the site of the battle of Mühlberg. The principled Hans von Brandenburg-Küstrin quit the meeting in disgust, because Moritz had insisted on including the thoroughly unprincipled Margrave Albrecht-Alcibiades. This first meting did not bring agreement, but progress was made in a subsequent discussion at Dresden (December 1551); Moritz by this time needed money badly, for the troops he had decided to keep under arms following the submission

9 Lutz, *Chistianitas Afflicta*, 40–44.

of Magdeburg. In the 15 January 1552 Treaty of Chambord, signed at the Loire chateau by Henry II and by Albrecht-Alcibiades on behalf of the confederates, France was to provide a subsidy of 70,000 gold crowns per month, in return for recognition by the confederates of the king's rights as "imperial vicar" for imperial cities that were not of the German tongue: that is, "Cambrai [in the Low Countries], Metz, Toul, Verdun [all in Lorraine], and any others there may be." In the version of the treaty published in France, the confederates promised not to attack the lands of ecclesiastical princes in Germany; the version published in his own name by Albrecht-Alcibiades was a manifesto for attacks of precisely this kind.[10]

By the time Mary sent Charles word that Moritz was in contact with anti-Interim princes (October 1551), the emperor was on his way from Augsburg to Innsbruck, the capital of Habsburg Tyrol. Mary had recommended Worms or Speyer as the appropriate vantage point for observing German affairs, because the "force" of the empire was to be found in the Rhineland, where he would also be close to the Low Countries. Instead, Charles chose Innsbruck, since by keeping to the House of Austria's home ground he could save money by dismissing most of the troops he had maintained while at Augsburg. Relatively isolated in Innsbruck, with no one among his advisers who had Granvelle's instinct for imperial politics (the bishop of Arras was no match for his father), Charles had no inkling that the settlement he had imposed on Germany a mere four years earlier was about to collapse. In late March 1552, when he was forced to acknowledge that Henry II and Moritz were acting in concert, he had nowhere to go; if he tried to reach the Netherlands via the Rhineland, he might be met by a French army. But the (unwarranted) doubts he now had about Ferdinand's loyalty prevented him from going to Vienna. As he explained to Philip, he would remain in Innsbruck to await the arrival of troops from Italy.[11]

At the beginning of April Henry II mustered an army of some 37,000 men. In Nancy, capital of the duchy of Lorraine, he paused long enough to constrain the dowager duchess to name men favorable to France to the regency council for her ten-year-old son. He then marched his army down the Moselle and on 17 April entered Metz, which had already submitted to Montmorency; three days later, he set off again for the Vosges, planning

[10] Ibid., 62–70.

[11] Mary to Arras, 5 October 1551, and Mary to Charles, 24 September 1551, Lanz, Letters 739 and 742, III, 77, 76; Charles to Mary, 4 October 1551 and 9 March 1552, Lanz, Letters 741 and 752, III, 77, 112; Charles to Philip 11 January 1552, Corpus Documental, Letter DXXV, III, 400–401; Rodriguez-Salgado, The Changing Face of Empire, 45–46, citing Charles's unpublished instructions (29 March 1552) to Juan Manrique de Lara for his mission to Philip. Lutz, Christianitas Afflicta, 72–84, speaks of a loss of competence in the emperor's inner circle following Granvelle's death in 1550.

to strike into Alsace, whose cities he hoped would (like Metz) accept the argument that France was the protector of their "liberties." Meanwhile, Moritz of Saxony began a double game that played one Habsburg brother off against another, threatening to attack Charles while holding out to Ferdinand a promise of the military cooperation he needed in the east. Preoccupied by the Ottoman march against Transylvania, Ferdinand had asked Moritz for a meeting to resolve differences standing in the way of common action against the Turks. Even though he was then mustering his French-paid troops for a march to the south, Moritz agreed (24 March 1552) to meet with Ferdinand at Linz on 18 April. But, as Charles noted in a letter to Ferdinand, Moritz was not behaving like a man preparing for peace; for example, he had met with Albrecht-Alcibiades, to encourage the campaign of terror the margrave and his rogue army were waging against the episcopal principalities of Bamberg and Würzburg in the Main valley. Moritz also sent four banners of infantry and 300 horse toward Füssen, dangerously close to Innsbruck. Nonetheless, he did come to Linz, bringing with him the French ambassador (the same Jean de Bresse). The discussions at Linz (18 April–6 May) were inconclusive, and to gain time both sides agreed to a further meeting at Passau on 26 May and to a fifteen-day truce that in Moritz's view (if not Charles's) did not start until 26 May. Moritz then marched his men toward the valley of the Lech. South of Füssen, they surrounded and routed (19 May) several companies of *Landsknechte* Charles had engaged to guard the fortress of La Chiusa at the Ehrenberger Narrows. Realizing that enemy cavalry could be in Innsbruck "within twenty-four hours," Charles and his entourage "rode all night" to the south, crossing the Brenner Pass to reach Sterzing at dawn; from here they continued east through the Pustertal to the valley of the Drave, which they followed to Villach in Austrian Carinthia.[12] The emperor had suffered the double indignity of being driven to flight by an enemy with whom he was not even formally at war.

Ferdinand wanted a peace agreement at Passau; Moritz had offered to command Habsburg forces in Hungary if there were a negotiated settlement. But as Charles wrote Mary, he determined, while en route to Villach,

> to put into effect the decision I made before leaving Innsbruck, to prepare myself against the said Duke Moritz, both in order to be able to negotiate with more authority at Passau or, if things come to a rupture, to use the forces I can gather either against him or, if an agreement is reached, against the king of France, if one sees that there is need.

---

[12] Baumgartner, *Henri II*, 150–152 (Henry II's troops were well received by the imperial cities of French-speaking Lorraine, but not by those of German-speaking Alsace); Brandi, *Emperor Charles V*, 608–611; Charles to Philip, 9 April 1552, *Corpus Documental*, Letter DXXXIV, III, 421, and Charles to Mary, Villach, 30 May 1552, Lanz, Letter 793, III, 202–208.

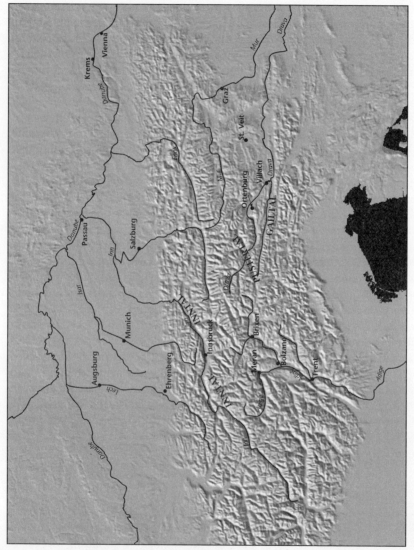

Map 11.1. Charles's retreat to Villach

Charles knew by now that Henry II, having found no support in Alsace, had turned back (13 May) across the Vosges to the Moselle valley, where he occupied several towns in Habsburg Luxemburg, but this letter does not indicate what form a campaign against France might take. The emperor sent out orders to muster seven "regiments" of *Landsknechte*, plus a large force of German cavalry, and light horse from Poland. Because he could not be certain that German troops would not be sympathetic to Moritz's cause, he also wanted as many Spaniards as he could get. Already on 9 April he had sent word for Philip to have twenty captains raise 300 men each; isolated in Innsbruck (even more so in Villach), he could not have known that the duke of Alba was even now mustering a somewhat larger number of men for the voyage to Genoa. Charles also summoned the Spanish infantry that had recently been serving in the siege of Parma.[13] He was organizing a huge army, the largest to date, without a clear idea how he would use it.

Philip and his councillors did heroic service in raising the sums Charles needed for this force, even though this was the worst possible time to enter the financial markets, owing to the "tightness" (*stretezza*) of money in Genoa, Augsburg, and Antwerp. Meanwhile, in preparing for the 26 May meeting at Passau, Ferdinand persuaded Charles that, instead of speaking for both brothers (as at Linz), he should speak only in his own name, allowing Charles's commissioners to speak for the emperor. In Passau the negotiators were joined by a delegation of Rhineland princes, who had made it clear that they favored neither a French invasion of Germany nor a civil war in the empire. Ferdinand surprised everyone by declaring that he too hoped to play a mediating role. By the end of June all the parties except Charles's commissioners had agreed to a text that resembled recent recesses of imperial diets, save on one key point: the truce between adherents of the Catholic religion and of the Augsburg Confession was to be perpetual, not (as on all previous occasions) limited to an interval that would end with the convening of the next diet. Just before leaving Passau to rejoin his army (5 July), Moritz indicated that he could accept this agreement. Ferdinand journeyed to Villach for three days of conversation with Charles (8–11 July). Charles was willing to release Philip of Hesse and John Frederick of Saxony from captivity, as the confederates had long demanded, but he would not sign off on a perpetual truce that would effectively legitimize heresy in the empire, an act he believed would imperil his immortal soul. A dejected Ferdinand brought the news back to those who remained at Passau: the treaty was acceptable only if revised to have the religious truce end with the next diet. Assuming that Moritz would press the attack rather than agree

---

[13]   Charles to Mary, Villach, 30 May 1552, Lanz, Letter 793, III, 202–208; Charles to Philip, 9 April 1552, *Corpus Documental*, Letter CXXXIV, III, 421. Maltby, *Alba*, 78–79.

to these terms, Charles retreated one step further, following the valley of the Adige/Etsch River south to Bozen/Bozano. Only when Alba and the 7,000 Spaniards joined him did he retrace his steps, north to Villach, then west and north again to Innsbruck. It was in Innsbruck (6 August) that he received word that Moritz of Saxony and his allies had accepted the revised Treaty of Passau; as he had promised, Moritz himself was now en route to join Ferdinand's forces in Hungary.[14]

There was now disturbing news from Italy, where a surprise attack by anti-Spanish and anti-Medici exiles had overwhelmed the Spanish and Florentine garrison of Siena (27–28 July); French troops stationed in a small principality held by Ottavio Farnese marched at once to their aid. Ironically, Siena was now the more securely French because of the citadel and new-style fortifications that Spanish gold had recently built in order to keep the restive city under Florentine and Medici control. At Innsbruck some in the council of war wanted to take the Spaniards and the German levies now arriving back across the Alps to face this danger, but Charles demurred. He considered rejecting the Treaty of Passau (even as amended), so as to attack Moritz and his allies, but on reaching Augsburg (15 August) the emperor signaled his ratification. This left only two possible enemies for the multinational force that was still converging on various mustering points: Margrave Albrecht-Alcibiades or Henry II of France. The choice seemed clear. Mary had been asking Charles to relieve pressure on the Netherlands by bringing his army closer, and Albrecht-Alcibiades, continuing his depredations in the Rhineland, was besieging the capital of the prince-archbishop of Trier (the city capitulated on 28 August). But the emperor now played his own double game. On the one hand, he wrote to several German princes that he would direct his army against the rogue margrave. He also officially annulled (12 September) the iniquitous "treaties" by which Albrecht-Alcibiades had forced the prince-bishops of Bamberg and Würzburg to promise huge indemnities to spare their territories from further plundering. He planned to cross the Rhine at Speyer, but since Albrecht-Alcibiades had burned all the boats from which a bridge might be made, he detoured south to the bridge at Strasbourg. On the other hand, during these weeks his emissaries made contact with Albrecht-Alcibiades to explore a possible alliance against France.[15]

---

[14] Lutz, *Christianitas Afflicta*, 86–103; Brandi, *Emperor Charles V*, 611–614; Fichtner, *Ferdinand I*, 195–201.

[15] Pepper and Adams, *Firearms and Fortifications*, 58–78; Lutz, *Christianitas Afflicta*, 104–108; Gaston Zeller, *La réunion de Metz à France, 1552–1648. Ière partie, L'occupation* (Paris, 1926), 404–406.

The Siege of Metz

From Wissembourg, just north of Strasbourg, Charles wrote Mary (23 September) that he was now thinking of a campaign to recover Metz for the empire. This was indeed a worthy strategic objective, because Metz in French hands would be a springboard for invasions down the Moselle valley into Luxemburg, meant to cut off the route by which mercenary troops recruited in Germany came to the Netherlands. But Mary was horrified by the thought of beginning so late in the season the siege of such a large city that had now been refortified by the French. She recommended (in vain, as usual) a more sensible plan: let Charles garrison his men for the winter in various towns and begin the offensive in the spring. Scholars have attributed the decision for Metz to the duke of Alba, whom Charles had made his overall commander, as in the First Schmalkaldic War, but Spanish sources point to the emperor himself. Albrecht-Alcibiades' decision to withdraw from Trier (28 September) may have encouraged Charles to take more seriously the idea of adding the margrave's men (about 15,000 infantry) to his own force. Duke Francis of Guise, Henry II's commander in Metz, was also interested in recruiting Albrecht-Alcibiades, but the duke of Alba took personal charge of the negotiations for the imperial side that led to a treaty of alliance signed on 10 November. Charles had no money for the monthly wages for Albrecht-Alcibiades' men; to solve this problem he reversed his own action of a few months earlier, solemnly ratifying the ransom treaties the margrave had extorted from Bamberg and Würzburg.[16]

Within Metz, Guise and his 6,000 men had been busy since August repairing and rebuilding the fortifications whose weakened condition had been one of the reasons the city fell so easily to the French in the spring. Alba appeared before the walls with an advance party of 4,000 infantry and 4,000 cavalry, but Charles was delayed for weeks by severe attacks of gout. On 23 October he was to be carried by litter across a makeshift bridge into Diedenhofen/Thionville (in Luxemburg, just downriver from Metz) for a rest, but when the emperor and his party arrived on the right bank, the bridge was not ready; embarrassed citizens had to scramble to get him across in proper style. Once in Thionville, he stayed for two weeks, while his army took up positions around Metz. Some observers noted signs of disorder in the camp, not to mention the fact that the Spaniards and Italians in particular were suffering the effects of an unusually severe winter. Nonetheless, forty heavy cannon that had come by water (down the Rhine, then up the Moselle from Coblenz) began bombardment on 9 November, and by 17 November they had battered a breach in the walls some fifty paces wide. To their dismay, the besiegers found that Guise and his men (like the defenders of Marseilles in 1524) had built a high earthen rampart or *retirata* behind this weak point in the city's defenses. Charles wanted to order a charge through the breach, despite guns bristling from the rampart, but his commanders dissuaded him. The cannon were moved to a different vantage point and opened a second breach, only to disclose another *retirata* behind it. By this time, in early December, some men were deserting; others lay dying. Charles refused to give up, but by 1 January 1553 he admitted the truth and gave orders to abandon the siege. For France and the duke of Guise this was a great victory. For Charles it was his worst defeat: the largest of all his armies had achieved nothing.[17]

Sinews of War

The siege of Parma began in May 1551 and lasted through April of the following year. To support the pope's troops, Charles promised 200,000 scudi but may have provided no more than 165,000 (154,011 ducats).[18] Charles wrote Mary that the 8,000 *Landsknechte* and 1,500 cavalry he was raising for Parma would cost 30,000 ducats a month, but contemporary financial summaries in the Low Countries indicate the cost would have been about twice this much, 61,080 a month.[19] If one assumes these men served at Parma only for the seven-month period projected in Charles's letter to Mary, the cost would have been 429,590 ducats. In another letter to Mary just after the siege was broken off (May 1552), Charles mentions a further 4,000 Italians who had been serving at Parma under the marquess of Marignano, and 2,000 Spaniards, presumably brought from Lombardy when Gonzaga was named commander of the siege army (6 June 1551). Because Marignano, one of Charles's colonels, was present also at the beginning of the siege, it seems likely all of these men will have been on Charles's payroll for eleven months (June 1551–May 1552), at a cost of 220,000 ducats.[20] One should also add the usual 20% for officers' pay, victuals, and the artillery and baggage trains for the men serving under

---

[17] Baumgartner, *Henri II*, 151–159; Maltby, *Alba*, 80–81; Zeller, *La réunion de Metz à France*, 413–415; Brandi, *Emperor Charles V*, 615–622.

[18] Compare Pastor, *Geschichte der Päpste*, VI, 101, with the three loans mentioned in this connection by Carande Thobar, *Carlos V y sus banqueros*, cited in note 8.

[19] Aud. 650, 529–531, the wages projected in winter 1552 for a campaign the next year are: for High Germans (*Landsknechte*), the equivalent of 5.47 ducats a month; for German heavy cavalry, 13.12 ducats; and for light horse, 9.654 ducats. By the extrapolation process used hitherto (Chapter 7, note 39), this would mean, respectively, 5.29 ducats a month for the *Landsknechte* in 1550, and about 12.7 ducats for the cavalry, or 42,320 for 8,000 infantry and 19,050 for the 1,500 cavalry.

[20] To allow for some inflation in their pay as well, I count them at 5 ducats a month, as opposed to my estimate of 4.5 for the First Schmalkaldic War (Chapter 10, note 53).

the imperial banner, or 129,918 ducats. With the money for papal troops, Charles will probably have spent as much as 779,508 ducats for the siege of Parma.

Even before retreating from Innsbruck to Villach, Charles summoned from Naples 4,000 Spanish infantry; these were apparently not at Parma, but it seems they did join the emperor north of the Alps, because he later requested Philip to recruit 3,000 men in Catalonia and the Balearic Islands for the needs of Naples.[21] In addition to these men, and the 7,000 Spaniards brought by Alba, he joined to his army the 2,000 Spaniards and the 4,000 Italian infantry (under the marquess of Marignano) that had been serving at Parma.[22] One can assume all these men were on the imperial payroll at least from 1 June. Having this many Spaniards and Italians gave Charles the confidence to build a large German army, plans for which he described in detail in a letter to Mary from Villach (30 May 1552). There were to be seven colonels, each with a regiment of ten banners of *Landsknechte*, or 4,000 men; six of the colonels are named: Conrad von Bomelberg, to muster his men at Lake Constance or "the Black Mountain" (Black Forest); the count of Eberstein, to muster in Regensburg, where he will incorporate into his regiment the two banners now serving there on Ferdinand's payroll; Conrad von Haynstein, to muster at Frankfurt; Joost Claes de Sollersen, baron of Thurn und Tassis; Count Johann von Nassau; and Hans Walter, who would have to re-form a regiment, because his seven banners were routed by Duke Moritz at the Ehrenberger Narrows a few weeks earlier. There were also to be 2,000 light horse from Poland and 6,000 German heavy cavalry, including 2,500 to come from Bohemia, 2,000 from Franconia, 1,000 whose services were currently retained by "the duke of Holstein,"[23] and 400 to be raised by the count of Oettingen.[24]

All of these units were to be ready by 30 June, and there are indications in subsequent letters that the *Landsknechte* were mustering during the course of the month; for example, Bomelberg had "filled" five of his banners by 22 June. The cavalry was slower in coming together: the 1,000 men previously retained by Holstein had still not arrived as of 31 August, and Margrave Hans of Brandenburge-Küstrin (now back in Habsburg service) brought only 1,100 or 1,200 cavalry, in place of the larger number

[21] Charles to Philip, 9 April and 18 September 1552, *Corpus Documental*, Letters CXXXIV, CLV, III, 421, 489–491.
[22] Maltby, *Alba*, 79–81; Charles to Mary, 30 May 1552, Lanz, Letter 792, III, 202–208.
[23] Charles probably means King Christian III of Denmark (r. 1534–1559), whom he may not have thought to call by his proper title, despite the 1544 Treaty of Speyer in which he had recognized Christian as king, notwithstanding claims by descendants of a previous king (Christian II) who had married Charles's sister.
[24] Charles to Mary, 30 May 1552, cited in note 13, and, for the count of Oettingen, Charles to Ferdinand, 30 June 1552, Lanz, Letter 836, III, 312–318.

for which he had contracted, because some of his captains (*Rittmeister*) refused to appear when summoned. To adjust for these difficulties, I will assume that Charles had only 5,000 heavy cavalry under his command, not the 6,000 he wanted. From 1 June through the end of December, with January 1553 as the going-home month, he will have been responsible for 17,000 Spanish and Italian infantry, 28,000 *Landsknechte*, 5,000 German cavalry, and 2,000 light horse, all at the higher rates of pay now prevailing.[25] The cost for this abortive campaign would have been 2,584,544 ducats, or 3,276,473 in all, adding in the usual 20% for victuals, officers' pay, and the baggage and artillery trains, plus 175,000 for the emperor's household.[26]

* * *

Just when Charles's credit was at a low point, there was again good news from the Indies. The flow of silver from the promising new mine at Potosí (modern Bolivia) had been interrupted by the rebellion of Hernando de Pizarro, son of Peru's *conquistador*. The *licenciado* Pedro de La Gasca, sent from Spain to deal with the problem, talked some of the rebels into submission, then formed an army to defeat Pizarro and his allies (April 1548). Charles had advance word of these events in December 1548 and received further details from La Gasca's emissary, who arrived in Seville in January 1549. Resistance to the idea of a further sequestration of the huge amount of private treasure that could now be expected was quickly overcome. In Peru it took more than a year to sort out the confiscation of rebel treasure for the crown's benefit and to process the silver bars for shipment to Nombre de Dios (Panama). But starting in October 1550, La Gasca's ships brought some 2 million ducats in silver safely to harbor in Spain, of which the royal fifth would have been about 400,000. Some of the treasure – 98,345 ducats – went to help pay off 325,532 ducats in principal and interest still due for loans contracted between December 1546 and February 1549. In part to shore up Spain's defenses in Italy – Lombardy, Piacenza, and Siena – Charles contracted for 583,288 in new debts during 1550; a further 211,335 ducats in Peruvian silver went toward the 717,988 ducats the treasury eventually paid out in interest and principal for these loans. He had ideas about holding a portion of the treasure in reserve, but

---

[25] For *Landsknechte*, light horse, and German heavy cavalry I use the rates used by military planners in the Low Countries for 1552–1553 (note 19); for Spanish and Italian infantry I count five ducats per month (note 20).

[26] A cost of 1,225,280 for the 28,000 *Landsknechte* for eight months, 154,464 ducats for 2,000 light horse, 680,000 for 17,000 Spanish and Italian troops, and 524,800 for 5,000 heavy cavalry. Charles did not have to find a further 246,150 to pay Albrecht-Alcibiades' approximately 15,000 *Landsknechte* for three months, because he gave the rogue baron license to collect the sums he had extorted from two prince-bishops.

when the war against Parma began the next summer, he ordered a new sequestration of 600,000 ducats in privately owned silver, and this was only the beginning. Of the 542,268 ducats he borrowed to support the papal siege of Parma,[27] nearly half the principal (262,250 ducats) was repaid in New World silver. Perhaps because he seems also to have appropriated for the Parma war a reserve of 500,000 Carolus gulden (273,375 ducats) accumulated by Mary in the Low Countries to pay off her debts, he borrowed 367,695 ducats for the needs of the Low Countries, all of which was repaid from the recent shipments of *oro y plata*. Finally, there were direct remittances to Italy of 550,000 ducats in specie, at least some of which came to Genoa in silver bars, to avoid the exchange fees for transfer from one currency to another.[28]

By December 1551 Charles had managed to expend 1,891,846 ducats, all but about 100,000 of La Gasca's treasure, a good part of it in the vain effort to wrest Parma from Ottavio Farnese. More ominous for the long term, this vast sum had not diminished Castile's overhang of debt, because of new loans from the bankers, and a huge sum added to the kingdom's long-term debt in order to compensate the holders of private treasure with *juros*. In November 1551 Philip projected unavoidable expenses of 1 million ducats over the next two years, as against 611,000 ducats in disposable revenue, of which he had already spent 111,000 for the defense of Spain's frontiers.[29] In the spring of 1552, when Charles was beset by the greatest crisis of his reign, Castile's cupboard was bare.

The Low Countries now had a French war of its own to deal with in 1552, but Castile and Naples both came to their sovereign's aid. In May 1552 the Parlamento of Naples granted a *donativo* of 880,000 scudi payable over two years, of which bankers may eventually have remitted to the emperor as much as 528,000 scudi or 492,835 ducats (see Chapter 13), even though Charles himself expected that some of the money would be held back to defend Naples against Barbarossa's successor, Turgut Reis.

---

[27] Charles to Mary, 13 June 1551, *Corpus Documental*, Letter CD, III, 295–298, speaks of charging the cost for the 8,000 *Landsknechte* and the 1,500 cavalry he is raising for Parma against Milan's revenues for 1552 and 1553, because the income for 1551 is spent already. But Milan's treasury was exhausted during the years 1550–1555, and expenses relating to the defense of Lombardy had to be supported from Castile or Naples: Chabod, *Lo stato e la vita religiosa a Milano nell' epoca di Carlo V*, 132. On the sequestrations of 1551, Carande Thobar, *Carlos V y sus banqueros*, III, 313–316, and *Estudios de Historia* (Barcelona, 1989), 219.

[28] Carande Thobar, *Carlos V y sus banqueros*, III, 313–321, 359–365; Charles to Maria and Maximilian, 20 October 30 December 1550, and to Maria alone, 9 June 1551, *Corpus Documental*, Letters CDLXXVI, CDLXXX, and CVI, III, 243–244, 251–252, 341–344; Rodriguez-Salgado, *Changing Face of Empire*, 58.

[29] By Philip's count, there were 131,000 ducats left, which was to be sent on to the emperor in specie as he had instructed: Philip to Charles, 19 November 1551, *Corpus Documental*, Letter CXIX, III, 380–383.

It was the money from Naples that saved Charles in his hour of need.[30] Meanwhile, before he had to flee Innsbruck for Villach, Charles had sent Juan Manrique de Lara, a trusted military adviser who had served recently as ambassador to Genoa, to bring back 500,000 ducats in cash. To meet this demand and send Manrique on his way (apparently in June 1552), Philip and his councillors scooped up the money by "taking" what was on deposit in episcopal chanceries, monasteries, and universities around the kingdom, and by negotiating with various "burghers of Seville" for a further 136,000 ducats in loans. Because there were no assignations left for these new debts, the treasury attempted to create new streams of revenue by offering urban magistracies for ambitious gentlemen, township charters for villages, and licenses for the import of French goods in time of war. Some months later fifteen grandees and prelates promised a further 200,766 ducats. Even though these transactions added to the burden on the treasury (save for 72,000 ducats of the last sum designated as contributions that Charles need not repay), they were invaluable in reducing the amount that Charles had to get from skeptical bankers who probably understood the state of the treasury better than he did. Indeed, at least in one case, bankers accepted in part payment of their loans the 40,000 ducats promised by the archbishop of Toledo.[31]

During 1552 contracts were signed for 3,669,449 in loans charged to the treasury of Castile, by far the largest total for any year in Charles's reign.[32] As indicated in Table 11.1, nearly 30% of this money (1,107,140 ducats) was borrowed during the first four months of the year, for the needs of Italy (including the Parma war), the Low Countries, North Africa, and the galley fleets that keep up the fight against Muslim corsairs. Sums that can be identified as borrowed for the army Charles built and maintained during the last eight months of the year amount to 2,398,174 ducats. The fact that Philip and his officials had to scrape to find the cash for Manrique's

---

[30] Rodriguez-Salgado, *Changing Face of Empire*, 51; D'Agostino, *Parlamento e società nel regno di Napoli*, 286; Charles to Mary, 30 May 1552, Lanz, Letter 793, 202–208, and Charles to Philip, June 1552, *Corpus Documental*, Letter DXXXIX, III, 443–444.

[31] Philip to Charles, May? 1552, "Relacion de Prestamos Particulares al Emperador," 31 August 1552, Charles to Philip, 18 September 1552, and Philip to Charles, 7 October 1552, *Corpus Documental*, Letters DXXXVI, DL, DLV, and DLVIII, III, 426–433, 468–470, 489–491, 503–515; Carande Thobar, *Carlos V sus y banqueros*, loan 376, and III, 382, 396; Fernández Alvárez, *Charles V*, 153–154. Charles did not thank Philip for sending Manrique and the 500,000 ducats until September (18 September 1552, *Corpus Documental*, Letter DLV, III, 488–491); because his previous letter to Philip (at least in the published correspondence) was in June, it seems Manrique reached the emperor in July or August.

[32] According to Carande Thobar's figures, the next highest totals were for 1553 (2,261,208 ducats, including loan no. 412, a contract in which Genoese bankers paid off 445,000 ducats in debts held by other bankers), 1546 (1,805,219 ducats), 1546 (1,805,219 ducats), 1543 (1,742,01 ducats), 1551 (1,470,195 ducats), 1544 (1,424,778 ducats), 1555 (1,223,063 ducats), and 1554 (1,137,118 ducats).

Table 11.1. *Loans Charged against the Treasury of Castile in 1552*

Use of Funds	January–April	May–December[a]	Totals
Defense of Italy	324,938	91,468	416,406
North Africa		80,000	80,000
Galley fleets	65,000		65,000
Spain	126,000	28,667	154,667
Flanders	221,000	*81,114*	302,114
Genoa	190,542	*181,688*	372,230
Germany	143,660	*2,135,372*	2,279,032
TOTALS	1,071,140	2,598,309	3,669,449

Notes: Based on Carande Thobar, *Carlos V y sus banqueros*, III, 369–402, 472–478 (loans 360–398). I count as available for Charles's use in Germany one loan for 300,000 ducats with delivery of funds in Spain (no. 387), on the assumption that Philip and his council would not have contracted so large a loan at this time save for Charles's urgent needs.
[a] Monies available for the Second Schmalkaldic War are in given italics. Total available for Second Schmalkaldic War is 2,398,174.

mission shows that the kingdom's important revenues were already pledged well into the future; there was nothing left for 1553, 1554, or 1555.[33]

How could there be assignations for still more loans? Had it not been for more silver from the Americas in 1552 – 849,499 ducats worth, of which the royal fifth would have been about 158,000 – there would have been nothing on which to assign repayment of the 136,000 ducats lent by burghers of Seville as part of the 500,000 brought by Manrique, not to mention new bankers' loans. For the 1,479,335 ducats in loans contracted with the Fugger, Schetz, Doria, and Spinola between March and December 1552, roughly half the principal sum (743,501 ducats) was to be repaid in *oro y plata*.[34] But as he did with all his revenues, Charles was promising more than the treasure ships brought in. Anton Fugger, who fled with the emperor to Villach, attempted to arrange loans for 400,000 ducats that would require two Genoese bankers, Antonio Maria Grimaldi and Domenico Grillo, to forgo the 250,000 in Indies silver they were to have in repayment for their loans for imperial troops at the siege of Parma (December 1551).[35] Grimaldi and Grillo refused, perhaps because of delay in yet another loan contract that was to have been settled in *oro y plata*. Thus Fugger lent but 150,000, including a mere 50,000 in cash (payable in Venice) plus 100,000 for the prolongation of unpaid debts. Meanwhile, Philip and his councilors promised an additional 100,000 in specie to a

[33] Carande Thobar, *Carlos V y sus banqueros*, III, 396, with Philip to Charles, May? 1552, *Corpus Documental*, Letter CD, III, 428–433.
[34] Carande Thobar, *Carlos V y sus banqueros*, loans 372, 375, 381, 383, 385, 387, 388, 394, 396bis, 397, and III, 395–413.
[35] For this loan, Chabod, *Lo stato e la vita religiosa a Milano*, in *Opere*, III,132.

Spanish merchant who proved willing to "anticipate" his 300,000 payment for various commercial privileges (including control of Castile's African slave trade). For another of their loans, the Fugger were promised 80,000 ducats from the royal fifth for treasure arriving in 1552, but, as noted earlier, this money was already claimed – 136,000 for the burghers of Seville, plus 22,000 ducats urgently needed to "resist the Turks" (i.e., Turgut Reis). Because there was no sequestration of private silver in 1552, Charles had only the royal fifth, but he pledged a total of 1,001,501 ducats in *oro y plata* to repay the bankers for loans of this year. Hence, much of the 600,000 in *oro y plata* sequestered from private owners in 1553 will have gone for settlement of loans contracted the previous year.[36]

In all, Charles seems to have had some 3,391,009 ducats available for the army of 1552: 492,835 from Naples, 163,234 in either interest-free loans or revenue from the sale of offices in Castile (part of Manrique's 500,000 ducats), 2,398,174 in bankers' loans, and 336,766 in private loans to make up the rest of Manrique's 500,000 ducats. I do not count the 158,000 ducats for the royal fifth, because it went either to repay some of the private loans or for purposes other than the war in Germany. Of the 2,398,174 in bankers' loans, it may be estimated that about 756,000 ducats was shifted over to the kingdom's long-term debt – 256,000 in *juros*, which the Schetz of Antwerp accepted as part payment for their loans, and perhaps 500,000 of the 600,000 in private treasure sequestered in 1553, to make good on a least some of the emperor's promises to repay the war loans of 1552 in *oro y plata*.

Debt cascaded from one level of the kingdom's financial structure down to the next. Because bankers no longer trusted assignation on extraordinary revenues like the *servicios* and the *maestrazgos*, known to be pledged years into the future, they demanded repayment in *oro y plata*, only to find that even this source of royal income was overpledged. The alternative was to accept in payment of their loans *juros* at 5% to 7%, charged against the dwindling portion of the kingdom's ordinary revenues that was not yet pledged. This was particularly true for members of the Schetz family in Antwerp, who accepted a total of 256,000 ducats in *juros* in partial settlement of loans for 221,760 ducats (May 1552) and 300,000 ducats (December 1552).[37] By the 1550s it was quite common for bankers to receive what were called *juros de caution* equivalent to the face value of their loans, with interest; Genoese bankers like Ansaldo Grimaldi had set the pattern in the 1530s (Chapter 8). Bankers were permitted to sell these *juros* (e.g., to ecclesiastical corporations, which usually had cash on hand) if the due dates for their loans elapsed without payment. But as Philip reported to his father during this terrible year, bankers now demanded license to sell their cautionary *juros* if the ships on which the specie portion of repayment was assigned had not

[36] Philip to Charles, 7 October 1552, *Corpus Documental*, Letter DLVIII, III, 503–515.
[37] Carande Thobar, *Carlos V y sus banqueros*, loans 376 and 394, also III, 382, 402.

Table 11.2. *Sources of Funds (in ducats) for Charles's Campaigns, 1543–1552*

	Windfalls	Italy	Empire	Long-Term Debt	Short-Term Debt	Totals
1543	370,900			191,600	435,000	997,500
1544	227,706	250,000[a]	334,320		781,604	1,593,630
1546–1547	777,340	186,668[b]		150,000	1,563,431	2,677,429
1552		373,336[a]		2.001,613[c]	1,398,673	3,773,622
TOTALS	1,375,946	810,004	334,320	2,343,213	4,178,698	9,042,181
	(15.2%)	(9%)	(3.7%)	(25.9%)	(46.2%)	(100%)

[a] Naples.

[b] Papal subsidy.

[c] I count toward long-term debt not only the 256,000 which the Schetz family accepted in *juros* in part payment of its short-term loans, but also the 743,501 ducats of short-term debt repaid in New World treasure, on the assumption that this treasure will mainly have been "taken" from private owners compensated with *juros*.

arrived by a fixed date. Philip resisted this pressure but not for long. By the early years of his reign (1556–1598), bankers were selling cautionary *juros*[38] as soon as they received them, in effect soaking up whatever capital was available for these investments, and crowding out the crown as a potential seller. The year before Charles came to the throne, the annual *juro* interest charges against the kingdom's *rentas ordinarias* amounted to 349,608 ducats. By 1554, the annual charges were 878,210 ducats. If we assume an average rate of 6.25%, the latter figure would mean a capital debt of 14,051,376 ducats, more than fourteen times as much as the estimated income for *rentas ordinarias* that was not eaten up by traditional fixed expenses. Less than two years into his reign, Philip II forcibly converted outstanding bankers' loans into *juros* at 7%, charged against the small fraction of ordinary income that was still available. Scholars are agreed that, in taking this step, Philip was only doing what Charles should have done – indeed, was advised to do – several years earlier. Philip understood, if Charles did not, that the cost of honor and reputation had been to bring one of Europe's richest kingdoms to the very brink of bankruptcy.[39]

* * *

In financial terms, the campaigns of 1543–1552 differ in two striking ways from the campaigns of 1529–1541, as may be seen from a comparison of Table 11.2 and Table 8.1, which provide estimates of where Charles got the money to fight his wars in both periods. First, the later series of wars cost

[38] Known as *juros de resguardo*: Modesto Ulloa, *Le hacienda real de Castila en el reinado de Felipe II* (Madrid, 1977), 120.

[39] Toboso Sanchez, *La deuda pública castellana*, 90–105; Carande Thobar, *Carlos V y sus banqueros*, II, 90–93.

nearly twice as much overall. Over the years Charles mustered more men for his campaigns. Perhaps more important, the cost of retaining their services rose faster than the contemporary inflation in prices; between 1529–1530 and 1552–1553, the monthly wage for *Landsknechte* increased from 3.53 ducats to 5.47, or about 55% in less than twenty-five years[40] (e.g., 5.47 ducats a month for *Landsknechte* in 1552, as opposed to 3.53 in 1529). Second, for the larger sums needed for his later wars Charles depended noticeably more on credit. "Windfalls" provided nearly 30% of what the emperor needed in the first period, but less than 20% in the latter period; conversely, long-term borrowing against the treasury of Castile paid for over half the costs of war between 1543 and 1552, as opposed to a bit more than a fourth between 1529 and 1541. The thing to keep in mind is that Charles left Castile in 1543 and did not return again until early 1556, after his abdication. So long as the emperor had Castile as his principal place of residence, he paid some attention to the admonitions of his Consejo de la Hacienda; for example, he waited until he had some assurance that Castile would not have to bear the full cost before launching his enterprises (as in 1529, 1532, and 1535). Once he left Castile behind him, and perhaps especially after the trusted Cobos had died (1547), he was increasingly less receptive to the ever sensible and now more urgent remonstrances of Philip and his advisers. If loyal councillors were dismayed by the emperor's recklessness – and not just in Castile – what reactions to Charles's wars might be expected from loyal subjects, who lacked an insider's grasp of high politics, and yet had to pay the taxes that were sooner or later required to satisfy the bankers' demands? This question is addressed in Part III.

[40] Chapter 7, note 39, and note 19 in this chapter; for contemporary inflation in Spain, where prices were rising faster than elsewhere in Europe, see Part III, note 4.

PART THREE

War Taxation in the Core Provinces, Naples, and Castile

B efore taking up issues peculiar to each realm, it will be useful to glance at overall trends. Table III.1 compares the nominal value[1] of subsidies granted by the parliamentary bodies of the Low Countries,[2] Naples, and Castile during Charles's reign. One sees at once that the increase for the *donativi* of Naples was quite dramatic. This was due not just to the interplay of baronial politics in the kingdom (Chapter 13), but also to an artificially low starting point, for the *donativi* were a relative novelty at the beginning of the sixteenth century. Conversely, the overall upward trend for *beden* in the Low Countries is partially masked by a high starting point. Although the ordinary subsidies granted year by year increased only slightly during Charles's reign,[3] the core provinces approved larger and larger extraordinary subsidies during each succeeding military crisis, starting with the invasions of the Low Countries from both France and Guelders during the 1520s. Finally, because Table III.1 gives the totals in five-year periods, the starting point for Castile's *servicios* is also a bit low, since (owing to the Comuñero revolt of 1520–1521) there was no *servicio* income for two of the first five years. Thus although subsidies were rising in all three realms, differences in the rates of increase were not so great as they appear here. It would give a fairer picture of the overall trend realms to measure the shorter, two-decade interval between 1529–1533 and 1549–1553. This would mean nominal increases of 84% for the Low Countries, 147% for Naples, and 78% for Castile. Making the necessary adjustments for inflation rates that

---

[1] For various reasons (e.g., the rebates granted to towns with voting rights), the sums granted by parliaments were rarely if ever collected in full.

[2] Brabant is not included in Table III.1 because there is no study of its finances for this period. Owing to a fire that destroyed the old archducal palace in Brussels in the 1660s, the archives of Brabant are less well preserved than in Flanders or Holland.

[3] By only 25% in the two provinces mentioned in Table III.1. The ordinary subsidies were 240,000 gulden for Flanders and 80,000 for Holland in 1518, and 300,000 and 100,000 in the 1550s.

Table III.1. *Average Annual Subsidies of the Core Provinces, Naples, and Castile, 1519–1553 (nominal amount, expressed in Spanish ducats)*

Years	Low Countries *beden* (ordinary & extraordinary)[a]			Naples *donativi*[b]	Castile *servicios*[c] (ordinary & extraordinary)
	Flanders	Holland	Sum		
1519–1523	199,536	108,304	307,840	56,006	128,711
1524–1528	115,676	98,972	214,648	0	168,733
1529–1533	125,298	73,299	198,597	105,785	226,933
1534–1538	186,963	76,534	263,497	248,286	164,267
1539–1543	262,135	114,417	376,252	315,419	419,220
1544–1548	288,644	82,132	370,776	153,078	348,800
1549–1553	231,790	133,708	365,498	261,352	404,267
35-YEAR TOTALS	7,050,210	3,436,830	10,487,040	5,699,630	9,304,655

[a] For Flanders: Maddens, *De Beden in het Graafschaap Vlaanderen.* I add to Maddens's totals for 1543 a figure of 300,000 pounds of 40 silver groats for the two tenth pennies in Flanders that year (Aud. 650,298), and to his figures for 1552 480,000 pounds (262,404 ducats) for a Flanders *extraordinaris bede* (Aud. 650,299). For Holland, see Tracy, "The Taxation System of Holland," 108.

[b] Figures from D'Agostino, *Parlamento e societa nel regno di Napoli*, 272–274.

[c] Carande Thobar, *Carlos y sus banqueros*, II, 536–537.

have been calculated for each realm,[4] the nominal value of subsidies would have increased over these two decades by about 42% in the Low Countries, 73.5% in Naples, and 49% in Castile.

Did generosity have its rewards? Table III.2, pinpointing the dates at which subsidies rose appreciably, gives an indication of how different parliamentary bodies used their power of the purse. When either Flanders or Holland approved large totals of extraordinary subsidies within a single year, it was usually to respond to invasions of the Low Countries from France and/or the Rhineland, as in 1521–1523, 1527–1528, 1543–1544, and 1552–1553. The threats in question were often of special interest to the individual province; thus in the early 1520s Flanders paid for 10,000 infantry engaged in recapturing from France the nearby city-province of Tournai, while Holland paid for the army that was imposing Habsburg rule on Friesland, across the Zuyder Zee, a frequent springboard for

[4] Charles David Hendricks, "Charles V and the Cortes of Castile: The Politics of Renaissance Spain," Ph.D. dissertation, Cornell University, 1976, 223, calculates a wage–price inflation rate of 32% for these two decades in Castile; for my assumption that prices increased by 2% a year in Naples during the same period, see Chapter 13, note 26; in the Low Countries, butter and rye prices increased by approximately 100% between 1500 and 1550: E. Scholliers and Chr. Vandenbroecke, "Structuren en conjuncturen in de zuidelijke Nederlanden, 1400–1800," in Blok, (*Nieuwe*) *Algemene Geschiedenis der Nederlanden*, vol. V, 278.

Table III.2. *Largest Parliamentary Grants (in Spanish ducats)*
during Charles's Reign

Year	Low Countries *beden* (extraordinary)		Naples *donativi* (multiyear)	Castile *servicios* (multiyear)
	Flanders	Holland		
1521	166,735	129,776		
1522	191,335			
1523		271,853		
1525				810,667
1528		300,222		
1530	177,122	176,400		
1532			600,000	
1536			1,000,000	
1537	292,471			
1538				1,210,667
1541			800,000	
1543	687,648	316,482		
1544	650,010	173,518	600,000	
1549			600,000	
1552			800,000	
1553		450,000		

Sources: See Table III.1.

hostile incursions.[5] In Castile, the crucial year was 1538–1539, when noble deputies representing the towns with voting rights in the Cortes gained concessions that were important for their towns as well as themselves.[6] In Naples, by contrast, when the Parlamento agreed to unusually large *donativi*, it was either because the barons hoped in this way to rid themselves of a hated viceroy or lieutenant (1532, 1536), or because of urgent needs of the sovereign, lying beyond the borders of Naples (1541, 1552).[7] In other words, the Neapolitan assembly not only approved subsidy increases at a higher rate than the parliaments of Castile and the Low Countries but also demanded less in return.

The amounts of subsidy income raised in each realm may seem surprising in light of population estimates for 1550 mentioned in Table 5.2 – approximately 5,900,000 for Castile, 2,130,000 for Naples, and 2,175,000 for the

[5] Maddens, *Beden in het Graafschap Vlaanderen*, 426; cf. AJ 9 February 1528: Audiencer Laurent Dublioul reminds the deputies that once Utrecht has become part of the Habsburg Netherlands, "Holland will no longer be a frontier"; Brandi, *Emperor Charles V*, 384–385.

[6] The "capitation" of the *alcabala*, as described in Chapter 14.

[7] For all these points, see Chapter 13.

three core provinces. Flanders and Holland, the two provinces represented in Table III.1,[8] had a combined population of perhaps 1,250,000, a bit more than half that of the Kingdom of Naples, and about a fourth as much as Castile. Yet these two provinces provided more subsidy income than Castile, and nearly twice as much as Naples. This does not necessarily mean that Flanders and Holland were overtaxed in real terms, as fiscal historians would be quick to point out.[9] But in the politics of taxation, perceptions are what count; in this respect, one may be sure that Charles's Low Countries subjects would not willingly have traded places with taxpayers in Castile,[10] who had to pay the *alcabala*, the traditional sales tax reckoned at 10% of the value of all transactions, plus the *tercia*, a levy equivalent to two-ninths of the church's tithe income, collected by the crown with papal permission. In Naples commoners liable to the *donativi* also had to pay the annual hearth tax, plus excise taxes, which viceroys could impose at will.[11]

From a banker's perspective, what mattered was the total package of a prince's disposable revenue, in which parliamentary subsidies formed the lion's share in the Low Countries, but only a fraction in Castile and Naples (see Table 5.2). In Castile, bankers were quite happy to "anticipate" revenues for *servicios*, even if this was only a part of their business with the crown.[12] There were also tax-farming contracts for *maestrazgo* lands[13] and, for the church revenues dependent on permission from Rome,

---

[8] In Lodewijk van Schoer's summary of all *beden* to which the various provinces had consented between May 1542 and December 1543 (Aud. 650, 299), Flanders and Holland accounted for 47% of the total (2,475,000 gulden out of 5,250,900), or 51% of the extraordinary subsidy which in May 1542 was approved "in case of war" (230,000 out of 447,000).

[9] Gelabert, "The Fiscal Burden," 539–576; see also James D. Tracy, "Taxation and State Debt," in Brady, Oberman, and Tracy, *Handbook of European History*, 576–580. For Castile, Hendricks, "Charles V and the Cortes of Castile," argues that the total tax burden on commoners was actually a bit less at the end of Charles's reign than it was at the beginning. José Ignacio Fortea Perez, *Monarquía y Cortes en la corona de Castilla: Las ciudades ante la política fiscal de Felipe II* (Salamanca, 1990), 452–456, suggests caution in accepting Hendricks's conclusions, because there have not been enough local studies to check the assumptions he makes about how certain taxes were collected at the municipal level.

[10] The common feeling in the Low Countries that Castile's *alcabala* was a form of tyranny helps explain the massive resistance in 1572 to the duke of Alba's "Tenth Penny" sales tax, which touched off the Dutch Revolt. See Ferdinand H. M. Grapperhuis, *Alva en de Tiende Penning* (Zutfen, 1982).

[11] Sales and hearth taxes levied for the profit of the central government, though not unknown in the Low Countries, were put in place only when the provinces agreed to raise an extraordinary subsidy by these means.

[12] Compare Carande Thobar, *Carlos V y sus banqueros*, II, 255 (*rentas ordinarias*) and 536–537 (*servicios*). Taking the year 1536 as an example, and converting into ducats the figures Carande Thobar gives in *maravedis*, the former had a nominal value of 1,099,432 ducats for that year, the latter 166,667. The *rentas ordinarias* (including the *alcabala*), though nominally worth much more than the grants by the Cortes, were not of much interest to bankers, because they were increasingly pledged to pay interest on the crown's long-term *juro* debt.

[13] Kellenbenz, *Die Fuggersche Maestrazgopacht (1525–1542)*.

the *cruzada* and the clerical *subsidio*. Most of all, of course, bankers coveted for their loans assignation on the crown's share of gold and silver from Peru and Mexico, even if shipments were sparse in some years, including the period 1541–1545.[14] In Naples, bankers seem to have preferred the old *focatico* to the new *donativo*, because the nominal value of the former was almost always higher than the latter in any given year.[15] Even though the traditional hearth tax was reduced to a fraction of its value by old debts,[16] *cambios* for the needs of Spanish garrisons in Milan and elsewhere were more likely to be charged against the *focatico* than the *donativi*.[17] In the separate provinces of the Low Countries, however, there was no revenue worth comparing with the ordinary and extraordinary subsidies. Because the provincial parliaments came to control these revenues by the end of Charles's reign, bankers preferred to deal with their spokesmen, turning a cold shoulder to the agents of the central government with whom they had always dealt in the past.[18]

Needless to say, parliamentary bodies that negotiated directly with the bankers had more leverage in dictating how their money would be used: the provincial states of the Low Countries were not only able to direct most of their subsidy income to local needs; they also forced Mary's government to yield control of these key revenues into their hands (Chapter 12). In Castile, where subsidies were at times (if not always) a key source of assignations for bankers' loans, the towns represented in the Cortes were also able to gain some control over important revenues, if not to restrict the amount of subsidy income that went to pay for Charles's overseas wars (Chapter 14). By contrast, the Parlamento of Naples, where neither towns nor provinces had any effective representation, the dominant nobles bargained in their own behalf, but not for any larger interest (Chapter 13). Thus, although all three realms were responding to the same war-generated fiscal pressure, the end result in each case reflects a unique balance of political and social interests.

[14] Carande Thobar, *Carlos V y sus banqueros*, I, 240.
[15] See Coniglio, *Consulte e bilanci del Viceregno di Napoli*, Document 6, 134–164: the nominal yield for the hearth tax in 1508–1509 was 403,667 scudi or Neapolitan ducats. This sum was exceeded by the annual face value of a *donativo* only in 1535, owing to the Parlamento's grant of 1 million ducats, of which 500,000 was to be collected during the first year of a six-year *donativo*: see Chapter 13.
[16] Including alienation by the crown of the right to collect it in certain communities: Chapter 3, notes 18, 19.
[17] See Chapter 13.
[18] See Chapter 12.

Chapter 12

Fiscal Devolution and War Taxation
in the Low Countries

Chapter 4 described a build-up of mutual suspicions between Margaret of Austria's government and the states of the core provinces. This chapter focuses on a process of mutual accommodation, in which two sides that still mistrusted each other had to cooperate because of the pressure of war. In stages, the hammer blows of invasion in the 1520s, 1540s, and 1550s forced the birth of a new fiscal order in all three core provinces, as will be discussed here with special reference to Holland.[1] The states accepted novel forms of taxation, in return for the government's willingness to relinquish to them effective control of the new revenues. By the end of Charles's reign, it was the provincial parliaments that collected huge sums in taxes, using their own officials, and negotiated with the bankers about new loans, while Mary of Hungary and her fiscal agents were left with a mountain of old debt not assignable to any revenues the central government controlled.

Borrowing from the Future: "Renten" on the Subsidies, 1521–1529

In April 1521 one French ally invaded Luxemburg, while another launched an attack on Spanish Navarre.[2] Once begun, this Habsburg-Valois war would continue until the Peace of Cambrai (September 1529), save for a two-year hiatus following the capture of Francis I at Pavia in January 1525. This level of military engagement demanded more money. According to summaries prepared by the receiver general and the Council of Finance for the years 1520–1530, average annual income for 1521–1529

---

[1] Sources for Holland include AJ; RSH; and the correspondence of Antoine de Lalaing, count of Hoogstraten, *Stadtholder* or provincial governor of Holland, 1522–1540, and of Lord Gerrit, lord of Assendelft, First Councillor of the Council of Holland, 1527–1558, both to be found in Aud.

[2] Knecht, *Renaissance Warrior and Patron*, 165–177; Brandi, *Emperor Charles V*, 154–160.

(989,298 Carolus gulden) was about one-third higher than for the previous nine years.[3] Between 1521 and 1529, some 61% of all expenditures went for armies, artillery, fortifications, and warships.[4] In 1528 alone, fighting on two fronts, Margaret and her ministers calculated that they spent between 1.3 million and 1.4 million gulden to keep two armies in the field.[5]

Waging war also required borrowing against future revenues. In the Low Countries, unlike in Castile or Naples, the ordinary subsidies of the three core provinces were the single most important revenue, providing a bit more than half of the government's gross annual income during the 1520s: 240,000 per year for Flanders, 200,000 for Brabant, and 80,000 for Holland (with subtractions for "graces" or rebates, the total disposable income was about 360,000).[6] Traditionally, there were two ways to borrow against future subsidy income. First, one could ask the states to "anticipate" what they owed for one or more half-year terms of the current ordinary subsidy.[7] The provincial parliaments were often willing to do so in time of war,[8] but this meant they were less likely to consent to the extraordinary subsidies that were also needed in time of war. Extraordinary subsidies were usually collected on the basis of the provincewide assessments used for ordinary subsidies, like the *transport* in Flanders or the *schiltal* in Holland, and one could not go too often to the same well. The government sometimes tried alternate means of collecting extraordinary subsidies (like the provincewide excise tax approved by the States of Holland in 1523) but with discouraging

---

[3] Aud. 867, 35–38.

[4] Aud. 873, a 315-page summary of income and expenses for 1520–1530, said at the end to have been presented to the emperor in Brussels in March 1531 by the count of Hoogstraten (president of the Council of Finance and *Stadtholder* in Holland) and receiver general Jean Micault, and "seen" by Charles in the presence of Jean Carondolet, archbishop of Palermo and president of the Council of State, and Laurent Dublioul, *Audienceur* or head of the chancery. To reach a total income for these years of 12,543,258 Carolus gulden, I have reduced the stated total income (15,113,493) by the amount listed for "graces" or rebates on the subsidies (2,570,235; in the accounting practice of the period, the amount due for subsidies was always entered as income, and rebates were entered as expenditures). To arrive at a total of 7,658,803 (61.06%) gulden spent on war-related expenses, I have added the expense categories for payments by the treasurer of war (6,562,403), payments by the master of artillery (311,865), payments for fortifications (70,943), payments for Spanish infantry (13,406), and payments by provincial receivers of subsidies (chiefly in Brabant and Flanders) that went directly for warships or other military needs, without passing through the hands of the receiver general (700,186).

[5] Aud. 876, 132–136.

[6] Calculations for the year 1531: Aud. 875. In government accounts, the amount due was entered as income and rebates were entered as an expense.

[7] Subsidies were approved by the states for periods of two to six years, with payment due on St. John's Day and at Christmas.

[8] For the years 1520–1530, Aud. 873, 53v–57v, lists 405,889 gulden in "anticipations from future *aides* [subsidies] and loans from officers," plus a further 33,691 in anticipations by the States of Brabant.

results.[9] Receivers could either advance money against what they expected to collect for future terms of the ordinary subsidy or pledge their "receipts" for a coming year as security for a loan by bankers in Antwerp. But deputies to the states could make an awful ruckus if told that money for a given year was already "gone" as a result of transactions like these, to which they were not privy.[10]

Moreover, both the receivers and the bankers demanded high rates for short-term loans. In this respect, the government's best strategy was to expand its funded or consolidated debt. Since the thirteenth century, town governments in the Low Countries had been issuing bonds or "incomes" (*rentes* or, in Netherlandish, *renten*) against their choicest revenues, usually excise taxes on beer and wine that they collected with the approval of the princely government. As with the *juros* in Castile, there were two kinds of bonds. Redeemable or *losrenten* passed on from generation to generation, even from century to century, until such time as the principal was redeemed. *Lijfrenten* paid higher rates but were extinguished by the death of the named beneficiary. Although some towns ran their debts up to levels that caused problems, resulting in an occasional suspension of payments, many had built up solid credit ratings, so that their bonds were highly sought as investments by nobles and burghers well beyond the town walls.[11] The Burgundian dukes began issuing *renten* against lucrative parcels of domain income during the reign of Philip the Bold (d. 1404), if not earlier. Instead of borrowing from bankers on the Antwerp exchange, Margaret of Austria preferred to raise money by selling *rentes* on these familiar government revenues. But when Charles summoned rich creditors to find money for his journey from the Low Countries to Spain in 1522, there were no takers for *renten* on the domains of Brabant. Some wanted to buy parcels of domain outright, which in Margaret's view would have caused Charles "to lose *reputación* and obedience in the said province." On another ocasion, Margaret persuaded Adolph of Burgundy (d. 1540), hereditary admiral of the Low Countries, to accept a *rente* in payment of what he had spent putting warships to sea in defense of the fishing fleet against French privateers during the

---

[9] Burgher deputies liked the idea of a tax that would have to be paid by normally exempt nobles and clergy, but the nobles and the clergy were evidently not the only ones who objected to this novelty: most of what was expected from the excise had to be collected instead "according to the *schiltal*": AJ 9 December 1522, 30 March–7 April, 17, 30 July, 5, 9 August, 10 September 1523.

[10] Loans by the receivers themselves seem to have been small during the 1520s. See Aud. 873, 135–144, "Frais comptez par receveurs particuliers"; these were sums for which provincial or other local receivers accounted directly to the auditors of the Council of Finance, rather than through the receiver general or the treasurer of war, each of whom provided local receivers with quittances for transmittal to the auditors.

[11] Tracy, *A Financial Revolution*, 7–31.

previous two years. In the tense summer months of 1528, when money was needed for campaigns on two fronts against France and Guelders, Margaret and her Council of Finance found buyers for 100,000 in new domain *renten*.[12]

Renten secured by the much larger income from ordinary subsidies promised a wider market. In Brabant, Antwerp's capital market showed the way for the placement of such *renten*. At Emperor Maximilian's request, and using Antwerp's portion of the ordinary subsidy as security, the city government found buyers for *renten* with a capital value that may be estimated at 157,332 gulden (1512–1514). In Brussels, the church wardens at Our Lady of the Sandhill put 1,600 gulden into a *losrente* secured by their city's portion of the ordinary subsidy (1520). In such cases, the town treasurers simply withheld from their payments to the provincial receiver of subsidies the sums needed for interest payments and redemption of principal.[13] In Flanders, Ypres reported that its "rich and powerful" would not entrust any of their money to *renten* of this kind, but the magistrates of the Franc of Bruges found buyers for 32,000 in *losrenten*, secured by the Franc's ordinary subsidy quota.[14]

Holland too had a tradition of long-term borrowing on the government's behalf. In 1482, to finance a war against the ecclesiastical principality of Utrecht, the States of Holland voted an extraordinary subsidy in the form of a large issue of *renten*; the states obliged the province as a whole for principal and interest, based on domain revenues that Maximilian's government entrusted to Holland for this purpose. Because this debt was not retired until 1526, the precedent was not encouraging. Nonetheless, the states agreed in 1515 to an extraordinary subsidy in which they pledged the province's collective faith and credit once more, for an issue of 22,400 gulden in *losrenten* secured, this time, by the ordinary subsidy. As in 1482, prosperous Amsterdam insisted on separate responsibility for its portion of the sale; according to the laws of reprisal, its merchants would thus be subject to arrest in "foreign" towns only for arrears on the *renten* for which Amsterdam itself was liable, not for those on which Holland's other five "great cities" were collectively liable.[15]

---

[12] Margaret's instructions for Vaytel's mission to Ferdinand, 6 June 1528, *Familienkorrespondenz*, Letter 192, II, 237–242; Margaret to Charles, 21 February 1524, Lanz, Letter 49, I, 94; Margaret to Charles, 7 July 1528, Lanz, Letter 110, I, 278–279, the 100,000; with the advice of the Council of Finance, Margaret raised another 100,000 by loans from the great lords (the cardinal of Liège advanced 60,000), and was to ask an assembly of the clergy for 100,000 more.

[13] Aud. 873,126–129. The fourteenth-century church now known as Notre Dame du Sablon was Onze Lieve Vrouw van de Zavel in the sixteenth century.

[14] Aud. 873,129–129v; Maddens, *De Beden in het Graafschap Vlaanderen*, 349–361, especially 359, n. 116.

[15] "Foreign" in this context meant any place outside Holland, including, for example, Bruges in Flanders, an important market for *renten*: Tracy, *A Financial Revolution*, 57–60. Interest was paid in

To meet her needs during the 1520s, Margaret developed these precedents further. A summary for 1520–1530 reports that capital in the amount
of 1,016,051 was raised through sales of *renten* on provincial subsidies, as
opposed to 292,034 through sales of new *renten* on domain income. Most
of the subsidy *renten* were issued in Brabant and Holland. The States of
Brabant raised in this way extraordinary subsidies[16] of 240,000 gulden in
1522, 176,000 in 1525, and 42,848 in 1527; there were also numerous local
transactions in which Antwerp and other towns agreed to sell *renten* against
their own ordinary subsidy quotas.[17] Meanwhile, the States of Holland
consented to *renten* sales with a capital value of 32,000 in 1522, 128,000 in
1523, and 176,000 in 1528. Because Holland's wealth was rated at only about
40% of Brabant's – the current ordinary subsidies for the two provinces were
80,000 and 200,000 gulden respectively – the size of these Holland *renten*
sales is surprising. But Friesland was being brought under Habsburg rule
in 1522–1523, and Utrecht and Overijssel (the lands of the prince-bishop
of Utrecht) in 1528. Hollanders apparently accepted the argument that
having these territories as buffers between their province and the bellicose
duke of Guelders was worth paying for.[18]

---

semiannual installments, and the party issuing the *rente* was considered in default if interest was not
paid within six months of the due date. The solidity of Amsterdam's credit may be seen from a
transaction in 1522, when Amsterdam and three other cities agreed to find buyers for 16,000 in
renten on their ordinary subsidy quotas: Amsterdam's entire portion (8,000) was bought by no less
a personage than Jean Micault, receiver general for all finance (ibid., 45).

[16] Such transactions may been seen as anticipations of the ordinary subsidy when principal was
promptly repaid from the ordinary subsidy according to the original agreement; this was likely to
happen in cases (as in Flanders) when *renten* were issued against its own quota by a town or locality
that had its own officials deduct principal as well as interest payments from future subsidy payments
to pay down the debt. They are better seen as extraordinary subsidies, distinct sources of income for
the government, where little if any of the principal was repaid; this was likely to happen in cases
(as in Holland) when *renten* were issued by the states against the province's quota, so that while
towns deducted their share of interest payments from their ordinary subsidy quotas, the repayment
of principal fell to the government's receiver of subsidies, who always had more pressing demands
on his receipts. This distinction between the two provinces explains why Maddens, *De Beden in
het Graafschap Vlaanderen*, prefers to speak of anticipations, while I follow the usage of the States of
Holland in speaking of sales of *renten* as extraordinary subsidies.

[17] Charles to Margaret, 31 October 1522, Lanz, Letter 40, I, 70–72; Aud. 873, 126–129.

[18] Tracy, "The Taxation System of Holland," 108. AJ 9 February 1528, in reference to the government's
request for Holland to raise an extraordinary subsidy of 80,000 by issuing 5,000 in *losrenten* at the
usual rate of 1:16: Holland's advocate, Aert van der Goes, asserts that because his imperial majesty
will profit from the conquest of Utrecht, he and the other provinces should pay for it; Audienceur
Laurent Dublioul responds for the government that Flanders and Hainault and Luxemburg have
enough to do against France, and that Holland itself will have the benefit of this conquest, through
an increase of its trade, and because Holland will no longer be a border province. Cf. *RSH* 3 July
1528, the states propose that Utrecht, now conquered, be made a part of Holland, just as Tournai
had been made a part of Flanders when government forces in 1522 ejected the English army that
had occupied it since Henry VIII's campaign against France in 1511.

But the government was seldom able to exercise its option to redeem heritable *renten* and thus clear the ordinary subsidy of debt. The usual agreement was that the *renten* were to be redeemed from ordinary subsidy collections over the next two or three years; during this period the province issuing the *renten* assumed responsibility for interest payments, "lest his imperial majesty have nothing to be grateful for." Once this time limit had passed, interest was deducted from the ordinary subsidy. But the receiver of subsidies, charged with making redemption payments, always had more demands on his "receipt" than he could handle; thus redemptions were postponed indefinitely, while interest charges mounted with each new issue of *renten*. By 1531 *renten* interest payable from the ordinary subsidy receipts had risen to 42,092 for Brabant, 22,310 for Holland, and 6,466 for Flanders and other provinces.[19] Because there were also subtractions for "graces" enjoyed by the towns, the ordinary subsidy for Brabant and Holland netted the government less than half of its nominal value. Meanwhile, town deputies were besieged with complaints from wealthy burghers who had in many cases been "constrained" to buy and at least wanted their money back on time. But because the semiannual ordinary subsidy collections were the only reliable source of ready cash, they also had to worry about having the province keeping some money on hand for emergencies.

Hence the budgets[20] that were always presented when the government requested an extraordinary subsidy in the form of a sale of *renten* against the ordinary subsidy drew keen interest. No other issue brought out more sharply the basic conflict between the countrywide perspective of the government and the local interests of its provinces and towns. To Charles and his officials, it was obvious that money from the 240,000 sale of *renten* in Brabant in 1522 should be used "to discharge my debts" as well as to station men-at-arms on the frontier. After all, as Chapters 6 through 11 have shown, there was no hope of borrowing for the current war unless the debts of past wars were cleared. But burghers saw it as a waste of precious resources when money that might protect lives and property was used to satisfy the bankers. After all, in the "propositions" by which subsidies were requested, the government iself always gave first priority to "defense of the land." In Holland matters came to a head in 1523. In 1522 and 1523, the states raised a total of 80,000 gulden in support of Habsburg claims to the province of Friesland, contested by Guelders, by issuing 5,000 in *losrenten* at the rate of 1:16 (6.25%). When government officials requested a

---

[19] Tracy, *A Financial Revolution*, chap. II, especially table V, p. 66; Aud. 873, 126–129: for an extraordinary subsidy of 240,000 gulden agreed to by the States of Brabant in 1528, Antwerp's treasurers were authorized to deduct from their payments to the receiver of subsidies, over and above the city's rebate, a total of 28,125, representing *losrenten* sold by Antwerp against its own quota and that of surrounding rural areas, in order to raise money promptly. See note 16.

[20] Called *état* in French or *staat* in Netherlandish.

further issue of 5,000 for Friesland, Ruysch Janszoon, one of Amsterdam's elder statesmen, asked what had happened to the first 80,000 gulden: "I know where the money has gone, it has been used to purge the wounds and scars of old debt; for the garrisons in Friesland, which ought to be paid from the receipts of the emperor's domains, have been paid instead from Holland's extraordinary subsidies [i.e., the previous issue of 5,000 in *losrenten*]." Janszoon had been given access to the accounts of Willem Goudt, Holland's receiver of subsidies, but this did not resolve his questions, for the expenditures listed in Goudt's accounts were mainly in the form of remittances to the receiver-general for all finances or to the treasurer of war, with no indication as to how these officials of the central government had spent Holland's money.[21] In the end, it took four months of wrangling to win approval of the second issue of 5,000 in *renten*. The states agreed to release 12,000 gulden for "old debts" in Friesland (not the 32,000 requested by the government); Hoogstraten, the Stadtholder, was to be reimbursed for the 16,000 gulden he claimed to have spent from his own pocket to hire soldiers, but only insofar as he documented his expenses to the satisfaction of the deputies.[22]

These years mark a low point in relations between officials sent to negotiate with the Hollanders and members of the small burgher elite who spoke for their towns. In a private meeting with Amsterdam's delegation, Hoogstraten complained that "these people do not trust me," for they had "sent to the emperor in Spain" to have him removed as *Stadtholder*. The town secretary made a guarded reply: "My lord, no such thing was attempted against you by the town government [*consilio publico*], and the city is not responsible for what individuals may do."[23] Playing on the sinister motives imputed to the government, Hoogstraten and others sometimes tried to get their way with threats and innuendos. Thus a truce with Guelders (1524–1526) "was not so well made" that the *Stadtholder* did not know how to break it. Meester Vincent Corneliszoon, a Hollander who served with Hoogstraten on the Council of Finance, merely "smiled" when asked why troops were gathering near the border during the truce. On behalf

---

[21] AJ 20 October 1523. Janszoon was correct. Receivers accounted for expenses by listing the *décharges* or quittances they had been issued for remittances to (or payments on the account of) other named officials. The point was not to explain to burghers how the government's finances worked, but to ensure that the receiver could indeed "account for" all of the income he was entitled to collect. For Goudt's accounts as Holland's receiver for the subsidies between 1515 and 1542, see GRK, nos. 3417–3442.

[22] AJ 9, 15, 20, 25 October, 21–23 November, 17–18, 28–29 December 1523, 25–28 January, 8–10, 14–15 February 1524.

[23] AJ 4 June 1524; cf. AJ 12 May 1530: the lord of Renesse tells Hoogstraten that Holland's deputies had said to him that "Hollanders were unlucky to have as their *Stadtholder* a man who was also head of the Council of Finance, for such a man is divided in two."

of the regent herself, Audiencer Dublioul hinted that, though Margaret had never been "rewarded" for helping Holland maintain its commercial position in the Baltic, she understood well enough how to "disrupt the eastward trade." During the Habsburg siege of Utrecht (1528), Hoogstraten threatened to have the Amsterdam merchants he suspected of "feeding" the enemy sewn up in sacks and drowned; "do it, my lord," spoke up burgomaster Pieter Colijn, "we ask you to." When Amsterdam demanded trade concessions for its consent to the 1529–1530 "coronation subsidy" (see Chapter 6), the *Stadtholder* "started up like a man beside himself, saying, 'I will lay you out flat,' pointing to the ground, 'like a dog.'"[24]

When the parties to an adversarial relationship are bound together by powerful common interests, "frank"[25] exchanges of this kind can help to clear away misunderstandings. In this case, the needs of defense demanded finding ways to cooperate. Beginning with the second 5,000 in 1524, budgets for new issues of *renten* had to be approved by the states. Requests by the deputies to have their people oversee disbursement of funds raised in this way were at first ignored, but in 1528 the states named two of their number to "stand alongside" Willem Goudt, the receiver of subsidies, as he made out payment orders. They also appointed two "masters of the muster" to keep muster rolls for the banners of mercenary troops recruited for service in Holland; two Amsterdam burgomasters were chosen, including the previously mentioned Pieter Colijn, whom Hoogstraten had recently threatened to remove from office. When the government wanted yet another issue of *renten* to help complete the victory in Utrecht, the Council of Holland[26] sensed immediately that the states would not agree without having more information; they wrote Hoogstraten to have the treasurer of war's clerk send copies of the accounts that would show how the money from previous sales had been spent.[27]

There were also direct contacts between burgher deputies and military commanders. In Holland, the states promised Floris van IJsselstein, the count of Buren, 1,000 gulden as soon as his men captured the city of Utrecht. In Flanders, the Four Members approved an extraordinary subsidy of 150,000 gulden (1521) but only on condition that 32,000 of this sum be placed in the hands of their own commissioners, for hiring 1,000 cavalry

[24] AJ 27 June–3 July 1524, 21 July 1525, 11 October 1526, 22–22 March 1528, 11 February 1530.
[25] AJ 19–23 February 1524: following a session in Brussels at which Holland's deputies complained that Margaret was asking the provinces to carry burdens the government itself should bear, "the *Stadtholder* and our Gracious Lady [Margaret] thanked the States of Holland for speaking so freely, and pointing out the [government's] failings."
[26] The central government's court of appeals and administrative organ for the province, based in The Hague.
[27] AJ 17–18 December 1523; *RSH* 21–23 March 1528; AJ 31 March–9 April 1528; and Council of Holland to Hoogstraten, 9 July 1528; Aud. 1524.

and 3,000 infantry to guard the frontier between Flanders and Artois. The following year, Margaret reported to Charles that the Four Members had taken control of the current ordinary subsidy in Flanders, to make sure the troops were properly paid; this meant that lenders who had been assigned on the ordinary subsidy for repayment were reluctant to make further loans, because the receiver of subsidies whose pledge of repayment they had accepted now had no access to the money. In Brabant, Antwerp and 's Hertogenbosch loyally supported the war against Guelders, but Louvain and Brussels did not; it seems there was disagreement over how to allocate the 288,000 gulden in extraordinary subsidies approved by the states in 1528. "Without the knowledge of the Council of Finance," two friendly members of the Council of State, the prince-bishop of Liège and the lord of Bergen-op-Zoom, gave written approval to transactions in which the magistrates of Antwerp and 's Hertogenbosch received 186,682 in subsidy funds for money they had spent on the Guelders war.[28]

Hoogstraten captured the reality of Low Countries politics in one of his earthy metaphors, meant to convey to deputies that his interests and Holland's were one and the same:

> I am not so stupid as you think. If someone gives me this much satisfaction (pointing to his hand), I will do the same, and likewise if someone gives me this much satisfaction (pointing to his elbow). Similarly if someone gives me this much trouble (pointing in the same way) I will repay in like fashion. Do you imagine that I want others [i.e., governors of other provinces] to have flocks of sheep to shear, while I have only a herd of swine?

If Hoogstraten defended Holland's interests in Brussels, he expected his "sheep" not merely to provide him a handsome annual gratuity but also to strengthen his credibility at court, for example, by approving the regent's requests for subsidies.[29]

The Habsburg-Burgundian state always depended on a game of mutual interests. For generations, families like Hoogstraten's traded loyalty to the prince for a near monopoly on the most lucrative and prestigious offices of state. In the same way, towns were accustomed to trade consent to subsidies for rebates and other privileges. Now the game had an added level of complexity: towns were asked to put their credit ratings at the

---

[28] AJ 30 April 1528; Maddens, *De Beden in het Graafschap Vlaanderen*, 365–411; Aud. 873, 123v, an entry in the category of expenses called "Parties prinses en despense par les comptes des receveurs particuliers des aydes," which includes payments that provincial receivers of subsidies made without the written authorization of their superior, the receiver general of all finances.

[29] AJ 7 June 1537; cf. 11 February 1530, a similar comment juxtaposed to a threat to have Pieter Colijn and one of his colleagues removed as Amsterdam's burgomasters: "Si vous faictez bien je vous entretiendray. Si aultrement je trouveray des aultres." For cases in which the *Stadtholder* promoted Holland's interests at court, AJ 21 October 1535, 4–8 February, 14 May 1536.

Table 12.1. *Charges against the Ordinary Subsidies in 1531*

	Gross	Expenses	Rebates	*Renten* Interest	All Deductions	Net
Brabant	200,000	6,072	65,807	42,092	113,971	86,029 (43%)
Flanders	200,000	26,525	69,659	3,000	99,184	101,816 (51%)
Holland	80,000	10,967	25,674	22,312	58,953	21,047 (26%)
All others	99,251	1,000	23,622	4,849	29,471	68,781 (69%)
TOTALS	579,251	44,564	184,762	72,253	301,579	277,672 (48%)

Source: Aud. 875.

service of the government. By issuing *renten* against their subsidy quotas, towns shielded a portion of the government's borrowing needs behind guarantees that investors trusted. What they got in return was more of a say in how the government managed its war budget.

The "Novel Expedients" of 1542–1544

In 1531, for which a detailed summary survives, Mary of Hungary's government recorded an income of 1,229,292 Carolus gulden, including 579,251 gulden (47%) for the amount due that year in ordinary subsidies, and a further 393,000 gulden (32%) in the form of "anticipations" of the ordinary subsidy receipts of future years.[30] The three core provinces accounted for 82.9% of the ordinary subsidy, and 82.4% of the anticipations.[31] Table 12.1 shows the extent to which this most important of the government's revenues was eaten away by rebates, *renten* interest, and other charges against the ordinary subsidy. In Flanders, where sales of *renten* against the subsidies had been relatively small, various castleries agreed to new issues during the 1530s, some of which were redeemed on schedule, but most of which were not.[32] But in Brabant and Holland new issues were resisted by the states. In 1530, for example, the States of Holland were willing to issue 3,000 in new *renten* at 1:16 only if this new debt were secured by domain revenues placed under Holland's control. But the government wanted the domain revenues as security for its own issues of *renten*.[33] In the end, new buyers were found to take over Hoogstraten's 3,000 gulden in States of Holland *renten*, while the collectors of various domain revenues issued the

[30] Aud. 875. The anticipations are mainly in the form of loans by bankers or officials, assigned for repayment on future ordinary subsidies. For example, a certain Jehan Mos lent 100,000 gulden against receipts in Brabant, while the (unnamed) receiver of subsidies in Brabant advanced 100,000 against receipts for the Franc of Bruges in Flanders.

[31] These percentages are a bit higher than usual because the province of Zeeland, struck in 1531 by a devastating flood, was relieved of responsibility for its ordinary subsidy that year.

[32] Maddens, *De Beden in het Graafschap Vlaanderen*, table XII, 356–357.

[33] Chapter 5, note 3.

Stadtholder new "letters"[34] for his 3,000 in annual interest. This complicated transaction raised the capital sum needed (48,000) without adding to the total charge against Holland's ordinary subsidy.[35]

As war debts mounted with a new invasion from France in 1536, Mary's advisers groped for other sources of revenue. In October, the provincial states sent representatives to Brussels to hear a "general proposition" calling for national excise taxes on sales of wine, domestic and foreign beer, cloth of gold, bolts of woolen cloth, and other items of common consumption. Sales or excise taxes of this kind had long been collected by the towns, with the approval of the government – this was how towns funded their own issues of *renten* – but collecting them at a province- or countrywide level would have been a real novelty. To sweeten the pill, the government sought to play on burgher resentment of tax exemptions enjoyed by the nobles and the clergy, assuring deputies that no one would be exempt from these new excises, except for members of the mendicant orders. When the States of Holland met in The Hague to discuss this proposal, some towns objected to its "novelty," while others had concerns specific to their own trades; for example, Delft and Gouda worried lest their beer might be taxed at the higher "foreign" rate, as other brewing cities in the Low Countries did in levying their town excises. The next meeting of the States General, set for 26 October in Brussels, was delayed until 20 November because deputies from Flanders, where Ghent's refusal to pay taxes approved by the other three members was just beginning to cause problems, were slow in arriving. When the session opened, because no province was willing to be the first to declare its "mandate" on the excise proposal, the whole idea had to be dropped. As for the provincial assemblies that preceded this meeting, Mary reported to Charles that none of the deputies had dared to relay "to their people" the details of the government's proposal, "not even those of Artois, which is closest to the fire."[36]

Charles's firm suppression of Ghent's four-year tax rebellion (February 1540; see Chapter 8) strengthened Mary's hand in dealing with the states. So did Dr. Lodewijk van Schoer, a tough-minded burgher jurist who presided over Mary's Council of State from 1540 until his death in 1548.[37] Even so,

---

[34] The Netherlandish term was *rentebrieven*. A *rentebrief* gave the principal and interest, the names of purchaser and beneficiary (*lijfrenten* in particular were often bought by parents for their young children), and the place where the beneficiary or his agent was to collect the interest twice a year. These instruments were negotiable, but I have found little information on the secondary market: Tracy, *A Financial Revolution*, 90 (n. 50), 119.

[35] AJ 19–24 August, 2–5, 9 October 1530; *RSH* 30–31 August, 8 September 1530.

[36] AJ 3–14, 22–24 October, 28 October–1 December 1536; *RSH* 23–26 October, 18 December 1536; Charles to Mary, 10 September 1536 (how to deal with Ghent), and Mary to Charles, 12 November 1536, Lanz, Letters 654, 658, II, 666–667, 668.

[37] Tracy, *A Financial Revolution*, 72–73.

Mary struggled to raise money to meet the "first shock" of invasion from France and the Rhineland when war broke out again in 1542. The three core provinces raised 710,000 gulden in extraordinary subsidies, including 340,000 levied according to the traditional assessments, and a further 370,000 through sales of *renten*. In this case, however, the *renten* were not to be charged against the ordinary subsidies; instead, each province would have to devise a new means of funding the *renten* before the first interest payments came due the next year. Mary also borrowed 300,000 gulden in her own name, and persuaded the provinces to "anticipate" ordinary subsidy payments due in 1543 and 1544, with a net value (minus deductions) of perhaps 500,000 gulden for the two years. By September 1542, there was not enough to give the troops their going-home wage,[38] and nothing at all for more fighting in subsequent years.

In these desperate circumstances, the government turned again to "imposts" or excise taxes of some kind. Except for Artois, all the provinces had rejected the idea a second time in February 1542. But in Flanders, the Franc of Bruges had created a land tax specifically for the purpose of retiring some of its *renten*. The States of Brabant – backed by their colleagues from Artois, Hainaut, and Lille – proposed something similar in subsequent conversations with government commissioners. At a joint meeting with the Council of State, presided over by Mary (11 November 1542), the Council of Finance estimated the combined expenses for outstanding debts, garrison wages for the winter, and the cost of another all-out campaign during the warm months of 1543 at the gargantuan total of 2.4 million gulden – nearly ten times as much as the net value of the government's chief revenue, the annual ordinary subsidy of the three core provinces. What was to be done? It was "notorious" that one could not squeeze more money from the provinces according to the traditional assessments, in which peasants were burdened unfairly because of rebates granted to the cities. Hence one could not "preserve the country" (*garder le pays*) without finding some "new expedient" (*nouvel moyen*) to bring in revenue. There might be a "capital levy" according to the value of real and personal property, but because subjects were loath to provide information about their personal property this would be "difficult to manage." A better idea was an "impost" equivalent to 10% of landed income, "according to the proposal of Brabant" and the other provinces; there might be a

[38] *RSH* 5 July, 11, 18 September 1542; Aud. 650, 295–298, a tally in the hand of Lodewijk van Schoer of war subsidies granted in the years 1542 and 1543. For verification from other sources of Schoer's figures for subsidies granted in 1542, see Maddens, *De Beden in het Graafschap Vlaanderen*, 427, and Tracy, "The Taxation System of Holland," 111. But Schoer's estimate of the net value of the ordinary subsidy at 336,000 gulden per year includes a deduction only for rebates, not for *renten* interest. Mary to Charles, 17 and 18 September 1542, HHSA-B, PA 33, Konvolut 1, Aud. 53, 288–292.

Table 12.2. *Sources of Funds Raised by the Core Provinces, 1543–1544*

	2 Tenth Pennies	Ordinary Subsidies	Extraordinary Subsidies[a]	*Renten*	Total
Brabant	1,227,675	140,598	193,377	—	1,561,650
Flanders	1,450,600	164,206	214,200	—	1,829,006
Holland	166,160	82,664	134,184	136,190	519,198
TOTALS	2,844,435	387,468	541,761	136,190	3,909,854
	(77.8%)	(9.9%)	(13.9%)	(3.5%)	

[a] Collected by means other than a sale of *renten*.

Sources: Aud. 650, 352–382, with details from Maddens, *De Beden in het Graafschap Vlaanderen*, and Tracy, "The Taxation System of Holland," 111.

similar levy on the profits of commercial transactions. On 28 November Mary wrote to Charles that her commissioners would present this plan to the deputies now assembling for a meeting of the States General. She also warned that if the provincial states approved any new kind of revenue, they would insist on having control over its collection and disbursement. In fact, money for the "anticipation" of the ordinary subsidies as well as from the current sales of *renten* was already being collected and disbursed by the provinces, through officials like Holland's receiver for the common territory, who, though appointed by the government, rendered his accounts to the States of Holland rather than to the Council of Finance. During the spring of 1542, the Four Members of Flanders gave their consent to an extraordinary subsidy only on condition that the money be collected by a man whom they would appoint – the same official who had been collecting extraordinary subsidies in Flanders, and rendering his accounts to the Four Members, since 1537.[39]

On 2 December Lodewijk van Schoer read out to the States General a "general proposition" calling for a 10% impost on the income from real property, a similar "tenth penny" on commercial profits, both to be collected by receivers answerable to the provinces, and a "hundredth penny" or 1% duty on the value of exported goods. According to the Council of Finance, the three measures would yield 1 million of the 2.4 million gulden that was needed. In subsequent months, all three of these "novel

[39] Aud. 650, 484–493, a document bearing the heading "Correction," summarizing the joint meeting of 11 November 1542; the strategy of this document follows that outlined in a memorandum of about 1540 in the hand of Meester Vincent Corneliszoon van Mierop, a Hollander on the Council of Finance (Aud. 868, 120–128). Mary to Charles, 4 February, 28 November 1542, Aud. 53, 57–57v, 340v–341v. In Holland, accounts for two sales of *renten* in 1542 and 1543 were kept by receiver of the common territory: Rijksarchief van Zuid-Holland, The Hague, IIIe Afdeling, "Staten van Holland voor 1572," nos. 2275, 2276. Maddens, *De Beden in het Graafschap Vlaanderen*, 370–371, 401–409.

expedients" were either approved by the provincial states, or imposed by the government. The 1% export tax was disappointing, yielding a bit less than the 200,000 gulden Mary's loan broker, Gasparo Ducci of Lucca, had advanced for the right to collect it. But as Table 12.2 shows, however, the two tenth pennies in Flanders and Brabant, especially the levy on real property income, brought in over 2.6 million in 1543 and 1544, nearly half of what was needed for two further years of campaigning. Extraordinary subsidies of one kind or another brought in a further 677,851. Once the fighting was done, Schoer calculated for 1543–1544 war expenditures of 5,405,387 gulden, and a deficit slightly in excess of 1 million. If one considers that peacetime deficits in the 1530s could rise as high as 1.4 million gulden, this was a remarkable achievement. It is not too much to say that the disaster that seemed to loom as Mary met with her closest advisers in November 1542 was warded off by the "novel expedients" proposed to the States General a few weeks later.[40]

As Mary had warned Charles, the provincial states took control of the new revenues. In approving the two tenth pennies some months later, the Four Members insisted that the money be spent only for the defense of Flanders itself, or neighboring Artois, regardless of what the threats might be to other provinces. Mary agreed to this awkward condition because, owing to the system of collection, she would have no control in any case over how the money was disbursed. In Holland, the receiver of the common territory, though accountable to the States, was also the son of the previously mentioned Meester Vincent Corneliszoon. He showed his colors when he contravened the direct orders of the States by using 31,000 gulden from his receipts to pay a government debt chargeable against Holland's ordinary subsidies. Accordingly, the States entrusted the collection of further new revenues to another man, one who knew how to obey instructions, and soon succeeded to the position of receiver of the common territory.[41]

The "novel expedients" had an important spillover effect as well, because the provincial states were faced with the need for funding the new *renten* issues of 1542. In order to do so, they approved provincewide "imposts" of one kind or another, to be collected and disbursed by officials accountable to the provincial states. In Holland, rural folk were to pay a tax on the value of land (divided between owners and renters), while the burghers of walled cities paid "excises" on beer and other commodities. In contrast

---

[40] Tracy, *A Financial Revolution*, 77–91; Maddens, "De Invoering van de 'Nieuwe Middelen' in het Graafschap Vlaanderen tijdens de Regering van Keizer Karel," *Tijdschrift voor Filologie en Geschiedenis/Revue Belge de Philologie et d'Histoire* LVII (1979): 342–363, 861–898; Aud. 650, 398–400.

[41] Maddens, *De Beden in het Graafschap Vlaanderen*, 370–371, 401–409; Tracy, *Holland under Habsburg Rule*, 118–123.

with many of the older *renten* funded by the ordinary subsidies, the new issues were retired more or less on schedule. For example, *renten* issued by Holland in 1542 – and again in 1543 and 1544 – were fully redeemed by 1548. The reason for the difference is clear: because the funding revenues were now controlled locally, there was no reason not to repay the debts owed to burghers and wealthy peasants who had been "constrained" to put some of their funds in Holland *renten*.[42]

Meanwhile, the receivers of subsidies, serving at the pleasure of the Council of Finance, had nothing to collect except the ordinary subsidies, diminished in value for the reasons indicated in Table 12.1. Yet the receivers, anticipating future receipts that had now been entrusted to others, had overextended themselves by issuing "letters of obligation" to guarantee loans that could not be repaid from the ordinary subsidies alone.[43] Bankers in Antwerp were of course not slow to notice that the choice revenues were no longer in the keeping of government officials. In Flanders, lenders made contact with local authorities as early as 1544, when various towns and castleries issued "letters of obligation," guaranteeing that a particular loan would be repaid from their quota of future subsidies. Holland was as yet a bit removed from the sophistication of credit markets in Bruges and Antwerp. In 1537, when Mary of Hungary requested that Holland send "letters" on future subsidies that bankers would accept as surety for their loans, the president of the Council of Holland had no idea what kind of letters were meant – or so he said. By 1553, however, the States of Holland were issuing "letters of obligation" binding future subsidies to the repayment of a stated loan. In keeping with the impersonal logic of finance, bankers bypassed the familiar but now impecunious revenue officers of the central government in favor of provincial officials with revenues at their disposal.[44]

The 1550s: A Free Market in Provincial *"Renten"*

King Henry II's occupation of Metz initiated the longest and costliest of the Habsburg-Valois wars (1552–1559). If Lodewijk van Schoer calculated a total of 5,405,387 gulden for all military expenses during 1543 and 1544, estimates in the 1550s ranged from 4,079,952 to 5,377,420 gulden for the six-month campaign season of a single year.[45] To raise sums of this magnitude year after year, Mary strained every resource. The floating

---

[42] Tracy, *Holland under Habsburg Rule*, 118–123.

[43] E.g., the 31,000 gulden mentioned in the previous paragraph was for a loan that Willem Goudt, Holland's receiver of subsidies, had contracted against his future receipts but could not pay.

[44] Tracy, *Holland under Habsburg Rule*, 118–123.

[45] See note 40; Aud. 650, 159–162 (estimate for the campaign season of 1558) and Aud. 650, 529–530 (undated estimate preceding a calculation of how much in war subsidies should be asked of the provincial states for 1553).

or bankers' debt of the Habsburg government in the Netherlands swelled from approximately 1.5 million gulden in 1545 to as much as 7 million in 1555. In addition to the loans she charged to the revenues still under her control, Mary used her influence with Charles to assign other loans for repayment on the treasury of Castile, despite the strong opposition of Philip and his Council of Finance. When Philip himself assumed control in Brussels, following the joint abdication of Mary and Charles, he soon accepted the realities Charles had refused to face. If Castile's treasury unilaterally converted high-interest loans into 5% or 7% *juros* in 1557, holders of 12% government loans in the Low Countries were asked to accept 5% in 1558. Philip's only consolation was that his enemy was having similar problems; in the fall of 1557 Henry II had to suspend the quarterly payment due in Lyon on the great consolidated loan known as the Grand Parti. Yet the bankers in Lyon kept on lending to the crown, and the stream of money from Spain to the Low Countries continued flowing. According to a "General Proposition" read to the States General in 1559, the equivalent of 12 million gulden had been transferred from Spain since January 1556, not counting a further 3 million for exchange fees and armed escort for shipments of specie.[46]

During this war, spanning the reigns of Charles and Philip, the provinces regularly used future revenues under their control for loan guarantees. In 1557 the three core provinces together were estimated to carry a total debt of 10 million gulden, a figure that does not count the debt carried in behalf of the central government by individual cities. The provinces also agreed to extraordinary subsidies at unprecedented levels. In Holland, where the states had consented to 577,682 gulden in extraordinary subsidies for the years 1542–1544, the total for the years 1552–1555 was 1.2 million gulden. Much of the money raised for extraordinary subsidies, and much of the debt carried by the provinces, came through sales of *renten*. In 1554, for example, 333,497 was brought in through sales of *renten* by Lille, Tournai, Hainaut, and three of the Four Members of Flanders, funded either by the ordinary subsidies of these provinces, or by domain revenues entrusted to their administration for this purpose. By 1553, the ordinary subsidy of Flanders was obligated for 52,944 in annual *renten* interest, that of Brabant for 57,200. It seems likely that still larger sums were raised through sales of *renten* backed by the revenues controlled by the provincial states – that is, the provincewide excise and land taxes dating from the 1540s. In Holland, where the ordinary subsidy had long been considered overburdened, *renten* were sold in the 1550s only on this new basis. The difference in volume for the two series of Holland *renten* is striking: 582,590 gulden for all sales

[46] Rodriguez-Salgado, *Changing Face of Empire*, 54–60, 232–242; Baumgartner, *Henri II*, 86–87; Aud. 650, 110–114, 232; Tracy, "The Taxation System," 111–113.

backed by the ordinary subsidy between 1522 and 1544, as opposed to 1,066,631 for sales funded by the excise and land taxes between 1552 and 1558. Perhaps even more remarkable is the fact that, in contrast to the older series of *renten*, a fair portion of the new and larger debt was retired on schedule.[47]

Control of key revenues by the states – not by the central government, with its multiple priorities – also created a better market for provincial *renten*. In Holland during the 1520s, the forced sale of annuities was but a different version of the practice of forced loans familiar in the Italian city republics.[48] One of Dordrecht's magistrates put the matter succinctly: when putting money into *renten* backed by the government's ordinary subsidies, people had no confidence of getting it back. Towns disliked dealing with angry burghers whose investments were not redeemed on schedule and tried to avoid compelling their own citizens to "buy." In 1528 Amsterdam secretly agreed to "find" buyers for its portion of a *renten* sale only because the government gave the city authority to "constrain" the Carthusian monastery outside its walls to buy, along with certain "wealthy peasants." Delft and Leiden gave their consent to a sale only after they were promised that certain tax-exempt nobles would be forced to buy Holland *renten*. One could also sell Holland *renten* in "foreign" markets like Bruges, but this was problematic for a different reason: owing to the principle of collective responsibility, *renten* holders in Bruges and elsewhere could have Holland merchants and their goods seized and held under arrest whenever interest payments fell behind.[49]

When *renten* sales resumed on a new basis during the 1540s, the practice of forced buying was continued. By 1549, however, the timely redemption of *renten* sold over the previous few years was beginning to have an impact on investor psychology. Meeting in Brussels in April of that year, Holland's deputies put off requesting the government's permission to constrain buyers for a new issue, on the grounds that coercion might not be necessary. In August 1552, when the states signaled their approval for a sale of *renten* with a capital value of 200,000 gulden, the largest issue to date, the deputies sent on to Brussels the usual request for permission to constrain buyers in Holland; without explanation, Mary of Hungary said no. The question was discussed again at a meeting in Brussels in October. This time, the deputies dropped the idea of constraint; according to the travel diary of

[47] Aud. 650, 338–351; Tracy, "The Taxation System," 111–113.

[48] For Florence and Venice: Anthony Molho, *Florentine Public Finance in the Early Renaissance* (Cambridge, Mass., 1971), and Pezzolo, *L'oro dello stato. Società, finanza e fisco nella Repubblica veneta del secondo'500*.

[49] AJ 13 February, 7–11 March, 21–23 November, 29 December 1523, 25–28 January, 14–15 February 1524, 1–6 December 1527, 19 February, 31 March–9 April, 29 May, 18 November 1528, 5 September 1532.

Amsterdam's city attorney, Adriaan Sandelijn, it was at his suggestion that they did so. Viglius van Ayta, president of the council, agreed that under the present circumstances constraint was "unreasonable." In fact, the large sums raised through *renten* sales in the 1550s reflect an explosion of interest among wealthy and not-so-wealthy buyers, not just in Holland but in the neighboring provinces of Utrecht and Zeeland, hitherto not represented among purchasers of Holland annuities. Resort to the credit markets of Bruges, always suspect in Holland, was no longer necessary.[50] To an extent the central government had never achieved, Holland and other provinces gained the confidence of investors. The "faith and credit" of these provinces was trusted by the bankers who needed reliable guarantees for their 100,000 gulden loans, and trusted also by thousands of men and women with sums as small as 100 gulden at their disposal, eager for safe investments promising a decent return.

Cui Bono?

Of these added resources provided by the provinces, how much was Charles able to claim for himself and his personal campaigns? Very little, it seems. To my knowledge, there were only two occasions when he got large sums from the provincial subsidies of the Low Countries. The first was the coronation subsidy of 1529–1530, yielding some 348,000 gulden (190,706 Spanish ducats) for the German infantry and Low Countries cavalry that joined the emperor in Italy (Chapter 6). The second was in 1531, when the emperor was preparing to leave the Low Countries for Germany. Although he told the States of Holland (in Brussels for a meeting of the States General) he was not taking more than 200,000 from the subsidies of all the provinces, a summary for income and expenses for 1531 to 1536 shows that he in fact used 162,600 gulden for the arrears of the *compagnies d'ordonnance* that were to accompany him and had a further 408,881 gulden remitted to him in Germany, counting exchange fees. These sums amount to a hefty 58% of all the subsidy income recorded for 1531, which included large "anticipations" of receipts due in subsequent years. For example, 100,000 gulden of the remittances to Germany was assigned on the ordinary subsidies of Brabant; in Holland, Charles may have taken as much as 160,000 gulden, or two full years of the face value of a six-year ordinary subsidy running from 1531 through 1536. But measures of this kind also provoked a hefty response. In 1532 Holland's deputies professed to be outraged to learn that money they had counted on for the defense of Holland's frontiers

---

[50] *RSH* 11 April 1549; Adriaan Sandelijn, "Memoriaelboek," 4 vols., Gemeentearchief Amsterdam, I 31 (9 August 1552), I 329 (22 October 1552); Tracy, *A Financial Revolution*, chap. IV.

was already "gone" because of the emperor's trip to Germany.[51] Even an emperor could not ignore such reactions, no more than he could ignore the uproar in Castile over his sequestrations of private treasure coming from the Indies. The account just mentioned does not show any further remittances to Charles for the years 1532–1536.

Might Charles have "taken" more from the provincial subsidies if he spent more time in the Low Countries? One assumes that he would have. But complaints by the provincial parliaments were not the main reason that prevented him from making of the Low Countries the cash cow that his subjects thought it was. The real problem was military and geopolitical. If Castile and Aragón were sheltered behind the Pyrenees, the Low Countries had no natural boundary to define its border with France. Moreover, even the provinces closest to France, not so urbanized as the core provinces farther north, still offered more wealth per square kilometer to be ravaged by enemy armies than Spain did – hence the enormous growth in military expenditures during Mary of Hungary's tenure as regent, as mentioned in passing here. Even in 1543–1544, when Charles and his army were helping to shield the Low Countries from attack, the accounts of provincial revenue collectors (at least in Holland) show money being spent for local defense needs, not the grand strategy of empire.[52] Instead of the Low Countries coming to the aid of their sovereign, it was again and again Castile that came to the aid of the Low Countries, by Charles's command.

One of the ironies of history is that the Habsburg dynasty had no joy from this net transfer of large sums from Spain to the Low Countries. Within ten years of Charles V's death (1558) Philip II had to face a rebellion, which from 1572 was concentrated in the north and led by Holland. The ultimate success of the Dutch Revolt, gaining full independence for the northern provinces, was recognized provisionally by the Twelve Years Truce of 1609–1621 and definitively by the Peace of Westphalia in 1648. There is no simple answer to the question of how these small territories were able

---

[51]　Aud. 875, summary of income and expenses for 1531–1536. GRK no. 3436, Willem Goudt's thirty-fourth account as receiver for the subsidies in Holland (in his initial summary of the sums accounted for here, Goudt says Charles "took" the first four half-year terms of the ordinary subsidy of 80,000 gulden per year); AJ 24/25 October 1531 (Charles tells the States of Holland he has not taken "more than 200,000 pounds" in subsidy revenue), 6 August 1532.

[52]　One may take as an example GRK no. 3444, the account (rendered by Willem Goudt's widow) for an extraordinary subsidy of 120,000 gulden, approved by deputies from Holland at the meeting of the States General in Mons, attended by Charles himself (Chapter 9, note 24) The widow Goudt reports 121,500 gulden in income and 112,981 in expenditures, including 106,386 in payments to Jan Carpentier and Hendrik Sterck, treasurers of war in the Low Countries. This total includes a payment of 30,000 for troops, without further description, and another for 7,500 for garrisons in Artois and Flanders, but the other expenditures all relate to Holland itself or provinces bordering on Holland.

to stand off the mighty Spanish monarchy, but part of the story hinges on another irony. At the beginning of the revolt, the rebel States of Holland solved their most urgent problem by dedicating to the payment of garrison wages the familiar land and excise taxes by which *renten* issued in the 1540s and 1550s were funded. This meant that payment on still-outstanding *renten* from this period had to be suspended for several years, with unpaid interest added to the capital. But when new "imposts" were created to service the old debt, Holland slowly regained the confidence of potential investors, despite the constant burden of paying for a war that grew more costly with each passing year. From 1595 new issues of States of Holland *renten* found a ready market not just among wealthy Hollanders but throughout the borders of the rebel provinces and beyond their borders.[53] In effect, Margaret of Austria and Mary of Hungary had given their provinces a fiscal armature that would one day be turned against the Habsburgs: rebel Holland's ability to manage state debt was surely an indirect legacy of the fiscal devolution of Charles V's reign. Although never imagined by anyone at the time, this surprising turnabout was the most important long-term consequence of Charles V's wars in the Low Countries.

[53] Tracy, "Keeping the Wheels of War Turning: Revenues of the Province of Holland, 1572–1609," in Graham Darby, ed., *Origins and Development of the Dutch Revolt* (London, 2001), 133–150.

Chapter 13

Baronial Politics and War Finance in the Kingdom of Naples

In the emperor's continuing absence from Naples, save for the brief visit of 1535–1536, everything depended on the viceroy. Following Raymón of Cardona's death in 1522, Charles chose men of proven loyalty to himself. As noted in Chapter 3, Charles de Lannoy (r. 1522–1527) and Philibert de Châlons, prince of Orange (r. 1527–1530), were busy with the emperor's Italian wars and had little time for the internal affairs of the kingdom. In a letter sent from Naples in 1529, Iñigo López de Mendóza, bishop of Burgos, echoed earlier petitions from the Cortes of Castile by pleading for a Spanish viceroy: "Since the kingdom was conquered by Spaniards,[1] it seems that only they have the *reputación* on which his majesty's position in Italy is founded." The Dominican friar Garcia de Loaysa, Charles's confessor and a member of the inner circle, thought he had the right candidate: the marquess of Villafranca, Pedro Alvárez de Toledo, a younger son of Fadrique Álvarez de Toledo, second duke of Alba, a senior member of the inner circle. Instead, Charles tacitly accepted the fact that Cardinal Pompeo Colonna, lieutenant of the realm, had taken the reins of government into his own hands following Orange's death at the siege of Florence (3 August 1530). One of Rome's two great families, the Colonna had been imperial partisans for centuries; Ascanio Colonna, the head of the clan, duke of Tagliacozzo, held one of the wealthiest baronies in the kingdom, and his younger son, Cardinal Pompeo, hoped to gain appointment as viceroy.[2] But López de Mendóza, still in the kingdom, was harshly critical

---

[1] A reference to Gonsalvo de Córdoba's conquest of Naples in 1503.

[2] Hernándo Sanchez, *Castilla y Napoles*, 188–189; D'Agostino, *Parlamento e società nel regno di Napoli*, 219–220; Coniglio, *Consulte e bilanci del Viceregno di Napoli*, 380–383 (1520 list of the expected receipts for the adoa, a tax on baronial income); Colmeiro, *Cortes de los Antiguos Reinos*, II, 123 (petition from the 1523 Cortes of Valladolid). For the membership on the Consejo de Estado of Garcia de Loaysa (1523–1530) and Fadrique de Toledo (from 1526 until his death in 1531), Kohler, *Karl V*, 126, 135. The Orsini, rivals of the Colonna, were equally well known for their support of the papacy over the centuries.

of Colonna's venal and incompetent administration. When the Parlamento of 1532 agreed to a *donativo* of 600,000 scudi (Chapter 4), the parliamentary committee deputed to negotiate with Colonna was mainly interested in securing his permission for sending to Spain an "ambassador" of its choice, so that Charles could be fully informed of the Parlamento's complaints against the lieutenant.[3] Nonetheless, it was not until July 1532, as Pompeo Colonna lay on his deathbed, that Charles decided on a viceroy who could impersonate the prestige of the kingdom's Spanish conquerors. While at the Diet of Regensburg, the emperor signed Pedro de Toledo's commission; his instructions for the post were drafted by Garcia de Loaysa, now representing Charles at the papal court.[4]

Toledo clearly had a mandate to bring Naples more firmly under Habsburg control. But his autocratic style of governing has led to a debate among scholars as to whether he was (in the French saying) more royalist than the king. According to one interpretation, Charles and his advisers meant to assert his "absolute power" in the kingdom – for example, in ordinances that claim for the crown the right to dispose of fiefs, contrary to all previous grants by Charles's predecessors or their viceroys. The newer and more plausible view is that if Toledo did at times exceed his authority, the pattern of his "rigor" was not any different from those who ruled for Spain in Sicily or Milan. Toledo may have been "intransigent" in his insistence that noble accused malefactors be treated the same way as commoners, but he operated within the limits of a program emanating from Charles, focused on the need for extracting revenue for the emperor's grand plans. The immediate reason Naples needed a strong viceroy in Naples in the summer of 1532 was to advance preparations for Doria's armada.[5]

The kingdom's political elite was not pleased to have an assertive foreigner as viceroy. The most important families were the holders of hereditary sinecures known as the "seven great offices of the realm," including Alfonso de Avalos, marquess of Vasto, grand chamberlain; Ascanio Colonna, duke of Tagliacozzo, grand constable; and Andrea Doria, recently named prince of Melfi and grand protonotary. Although loyal to Spain, these men were immediately offended by Toledo's authoritarian manner, as when, on arrival in the capital, he sent word to Vasto that "although he has until now honored the marquess as his patron, the marquess must henceforth obey him as a subject." Within a year Toledo had gained the enmity of Doria as well. Because it served his purposes never to depend on a single adviser, Charles had Toledo send his own man to Coron

[3] Coniglio, *Regno di Napoli*, 63–65; D'Agostino, *Parlamento e società nel regno di Napoli*, 221–231.
[4] Hernándo Sanchez, *Castilla y Napoles*, 204.
[5] Contrast Cernigliaro, *Sovranita e feuda*, 130–138, 236–237, with Hernándo Sanchez, *Castilla y Napoles* (1994), 194, 201–204.

to check Doria's assessment; this was to be a secret mission, but evidently it was not.[6] There were also high civil officials to deal with. Viceroys traditionally relied on what was now called the Collateral Council, including three great nobles and three senior civil servants known as regents of the Chancery. Though not a member, the first president of the Sommaria regularly met with the council. Toledo sought to limit the Sommaria's political influence by excluding its president from meetings of the council. He was in effect following through on a recommendation by Charles Leclerc, who saw in the president's repeated absences from the Sommaria a cause of interminable delays in proceedings against fiscal malefactors. Toledo took pains to cultivate the regents of the Chancery, for example, by creating offices for their benefit. But enemies accused him of bypassing the three noble members by summoning full meetings of the council as infrequently as possible and by using secretaries for the dispatch of orders traditionally issued by the council.[7] Could a viceroy who so easily alienated the great men of the realm achieve Charles's larger objectives for Naples?

A Baronage Tamed?

In relations between the barons and their sovereign, if not between barons and their subjects, the Habsburg era made an important difference. By reputation, the barons of Naples were notoriously anarchic. Despite upholding the traditions of Europe's military caste, they could not be counted on to defend the kingdom against attack, for they were just as likely to make bargains with the invader. Most barons showed no affection for any ruling house, not even for the dynasty to which they owed their position. Their influence over urban centers (even those of the royal domain) drew the towns into petty baronial feuds, while the barons themselves gave evidence of no political conception higher than self-interest.[8] But under Charles V, the first Holy Roman Emperor to rule here since Frederick II (d. 1250), the barons of Naples came to be known for loyalty to the dynasty. This was partly due to the outcome of the rebellion of 1527–1528. The ninety nobles whose lands were confiscated for their participation in the revolt constituted no more than a fraction of the kingdom's titled and untitled

---

[6]   Chapter 7, note 24.

[7]   Hernándo Sanchez, *Castilla y Napoles*, 209–218; Croce, *Storia del regno di Napoli*, 108; Morial, *El Virrey de Napoles*, 103–105; Leclerc, "Rapport et Recueil," chap. xliii, 175–177, "Abuz et desordres audit royaulme." Toledo may have been following in Naples a tendency common in Castile since the time of the Catholic kings, by which great nobles were excluded from the high councils of state, in favor of lesser nobles and men of bourgeois origin: Carande, *Estudios de Historia*, 86.

[8]   This characterization of the baronage in Croce's classic work (*Storia del regno di Napoli*, 12–14, 61–73) seems not to be disputed by later writers.

baronage,[9] but they included the leadership of the "Angevin" faction that had never reconciled itself to Alfonso V of Aragón and his successors. The spoils were distributed among Habsburg supporters, including Genoese bankers and army commanders. For example, the title of prince of Melfi, involving control of lands valued at 371,000 ducats, was awarded first to Orange himself and, following his death, to Doria.[10]

But it was not just a question of leavening the ranks of the baronage. Before, during, and after the revolt, barons of Naples were conspicuous for their service in the emperor's campaigns, within the kingdom and beyond its borders. The emperor's victories in Italy depended heavily on Neapolitan levies as well as the Spanish *tercios* normally based in Naples. Four commanders in the Lombard wars, all from families ennobled by Aragonese monarchs, were of particular importance: Ferrante de Avalos, marquess of Pescara, and his nephew, Alfonso de Avalos, marquess of Vasto; Antonio de Leyva, prince of Ascoli; and Fernando de Alarcon, marquess of Rende. Even though French invaders in 1527–1528 had the upper hand for a time, many barons displayed exemplary devotion to the sovereign. Giambattista Carraciolo refused a rich offer from Francis I's commander, "lest I be found wanting in fealty to my lord." Another Caracciolo, the marquess of Laino, returned a memorable answer to besiegers who captured and threatened to kill his son: "I have four other sons, all ready to die in the service of their lord." For the expedition against Tunis in 1535, several great barons armed galleys at their own expense in order to participate. Others met their death on a second expedition to Tunis in 1544, attempting (in vain) to dislodge the rebellious son of Mulay Hassan, whom Charles had left in control of the city in 1535.[11]

This new culture of fealty was no doubt enhanced by constant communication among the great barons. Although their estates were spread out across the kingdom, most of the important titled families had palaces in Naples, where they lived for much of the year, and competed for influence in one or another of the capital city's five noble *seggi* (together with the Seggio del Popolo, these traditional corporations formed the governing body of the capital). This was not an unmixed blessing for Toledo, for he had to reckon with the fact that his enemies were in daily contact with one another. So as not to have dealings with Toledo, the marquess of Vasto

[9] For confiscation of these holdings, and their distribution among loyal supporters of Charles's rule in Naples, see Pedio, *Napoli e Spagna*, 274–289; those affected included one prince, four dukes, three marquis, four counts, and seventy-eight untitled barons. Leclerc, "Rapport et Recueil," chap. xxiii, 88–94, "Lestat des nobles," counted four princes, sixteen dukes or duchesses, thirteen marquis, fifty counts, and 538 untitled barons.

[10] Cernigliaro, *Sovranita e feudo*, I, 126–133, describing this redistribution of baronial holdings as "a true juridico-political revolution."

[11] Croce, *Storia del regno di Napoli*, 109–117.

avoided the capital; but when he retired to his estate on the isle of Ischia, in the Bay of Naples, it seemed that "all Naples came to see him." As a younger son of the second duke of Alba, who spent years attending on the person of the emperor, Toledo understood better than most men that the exercise of authority depended on having his own coterie of supporters. Colantonio Caracciolo, marquess of Vico, chanced to be at court in Regensburg in July 1532; he accompanied the new viceroy on his journey to Naples and was a reliable friend ever after. So was the influential Fernando de Alarcon, marquess of Rende, who had met the marquess of Villafranca at Charles's court in 1525, when he accompanied the captive Francis I to Spain. If Ferrante de Sanseverino, prince of Salerno, was a leader of the opposition to the viceroy, along with Andrea Doria and the marquess of Vasto, Toledo managed to gain the friendship of Salerno's kinsman, Pietro Antonio de Sanseverino, prince of Bisignano. For strategic reasons, Toledo cultivated Fernando de Castriota, marquess of Atrapalda and governor of the province of Otranto; a descendant of Scanderbeg, the fifteenth-century Albanian mercenary commander, Atrapalda maintained contacts with compatriots on the other side of the Adriatic and was thus a source of invaluable information on Ottoman naval and military activity.[12]

Marriage was the best way to cement ties with families of comparable rank. Garcia de Toledo, the viceroy's younger son, married Vittoria de Colonna, daughter of Ascanio Colonna the younger, marquess of Tagliacozzo, elder brother of the late Pompeo Colonna. Isabella de Toledo, one of the viceroy's daughters, wed Fernando Spinelli (of the Genoese banking family), duke of Castrovillari. The Spinelli-Toledo connection was strengthened when the widower-viceroy, despite his resolve to set a high moral tone, formed an illicit relationship with a married woman who happened to be Fernando's sister, Vincenza Spinelli. Upon her husband's death Vincenza took up residence at the viceroy's villa in Pozzuoli, outside Naples, and it was only at Fernando's insistence that the couple were married some years later. Toledo's real marital coup came through an alliance with the Medici. Since its surrender to an imperial army and its restoration to the Medici (1530), Florence had been a Habsburg client state. Upon the assassination of Duke Alessandro (1537), many of Charles's advisers argued for excluding the Medici from power, but Charles endorsed the succession of Cosimo de Medici, as Toledo among others had recommended. Two years later, Duke Cosimo wed the viceroy's youngest daughter, Leonor de Toledo. In subsequent years, Cosimo used his information network to apprise Toledo of plots by Neapolitan exiles, while Toledo used his connections at the Spanish court to help Cosimo regain the two

[12] Hernándo Sanchez, *Castilla y Napoles*, 99–100, 269–271, 276, 278, 359–362.

fortresses he had had to surrender to Spanish troops as a condition of his accession.[13]

Loyalty to the viceroy was built up from these personal connections, just as fealty to the dynasty was built up by the participation of so many Neapolitan barons in Charles's campaigns. But how could one mount an assault on the privileges of the barons who were ready to give their life and blood in service of the sovereign? Even in 1528, when there was a welcome opportunity to replace leaders of the Angevin faction with Habsburg loyalists, Charles's government made no effort to change the way that loyalist barons ruled their baronies. Similarly, how could Toledo presume to undermine the social position of those on whose support he depended? For example, Alonso Sanchez's stewardship of the treasury was the subject of frequent criticisms; but Sanchez was also a reliable ally, because his brother Luis was married to Maria de Toledo, the viceroy's sister.[14]

Charles's visit to Naples (October 1535–March 1536) was among other things a test of wills between Toledo and his enemies. The kingdom's titled barons claimed the privilege (enjoyed by some grandees in Castile) of appearing covered in the presence of the sovereign, that is, not removing their caps. Charles let it be known that he recognized no such privilege in Naples, but as a personal favor he allowed certain conspicuously loyal barons – like the previously mentioned prince of Bisignano, a friend of Toledo – to appear covered in his presence. In November, when he came within sight of the capital, the triumphal arches for the royal entry were not yet ready, so the emperor lodged for three days in the small town of Pietra Blanca. According to Gregorio Rosso, *eletto* or spokesman for the Seggio del Popolo in Naples, "many people, not just lords and knights and gentlemen, but members of the popular class and even the dregs of the population [*vile plebe*] of Naples, came out to Pietra Blanca, where they stood in the street and waited to see the emperor pass by or come out of his house, for they did not have the patience to wait and see him in the capital." Toledo scored a coup by arranging that, for his solemn entry into Naples (November 25), Charles should be immediately followed by the viceroy, not by his enemy, the marquess of Vasto, who as grand chamberlain claimed pride of place among the seven great officials of the kingdom.[15]

Although he was now preoccupied with preparations for the coming campaign against France,[16] Charles had come to Naples to form his own impressions about the state of the kingdom, and in this process Rosso as *eletto del popolo* had a role to play:

---

[13] Ibid., 95–101, 118–133.

[14] Tommaso Astarita, *The Continuity of Feudal Power: The Caracciolo of Brienza in Spanish Naples* (Cambridge, 1992), 14, 38–41; Hernándo Sanchez, *Castilla y Napoles*, 361.

[15] Rosso, *Istoria delle Cose di Napoli*, 59–61; Hernándo Sanchez, *Castilla y Napoles*, 288.

[16] See Chapter 8.

On Tuesday 16 December, the emperor, wanting to know the condition of the people of the city of Naples, and what he could do to help them, bade me speak. I told him the people were most faithful and loving of his crown, and that to keep them content nothing was needed but to avoid infringement of their material well-being, and to give everyone due justice, and that the people were of late resentful and disgusted because of the new excise taxes [*gabelle*] imposed by the viceroy.

Not surprisingly, as Rosso continues, "for speaking freely in this way, and according to my conscience, I was on 17 December removed from my post as *eletto*, and replaced by Andrea Stinca, one of the secretaries of accounts, a man in all things dependent on the viceroy." Rosso was surely not alone in blaming Toledo for the problems of the city and the kingdom, even if his claim that "the greater part of the city" opposed the viceroy is best taken with a grain of salt.[17] The point to be emphasized is that while in Naples Charles demonstrated continuing confidence in his chosen vice-regent, despite the opposition of senior and important military commanders like Vasto, and the unpopularity that Toledo seemed to evoke in the capital. Charles needed from Naples the added financial support he was not getting from the Low Countries, and for this he needed a viceroy strengthened by the visible endorsement of the sovereign.

A Competition in Generosity: The Parlamento and the *Donativi*

The prince of Bisignano, sent by the Parlamento of Naples to bring Charles the *capitoli* on which the *donativo* of 600,000 scudi was conditioned (Chapter 4), caught up with the emperor at Regensburg in July 1532. Charles formally approved most of the *capitoli*, including the proviso that no further *donativo* could be requested while the 600,000 was being collected. As Bisignano and the marquess of Vico accompanied the new viceroy on his journey from Regensburg to Naples, one may surmise that Toledo formed some initial impressions about the delicate business of obtaining consent for *donativi* – possibly even the idea that one could manage a few key men more easily than a large assembly. The *capitoli* of 1531–1532 would have prevented him from even summoning a Parlamento until 1536. But the ominous news that Barbarossa had sailed out from Istanbul with a fleet of seventy galleys (May 1534) meant that money had to be found somehow. Toledo summoned for a special meeting all barons residing in the capital, or close enough to respond within forty-eight hours. As if they constituted

[17] Rosso, *Istoria delle Cose di Napoli*, 65, 68–69; Hernándo Sanchez, *Castilla y Napoles*, 251. It seems the *gabelle* at issue are the new levies on sales of wine, grain, meat, and fish, imposed by Toledo in 1533 to raise funds for building projects in the capital, and maintained subsequently, despite an uprising in several of the city's popular quarters: Hernándo Sanchez, *Castilla y Napoles*, 249.

a Parlamento, those assembled agreed to a new *donativo* of 150,000 ducats over one year; collection was not to begin until September 1534, but by assigning this prospective income to the bankers Toledo got what he needed to strengthen the kingdom's defenses – if not to prevent the humiliation of Barbarossa's raid at Fondi.[18]

When Charles himself came to Naples he brought an updated version of the plan for a large *donativo* that would be applied to the kingdom's debts, broached by Habsburg officials in 1518 (Leclerc's instructions) and again in 1529 (the memorandum carried by Sanchez). A Parlamento was convened in the cloister of San Lorenzo on 8 January 1536, with appropriate ceremony:

> A platform for the emperor was set up outside the usual meeting hall, in the refectory of San Lorenzo, and there he seated himself under a *baldacchino*, surrounded by the seven great officers of the realm. On two benches to his left and right the titled barons were seated according to their order of precedence, with the *sindico* of Naples occupying the first seat.

"From his own mouth" the assembly heard of the emperor's great needs: 500,000 scudi at once, for the expenses of his coming campaign in France, and a further 3 million over nine years to "disengage and recover" towns and villages alienated from the domain. According to the reports of foreign ambassadors, a twenty-four-man deputation met to frame a reply to Charles's request, with two of Toledo's chief enemies, Andrea Doria and the marquess of Vasto, included among the six titled barons. They gave their answer the next day: Parlamento would grant 1.5 million in all, 500,000 over one year, and 1 million over the next five years. Though less than what Charles had asked, the 1.5 million scudi was, in Rosso's view, "a *donativo* [of a size] never heard of before, not in Naples, or anywhere else." To my knowledge, this was indeed more money than any parliament had ever consented to provide to a ruler. But what the size of the grant really indicated was how far Toledo's enemies were willing to go in order to be rid of him. The *capitoli* included a request that all high officials of the kingdom (obviously including the viceroy) be suspended at once, and that no one in future be appointed for a term longer than three years; in reply, Charles said only that he would consider the matter. In the end, 1.5 million scudi was also more than the kingdom could bear, as Charles recognized a few months later when he reduced the amount due to 1 million.[19]

Charles did agree that no new *donativo* would be asked for the next five years, but Toledo nonetheless summoned another Parlamento in 1538,

[18] D'Agostino, *Parlamento e società nel regno di Napoli*, 238–239; for Fondi, see Chapter 8.
[19] Rosso, *Istoria delle Cose di Napoli*, 66–68; D'Agostino, *Parlamento e società nel regno di Napoli*, 242–254; Caracciolo, *Uffici, difesa e corpi rappresntativi*, 204–207.

which agreed to a grant of 360,000 ducats over two years, the bulk of which was to go for an "enterprise" against the Ottomans, in which Charles's combined galley fleets would join with papal and Venetian forces. The expedition that this money presumably helped pay for turned out badly when Doria, despite his superior numbers, allowed the Turkish fleet that had been penned in at Prevesa to escape unharmed.[20] Yet the next year Charles demanded, for the enterprise against Istanbul he was planning (Chapter 8), 150,000 scudi for himself, and 110,000 for outfitting the fleet. By now Toledo had put together the network of supporters he needed to make things run smoothly. He summoned "reliable" barons to a private, preparliamentary discussion, "in such wise," as he boasted to Charles, "that before the Parlamento has convened, I already have a *donativo*." Perhaps because the planned naval expedition never materialized,[21] Toledo had trouble the next year with the Collateral Council, which refused to endorse his summons of yet another Parlamento. Even as barons from outside Naples were arriving in the capital for the announced assembly (November 1540), the viceroy postponed it until 1541 – but then he asked those who had come to consider ways of responding to the urgent needs of the emperor and the kingdom. Members of this ad hoc group took it on themselves to offer 170,000 ducats over the next year, a promise of sufficient weight that Toledo persuaded his bankers to accept on this sum an assignation of 70,000, which he used for the arrears of garrisons within the kingdom. The 170,000 should not, however, be counted as a *donativo*. When the postponed Parlamento finally did convene in July 1541, the three chambers agreed, with a rapidity that surprised even Toledo, to a grant of 800,000 ducats over three years, including the 70,000 that the viceroy had already spent, plus 730,000 in new funds. This was the *donativo* that helped pay for Charles's campaign against Algiers.[22]

The next time Charles demanded money, in 1543, the Collateral Council took an even stronger stand against calling a Parlamento, not only because the 800,000 grant of 1541 was still being collected, but also because monies raised by the *donativi* were chiefly expended beyond the borders of the kingdom, without regard for domestic needs. As in 1534, Toledo took the line of least resistance by calling a meeting of the barons then resident in Naples, who agreed that 150,000 ducats should be raised immediately. Toledo reported to the emperor that the barons had not asked for anything

[20] D'Agostino, *Parlamento e società nel regno di Napoli*, 254–255.

[21] Ibid., 265–266.

[22] Ibid., 272–274 (counting the 170,000 as a separate *donativo*); Caracciolo, *Uffici, difesa, e corpi rappresentativi*, 214–215, believes that the speed with which the 800,000 was granted shows that the Parlamento had by now abandoned its earlier claims to a "contractual" relationship, in which *donativi* would be granted only if the sovereign had observed the terms of previous *capitoli*.

in return for this grant, other than to be "recommended" to their sovereign; he also noted that it would be very helpful if at least some of the 150,000 could be held for the needs of the kingdom. When the full Parlamento convened again in 1544, the *donativo* granted in 1541 having now expired, the three chambers granted 600,000 ducats over two years, but only on condition that the bulk of the money be used within the kingdom. In 1546 the barons resident in Naples consented to a further 220,000; Toledo apparently tried his best to keep this money within the kingdom, but it seems his efforts were in vain.[23]

The strength of Toledo's position can be measured by the fact that his control of the Parlamento was not materially affected by an uprising (1547) against a tribunal of the Roman Inquisition that had been established in the capital at the instance of the viceroy himself. Doubting the success of his own efforts to stamp out Protestant ideas among the city's intellectuals, Toledo had called for the erection in Naples of a Roman tribunal, which was expected to proceed against heresy with more rigor than was displayed by the archbishop's inquisitorial court. But even in deeply Catholic Naples the inquisition was a sensitive issue; there had been a similar uprising under Ramón Cardona (1510), when the Aragonese viceroy was thought to be planning to introduce the Spanish Inquisition. Thus, when copies of the papal bull Toledo had requested were affixed to church doors, there were riots and demonstrations in various parts of the city. The *seggi* convened in emergency session and sent an envoy to Pozzuoli to tell Toledo of their firm opposition to the new tribunal. Toledo had to back down on the main point but, under cover of restoring order, he took advantage of the situation to impose a new excise for the maintenance of a Spanish garrison in Naples, as well as a humiliating ban on the bearing of arms within the city. The next Parlamento (1549) voted a grant of 600,000 ducats over two years, in return for the viceroy's promise to withdraw the garrison excise and the ban on bearing arms. Following the expiration of this *donativo*, the Parlamento of April–May 1552 voted a larger sum, 800,000 ducats over two years. This money, with deductions for interest and exchange fees, was what gave Charles V at Villach the resources to make a stand against his enemies.[24]

If one divides Charles's reign as king of Naples into two periods, before and after Toledo's appointment as viceroy, one finds a striking increase in the kingdom's willingness to respond to his demands for funds. Between 1518 and 1532, successive Parlamenti approved a minimum of four *donativi* with a total face value of 1,210,000 scudi or Neapolitan ducats, or 93,076

[23] D'Agostino, *Parlamento e società nel regno di Napoli*, 277–279.
[24] Pedio, *Napoli e Spagna*, 346–355; D'Agostino, *Parlamento e società nel regno di Napoli*, 281–292.

per year over thirteen years.[25] Between 1534 and 1552, ten assemblies (not all of which were parliaments in the full sense) granted a total of 5,020,000 ducats in *donativi*, or an average of 278,889 per year over eighteen years. The simple ratio between these two annual averages – roughly 3:1 – would not take inflation into account. But if prices in Naples increased by a total of, let us say, as 32% for the sixteen years between 1518 and 1534,[26] the average annual purchasing power of the later *donativi* would still exceed that of the earlier ones by a ratio of 2.27:1. The Toledo years made a difference – but not entirely because of the viceroy's skill at controlling the assemblies through his coterie of supporters. In some years, conspicuously so in 1536, the push for a large *donativo* came from Toledo's enemies. One might say that Charles's success in extracting money from the kingdom for his own needs depended on a local variant of the ancient maxim of *divide et impera*: after 1528, each of the shifting factions among the kingdom's great men competed for the favor of their lord – a sovereign who measured loyalty not just by bravery on the field of battle, but by the coin of the realm.

Cui Bono?

For the *donativi*, one must start with the fact that monies sent outside the kingdom were remitted by bankers who charged interest for sums advanced against a *donativo* to be collected over a term of years, as well as fees for exchanging money into the currency desired at the destination. One may also assume that the bankers deducted the bulk of these charges from what they remitted, rather than awaiting payment at a later date. In July 1537 Bartolommeo Camerario reported that of the 600,000 granted by the Parlamento in Pompeo Colonna's time (1531) and payable over the next four years, 200,000 had been "eaten" by interest paid to the bankers who "anticipated" the collection of the money. This estimate did not include further deductions for sums that had either not yet been collected, or that provincial collectors held back instead of sending on to the treasury.[27] Given the reports by Camerario and others on perennial shortfalls in hearth tax receipts, one may conservatively estimate that 40% of the projected

---

[25] For the period 1523–1530, Coniglio, *Il regno di Napoli*, 191, gives *donativi* of 300,000 in 1523, 50,000 in 1524, and 300,000 in 1530; I follow D'Agostino, *Parlamento e società nel regno di Napoli*, 213–216, who, noting the uncertain documentation of these years, gives only one *donativo* of 200,000 in 1528.

[26] Calabria, *The Cost of Empire*, 94–96, has data showing the cost of grain prices at Bari increased by roughly 200% between 1550 and 1600. If one assumes that the rate of inflation for the first half of the century would have been only half as great, or 100%, the increase over a sixteen-year period would be 32%.

[27] Coniglio, *Il regno di Napoli*, 234–236. Camerario explains that in order to maintain the emperor's credit, he had to pry 10,000 ducats loose from the provincial collectors and give it to certain bankers.

donativi income was either "eaten" by interest and exchange charges, or never collected. This would reduce the total *donativi* receipts potentially available for shipment outside the kingdom to 3,738,000 ducats: 726,000 for the period 1518–1532, and 3,012,000 for the years 1534–1552.

Information available in published sources offers a few clues as to how the sums that bankers provided for the *donativi* were allocated. In 1518, the 110,000 for the marriage of Charles's sister Eleanor (66,000 net) was clearly destined for use outside the realm. Conversely, it seems the 300,000 granted in 1520 (180,000 net) was indeed kept within the borders, because Leclerc found by other means the money needed to help pay for the expenses of the imperial election.[28] The 200,000 in 1528 (120,000 net) was presumably spent on the costs of the recent civil war. The 600,000 approved under Colonna in 1531 (360,000 net) was, according to a comment by Gregorio Rosso, used for the arrears of Naples-based troops who had fought in the siege of Florence the year before[29] – or for the bankers who paid their arrears. The 150,000 approved under Toledo in 1534 (90,000 net) went to strengthen the kingdom's defenses against Barbarossa's fleet. As to the 1 million for the *donativo* granted to Charles himself in 1536 (600,000 net), there may have been a rough split between the two purposes indicated in Charles's request to the Parlamento, half for his coming war against France and half to retire government debts in the kingdom. Of the 360,000 obtained by Toledo in 1538 (216,000 net), 80,000 is known to have been kept back for domestic needs, leaving 136,000 for Doria's naval campaign in Greece. Charles was presumably the beneficiary of the 260,000 (156,000 net) consented in 1539, for the voyage to the east he did not undertake. As for the 800,000 approved in 1541 (480,000 net), Toledo had already spent 70,000 for troop arrears in the kingdom, meaning Charles could have claimed as much as 410,000 Neapolitan ducats (382,694 Spanish ducats) for his campaign against Algiers. In 1543 Toledo's plea that at least some of the 150,000 he had obtained (90,000 net) be spent in the kingdom makes it sound as if none of it was. On the other hand, it seems Charles did not claim more than half of the 600,000 (360,000 net) granted in 1544, all of which (according to the *capitoli*) was supposed to remain in the kingdom.[30] Finally, there is no reason to believe that any of the money from two of the last three *donativi* mentioned here – 220,000 in 1546 (132,000 net) and 880,000 in 1552 (528,000 net) – was held back in Naples.[31] But of the money expected from

[28] See Chapter 3, note 24.
[29] Pedio, *Napoli e Spagna*, 297.
[30] Coniglio, *Il regno di Napoli*, 245: 175,000 ducats from the *donativo* of 1544 was destined for the affairs of Germany.
[31] Ibid., 245, believes that about 500,000 ducats from the *donativo* of 800,000 in 1552 were destined for expenses in Germany and Lombardy.

the 600,000 *donativo* of 1549 (360,000 net) only about half was assigned for payments abroad, and the rest was kept for further redemptions of debt.[32] By these estimates, some 1.2 million Neapolitan ducats (112,800 Spanish ducats) in *donativi* money would have spent within the kingdom during Charles's reign (19% of gross receipts or 32% of the net), as opposed to 2,538,000 expended beyond its borders (41% of gross receipts or 68% of the net). Roberto Mantelli has come to a similar conclusion by different means: in his view, roughly 40% of the gross receipts for *donativi* approved between 1541 and 1559 went for payments outside the kingdom.[33]

In fact, the sums taken from Naples during the course of the reign greatly exceeded what could have come from the *donativi* alone. Charles got money from other sources of revenue in the kingdom by the simple expedient of referring his bankers to Naples for payment and inducing the viceroy to accept these often unexpected assignations. In 1544 he thought he had persuaded Toledo to accept a responsibility for a loan for 72,500 ducats, contracted with the Fugger in Augsburg on Charles's behalf by Vásquez, stipulating payment could be expected in Naples if not in Spain, though it seems this loan was eventually repaid in Castile.[34] Toledo is known to have refused assignations on some occasions – for example, a *cambio* for 50,000 scudi in 1549 and another for 52,000 assigned on the *donativo* of 1552.[35] No one has yet attempted to calculate how much Naples contributed to expenses beyond its borders during Charles's reign. There is, however, a Spanish account of sums "taken out of the kingdom [of Naples] from 1540 through 1560," which lists a total of 2,659,495 Spanish ducats for the years 1541 through 1552. The preceding estimate of funds for *donativi* during the same years sent out of the kingdom (1,120,080 ducats) would thus account for only 42% of the monies actually exported.[36] How could

[32] Roberto Mantelli, *Burocrazia e finanze pubbliche nel regno di Napoli a meta del cinquecento* (Naples, 1981), 356–358: the Parlamento destined 247,592 ducats for payment abroad, 238,578 for repayment of debts. Mantelli does not reduce the sums mentioned to take account of bankers' interest and exchange fees, or shortfalls in collection.

[33] Ibid., 356–358.

[34] Charles to Philip, 17 October 1544, *Corpus Documental*, Letter CCXCII, II, 289, responding to Philip's complaints about the fact that Charles had accepted an assignation on Castile for Mary's loan of 161,000 crowns (Chapter 9), Charles says he will write the viceroy to Naples to be sure to pay two other *cambios*, the first for 38,550 ducats negotiated by Mary, the second for 72,500 ducats negotiated by Vazquez, payable in Naples if not Spain; Charles to Philip, 13 January 1545, *Corpus Documental*, Letter CCCV, II, 328–329: he believes the viceroy of Sicily will accept responsibility for at least 50,000 ducats of Mary's large loan, while Toledo in Naples has the other loan, payable in Naples or Spain. Cf. Carande Thobar, *Carlos V y sus banqueros*, loan no. 236, 23 September 1544: Anton Fugger's loan of 62,500 scudi, repayable in Naples, was repaid in Castile.

[35] Coniglio, *Il regno di Napoli*, 248.

[36] This document is the principal source for Chapter 10 of Mantelli, *Burocrazia e finanze*, "Le rimese all'estero della tesoreria generale del regno di Napoli dal 1541 al 1559." For the years 1541–1559,

this much be extracted from a kingdom already struggling with debt? It seems likely that more domain towns or villages had to be sold in order to satisfy the bankers. In this case, the *donativi* may have had a further indirect role in sending money abroad, for the portion set aside for debt redemption could have been used to reclaim recently alienated lands, which could then be sold once again to pay for the next round of *cambi*.

The great barons of Naples, with palaces in the capital as well as castles in their baronies, had in some degree a perspective of the whole realm – hence the Parlamento's repeated demands that money from the *donativi* be kept back for the needs of the kingdom. The barons were also good at bargaining for individual concessions or privileges, in return for their support of the crown's fiscal demands.[37] What this assembly lacked was the vigorous representation of local interests – provinces in the Low Countries, or, as will be seen in the next chapter, town-states in Castile – that could serve as a check on the ambitions of the crown. Towns in Naples often offered large sums to buy their way back into the royal domain, or for guarantees that they would not be alienated; but they had to compete against the riches of titled barons who knew how lucrative the business of lordship could be.[38] Naples was dominated by its barons long before Charles V came on the scene, but scholars have seen in his reign a potential turning point, a road not taken in the history of the kingdom's parliamentary institutions. In the Low Countries, the wars of this era made provincial parliaments more important by inducing them to develop their own capacity for the management of state debt. In Naples, where the same wars gave the Parlamento an opportunity to bargain for concessions, the opportunity was squandered, because those who counted in the politics of the kingdom – the titled barons – represented no local interest at all but only the personal interests that led them to curry favor with the sovereign, even if it meant offering more than was asked.

Mantelli, 356–358, estimates that more than half of the money sent abroad had to come from sources other than the *donativi*.

[37] A point made by Giovanni Muto, "Taxation in the Kingdom of Naples," in Blockmans and Mout, *The World of Charles V.*

[38] Croce, *Storia del regno di Napoli*, 83–84, Capri tore down the castle of its baron and offered the crown a large sum to buy its way back into the domain, alleging that "Nihil gravius populis et praesertim solitis regio fastigio submitti, quam aliam dominationem habere quam regiam majestatem"; Leclerc, "Rapport et Recueil," c. xli, 170–172v: Iserna purchased for 4,500 ducats the privilege of not being alienated from the domain, according to a letter patent signed by Charles at Worms, 21 May 1521; Coniglio, *Consulte e bilanci*, Document 35, Lopez de Mendóza's instructions for Sanchez's mission to Spain in 1529: "There is no village [*terra*] which your Majesty has wanted to sell which has not been so destroyed that in order to redeem itself from vexation it would not offer more to become part of the domain than the baron gave for it."

In the judgment of one scholar,[39] Toledo was so successful in managing the Parlamento through his coterie of supporters that the assembly was by the time of his death reduced to a tame instrument of the viceroy's will. Under Philip II and his successors, the Parlamento played even less of a role in the affairs of the kingdom, even though the *donativi* demanded of it continued their steady increase. In time, it came to be felt that the representatives of the six *seggi* of the capital city had, by themselves, sufficient standing to speak for the kingdom as a whole. In 1642, as the States General of the United Provinces were managing the last phase of their long war against Spain, the old-regime Parlamento of Naples was summoned for the last time ever.[40]

[39] See note 22.
[40] Elena Croce, "I parlamenti napoletani, sotto la dominazione spagnola," *Archivo Storico per le Provinze Napoletane*, n. s., 22 (1936): 358.

Chapter 14

Town Autonomy, Noble Magistrates, and War Taxation in Castile

Aristocratic privilege and urban autonomy were to be found in other parts of Europe, but in Castile these two common elements of the European social heritage formed a unique amalgam. As Christendom's anointed leader in the great struggle against Islam, Charles had the sympathy of Castile's nobles, who, like their counterparts in Naples, rallied to his maritime crusades; indeed, in Castile they came in such great numbers that extra ships were required to carry them.[1] But as a ruler demanding money from his realm and especially its chief towns, he faced many of the same nobles who, unlike their Neapolitan brethren, served as urban magistrates in major towns throughout the realm and often represented the interests of their cities in the Cortes. This tension set the framework for the reign of the king whom Castilians knew as Carlos I.

Overcoming the Legacy of Revolt

The bitter divisions of Castile's civil war did not extend much beyond the emperor's return to the kingdom in 1522. Loyalists and rebels were never totally at odds, because they had some common goals, such as inducing their sovereign to make a proper marriage. For his part, Charles did not object to the fact that many towns sent former rebels as *procuradores* to the Cortes, because he needed the towns as a counterweight to certain of the great nobles who had grown even more powerful as a result of their role in suppressing the revolt. Some years on, as Santa Cruz tells the story, Charles was not even interested in learning the whereabouts of condemned rebels who were still at large: "Better you should tell Hernando de Avalos to make himself scarce than to try and get me to have him captured."[2]

---

[1] See Chapters 4, 7 and 8.

[2] Hendricks, "Charles V and the Cortes of Castile," 175–183; Santa Cruz, *Crónica del Emperador*, III, 11, an incident that happened just before Charles's departure for Barcelona in 1529, en route to Italy.

At the Cortes of Toledo, in the summer of 1525, both the king and the *procuradores* had their minds on foreign affairs. With Francis I now captive in Spain, Charles was eager to capitalize on the prestige of the great victory at Pavia. Just for this reason, Castile's political elite was anxious for a suitable royal marriage, so Charles would have a person of authority in whose hands to leave the kingdom when and if he insisted on embarking for Italy. While at war with France, Charles had obligated himself in the Treaty of Windsor (1522) to wed Mary Tudor, in return for a rich dowry promised by Henry VIII. Mary herself was then only six years old, but Margaret of Austria, not easily ignored in such matters, continued to promote the English match. The *procuradores* in Toledo had other ideas. One of the demands of the Comuñeros in 1520 had been a match between Charles and Isabella of Portugal, said to have inherited the character of her and Charles's grandmother, Isabella of Castile. Isabella herself favored the idea, as did her father, Manuel I (d. 1521), and her brother, John III (r. 1521–1557). The first of seventy-one petitions drawn up by the Cortes of Toledo was that "your majesty be pleased to do us the signal favor of marrying, as you have promised in past Cortes, and please remember that Doña Isabella, the sister of the king of Portugal, is one of the most excellent persons there has ever been in Christendom." To be sure, there was no more talk (as at Valladolid in 1523) of having Charles respond to petitions before the Cortes voted a *servicio*. But the *procuradores* surely understood that there were now good reasons for abandoning the English princess. With France seemingly pacified, England's help was no longer so necessary; and, if Charles wanted to get to Italy any time soon, he could not wait for the ten-year-old Mary Tudor to reach a suitable age not just for marriage but for the regency of Castile. In April 1525 he had sent one of his Burgundian confidants, Jean Poupet de la Chaulx, to negotiate the terms of a Portuguese marriage treaty. At about the same time, he sent another envoy to Henry VIII's court to make appropriate excuses. Thus in his response to the Cortes's petition (4 August 1525), Charles only had to allude to the need for breaking off one match before concluding the other: "To this we say that our Grand Chancellor [Gattinara] has already responded on our behalf when he gave you a report of the state in which things stand between us and the king of England."[3] Charles and Isabella were wed in Seville seven months later (10 March 1526). She proved to be the mother of royal children and trusted governess of the realm that Castilians hoped for, and a wife whom Charles loved dearly; her early death in childbirth (1539) was perhaps his greatest sorrow.

The signal favor the *procuradores* did for Charles was to approve a grant of unprecedented size, totaling 810,666 ducats. The 410,666 for an ordinary

---

[3]   Colmeiro, *Cortes de los Antiguos Reinos*, IV, 404–405; Fernández Alvarez, *Carlos V*, 325–339.

servicio to run from 1527 through 1529 was no more than had been granted in 1523, but the extraordinary *servicio* of 400,000 ducats to be collected from 1526 through 1529 was a novelty. No large loans were contracted by the treasury of Castile at this time, and I have not seen any indication how the 810,666 ducats were allocated. But it seems likely the money was needed in Italy. In a letter written from Toledo while the Cortes was in session (21–30 July 1525), Charles explained to Ferdinand how he expected to get what he needed to cut expenses in Italy by giving most of his troops their going-home pay. Venice had promised 100,000 ducats in return for renewal of a treaty, while Francesco Sforza agreed to pay 600,000 ducats over a period of years in return for Charles's recognition of him as duke of Milan.[4] But Venice may not have paid this sum,[5] and even if Milan's meager revenues could have supported the amount pledged, Sforza himself was soon in communication with Charles's enemies.[6] When the League of Cognac revived the hopes of anti-Habsburg partisans early the following year, the need in Italy was even greater; the two letters of exchange for 100,000 ducats each that Charles mentions in his correspondence (June 1526) may be related to the extraordinary *servicio* approved at Toledo, for which collection began in this year.[7]

While these *servicios* were still running, Charles summoned another Cortes for February 1527. According to the proposition read to the three "arms" or estates of the realm gathered in Valladolid, because the sums granted in 1525 had in effect already been spent, Charles asked all his subjects to help him as they could for the expenses of wars against France (in Italy), and against the Grand Turk, whose armies threatened Vienna. The response of the three estates was a flat negative. The nobles had never

---

[4] Carande Thobar, *Carlos V y sus banqueros*, II, 536–537, and the table of loans; no loans were contracted between May 1525 and January 1526. Charles to Ferdinand, 21/30 July 1525, *Familienkorrespondenz*, Letter 145, I, 313–317.

[5] As part of what he owed Ferdinand, Charles had assigned him 200,000 ducats due from Venice; but for complaints that he was not getting the money, see Ferdinand's instructions for Salinas's mission to Charles, 2 April 1525, *Familienkorrespondenz*, Letter 136, I, 288, and Ferdinand's instructions for Antoine de Croy's mission to Charles, 4 June 1529, *Familienkorrespondenz*, Letter 306, III, 423–427.

[6] In 1525, Charles assigned Ferdinand the revenue from Milan's salt tax, but Ferdinand found it unprofitable and asked for another assignation: Ferdinand's instructions for Salinas, 2 April 1525, and Ferdinand to Charles, 1 September 1525, *Familienkorrespondenz*, Letters 136 and 149, I, 288, 323.

[7] Hendricks, "Charles V and the Cortes of Castile," 202–210: the ordinary *servicio* approved at Toledo was to be collected starting the year following Charles's promised marriage to Isabella; the extraordinary *servicio* was requested to allow Charles to make good on subsidies he had promised Henry VIII in the Treaty of Windsor, but Hendricks thinks that in their euphoria over the upcoming royal marriage, the *procuradores* were probably not too concerned how the money was spent. Charles to Ferdinand, 27 July 1526, *Familienkorrespondenz*, Letter 216, I, 416–417: when the constable of Bourbon sailed from Barcelona for Italy on June 24, he carried a letter of exchange for 100,000 ducats, and Charles now sends a letter of exchange for another 100,000.

paid in the ordinary *servicios*[8] and were not minded to change. They professed to be ready to follow their sovereign to war, should he go, but because giving "tribute" would demean their dignity, they asked him to withdraw the request. The *procuradores* of the towns pronounced it impossible to raise another subsidy – villages in the rural districts were so poor that it was hard to collect even the *servicios* that had been approved at Toledo.[9] That deputies representing urban interests should make this argument is not so surprising as it may seem, for times were indeed hard in rural Castile. Moreover, the *caballeros* who spoke for the towns had a stake in the rural economy – the peasants who paid the portion of the *servicios* assigned to the countryside were also the tenant farmers on whom a good part of their income depended.[10]

At the Cortes of Madrid (April 1528), summoned to make formal recognition of the one-year-old Philip as Charles's heir, the *procuradores* granted another 410,666-ducat ordinary *servicio* but only 133,333 as an extraordinary *servicio*, both to run from 1530 through 1532. This time deputies had ideas on how the money should be spent:

> May it please your majesty to command that the *servicio* you demand be spent for the defense of this kingdom, for so it is said in the summons of the Cortes, and also that moneys from loans and from the *rentas ordinarias* and from the Indies be spent for defending this realm, and not for any other purpose. For if the realm be freed of other obligations, there will be much contentment, and a willingness to grant much larger *servicios*. On the other hand, the kingdom is much burdened by having to defend such a large area by sea and land against the Moors and other enemies of Christendom, and in such hard times, so that it will be hard to grant even small *servicios*.

Charles professed in his reply to accept this implied critique of his imperial policy: "It pleases us to devote the *servicio* our kingdom gives us for its protection and defense, as you have said, and to ward off any enemies who may attack it, and not for any other need of ours nor of any of our other kingdoms and lordships."[11] That he kept his word may be doubted, for Lautrec's invading army had crossed the border of the Kingdom of Naples on 4 February. Between November 1527 and April 1528, the emperor forwarded to Italy letters of exchange for 560,000 ducats, 460,000 for the

[8] Hendricks, "Charles V and the Cortes of Castile," 260: all Castilians of *hidalgo* status were exempt from ordinary *servicios*, but could be liable to pay in extraordinary *servicios*, depending on the circumstances.
[9] Colmeiro, *Cortes de los Antiguos Reinos*, II, 142–144.
[10] This point is made in debates surrounding the Cortes of 1538/1539, discussed later (see note 28).
[11] Colmeiro, *Cortes de los Antiguos Reinos*, II, 144–151, IV, 450.

Viceroy of Naples, Philibert de Châlons, and 100,000 for Ferdinand to use in sending *Landsknechte* across the Alps.[12]

Just before leaving the Low Countries for Germany (November 1531), Charles wrote asking Isabella to summon another Cortes for early the following year. He wanted "at least 200,000 ducats," arranged in such a way that the full sum could be "collected" or "cashed"[13] by May (1532). In fact, the *procuradores* who assembled at Segovia agreed to 490,666 ducats over two years (mid-1532 to mid-1534); this was the first time that the deputies had consented to raise a new subsidy during a year when a previously approved one was still being collected.[14] In return, they asked for definitive settlement of a matter on which Charles had already professed his willingness to meet the wishes of the Cortes.

Higher *Servicios* in Return For Stabilization of the *Alcabala*

At issue was a new way of collecting the *alcabala* and the *tercia*, the most important of the crown's *rentas ordinarias*. According to an estimate by crown auditors in 1534, the gross yield for the two revenues together that year was 847,924 ducats, mostly from the *alcabala*. During the same year, the gross yield for all of the *rentas ordinarias* was 1,090,597 ducats.[15] The *alcabala* was a tax on the exchange of goods, fixed by the Catholic kings at 10% of the value, normally paid in cash by the seller in his place of residence. Merchants and tradesmen bargained with local collectors to pay fixed sums at regular intervals, instead of having to report individual

[12] Charles to Ferdinand, 27 November 1527 and 19 April 1528, and Charles's instructions for the mission of Pedro de Córdoba and Salinas to Ferdinand, 29 April 1528, *Familienkorresponenz*, Letters 130, 174, and 175, II, 148–152, 204–206, and 208. During this period the treasury of Castile contracted loans totaling 611,334 ducats, mostly with Augsburg or Italian bankers: Carande Thobar, *Carlos V y sus banqueros*, loans 50–65. Note too that although the important border town of Fuerterrabía had been recaptured from France in 1524, its new fortifications were still not completed in 1532, according to a complaint by the *procuradores* at the Cortes of Segovia: Colmeiro, *Cortes des los Antiguos Reinos*, IV, 578–579.

[13] Charles to Isabella, 25 November 1531, *Corpus Documental*, Letter CXXVI, I, 329. The phrase he uses is, "de suerte y forma que esten cobrados por todo el mes de Mayo." *Cobrar* can mean "collect" or "cash." It seems Charles wanted a *servicio* of about 200,000 on which he could assign remittances by his bankers. Cf. Carande Thobar, *Carlos V y sus banqueros*, loans 94 and 95 (both in April 1532), for 100,000 scudi and 100,000 ducats respectively.

[14] Ibid., II, 535–536: during 1532, the treasury was to collect 50,000 and 16,667 ducats for the last year of the ordinary and extraordinary subsidies approved at Madrid in 1528, plus 54,000 and 40,000 ducats for the first year of the ordinary and extraordinary subsidies approved at Segovia.

[15] Ibid., II, 91, and 230–248. The *alcabala* and the *tercia* thus represented about 78% of the *rentas ordinarias*. The most important standing charge against the *rentas ordinarias* was of course interest on *juros*, which during the same year, according to Carande Thobar, amounted to 624,421 ducats, or 57% of the *rentas ordinarias*. With a further 28,000 ducats in deductions, the net value of all the *rentas ordinarias* was 438,176 ducats, still quite a bit more than the *servicio* income (90,000 ducats for 1533, 79,000 for 1535; none was collected in 1534: ibid., 536–537).

transactions as the law required. Although the clergy achieved substantial
exemption in 1491, this was a tax from which *hidalgos* were not exempt.
Since the fourteenth century, collection of the *alcabala* for each town and
its rural district was auctioned annually to the highest bidder. This "chief
tax farmer" (*arrendador mayor*) then sold rights for collecting the tax on particular commodities. Tax farmers were of course cordially hated wherever
governments had recourse to this method of collecting revenue. In Castile,
they had powers to place delinquents under arrest, and they had added reason to squeeze taxpayers because the crown offered bonuses to those who
remitted to the treasury sums larger than what they had contracted for.
In response to complaints, Ferdinand and Isabella began offering the possibility of "capitation" (*encabezamiento*), meaning that a town or village
guaranteed payment of what tax farmers paid the previous year, and then
apportioned the burden among residents in whatever way it chose. There
is some evidence the crown promoted capitation, possibly because having
revenues whose value was predictable year to year made it easier to sell
juros against the *alcabala*. Villages in the *tierra* of Córdoba paid by capitation
beginning in 1513, but the *alcabala* in the city itself – worth roughly four
times as much – continued to be farmed.[16]

The idea of capitation, inherited from the Catholic kings, remained
under discussion in the Council of Castile. In 1523, in advance of the
meeting of the Cortes of Valladolid, one member of the council urged
capitation on Charles as a way for his majesty to "secure" his income
against possible fluctuations. In fact, Charles offered the procurators a two-
point proposal: the *alcabala* would henceforth be collected by capitation,
and its total value would be fixed for fifteen years at a level somewhat less
than what had been brought in during the previous year. Procurators for
the eighteen cities could not come together on the details of this plan,
but at Toledo in 1525 crown and Cortes agreed on a modified version
of it: expected income from the *alcabala* was to be reduced by a stated
amount, and localities that agreed to switch over to the capitation method
of collection would be the beneficiaries of the reduction.[17]

---

[16] Fortea Perez, *Fiscalidad in Córdoba*, 35–43, and 125–133; for the years 1514–1519, the average annual value of the *alcabala* was 28,001 ducats for the city and 6,672 for the *tierra*; Edwards, *Christian Córdoba*, 69–77.

[17] Hendricks, "Charles V and the Cortes of Castile," 191–209 (for the idea of "securing" royal income through capitation, 195). Colmeiro, *Cortes de los Antiguos Reinos*, II, 157–162. In 1523 the Cortes of Valladolid petitioned for a general capitation of all the crown's ordinary incomes, renewable every ten years, with the understanding that head towns would pay interest on *juros* assigned to revenues in their districts: Carande Thobar, *Carlos V y sus banqueros*, II, 231–233, 240–241. This proposal was not approved, but in 1529 the treasury agreed that two Castilian merchants would receive in payment of their loan a ten-year "capitation" for the *alcabala* and the *tercia* in the diocese of Toledo, on the understanding that they would pay interest on and amortize *juros* and other debts assigned on this income.

What the Cortes of Segovia requested in 1532 was a "general capitation" of the *alcabala* and the *tercia* throughout the realm, but again there were disagreements over details. At the next Cortes (Madrid, October 1534), the procurators granted an ordinary *servicio* of 544,000 ducats over three years (1535–1537), for the emperor's planned campaign against Tunis, but no extraordinary *servicio*. It was at this Cortes that town procurators met with men from the Consejo de la Hacienda to begin what proved to be a two-year discussion on how to implement a "general capitation." The crown insisted that the *tercia* (equivalent to two-ninths of the ecclesiastical tithe) be farmed out as before, not "capitated." For capitation of the *alcabala*, the "kingdom" – as represented by the Cortes – had to accept liability for the full amount promised, regardless of what economic conditions might be. This meant that each locality was corporately liable for its quota and, in particular, for payment of annual interest for the *juros* funded by its portion of the *alcabala*.[18]

Before setting quotas for towns throughout the kingdom, royal auditors would hear reports from the rural communities; their decisions would then be proclaimed throughout the district by the *procuradores* of the main town. Each locality would have 120 days to provide royal officials with a written authorization (*poder*), pledging its faith and credit for the stated amount, failing which its *alcabala* would be farmed in the traditional way. With these modifications, both sides agreed in August 1536 to a "general capitation" of the *alacabala* at rates currently prevailing, for a period of ten years starting 1 January 1537. Towns and villages were free to raise their quotas by a head tax (capitation) or hearth tax or by any other means they chose. The question of how they actually did so has barely been studied for Charles's reign. It some cases, towns had, with the crown's permission, imposed a *sisa* or excise tax of their own, as a means of collecting their quota for an extraordinary *servicio*. It seems some towns now used this method to collect their share of the "capitated" *alcabala*. A *sisa* had some advantages for town councils, because it could reduce if not eliminate the need for a troublesome head or hearth tax on local residents; local merchants who had to pay the *sisa* would complain, but they complained less if nonresident merchants and tradesmen were made to pay at a higher rate.[19]

To historians cognizant of Castile's inflation rate, it seems obvious the crown made a bad bargain – or the towns a good bargain – because capitation "decoupled" the *alcabala* from market prices. Decades later, Philip II and his contemporaries certainly thought that Castilians were

---

[18] See the arrangements for a possible capitation discussed earlier (note 17).

[19] Carande Thobar, *Carlos V y sus banqueros*, II, 230–248; Hendricks, "Charles V and the Cortes of Castile," 240–241; Carretero Zamora, *Cortes, monarquía, ciudades*, 89; Fortea Perez, *Monarquía y Cortes*, 462–470.

taxed too lightly at rates fixed in the 1530s; when the costs of war in the Low Countries forced a second suspension of payments on the crown's short-term debt (1575), Philip persuaded the Cortes to accept a threefold increase in what was due for capitation of the *alcabala*. In Charles's time, however, the case was less clear. Actual *alcabala* income during the first thirty years of the sixteenth century had increased at only a fraction of the inflation rate. Thus the risk of lost revenue may have seemed a price worth paying for a guarantee that the *alcabala* would not fall below a certain level. In a letter of April 1536 Charles refers to the fact that Ansaldo Grimaldi of Genoa would not sign off on his loan contract unless given *juros* as a backup for the assignation he was to receive; others were making similar demands.[20] Bankers dealt in terms of relative certainty. Just as the crown of Castile had confidence in town governments as collectors of taxes,[21] bankers may have preferred to have their *juros* backed by the faith and credit of Castile's towns, through the capitation, in the same way that bankers in the Low Countries came to have more confidence in the promissory notes of the provincial states (Chapter 12).

Meeting as the new system was going into effect, the Cortes of Valladolid (April 1537) granted, as at Madrid, an ordinary *servicio* with a total value of 544,000 ducats (this time payable over only two years, 1538 and 1539) but no extraordinary *servicio*.[22] In theory, Charles should not have expected a further *servicio* until 1540. But having concluded at Nice a ten-year truce with France, the emperor saw a golden opportunity to launch a great maritime crusade against the Grand Turk. Many in Castile shared his enthusiasm, including a nobleman who hoped it would "please God to grant your majesty lordship over the infidels." It was too late for him to sail in person with the armada of the Holy League, which at Prevesa missed a chance to do real harm to an Ottoman fleet inferior in numbers (September 1538). Instead, Charles dreamed of leading an even larger armada against Istanbul itself the following year (Chapter 8). Thus in September 1538 he called all three "arms" of the realm to a Cortes at Valladolid the following month.

To raise the money for his great venture, he proposed an excise tax (*sisa*) payable throughout Castile and by all classes. Because this would require approval by the privileged estates, Charles insisted on summoning the nobles and the clergy, despite the misgivings of his advisers, who remembered all too well the recalcitrance shown by the nobles the last

---

[20] See Chapter 8, note 48. Fortea Perez, *Fiscalidad en Córdoba*, 42; Ulloa, *La hacienda real*, 787–791; Charles to Isabella, 18 April 1536, *Corpus Documental*, Letter CXCVII, I, 486–487 (because Ansaldo Grimaldi has promised to lend up to 200,000 ducats free of interest, Charles asks that his terms be met, including "para le seguridad de la paga se le den los juros;" cf. Carande, Thobar, *Carlos V y sus banqueros*, loan 115, for 221,530 ducats).

[21] Hendricks, "Charles V and the Cortes of Castile," 217.

[22] Carande Thobar, *Carlos V y sus banqueros*, II, 535–536; Colmeiro, *Cortes de los Antiguos Reinos*, II, 180–186.

time they had been called (1527).[23] The clergy supported the idea of a
sisa, provided that its payment by the clergy was approved by the pope,[24]
but everything depended on the nobility, especially its most prestigious
members. In the order of precedence, the grandees who ranked highest were: Pedro Hernández de Velasco, constable of Castile; Juan Esteban
Manrique de Lara, duke of Nájara; Iñigo López de Mendóza, duke of Infantado; Juan Alonso de Guzmán, duke of Medina-Sidonia; Francisco de
Zuñiga, duke of Béjar; Fadrique de Toledo, third duke of Alba (Pedro
de Toledo's nephew); Antonio Pimentel, count of Benavente; Beltrán de
la Cueva, duke of Albuquerque; Diego de Cárdenas, duke of Maqueda;
and Fadrique de Enríquez, admiral of Castile.[25] Grandees had not been
admitted to the royal council of Castile since the time of Ferdinand and
Isabella – Charles made exceptions for Alba and Béjar – but they always
added weight to important occasions by attending on the person of the
king.[26] Charles knew these men well and counted on their support.

He was to be sorely disappointed. To prepare their response to the petition for a *sisa*, the seventy-four nobles in attendance appointed a committee
of twelve, which after three weeks was unable to reach agreement. As the
full assembly deliberated on a response, it was decided that what it forwarded to the king would be approved by a simple majority, not, as Alba
and a few others wanted, by a two-thirds vote. The resolution then endorsed was presented to Charles by Nájara, Béjar, and the constable. Nobles
who agreed to a *sisa*, they said, would dishonor the memory of their ancestors, for "the difference between *hialgos* and commoners in Castile is
that yeomen [*labradores*] pay *servicios* and other fiscal burdens, but *hidalgos*
do not." The kingdom was indeed in dire financial straits but not for want
of revenue; the problem was that Charles had been at war for almost all of
his eighteen years on the throne. Let him therefore moderate his expenses,
remain at home, and live in peace for a time. Alba, Infantado, and fifteen
caballeros had either walked out before this resolution was approved or voted
against it. On the advice of Cobos, Tavera, and other members of his council, Charles dismissed the nobles immediately and never summoned them

---

[23] In a speech to the Cortes, as cited by Sanchez Montes, *Agobios carolinos*, 67, the constable of Castile claimed the idea of an excise came from proposals in the Low Countries for a tax on cloths and other goods.

[24] Hendricks, "Charles V and the Cortes of Castile," 231–235.

[25] The order of precedence for the first eleven of seventy-one nobles at the Cortes of Toledo in 1538, as given by Giron, *Crónica del Emperador Carlos V*, 143–144, substituting Iñigo López de Mendóza, fourth duke of Infantado (d. 1568), for his eldest son, Diego Hurtado de Mendóza, whose name Giron gives here.

[26] For example, when he anticipated that he and Francis I would meet face-to-face for peace talks, Charles had the constable, the duke of Infantado, the duke of Escalona, the duke of Béjar, and Pedro de Sarmiento, archbishop of Santiago, "hold themselves in readiness" in Barcelona all during the month of January 1538: Giron, *Crónica del Emperador Carlos V*, 126. Kohler, *Karl V*, 26.

again. This was to be the last time that either nobles or clergy ever appeared as a body at the Cortes of Castile.[27]

It was now all the more imperative to reach agreement with the *procuradores*. Town deputies had expressed interest in a modified version of Charles's proposal, in which the *sisa* was to be collected by town governments, not tax farmers or royal officials. They apparently liked even more the idea of an extraordinary *servicio* for which towns could raise their quotas by collecting a *sisa*, if they wished to do so. On this understanding, someone in Charles's council prepared a memorandum suggesting that in return for a further ten-year extension of the capitation of the *alcabala* (i.e., from 1547 through 1556), the towns might be expected to grant a sum sufficient "to free crown incomes of debt, and meet the present need, or at least the greater part of it." At the beginning of February 1539, Charles sent one *procurador* from each town back to his council with a proposal: if the towns approved an extraordinary *servicio* for either 533,333 ducats over two years or 400,000 in one year, in addition to an ordinary *servicio* of 810,666 ducats over three years, they could have capitation extended for ten years more. Eleven of the eighteen municipalities agreed almost at once to the 810,666 ducats in three years and the 400,000 ducats in one year that Charles preferred. Seville, Córdoba, and Segovia were slower. In Segovia, a zealous *corregidor* clapped a few troublesome *regidores* in jail, only to be told in a letter from Charles that the emperor wanted his subjects "convinced, not incarcerated." All three towns returned acceptable replies by the end of the month. But Salamanca, Burgos, and Valladolid could not be induced to consent to the extraordinary *servicio*. According to records of *ayuntamiento* debates, *regidores* in these urban centers of Old Castile contended that their rural subjects could not keep up with the current *servicio*, not to speak of the higher ones now demanded. In some places, they said, tenants had sold their cattle and mules and gone off begging, leaving the *caballeros* without anyone to farm their lands. Elsewhere, even yeomen farmers (*labradores*) were said to languish in debtor's prison because they did not have the cash for their quota in the *servicio* – a levy from which "the rich and powerful" were exempt. But even though men had fresh memories of the Comuñero uprising, sparked by a few municipalities, it was not really necessary to gain the consent of all the towns. There was a more than sufficient majority for the largest sum ever approved, an extraordinary subsidy for 400,000 ducats (1539–1540), plus the ordinary subsidy of 810,666 (1540–1542). This grant was to set a pattern for the rest of Charles's reign.[28]

---

[27] Sanchez Montes, *Agobios carolinos*, 56–69; Colmeiro, *Cortes de los Antiguos Reinos*, 187–189; Maltby, *Alba*, 40–42.

[28] Sanchez Montes, *Agobios carolinos*, 78–25; Colmeiro, *Cortes de los Antiguos Reinos*, II, 197; Hendricks, "Charles V and the Cortes of Castile," 236–241; Carande Thobar, *Carlos V y sus banqueros*, II, 536–537.

When the urban procurators proposed a general capitation at Córdoba (1532), they described it as a means "by which your majesty can free your subject from many vexations and many lawsuits," and also as beneficial to the treasury, "for it has been seen by experience that capitation increases revenues, for if they are farmed out in the usual way the tax farmers are continually going bankrupt, so that revenues diminish."[29] But everyone surely understood that other interests were in play. All men of noble rank (including most *procuradores* and *regidores*) had a stake in the eventual trade-off at Valladolid (1539), putting an end to the traditional *alcabala* in return for higher-than-ever *servicios*, for nobles paid in the *alcabala* but not in the ordinary *servicios*. To be sure, nobles did have to pay if they were residents of a town that chose to collect its portion of the extraordinary *servicio* by levying a *sisa* in which all were taxed alike.[30] But pending further study of how the towns actually collected their quotas, it seems best not to assume that this qualification materially affected an overall shift in the burden of taxation from wealthy nobles to poor-to-middling commoners. Like the grandees who rallied to Charles's campaigns but rejected his fiscal demands in 1527 and again in 1538, the *caballeros* who ruled Castile's towns were loyal soldiers, but also conscious of their corporate dignity as magistrates, and their financial interests as nobles. What Charles got from the Cortes was not what he wanted, but what the kingdom's nobles thought its commoners could bear.

The other major beneficiaries of this shift in collection of the *alcabala* were the municipalities, for by ending the "vexations" of the king's tax farmers towns also increased their own fiscal autonomy.[31] Although substantial payments to the crown still had to be made annually, the level was now fixed and could be managed so as to suit local interests – for example, by varying as needed the sums raised through taxes of different kinds, or by keeping surplus revenue for such purposes as the *ayuntamiento* might devise. Moreover, because a great part of the outstanding *juros* had been assigned to the *alcabala*, each main town also assumed responsibility for servicing its share of the king's debt. In this way too, the towns played a role that may in some respects be compared with that of the provincial states of the Low Countries during the second half of Charles's reign. It seems likely that in Castile, as in the Low Countries, local units built a respectable credit rating even as Charles's wars dragged the national treasury ever deeper into debt.

---

[29] Colmeiro, *Cortes de los Antiguos Reinos*, IV, 573.

[30] Hendricks, "Charles V and the Cortes of Castile," 260–262: as a percentage of a package of taxation including the *alcabala* and the *tercia*, the *servicios* rose from 16.4% of the total for the years 1516–1520 to 30.2% for 1541–1555; but the effect of this shift was mitigated by the fact that at least some cities chose to collect their share of the extraordinary *servicios* by levying a *sisa*.

[31] Fortea Perez, *Monarquía y Cortes*, 450–456, summarizing previous discussion.

The last time Charles met his Cortes in person was at Valladolid in 1542, when war with France had already begun. In return for another ten-year extension of capitation (1557–1566), the assembly granted an ordinary subsidy of 800,000 ducats to be collected from 1543 through 1545, and an extraordinary subsidy of 400,000, payable in 1542 and 1543, at least part of which was to go for the defense of Perpignan, where the French were expected to concentrate their attack. Although the *procuradores* petitioned him not to leave the kingdom, Charles was already making plans for his Rhineland campaign the following year. While in Germany during the next summer, Charles was apparently wondering if his subjects might support yet another subsidy. In August 1543, Cobos reported on a joint meeting of the council of state and the council of the treasury to consider where money might be found. In their opinion, there was no point in calling a Cortes, for "new impositions" were not possible when the kingdom was "much burdened" by current *servicios* amounting to over 400,000 ducats for the year.[32]

By February of the next year, Philip and his advisers had overcome their misgivings and sent out letters summoning the procurators of the eighteen towns to Valladolid; another joint meeting of the two councils determined that there was "no other way" to find the 400,000 ducats Charles wanted as soon as possible.[33] Once assembled, the *procuradores* had many complaints, including the fact that some royal auditors had refused to enter in their records even the first ten-year extension of capitation granted by the crown in 1539. But they also agreed once more to a 800,000 ducat ordinary subsidy (for 1546–1548), and a 400,000 ducat extraordinary subsidy (1544–1545). Not without reason, Charles commended Philip for his good work at the Cortes of Valladolid.[34]

Charles wanted yet another Cortes summoned the following winter, to help him in resisting "the Turk and the Christians who have gone astray [*desviados*]," but Philip persuaded him it would be futile. The dangers posed by the Turks in Hungary and by the Christians gone astray in Germany "seem far away to these kingdoms"; moreover, owing to the "sterility" of recent years, the common people who bear the cost of the *servicios* cannot pay more; and even if a Cortes were to approve another subsidy, collection could not begin until 1549, meaning that the bankers who remitted the money to Charles would in the end collect interest equivalent to more than

---

[32] Colmeiro, *Cortes de los Antiguos Reinos*, II, 198–201; Cobos to Charles, 7 August 1543, *Corpus Documental*, Letter CCLX, II, 152.

[33] Philip to Charles, 4 February 1544, *Corpus Documental*, Letter CCLXVII, II, 190–191. Note that the total of *servicios* actually current in 1544 was 154,000 ducats, as opposed to 308,000 in 1543.

[34] Colmeiro, *Cortes de los Antiguos Reinos*, II, 203–208; Charles to Philip, third letter of 6 July 1544, *Corpus Documental*, Letter CCLXXX, II, 243–244.

the face value of the subsidy.[35] No Cortes was summoned until 1548, when rumors of Charles's illness at Augsburg caused great anxiety in Castile. A new 800,000 ducat ordinary subsidy was approved without difficulty for the years 1549–1551, but Philip had to prod the towns by sending special emissaries in order to get consent for another 400,000 ducat extraordinary *servicio*. Both grants were renewed in 1551 and again in 1555.[36]

Cui bono?

Procurators at the Cortes of Madrid in 1528 reminded Charles that money raised by the consent of his subjects was better spent on defending the kingdom than on foreign wars; in rejecting his *sisa* proposal ten years later, Castile's grandees delivered the same message a bit more forcefully.[37] Nonetheless, the "Castilianization" of Charles – his adoption of the country's language and customs as his own – evidently made enough of a difference that many Castilians saw the king's foreign triumphs as their own. Even during the long and difficult years of absence at the end of the reign, some speakers at meetings of the Cortes expressed their pride in the fact that Castile's wealth was supporting the glorious Christian emperor, who had now surpassed even Julius Caesar by his victories over the previously invincible Germans.[38]

How much of the wealth that supported Charles abroad came from the *servicios*? One must bear in mind that, during his reign, the *servicios* never brought in more than half of gross income for the *alcabala*, even though the former rose in value after 1539, while the yield of the latter was relatively fixed.[39] In certain years, moreover, income from both sources was dwarfed by the huge sums that Charles realized through sequestration of private treasure shipped from the Indies.[40] But *alcabala* income was increasingly eaten into by a rapidly rising *juro* debt; and *servicio* income was more predictable than the Indies fleets, especially after the Cortes of 1538–1539. From 1539 to 1555, the average annual value of the *servicios* was 470,980

---

[35] Philip to Charles, 13 December 1544, Charles to Philip, 17 February 1545, and Philip to Charles, 25 March 1545, *Corpus Documental*, Letters CCXIX, CCCVII, and CCCXIII, II, 312–315, 338–339, 357–359.

[36] Colmeiro, *Cortes de los Antiguos Reinos*, II, 213–214, 232–233; Carande Thobar, *Carlos V y sus banqueros*, II, 535–536.

[37] See notes 11, 27.

[38] Hendricks, "Charles V and the Cortes of Castile," chap. 9. The reference is perhaps not so much to the campaigns in Germany described in Caesar's *Gallic Wars* as to the annihilation of three Roman legions under Marcus Quintilius Varro by a German commander known to the Romans as Arminius (A.D. 9 – cf. Tacitus's *Germania*).

[39] Hendricks, "Charles V and the Cortes of Castile," 219–221.

[40] E.g., 800,000 ducats in 1535 (Chapter 7), nearly 2,000,000 in 1551 (Chapter 11).

ducats; for the previous seventeen years (1522–1538), the average annual value had been 293,689 ducats; this was an increase of 60% per annum in raw numbers, or about 37% with adjustment for inflation.[41] The one occasion for which published documents permit comparison of the value of Charles's various revenues for his foreign campaigns was in September 1544, when an auditor's report identified the assignations for about 1,870,000 ducats in *cambios* sent to the emperor during the previous eighteen months. Roughly 25% of the total was secured by the *servicios* granted by the Cortes of Valladolid in that year, more than for any other source of revenue, though not by much. Looked at from the other end, it seems that virtually all of the money *servicios* granted in 1542 was used to settle old war debts, while money from the grants of 1544 went for loans contracted during Charles's campaigns in the Rhineland and France.[42]

In sum, it seems there was a striking contrast between Castile's willingness to support the emperor's foreign adventures and the determination of officials at all levels in the Low Countries to keep back the country's revenues for its own defense. This difference is primarily to be explained by the military situation of both realms. To be sure, the raids of Barbary corsairs were a constant threat in Castile, as in Aragón; but apart from the French invasion of Navarre in 1522, resulting in the temporary occupation of Fuenterrabía, and the dauphin's failed assault on Perpignan in 1543, the costs of defending the Pyrenees frontier were not to be compared with those of defending the featureless boundary separating northern France from the Low Countries. Historians of a former era might have explained the generosity of Castile and the stinginess of the Low Countries in terms of the relative weakness of parliamentary institutions in the one realm and their strength in the latter. In fact, representative assemblies in both countries were able to hold their own in quid-pro-quo bargaining with demanding central governments. Moreover, as has been suggested here, the strength of representative institutions may in both cases have something to do with the fact that deputies represented local interests – the provinces in the Low Countries, and in Castile the town-states, some of which were as large as the smaller Low Countries provinces.

In this respect, there is a final parallel worth noting. In the Low Countries, Mary of Hungary found a way to marshal the creditworthiness of the provinces for the central government's war needs, inducing the provincial states to raise cash by creating debt funded by taxes of their own devising. Through capitation of the *alcabala*, Charles induced Castile's creditworthy towns to assume responsibility for the treasury's existing long-term debt but not for any new debt. This further innovation was left to

[41] Part III, note 4.
[42] Carnade Thobar, *Carlos V y sus banqueros*, II, 535–536; Chapter 9, note 62, and Table 9.1.

his son, Philip II. First, as noted previously, Philip persuaded the Cortes to agree in 1575 to a tripling of the sums due for capitation of the *alcabala*. Second, in 1589 he won consent for a new kind of subsidy, known as the "*servicio* of millions," because it was to raise the unheard-of sum of 8 million ducats over six years. Everyone was to pay, including nobles and clergy, and to pay according to their ability. As in the capitation system, each main town, with its rural district, was left to raise its assigned quota as local authorities might determine. As this system continued into the reigns of Kings Philip III (1598–1621) and Philip IV (1621–1665), more and more of the crown's long-and short-term debt was transferred to the new *servicios*, with local governments responsible for paying the interest assigned to their quotas – at least until Philip IV decreed a major reorganization in 1658.[43] Chapter 11 concluded with the observation that the Dutch Republic sustained its war for independence from Spain in part by improving on the fiscal arrangements inherited from Charles V's reign. This chapter may conclude with the suggestion that Philip II and his successors helped sustain Spain's side of the struggle by adapting the principle of fiscal devolution to a realm that was divided into town-states, not provinces. This common ground is one reason, among others, why these two Habsburg states, become enemies, had the will and the resources to fight early modern Europe's longest war.[44]

[43] Ulloa, *La hacienda real*, 505–510; Miquel Artola, *La Hacienda del Antiguo Régimen*, (Madrid, 1982), 111–115.

[44] In what the Dutch call the Eighty Years' War, there was intermittent fighting from 1568 to 1572, and continuous war from 1572 to 1609 and from 1621 to 1645, interspersed by the Twelve Years' Truce of 1609–1621, and a three-year lull leading up to the 1648 Peace of Westphalia, at which the United Provinces and the Spanish Netherlands – roughly, modern Belgium (with Luxemburg) and the Netherlands – were recognized as separate nations.

Conclusions

Hegemony of the House of Austria?

Charles successfully preserved for Philip and Ferdinand all the lands inherited from their ancestors, and also increased the European dominions of his family. Milan, symbol of his pacification of Italy, was for centuries the anchor of Spanish and later Austrian Habsburg power in northern Italy. In the Low Countries, his armies conquered the county of Friesland (1515); evicted the forces of the duke of Guelders from Utrecht and Overijssel, allowing the prince-bishop of Utrecht to make good on his pledge to cede these provinces to Charles (1527–1528); and reconquered the duchy of Guelders itself (1543), which had for a time broken away from Habsburg control. No one could know that these additions, giving populous Holland and Brabant a shield against attack from the east and north, would redound to the benefit not of the Habsburg monarchy but of its great enemy in the next generation, the Dutch Republic.

Charles was also presented with many other plans for extending his authority. Some he rejected, but some others, where dynastic interests were involved, he pursued avidly, if to no avail.[1] But if the emperor was not quite the pacific defender of inherited rights that he claimed to be, he was also less eager for expansion than his enemies thought. Whether seeking to acquire territory or merely to defend what he had, Charles was always in the position of bargaining for peace here on fronts A and B so as to concentrate his strength on front C, the point of present danger, or opportunity. With all the revenues of all his lands, he lacked the resources to fight simultaneously

---

[1] Charles to Ferdinand, 31 October 1531, *Familienkorrespondenz*, Letter 574, IV, 346, turning aside Ferdinand's proposal for intervention in the civil war between the outnumbered Catholic cantons of Switzerland and their Protestant foes; for Charles's determined pursuit of a Danish crown for his niece (a daughter of the deposed Christian II), against all manner of good advice from the Low Countries, see Doyle, "The Heart and Stomach of a Man but Body of a Woman," chap. 6.

against all the foes that might be arrayed against him. This leads to the question of what prompted so many European states to accept the risks of war against the grand emperor, with all his armies and all his gold.

Hemmed in by Habsburg Franche Compté to the east, and by the Habsburg Low Countries to the north and Habsburg Spain to the south, France was also Europe's largest and most populous centrally governed kingdom,[2] and thus the natural enemy of Habsburg power. The same "honor and reputation" that brooked so large in the strategic thinking of Charles and his advisers required the Valois kings to expend their kingdom's resources in a series of campaigns aimed at diminishing Habsburg power (1521–1525, 1527–1529, 1536, 1542–1544, 1551–1559).[3] But France could not have stood against the Habsburgs alone; French diplomats always found an audience for the argument that Habsburg power was not compatible with the relatively new idea that there ought to be a rough balance among the competing interests that made up Latin Christendom. In effect, the bare possibility of a single great power dominating Europe created a sense of common interest among multiple principalities that were more commonly at war with one another.

Because the Catholic Church faced in Germany a religious revolution of unprecedented magnitude, one might have expected the popes to join hands with the devoutly Catholic emperor to stem the advance of the Reformation. But they did so only at times, not consistently, because as temporal rulers the popes were no less anxious about Habsburg "tyranny" in the peninsula than other Italian potentates – especially at moments of Habsburg triumph, such as the victory at Pavia in 1525, which prompted Clement VII to adhere to France in the League of Cognac (1526), just as Paul III tilted toward the French when Charles's Italian commanders blocked the ambitions of his nephew, Ottavio Farnese, would-be duke of Parma and Piacenza. After Pedro de Toledo's tenure as viceroy, Naples might have seemed well under control but not in the mind of Pope Paul IV (1551–1555), a Neapolitan who chafed under foreign control of his native land, and so kindled the Italian ambitions of King Henry II, thus helping to prolong the war that overlapped the end of Charles's reign and the beginning of Philip II's.[4]

---

[2]   For the connection between a monarchy strong enough to hold a territory together and stable population levels (for France in this era, about 20,000,000), E. Leroi Ladurie, *The French Royal State* (Oxford, 1994), 8–11.

[3]   For coherent expositions of France's interests during the Habsburg-Valois wars (1494–1559), see Bernard Chevalier, "France from Charles VIII to Henry IV," in Brady, Oberman, and Tracy, *Handbook of European History*, I, 369–402; and Robert Knecht, "Francis I and Charles V: The Image of the Enemy," in Jan DeNolf and Barbara Simons, eds., *(Re)Constructing the Past* (Brussels, 2000), 47–68.

[4]   Some years earlier, Charles thought Paul III (despite his professed neutrality) was trying to rally Italian states to France, "as if we mean to tyrannize Italy": Charles to Juan de Vega, his ambassador

In Germany, the dukes of Bavaria were as Catholic as the pope, but Bavaria had long-standing territorial disputes with its neighbor, Habsburg Austria, and was not displeased by a political constellation in which the emperor's ambitions in Germany were held in check by the military arm of the Protestant Reformation.[5] The Schmalkaldic League was France's natural ally, so long as French kings muted their persecution of native Protestants and their appetite for imperial lands west of the Rhine.[6] Farther afield, France from 1525 regularly made alliances with the Ottoman Turks. The most conspicuous display of their collaboration came in 1543, when 110 Turkish galleys, with a French ambassador on board, raided along the coasts of Sicily and Naples en route to a warm reception in Marseilles, followed by a conquest of pro-imperial Nice by a joint Franco-Ottoman fleet. Toulon became for a time a Muslim city, used as a base by Ottoman galleys for further raids against the Spanish coast.[7]

With all these foes arrayed against him, Charles saw himself as the paladin of Catholic Christendom, responsible to God for its defense against the machinations of Lutheran heretics, Turkish infidels, perfidious Frenchmen, and faithless popes. But others saw Habsburg power as a colossus bestriding Europe, threatening an equilibrium of long standing. It is worth pondering that, when all is said and done, not even a Charles V could wrench Europe's ingrained state pluralism from its long course of development. Some students of global history have argued that a civilization based on rival states pays the price of more frequent internal wars but reaps the benefit of leap-frogging improvements in technology, commerce, and warfare. Thus Europe's traditional pattern of political fragmentation, not to be shaken even by a Charles V, gave it certain competitive advantages over the great centralizing empires that dominated most of the rest of early modern Eurasia – the Ottomans in the Middle East, the Safavids in Persia, the Mughals in India, and the Ming dynasty in China.[8] Paradoxically, it may be that the greatest significance of Charles's reign for European history lies not in what he did but in what he did not do: he either failed to achieve or did not even attempt the *monarchia* of which Gattinara had dreamed.

---

in Rome, January 1543, in *Staatspapiere*, Document lxvi, 346–358. For the propaganda war between the courts of Charles V and Clement VII, see Headley, *The Emperor and His Chancellor*, 97–102; for the Franco-Papal alliance of 1555, see Lutz, *Christianitas Afflicta*, 399–407.

[5] For Bavaria's position in the Habsburg Empire, see Kohler, *Anti-Habsburgische Politik*, 22–38.

[6] For the earliest contacts between France and leaders of the League, see ibid., 208–211.

[7] Knecht, *Renaissance Warrior and Patron*, 487–488.

[8] For versions of this argument, Eric Jones, *The European Miracle* (2nd ed., Cambridge, 1987), and Michael Pearson, "Merchants and States," in James D. Tracy, ed., *The Political Economy of Merchant Empires* (Cambridge, 1991), 47–116.

Power of the Purse, I: The Bankers

The simplest way to make sure one's troops were paid while on campaign was to gather a large sum beforehand and carry it along, in carefully guarded chests. Khair-ad-Din Barbarossa did this when he sailed from Istanbul with a great fleet of galleys in 1534; so did Charles V when he held up his departure for Italy (1529) until the arrival of the Portuguese gold, for which he had pawned his interests in the Moluccas. The Italian bankers who backed various Mediterranean campaigns in the fourteenth century seem to have provided their credit in the same way, all at once.[9] But during the first half of the sixteenth century, the length of campaigns and the increasing size of armies made it almost impossible to gather all that was needed at the start of a campaign. Thus in November 1524, Francis I, encamped in the Park of Mirabello opposite Pavia, was "expecting 1,400,000 francs next month,"[10] probably in the form of a shipment of cash across the Alps. Charles's problems in keeping cash flowing to his paymasters were more complicated, because he was often in the position of fighting at great distances from his most reliable source of income (i.e., Castile), and against an enemy with interior lines of supply, and interior lines of credit (e.g., against Cleves in 1543 or France in 1544). The emperor was able to fight his wars as he did only because, like no other prince before him, he made the fullest possible use of the transfer mechanisms that European banking houses had developed over the centuries. This meant, of course, that he had to absorb huge costs for currency transfers (in addition to interest charges), as Philip II did in the next generation, using essentially the same credit system to sustain his long battle against the rebel provinces of the Low Countries.[11] It meant too that the great banking firms on whom the emperor principally depended had all the more weight in shaping the policies of his governments to their liking. Not only were firms like the Fugger and the Welser and the Grimaldi the only ones who could supply as much credit as was needed: they were also the only ones with wide networks of reliable agents, to ensure the remittance of money for the emperor's paymasters more or less on schedule.

To begin with, no matter how high the debts mounted, the simple expedient of repudiation, to which rulers of the fourteenth and fifteenth centuries had sometimes resorted,[12] was unthinkable. The bankers had to be contented somehow, if only by counting unpaid loan balances as fictive

---

[9] Chapter 7, note 29; Chapter 6, note 9; Part I, note 6.

[10] Knecht, *Renaissance Warrior and Patron*, 218.

[11] Thompson, *War and Government in Habsburg Spain*, chap. III, "The Problem of Financing."

[12] Probably the best-known example (because of its repercussions on Florentine politics) is the repudiation of some 800,000 florins in debts owed to the Bardi-Peruzzi firm by England's Edward III in the 1330s: Armando Sapori, *Le crisi delle compagnie mercantili dei Bardi e dei Peruzzi* (Florence, 1926).

"advances" in a new contract.[13] One need not imagine that the principle of contractual agreements governed sixteenth-century capital markets to the same degree that it presently does. For example, Castile's monarchy still claimed power to restructure debt arbitrarily, as in 1557, when Philip II, by fiat, converted short-term loans into low-interest, long-term *juros*.[14] The point is that this restructuring was not, as is sometimes thought, a repudiation.

In some respects, the bankers, by the choices they made, did nothing more than help to consolidate developments that were already underway. For example, bankers in Naples in effect cast a vote for Pedro de Toledo's authority as viceroy when they advanced 70,000 ducats on the promise of a mere ad hoc group of nobles that there would be, at some point, a *donativo* of 170,000 ducats.[15] Bankers in the Low Countries put their stamp of approval on what has here been called fiscal devolution when they began approaching the provincial parliaments for their loan guarantees, bypassing the central-government revenue collectors with whom they had previously dealt.[16] To what extent did the bankers distort local economies, through protomercantilistic arrangements in which firms advancing money to the crown were rewarded with control of major national resources, like the *maestrazgos* in Castile and the *dogana di Puglia* in Naples, or lesser ones, like the monopoly contract for importing into the Low Countries the alum needed by cloth manufacturers as a color-fixing agent? Economic historians may have differing answers in each case, but what lies beyond doubt is that midlevel merchants and manufacturers, lacking the means to do business this way, saw themselves as unfairly disadvantaged by cozy relationships between "great purses" and the crown.[17] One can certainly make a case that bankers in Castile deprived the crown of a key resource by gaining an effective monopoly over the marketing of *juros* funded by the kingdom's *rentas ordinarias*.[18] No sensible fiscal administration would allow such a valuable means of cheap credit to pass out of its control, if it were possible to do otherwise. But the bankers, made powerful by the needs that Charles's wars created, were not to be denied.

[13] E.g., Chapter 10, note 69.
[14] Chapter 11, note 39.
[15] Chapter 13, note 22.
[16] Chapter 12, note 44.
[17] On the *maestrazgos*, Kellenbenz, *Die Fuggersche Maestrazgopacht*; on the *dogana di Puglia*, John Marino, *Pastoral Economics in the Kingdom of Naples* (Baltimore, 1988); on the alum monopoly, Hugo Soly, "De aluinhandel in de Nederlanden in de 16e Eeuw," *Belgische Tijdschrift voor Filologie en geschiedenis/Revue Belge de Philologie et d'Histoire* 52 (1974): 800–857; and on complaints about "great purses" and their arcane dealings with the crown, Tracy, *Holland under Habsburg Rule*, 51–52.
[18] Chapter 11, notes 37, 38.

Power of the Purse, II: The Parliaments

I hope it is clear from the foregoing chapters that parliamentary subsidies played a vital role in meeting the bankers' demands, even if other sources of income (especially in Castile) were often more important. But how is one to understand the political implications of incessant bargaining between government officials and the parliaments of each realm?

Not too long ago, the parliamentary history of the late medieval and early modern centuries was the center of interest for scholars. For liberal historians of the late nineteenth and early twentieth centuries, parliaments represented a nascent sense of the public interest, strong enough to check the overweening ambition of monarchs. For defenders of the absolute-monarchy thesis, by contrast, it was the king and his officials who stood for a coherent vision of the common good, against which the privileged classes with parliamentary representation fought a retrograde battle.[19] In the last generation or so, however, careful study of elites and their material interests[20] has made it seem that parliamentary leaders and royal officials were two peas in a pod, mouthing platitudes about the commonwealth while tending to the business of enriching themselves and providing for their kin. If this be so, why should debates about taxation, a battle of slogans signifying perhaps not very much, still be taken seriously?

There is a reason, if one is willing to follow the commonsense dictum of Georg Wilhelm Friedrich Hegel: in the process of history, ideal values advance only insofar as they are supported by material or selfish interests.[21] Depending on circumstances, one can find a genuine grasp of the larger public good either among government officials berating sullen parliamentary deputies, or among deputies stubbornly resisting the government's demands, quite irrespective of the fact that officials and deputies alike owed their position to a successful record of looking out for themselves.

In each of the cases touched on in Part III of this book, the balance of moral and material forces worked out somewhat differently. In Naples, the nobles dominant in the Parlamento developed during Charles's reign a sense of loyalty to the new dynasty but not a sense of responsibility to any interest larger than their own. The fact that the government had to take their private concerns into account was thus of no effect in braking the government's demands for higher subsidies or in keeping more than a

---

[19] These issues are touched on in Chapter 4, especially notes 62–67.

[20] E.g., Daniel Dessert, *Argent, pouvoir et societé au grand siècle* (Paris, 1984); Linda Levy Peck, *Court Patronage and Corruption in Early Stuart England* (Boston, 1990).

[21] Hegel is not usually invoked as a prophet of common sense, certainly not in the English-speaking world, but I invite readers to consult the introduction to his *Philosophie der Geschichte*, translated separately as *Reason in History, a General Introduction to the Philosophy of History*, tr. Robert S. Hartman (New York, 1953).

fraction of the money back for the needs of the kingdom. In Castile, the proportion of noblemen among *procuradores* to the Cortes was probably just as high as among those attending meetings of the Parlamento in Naples. Yet these noblemen were also the mandatories of sizable town-states whose leading men had a well-defined sense of their corporate as well as their individual interests. Hence, if they too were not overly concerned about subsidy money leaving the kingdom – for many of them too, like the nobles in Naples, fought in Charles's wars – they did bargain for a fiscal rearrangement that not only diminished the tax liability of the nobility in general but also gave the town-states new powers to manage the royal revenues for which they and their districts were responsible. In the Low Countries, where the states represented some sense of provincial interest as well as the more local interests of towns with voting rights, it is hard not to see the central government as the only party in a many-sided dialogue that could claim to represent the interests of the realm as a whole.[22] Yet the government represented as well the dynastic interests embodied in Charles's instructions, not seldom at odds with those of the realm. To this higher selfishness the localism of the provinces and towns formed an effective counterweight, partly because (unlike in Naples or Castile) subsidy income made up here the bulk of government revenue, and partly because (also unlike Naples and Castile) the constant fiscal demands of war at home brooked large in the minds of all. Hence the provincial states were able both to bargain for greater control of revenues raised within their borders and to limit the money that Charles "took" for his own purposes to a fraction of overall subsidy income.

In no case were these developments of Charles's reign without deep historical roots, but neither were they in any sense foreordained by the past. In effect, Charles's wars, and the fiscal demands they generated, were a catalyst, pushing the institutions of each realm to develop in a given direction, rather than others that might be imagined.

Christendom versus Islamdom

That Christendom had need of leadership there can be no doubt, for it was on Charles's watch, so to speak, that Ottoman power scored some of its most impressive advances: the conquest of the great fortress of Belgrade (1521) and the island citadel of the Knights of Rhodes (1522); the overwhelming victory at Mohács (1526); and the occupation of central Hungary (1541). Yet an examination of the emperor's campaigns makes it clear that he concentrated his energy and treasure on the struggle against the Most Christian King of France. Hungary and Habsburg Austria were the realms

[22] I discount the States General, which played a minimal role in Charles's reign.

most directly threatened by the sultan's armies. Despite Habsburg propaganda about Charles defeating Suleyman in 1532,[23] the two great armies never came within fifty miles of each other, and Charles turned his back on Vienna as soon as he decently could. He had to meet his obligations as emperor, but his participation in this *empresa* was clearly pro forma. One cannot say the same, however, for the war against Ottoman power at sea. Charles's correspondence shows an involvement in the details of the maritime campaigns not found for any of his wars on land. Also, the attack on Constantinople was the one *empresa* in which he persisted, despite the advice of almost all his councillors, only to pull back at the last minute. With Doria as his master planner, Charles hoped to achieve at sea victories that would make a difference in the perennial war against Islam; briefly, after Tunis, it seemed as if he had done so.

The way in which Tunis was conquered raises another question. Christian accounts seem untroubled by the fact that thousands of Tunisians were cut down in their homes, and thousands more enslaved, even as 20,000 or so Christian captives were liberated from Barbarossa's dungeons. The only hint that Moors might be entitled to the same consideration as Christians comes in the garbled account of an anonymous German broadside, praising the clement emperor for not allowing Tunis to be plundered.[24] What is one to make of Spanish and Habsburg crusades to put a stop to Ottoman slave raids, even as Doria's fleet joined the Knights of Malta in their slave raids along the Barbary coast? Can one in any way credit the claim of moral superiority implied by the Christian notion of a crusade, as represented (for example) by the Knights of Malta? Or that implied by the Muslim notion of *jihad*, as represented by the *ghazi* warriors who had for generations spearheaded the Ottoman advance against Balkan Christian infidels? I would answer with a qualified yes: despite the contradictions inherent in the idea of hardened soldiers fighting for a spiritual ideal, men are nonetheless lifted beyond their narrow horizons by struggling for a cause greater than their own aggrandizement. From the heirs of a twentieth century that failed to master its own inner demons, crusaders and *ghazi* warriors deserve a measure of respect.

In practical terms, it may seem at first sight that Charles had little impact on the ongoing struggle between Christian and Islamic powers. The prestige gained at Tunis was wiped out at Algiers, and the conventional wisdom is that the western Mediterranean was not made safe for

[23] See the Italian engraving (1532) of Charles's troops encountering Suleyman's army, and Maarten van Heemskerk's engraving, *Charles V Liberates Vienna from the Turks*, no. 5 in his series "Victories of Charles V": Navascués Palacio, *Carolus V Imperator*, 115, 218; cf. the sources cited in Chapter 7, note 31, including Charles's letter patent of 1 March 1535 to vassals of the crown of Castile.

[24] Chapter 7, note 37.

European shipping until the great Christian victory at Lepanto (1571) – if even then.[25] But in a broader perspective, the alliance between Spain and Genoa, personified in the working relationship between Charles V and Andrea Doria, changed the balance of forces in Mediterranean warfare. As Heinz Duchhardt has said, what was really at stake in the 1535 Tunis campaign was "the maintenance of a sort of geopolitical balance between Christendom and Islamdom."[26] During the fourteenth and fifteenth centuries, Christian naval offensives against Muslim states of the eastern Mediterranean were for the most part mounted either by the papacy, or by the Republic of Venice, or by the two working together.[27] When Mamluk Egypt was overwhelmed by Ottoman armies (1517), the navies of the East were combined under the sultan; the great victory at Rhodes (1522) may be seen as the first fruits of Ottoman maritime supremacy in the East. That Sultan Suleyman took the new Spanish-Genoese threat seriously is apparent from his co-option of the chief corsair of the Barbary coast, Khair-ad-Din Barbarossa, as his *kapudan pasha* or admiral of the sea (1534). Conducting operations against Ottoman territory at times when Venice had a truce with the Porte, Genoese and Castilian galleys made strikes that compelled the enemy to send out large war fleets and armies in response. Doria's seizure of Castilnuovo (Chapter 8) may not seem important, for the fortress was held by Spanish troops for barely ten months (28 October 1538–6 August 1539). But to dislodge the 3,500 Spaniards, most of whom died in the fighting, it took an armada larger than any yet commanded by Barbarossa (130 galleys and 200 sailing ships, according to Santa Cruz), plus 70,000 paid troops and 10,000 skirmishers under Bazan Pasha.[28] How many campaigns of this type could a state sustain, even a state as wealthy and well-administered as the Ottoman Empire of Suleyman I?

The galleys of Castile and Genoa were potentially even more effective when they cooperated with papal and Venetian forces; Prevesa (1538) was no great success, but Lepanto was. In the end, the struggle between the Ottomans and their European rivals was a war of attrition. During the so-called Long Turkish War (1593–1606), when Habsburg Austria had help from Spain and the papacy and various Italian states as well as from the princes of the empire, European diplomats at the Porte noted for the first

[25] Parker, *The Grand Strategy of Philip II*, 101, 123.
[26] Duchardt, "Das Tunisunternehmen Karls V," 56: "Es ging vor Allem um die Erhaltung einer Art weltpolitisches Gleichgewichts zwischen Christianitas und Islam." Without giving his reasons, Duchhardt treats the Algiers campaign of 1541 as being more "a national-Spanish, Habsburg concern" than a war between Christendom and Islamdom (p. 63).
[27] This is the argument of Setton, *The Papacy and the Levant*.
[28] Santa Cruza, *Crónica del Emperador*, pt. V, chap. lii (vol. III, 529–530); pt. VI, chap. iv (vol. IV, 29–35).

time major fissures in the structure of the Ottoman state and its revenue-gathering apparatus.[29] Charles V had of course nothing to do with this war that broke out thirty-five years after his death. But his Mediterranean policy did have an effect beyond his lifetime, by giving the Ottomans one more enemy to worry about. Thus Charles not only left Europe's ingrained state pluralism essentially as he found it; he also helped make a broader basis of collaboration possible, if and when Christian states could overcome their habitual antagonisms. This may be a modest accomplishment for one who claimed to be Christendom's anointed leader, but Charles V did make a difference.

Impresario of War

Looking at Charles's wars in sequence, one can discern a pattern in terms of how well he planned and executed his campaigns. The art of the impresario of war – his metier – had two parts. The first was to preside over working out the strategic possibilities of a given situation: how many men or ships of what kinds would be needed, by what routes the different units were to converge, and what were the alternate objectives they might usefully pursue once joined together. The second was, of course, to be on hand to watch over the coming together of the army, to preside over the forming of battle plans in light of possibilities on the ground, and, as needed, to keep up the courage of his men by joining in the thick of an engagement. Down through the campaign in France in 1544, all but one of his campaigns exemplified the war impresario's art to a high degree, raising the stakes for his competitors, and contributing significantly to what historians have called the "military revolution" of this era, involving steady growth in the size of armies and in the sophistication of armaments and fortifications. The Italian campaign of 1529–1530 did nothing for his personal *reputacion*, but Charles held his mainly German army together, and their exploits (notably at Florence) consolidated the Habsburg hegemony in the peninsula that his commanders had built up by earlier victories. Tunis was a triumph, even if its luster was later dimmed by failure at Algiers. The Rhineland campaign of 1543 achieved its objectives, and in France the following year he did indeed constrain Francis I to "see reason," as Charles would have said. Algiers was of course a disaster, and Charles's plan of campaign is surely to be faulted for leaving too narrow a margin for delay; but he did get into place the men and armaments that could well have achieved his objective, had it not been for "the wind of Charles." The one exception to his record of successful planning was the Provence campaign of 1536, when Charles was in effect

[29] Jan Paul Niederkorn, *Die europäische Mächte und der "Lange Türkenkrieg" Kaiser Rudolfs II (1593–1606)* (Vienna, 1993), 27–40.

outplanned by Constable Montmorency, whose defensive arrangements were proof against even a large force. As for the First Schmalkaldic War, as in France, he gained what he wanted by keeping in the field a force that was at all times at least equal and at crucial moments numerically superior to that of the enemy. But in this case one must question his strategic objective: did Charles really expect to bend Protestant Germany to his will by defeating its two military champions?

In contrast with this record of fair success, all of the military and political decisions that Charles made between the summer of 1548 and the end of 1552 were, from a practical standpoint, wrongheaded. The Augsburg Interim recognized at least to a degree the local autonomy that was an enduring feature of the imperial constitution, but – unlike Mary, who had warned him against trying to subdue the Reformation by force – Charles had no grasp of why the Interim was so heartily detested in Lutheran Germany. His complicated plan for dynastic succession clearly slighted the elective character of the imperial office, and the months of painful negotiating that eventually led Ferdinand to accept an unpalatable vision of the dynasty's future ended by giving his brother and the princes of the empire a basis for dealing, independently of Charles's wishes. South of the Alps, where Charles had in earlier years sought to minimize fears of Habsburg hegemony, his treatment of the Farnese clan was a direct affront to Italian sensibilities. In Germany, his decision to take up residence in Austrian Innsbruck (rather than the Rhineland, as Mary recommended) showed Charles behaving not as a crowned emperor, for whom there was always a residue of loyalty, but as a local dynast who could not feel safe outside his hereditary lands. He was too slow to act on reports (again from Mary, among others) that Moritz of Saxony was consorting with his enemies; when the crisis came, he was too quick in ordering a vast army raised, before he could discern whether such a force would be needed. Once this army was assembled, and once Moritz had accepted Ferdinand's terms of peace, as revised by Charles, what was he to do? Charles could have earned much credit in the empire by crushing Albrecht-Alcibiades and his horde of plunderers; instead, he embraced the margrave and his extortionate treaties, as part of a foolish plan to set down before a large city in the dead of winter.

Granvelle's death surely made a difference, but not all the difference. One is tempted to see Charles as a victim of his own success. In earlier years, he disciplined himself to take into account the best information he could get about political alignments and military possibilities. More important, he accepted the principle that was constantly reiterated by his best advisers, from Gattinara to Granvelle and Mary of Hungary: one could accomplish political objectives by main force, but only some of the time. But having defeated his enemies in 1543 and 1544 – decisively, as he thought – he gave more credence to the hard-line views of lesser men, like Pedro de Soto, who thought that only cowards sheltered behind the walls of Germany's Protestant towns; or Ferrante Gonzaga in Italy, whose solution to the problem of Piacenza was to assassinate Pier Luigi Farnesi; or the younger Granvelle, who thought Charles's glory was exalted by the demeaning imprisonment of two of Germany's leading princes. Indeed, once the Protestants too were defeated – decisively, it seemed – Charles abandoned himself to solipsistic dreams of family glory, paying little heed to the temper of imperial politics. For these lapses in judgment he paid a high price. As this book has shown, the price that his subjects paid was higher still.

Bibliography

ARCHIVAL SOURCES

Gemeentearchief, Amsterdam
"Andries Jacobszoon, Prothocolle van alle die reysen . . . bij mij Andries Jacops gedaen [1524–1538]"
Adriaan Sandelijn, "Memoriaelboek"
"Stads Rekeningen"
Algemeen Rijksarchief/Archives Généraux du Royaume, Brussels
"Papiers d'État et de l'Audience"
"Comptes des Receveurs Généraux de toutes les finances," film copy of "Chambre des Comptes," Series B, Archives du Département du Nord, Lille
Rijksarchief van Zuid-Holland, The Hague: IIIe Afdeling
"Graafelijksheids Rekenkamer"
"Staten van Holland voor 1572"
The British Library, London
Charles Leclerc, "Rapport et Recueil de tout le Royaulme de Naples," Egestorn Collection, no. 1905
Archivio de Simancas, Valladolid
Colecion Estado
Haus- Hof- und Staatsarchiv, Vienna
"Belgien"

PRINTED CORRESPONDENCE AND PAPERS OF CHARLES V

"Berichte und Studien zur Geschichte Karls V," *Nachrichten von der Akademie der Wissenschaften zu Göttingen, Philologische-Historische Klasse,* nos. I–XIX (1930–1941).
Karl Brandi, "Die Politische Testamente Karls V," II (1930), 258–293.
Fritz Walser, ed., "Fünf Spanische Denkschriften an den Kaiser," VI (1932), 133–181.
Karl Brandi, "Eigenhändige Aufzeichnungen Karls V aus dem Anfang des Jahre 1525," IX (1933), 220–260.
Karl Brandi, "Aus den Kabinettsakten des Kaisers," XIX (1941), 203–257.
Correspondencia del Cardenal de Osma con Carlos V y su Secretario Don Francisco de los Cobos = *Collecion de Documentos Ineditos para la Historia de España* XIV (Madrid, 1849).

Manuel Fernández Alvárez, ed., *Corpus Documental de Carlos V* (5 vols., Salamanca, 1973–1981).

Die Korrespondenz Ferdinands I: vol. I, Wilhelm Bauer, ed., *Die Familienkorrespondenz bis 1526* (Vienna, 1912); vol. II, Wilhelm Bauer and Robert Lacroix, eds., *Die Familienkorrespondenz 1527–1528* (Vienna, 1930); vol. III, Wilhelm Bauer, and Robert Lacroix, eds., *Die Familienkorrespondenz 1529 und 1530* (Vienna, 1938); vol. IV, Herwig Wolfram and Christiane Thomas, eds., *Familienkorrespondenz 1531 und 1532* (Vienna, 1973) = *Veröffentlichungen der Kommission für Neuere Geschichte Österreichs*, vols. 11, 30, 31, and 58, Lieferung 1.

Karl Lanz, ed., *Korrespondenz des Kaiser Karls V aus dem Königlichem Archiv und der Bibliothèque de Bourgogne zu Brüssel* (3 vols., Leipzig, 1844–1846).

———, ed., *Staatspapiere des Kaisers Karl V aus dem Königlichem Archiv und der Bibliothèque de Bourgogne zu Brüssel* (Stuttgart, 1848).

Karl Lanz and Franz Cheml, eds., *Actenstücke und Briefe zur Geschichte des Kaisers Karls V*, in *Monumenta Habsburgica* (5 vols., Vienna, 1853–1858), vols. IV and V.

Alfred Morel-Fatio, *L'historiographie de Charles-Quint. Première partie, suivie de memoires de Charles-Quint. Text portugais et traduction française* (Paris, 1913).

Enrique Pacheco y Leyva, ed., *La politica española in Italia. Correspondencia de Don Fernando Martín, Abad de Najera, con Carlos I* (vol. I, Madrid, 1919).

CONTEMPORARY ACCOUNTS OF CHARLES'S REIGN

Luis de Ávila y Zuñiga, *Commentariorum de Bello Germanico a Carolo V Caesare Maximo Augusto Libri III, translati per Gulielmum Malinaeum Brugensem, et iconibus illustrati* (Antwerp: Johan Streelsius, 1550; copy in Special Collections, University of Minnesota Library).

Otto Adalbert Graf von Looz-Corswaren, ed., *Bernabé de Busto, Geschichte des Schmalkaldischen Krieges* (Burg, 1938) = *Texte und Forschungen im Auftrage der Preussischen Akademie der Wissenschaften, herausgegeben von der Romanischen Kommission*, Band I.

Pedro Giron, *Crónica del Emperador Carlos V*, ed. Juan Sanchez Montes (Madrid, 1964).

Francesco López de Gómara, *Crónica de los Barbarrojas*, in *Memorial Historical Español: Coleccion de Documentos, Opusculos, y Antigüedades que Publica la Real Academia de Historia* (Cuaderno 23, Madrid, 1853), 329–439.

Francisco Guicciardini, *Storia d' Italia* (5 vols., Bari, 1929).

———, *The History of Italy*, tr. Sidney Alexander (New York, 1969).

Rerum a Carolo Augusto in Africa Bello Gestarum Commentarii (Antwerp: Johannes Bellerus, 1555; copy in the James Ford Bell Library, University of Minnesota).

Keyserlicher Majestät Eroberung des Königreiches Thunis (Nürnberg, 1535; copy in the James Ford Bell Library, University of Minnesota).

Jacobus Basilicus Marchetus, Despota Sami, *De Morini quod Terouanum Vocant atque Hedini Expugnatione, deque Prelio apud Rentiacum, & Omnibus ad hunc usque diem Vario Eventu inter Caesarianos et Gallos Gestis, brevis & vera Narratio* (Antwerp: Johannes Bellerus, 1555; copy in the James Ford Bell Library, University of Minnesota).

Juan de Mata Cariazo, ed., *Historia del Emperador Carlos V, por el magnifico caballero Pedro Mexia, veinticuatro de Sevilla* (Madrid, 1945).

[Antoine Perrenin] = Johannes Etrobius [Jean Bérot], *Commentarium seu potius Diarium Expeditionis Tuniceae a Carolo Imperatore Maximo Semper Augusto Susceptae* (Louvain, 1547; copy in James Ford Bell Library, University of Minnesota).

Pauli Iovii Opera (9 vols., Rome, 1956–1987), including vol. III, Dante Visconti, ed., *Historiarum sui Temporis, tomus primus* (Rome, 1957); vol. IV, Dante Visconti ed., *Historiorum sui Temporis, tomus secundi, pars prior* (Rome, 1971); and, vol. V, Dante Visconti and T. C. Price Zimmerman, eds., *Historiarum sui Temporis, tomus secondus, pars altera* (Rome, 1985).

Fray Prudencio de Sandoval, *Historia de la Vida y Hechos del Emperador Carlos V*, ed. Carlos Seco Serrando (3 vols., Madrid, 1955–1956) = *Biblioteca des Autores Españoles*, vols. 80–82.

Alonso de Santa Cruz, *Crónica del Emperador Carlos V*, vols. I–III, ed. Francisco de Laiglesia y Auser (Madrid, 1920–1925), vols. IV–VI, ed. Antonio Blázquez y Augelera and Richardo Beltrán y Rozpide (Madrid, 1928).

Nicholas Durand de Villegagnon, *Expeditio Caroli Imperatoris in Africam ad Argieram* (Paris, 1542; copy in the James Ford Bell Library, University of Minnesota).

OTHER PRINTED SOURCES

P. S. Allen, *Opus Epistolarum Desiderii Erasmi Roterodami* (12 vols., Oxford, 1906–1958).

Lelio Arbib, ed., *Storia fiorentina di Benedetto Varchi* (3 vols., Florence, 1838–1841).

Adrianus Barlandus, *Historia Rerum Gestarum a Brabantiae Ducibus* (Brussels, 1585).

Calendar of Letters, Despatches and State Papers, Relating to the Negotiations between England and Spain (13 vols., London, 1862–1874).

Manuel Colmeiro, ed., *Cortes de los Antiguos Reinos de Léon y Castilla* (4 vols., Madrid, 1883–1886).

Giuseppe Coniglio, ed., *Consulte e bilanci del Viceregno di Napoli dal 1507 al 1533* (Rome, 1933).

Albertus Cuperinus, *Chronicke*, in C. R. Hermans, *Verzameling van Kronyken, Charters en Oorkonden betrekkelijk de Stad en Meierij van 's Hertogenbosch*, vol. 1 ('s Hertogenbosch, 1848).

Deutsche Reichstagsakten, Jüngere Reihe, vol. X:1, *Der Reichstag in Regensburg... 1532*, ed. Rosemarie Aulinger (Göttingen, 1992).

Letters and Papers Foreign and Domestic of the Reign of Henry VIII, ed. J. S. Brewer (21 vols., Vaduz: Kraus Reprint, 1965).

Blaise Monluc, *The Habsburg-Valois Wars*, ed. Ian Roy (modernizing a 1674 translation of the *Commentaires*) (Hamden, Conn., 1972).

W. Prevenier and W. P. Blockmans, *Handelingen van de Leden en Staten van Vlaanderen* = *Commision Royale d'Histoire de Belgique, Publications in Quarto*, vols. 58, 64, 67, 72 (Brussels, 1961–1982).

W. Prevenier and J. G. Smit, *Bronnen voor de Geschiedenis der Dagvaarten van de Staten en Steden van Holland voor 1544*, vol. 1 (The Hague, 1987).

Resolutiën van de Staten van Holland, 1524–1795 (278 vols., Amsterdam, 1789–1814).

Antonio Rodríguez Villa, *El Emperador Carlos V y su Corte según las cartas de Don Martín de Salinas, embajador del Infante Don Fernando (1522–1539)* (Madrid, 1903).

Gregorio Rosso, *Istoria delle Cose di Napoli*, in *Raccolta di Tutti i Piu Rinomati Scrittori dell'Istoria Generale del Regno di Napoli* (Naples: Giovanni Gravier, 1770).

Marino Sanudo, *I Diarii*, ed. Rinaldo Fulin, Federico Stefani, et al. (58 vols., Venice, 1879–1903).

SECONDARY WORKS

Gabriella Airaldi, *Genova e la Liguria nel medioevo* (Turin, 1986).

Miguel Artola, *La Hacienda del Antiguo Régimen* (Madrid, 1982).

Tommaso Astarita, *The Continuity of Feudal Power: The Caracciolo of Brienza in Spanish Naples* (Cambridge, 1992).

Michel Baelde, "Financiële Politiek en Domaniale Evolutie in de Nederlanden onder Karel V en Filips II," *Tijdschrift voor Geschiedenis* 76 (1963): 14–33.

———, *De Collaterale Raden onder Karel V en Filips II, 1531–1578* = *Verhandelingen van de Koninklijke Vlaamse Akademie van Wetenschappen, Letteren en Schoone Kunsten van België, Klasse der Letteren*, 27 (Brussels, 1965).

Frederic Baumgartner, *Henri II, King of France, 1547–1559* (Durham, N.C., 1988).

———, *France in the Sixteenth Century* (New York, 1995).

Bartolomé Bennassar, *Valladolid au siècle d'or* (Paris, 1967).

Giovanni Evangelista Blasi e Gambacorta, *Storia cronologica de' Vicerè . . . di Sicilia*, introd. Illuminato Peri (5 vols., Palermo, 1974–1975).

W. P. Blockmans, "Typologie van de Volksvertegenwoordiging in Europa tijdens de Late Middeleeuwen," *Tijdschrift voor Geschiedenis* 87 (1974): 483–502.

———, *De Volksvertegenwoordiging in Vlaanderen in de Overgang van de Middeleeuwen naar de Nieuwe Tijd (1384–1506)* = *Verhandelingen van de Koninklijke Akademie van Wetenschappen, Letteren en Schoone Kunsten van België, Klasse der Letteren*, 90 (Brussels, 1978).

———, "The Emperor's Subjects," in Hugo Soly, *Charles V*, 227–283.

———, ed., *Het Algemeen en de Gewestelijke Grote Privileges van Maria van Bourgondië* (Heule, 1985).

W. P. Blockmans and M. E. H. N. Mout, eds., *The World of Charles V* (Netherlands Academy of Sciences, in press).

D. P. Blok et al., eds., *(Nieuwe) Algemene Geschiedenis der Nederlanden* (15 vols., Haarlem, 1977–1983).

P. J. Blok, *Geschiedenis eener Hollandse Stad* (4 vols., The Hague, 1910–1918).

Richard Bonney, ed., *Economic Systems and State Finance* (Oxford, 1995).

James C. Boyajian, *Portuguese Bankers at the Court of Spain, 1626–1650* (New Brunswick, N.J., 1983).

Ernle Bradford, *The Sultan's Admiral: The Life of Barbarossa* (New York, 1968).

Thomas A. Brady Jr., Heiko A. Oberman, and James D. Tracy, eds., *Handbook of European History during the Late Middle Ages, Renaissance, and Reformation, 1400–1600* (2 vols., Leiden, 1994).

Karl Brandi, *Kaiser Karl V, Werden und Schicksal einer Persönlichkeir und eines Weltreiches* (2 vols., 2nd ed., Munich, 1941) = *Emperor Charles V*, tr. C. V. Wedgwood (New York, 1938).

Fernand Braudel, "Les emprunts de Charles-Quint sur la place d'Anvers," in *Charles-Quint et son Temps*, 191–201.

Anthony Bridge, *Suleiman the Magnificent, Scourge of Heaven* (New York, 1983).

Michiel Brokken, *Het Ontstaan van de Hoekse en Kabiljauwse Twisten* (Zutfen, 1982).

Peter Burke, "Presenting and Re-Presenting Charles V," in Hugo Soly, *Charles V*, 393–476.

Antonio Calabria, *The Cost of Empire: The Finances of the Kingdom of Naples in the Time of Spanish Rule* (Cambridge, 1991).

———, "State Finance in the Kingdom of Naples in the Age of Philip IV," Ph.D. dissertation, University of California, 1978.

Antonio Calabria and John Marino, eds. and tr., *Good Government in Spanish Naples* (New York and Frankfurt, 1990).

Francesco Caracciolo, *Uffici, difesa e corpi rappresentativi nel Mezzogiorno in eta spagnola* (Reggio Calabria, 1974).

Ramón Carande Thobar, *Carlos V y sus banqueros* (3 vols., Madrid, 1943–1967). Vol. I (1943; 2nd ed., 1967); vol. II (1949); vol. III (1967). 3 vols., reprinted (Barcelona, 2000).

Juan Manuel Carretero Zamora, *Cortes, monarquía, ciudades. Las Cortes de Castilla a comienzos de la epoca moderna (1476–1515)* (Madrid, 1988).

Aurelio Cernigliaro, *Sovranita e feudo nel regno di Napoli* (2 vols., Naples, 1983).

Federico Chabod, *Machiavelli and the Renaissance* (New York, 1954).

———, *Lo stato e la vita religiosa a Milano nell'epoca di Carlo V = Opere* (3 vols., Turin, 1964–1985), vol. III, pt. 1.

Charles-Quint et son temps (Paris, 1959).

Bernard Chevalier, "France from Charles VIII to Henry IV," in Brady, Oberman, and Tracy, *Handbook of European History*, I, 369–402.

Giuseppe Coniglio, *Il regno di Napoli al tempo di Carlo V* (Naples, 1951).

Philippe Contamine, ed., *Guerre et concurrence entre les États européens du XIVe au XVIIIe siècle* (Paris, 1998).

Benedetto Croce, *Storia del regno di Napoli* (6th ed., Bari, 1965).

Elena Croce, "I parlamenti napoletani sotto la dominazione spagnola," *Archivo Storico per le Provinze Napoletane*, n.s., 22 (1936): 341–358.

C. G. Cruikshank, *Army Royal: An Account of Henry VIII's Invasion of France* (Oxford, 1969).

Guido D'Agostino, *Parlamento e società nel regno di Napoli, Secoli XV e XVI* (Naples, 1979).

Robert Dauber, *A Knight of Malta in Brazil: Ambassador and Admiral Fra François de Villegagnon, 1510–1571* (Malta, 1995).

R. Trevor Davies, *The Golden Century of Spain* (New York, 1965).

Jean Pierre Dedieu, *L'Espagne de 1492 à 1808* (Paris, 1994).

Jan DeNolf and Barbara Simons, eds., *(Re)Constructing the Past* (Brussels, 2000).

Raymond De Roover, *Money, Banking and Credit in Medieval Bruges* (Cambridge, 1948).

Daniel Dessert, *Argent, pouvoir et société au grand siècle* (Paris, 1984).

Jan De Vries, *The Dutch Rural Economy in the Golden Age* (New Haven, Conn., 1974).

———, "Population," in Brady, Oberman, and Tracy, *Handbook of European History*, I, 1–50.

Antonio Dominguez Ortiz, *El Antiguo Régimen: Los reyes catolicos y los Austrias* (Madrid, 1973).

Daniel Doyle, "The Heart and Stomach of a Man but the Body of a Woman: Mary of Hungary and the Exercise of Political Power in Early Modern Europe," Ph.D. dissertation, University of Minnesota, 1996.

Heinz Duchhardt, "Das Tunisunternehmen Kaiser Karls V, 1535," *Mitteilungen des Österreichischen Staatsarchivs* 37 (1984): 35–72.

Christopher Duffy, *Siege Warfare: The Fortress in the Early Modern World, 1494–1660* (London, 1979).

John Edwards, *Christian Córdoba: The City and Its Region in the Late Middle Ages* (Cambridge, 1982).

Amelio Fara, *Il sistema e la città. Architettura fortificata dell'Europa moderna dai trattati alle realizzazione, 1464–1794* (Genoa, 1989).

Manuel Fernández Alvárez, *Charles V, Elected Emperor and Hereditary Ruler*, tr. J. A. Lalaguna (London, 1975).

———, *Carlos V, el César y el hombre* (Madrid, 1999).

Santiago Fernández Conti, "El gobierno de los asuntos y la guerra en Castilla durante el reinado del Emperador Carlos V," in José Martínez Millán, *Instituciones y Elites de Poder*, 47–105.

Paula Sutter Fichtner, *Ferdinand I of Austria: The Politics of Dynasticism in the Age of Reformation* (New York, 1982).

Siegfried Fiedler, *Kriegswesen und Kriegsführung im Zeitalter der Landsknechte* (Koblenz, 1985).

Robert Finlay, "Prophecy and Politics in Istanbul: Charles V, Sultan Suleyman, and the Habsburg Embassy of 1533–1534," *Journal of Early Modern History* 2 (1998): 249–272.

Godfrey Fisher, *Barbary Legend: War, Trade, and Piracy in North Africa, 415–1830* (Oxford, 1957).

José Ignacio Fortea Perez, *Córdoba en el siglo XVI: La bases demográficas y económicos de la expansión urbana* (Córdoba, 1981).

———, *Fiscalidad in Córdoba. Fisco, económia y sociedad: Alcabalas, encabezamientos, en tierras de Córdoba* (Córdoba, 1986).

———, *Monarquía y Cortes en la corona de Castilla: Las ciudades antes la politica fiscal de Felipe II* (Salamanca, 1990).

Carlo di Frede, "Il processo di Bartolommeo Camerario," in *Studi in Onore di Ricardo Filangieri* (2 vols., Naples, 1959), II, 329–344.

Giuseppe Galasso, "Trends and Problems in Neapolitan History in the Age of Charles V," in Antonio Calabria and John Marino, *Good Government in Spanish Naples*, 13–78.

Robert Gardner, ed., *The Age of the Galley: Mediterranean Oared Vessels since Pre-Classical Times* (London, 1995).

Richard Gascon, *Grand commerce et vie urbaine au XVIe siècle: Lyon et ses marchands* (2 vols., Paris, 1971).

Juan Gelabert, "The Fiscal Burden," in Richard Bonney, *Economic Systems and State Finance*, 539–576.

Marie-Claude Gerbet, *Les nobles dans le royaume de Castile: Étude sur les structures sociaux en Estremadure 1454–1516* (Paris, 1979).

Fausto Gianini, *Mirabello di Pavia. Il parco, la battaglia, la parrochia* (Pavia, 1984).

Ralph Giesey, *If Not, Not: The Legendary Oath of the Aragonese and the Laws of Sobrarbe* (Princeton, 1968).

Benjamin González Alonso, *Sobre el estado y la administración de la corona de Castilla en el Antiguo Régimen* (Madrid, 1981).

A. Goris, *Étude sur les colonies marchandes méridionales à Anvers, 1488–1577* (Louvain, 1925).

Ferdinand H. M. Grapperhuis, *Alva en de Tiende Penning* (Zutfen, 1982).

Le Baron Guillaume, *Histoires des bandes d'ordonnance des Pays Bas = Mémoires de l'Académie Royale des Sciences, des Lettres et des Beaux Arts de Belgique, Classe des Lettres*, 40 (Brussels, 1873).

John Guilmartin, *Gunpowder and Galleys: Changing Technology in Mediterranean Warfare at Sea in the Sixteenth Century* (Cambridge, 1974).

Stephen Haliczer, *The Comuneros of Castile: The Forging of a Revolution, 1475–1521* (Madison, Wis., 1981).

Philippe Hamon, *L'argent du Roi. Les finances sous François I* (Paris, 1994).

Donald Harreld, "High Germans in the Low Countries: German Merchants and Their Trade in Sixteenth-Century Antwerp," Ph.D. dissertation, University of Minnesota, 2000.

John Headley, *The Emperor and His Chancellor: A Study in the Imperial Chancery under Gattinara* (Cambridge, 1983).

Jacques Heers, *Gênes au XVe siècle* (Paris, 1961).

Paul Heidrich, *Karl V und die deutsche Protestanten am Vorabend des Schmalkaldischen Krieges = Frankfurter Historische Forschungen*, vols. 5, 6 (Frankfurt, 1911).

Charles David Hendricks, "Charles V and the Cortes of Castile: The Politics of Renaissance Spain," Ph.D. dissertation, Cornell University, 1976.

Alexandre Henne, *Histoire du règne de Charles-Quint en Belgique* (10 vols., Brussels, 1858–1860).

Carlos José Hernándo Sanchez, *Castilla y Napoles en el siglo XVI. El Virrey Pedro de Toledo. Linaje, estado y cultura (1532–1553)* (Junta de Castilla y Léon, 1994).

Andrew Hess, *Forgotten Frontier* (Chicago, 1978).

Philip Hoffman and Kathryn Norberg, eds., *Fiscal Crises, Liberty, and Representative Government* (Stanford, 1994).

Judith Hook, *The Sack of Rome* (London, 1972).

J. A. van Houtte et al., eds., *Algemene Geschiedenis der Nederlanden* (11 vols., Utrecht, 1949–1958).

Halil Inalcik and Donald Quatert, eds., *An Economic and Social History of the Ottoman Empire* (2 vols., Cambridge, 1997).

Jonathan Israel, *History of the Dutch Republic: Its Rise, Development and Decline* (Oxford, 1995).

Hubert Jedin, *A History of the Council of Trent*, tr. Dom Ernest Graf (2 vols., St. Louis, 1957–1961).

Eric Jones, *The European Miracle* (2nd ed., Cambridge, 1987).

A. G. Jongkees, "Het Groot Privileg van Holland," in W. P. Blockmans, *Het Algemeen en de Gewestelijke Grote Privileges*, 145–235.

Richard Kagan, "Las cronistas del emperador," in Pedro Navascués Palacio, *Carolus V Imperator*, 183–212.

Henry Kamen, *Spain, 1469–1714: A Society of Conflict* (2nd ed., London, 1991).

———, *Philip of Spain* (New Haven, Conn., 1997).

———, *The Spanish Inquistion: A Historical Revision* (New Haven, Conn., 1997).

Hermann Kellenbenz, *Die Fuggersche Maestrazgopacht (1525–1542)* (Tübingen, 1967).

———, *Schwerpunkte der Kupferproduktion und des Kupferhandels in Europa, 1500–1650* (Cologne and Vienna, 1977).

Hayward Keniston, *Francisco de los Cobos, Secretary of the Emperor Charles V* (Pittsburgh, 1960).

Paul Kennedy, *Grand Strategies in War and Peace* (New Haven, Conn., 1991).

Lord Kinross, *The Ottoman Centuries* (New York, 1977).

Ellen E. Kittell, *From Ad Hoc to Routine: A Case Study in Medieval Bureaucracy* (Philadelphia, 1991).

R. J. Knecht, *Renaissance Warrior and Patron: The Reign of Francis I* (Cambridge and New York, 1994).

―――, "Francis I and Charles V: The Image of the Enemy," in Jan DeNolf and Barbara Simons, *(Re)Constructing the Past*, 47–68.

H. G. Koenigsberger, *Estates and Revolutions* (Ithaca, N.Y., 1971).

Alfred Kohler, *Anti-Habsburgische Politik in der Epoche Karls V: Die Reichsständische Opposition gegen die Wahl Ferdinands I zum Römischen König und gegen die Anerkennung seines Königtums* (Göttingen, 1982).

―――, *Karl V, 1500–1558. Eine Biographie* (Munich, 1999).

Martin Körner, "Public Credit," in Richard Bonney, *Economic Systems and State Finance*, 507–538.

Rudolf Kötzschke and Helmut Kretschmar, *Sächsische Geschichte* (Frankfurt am Main, 1965).

Francisco de Laiglesia y Auser, *Estudios Historicos (1515–1555)* (Madrid, 1908).

Frederick C. Lane, *Venice, a Maritime Republic* (Baltimore, 1973).

Stanford E. Lehmberg, *The Later Parliaments of Henry VIII, 1536–1547* (Cambridge, 1977).

Emmanuel Leroi Ladurie, *The French Royal State* (Oxford, 1994).

Giuseppe de Leva, *Storia Documentata di Carlo V, in correlazione all' Italia* (5 vols., Venice, 1863–1894).

P. H. P. Leupen, "De representatieve instellingen in het Noorden, 1384–1482," in D. P. Block et al., *(Nieuwe) Algemene Geschiedenis der Nederlanden*, IV, 156–171.

Heinrich Lutz, *Christianitas Afflicta. Europa, das Reich, und die päpstliche Politik im Niedergang der Hegemonie Kaiser Karls V (1552–1556)* (Göttingen, 1964).

N. Maddens, "De opstandige houding van Gent tijdens de Regering van Keizer Karel," *Appeltjes uit het Meetjesland* 28 (1977): 203–239.

―――, *De Beden in het Graafschap Vlaanderen tijdens de Regering van Karel V (1515–1550)* = *Standen en Landen/Anciens Pays et Assemblées d'état*, vol. 72 (Heule, 1978).

―――, "De Invoering van de 'Nieuwe Middelen' in het Graafschap Vlaanderen tijdens de regering van Keizer Karel," *Belgische Tijdschrift voor Filologie en Geschiedenis/Revue Belge de Philologie et d'Histoire* 57 (1979): 342–363, 861–898.

William Maltby, *Alba: A Biography of Fernando Alvarez de Toledo, Third Duke of Alba, 1507–1582* (Berkeley, 1983).

Roberto Mantelli, *Burocrazia e finanze pubbliche nel regno di Napoli a meta del cinquecento* (Naples, 1981).

José Antonio Maravall, *Las comunidades de Castilla* (Madrid, 1979).

John Marino, *Pastoral Economics in the Kingdom of Naples* (Baltimore, 1988).

José Martínez Millán, ed., *Instituciones y elites de poder en la monarquía hispana durante el siglo XVI* (Madrid, 1992).

Peter Matheson, *Cardinal Contarini at Regensburg* (Oxford, 1972).

Anthony Molho, *Florentine Public Finance in the Early Renaissance* (Cambridge, Mass., 1971).

Julian Montemayor, *Tolède entre fortune et déclin (1530–1640)* (Limoges, 1996).

José Maria del Morial, *El Virrey de Napoles Don Pedro de Toledo y la guerra contro el Turco* (Madrid, 1966).

John Munro, "Patterns of Trade, Money, and Credit," in Brady, Oberman, and Tracy, *Handbook of European History*, I, 147–196.

Giovanni Muto, "Taxation in the Kingdom of Naples," in W. P. Blockmans and M. E. H. N. Mout, *The World of Charles V.*

Helen Nader, *Liberty in Absolutist Spain: The Habsburg Sale of Towns, 1516–1700* (Baltimore, 1990).

Pedro Navascués Palacio, ed., *Carolus V Imperator* (Madrid, 1999).

Jan Paul Niederkorn, *Die europäische Mächte und der "Lange Türkenkrieg" Kaiser Rudolfs II (1593–1606)* (Vienna, 1993).

A. van Nieuwenhuysen, *Les finances du Duc de Bourgogne, Philippe le Hardi (1386–1404)* (Brussels, 1984).

Joseph O'Callaghan, *The Cortes of Léon and Castile, 1188–1350* (Philadelphia, 1990).

Oliver K. Olson, "Theology of Revolution: Magdeburg, 1550–1551," *Sixteenth Century Journal* 3 (1972): 56–79.

Arturo Pacini, *La Genova dell'Andrea Doria nell'impero di Carlo V* (Florence, 1999).

Geoffrey Parker, *The Grand Strategy of Philip II* (New Haven, Conn., 1998).

———, *The Military Revolution* (Cambridge, 1988).

Ludwig Pastor, *Geschichte der Päpste* (16 vols., Freiburg im Breisgau, 1891–1933).

———, *History of the Popes* (40 vols., St. Louis, 1913–1950).

Michael Pearson, "Merchants and States," in James Tracy, *The Rise of Merchant Empires*, 47–116.

Linda Livy Peck, *Court Patronage and Corruption in Early Stuart England* (Boston, 1990).

Tommaso Pedio, *Napoli e Spagna nella prima meta del cinquecento* (Bari, 1971).

Simon Pepper "Siege Law, Siege Ritual, and the Symbolism of Walled Cities in Renaissance Europe," in James D. Tracy, *City Walls*, 573–604.

Simon Pepper and Nicholas Adams, *Firearms and Fortifications: Military Architecture and Siege Warfare in Sixteenth-Century Siena* (Chicago, 1986).

Ciriaco Pérez Bustamente, "Actividad legislativa de Carlos V, en orden a las Indias," in *Charles-Quint et son temps*, 113–121.

Géza Perjés, *The Fall of the Medieval Kingdom of Hungary: Mohács 1526–Buda 1541*, tr. Márió D. Fenyö, *War and Society in Central Europe*, vol. XXVI (Boulder, Colo., 1989).

Sean T. Perrone, "The Castilian Assembly of the Clergy in the Sixteenth Century," *Parliaments, Estates and Representation* 18 (1998): 53–70.

Luciano Pezzolo, *L'oro dello stato. Società, finanza e fisco nella Repubblica veneta del secondo '500* (Treviso, 1990).

Vinzenz Pfnür, *Einig in der Rechtfertigungslehre?* (Munich, 1970).

Carla Rahn Phillips, *Ciudad Real, 1500–1750: Growth, Crisis, and Readjustment in the Spanish Economy* (Cambridge, Mass., 1979).

Carla Rahn Phillips and William D. Phillips, *Spain's Golden Fleece: Wool Production and the Wool Trade from the Middle Ages to the Nineteenth Century* (Baltimore, 1997).

William D. Phillips and Carla Rahn Phillips, *The Worlds of Christopher Columbus* (New York, 1992).

Ruth Pike, *Aristocrats and Traders: Sevillian Society in the Sixteenth Century* (Ithaca, N.Y., 1972).

Götz Freiherr von Pölnitz, *Anton Fugger* (4 vols., Tübingen, 1958–1967).

Walter Prevenier and Wim Blockmans, *The Burgundian Netherlands* (Cambridge, 1986).

———, *The Promised Lands: The Low Countries under Burgundian Rule, 1369–1520*, tr. Elizabeth Fackelman (Philadelphia, 1999).

René Quatrefages, "L'organisation militaire de l'Espagne, 1492–1592," Thèse de doctorat, Université de Paris-IV (la Sorbonne), 1989.

Horst Rabe, *Reichsbund und Interim. Die Verfassungs- und Religionspolitik Karls V und der Reichstag von Augsburg, 1547/1548* (Cologne and Vienna, 1971).

Susanna Peyronel Rambaldi, "Milano nel Tempo di guerre d'Italiai" in Franco Della Peruta, ed., *Storia Illustrata di Milano* (7 vols., Milan, 1992–1997), IV, 981–1000.

Otto Redlich, *The German Military Enterpriser and His Work Force* (Wiesbaden, 1964).

Baron de Reiffenberg, *Lettres sur la Vie Intérieure de l'Empereur Charles-Quint, Écrites par Guillaume van Male, Gentilhomme de sa Chambre* (Brussels, 1846).

Luis A. Ribot Garcia, "Les types d'armée en Espagne au début des temps moderne," in Philippe Contamine, *Guerre et concurrence entre les États européeens*, 43–82.

M. J. Rodriguez-Salgado, *The Changing Face of Empire: Charles V, Philip II, and Habsburg Authority, 1551–1555* (Cambridge, 1988).

Paul Rosenfeld, "The Provincial Governors from the Minority of Charles V to the Revolt," *Standen en Landen/Anciens Pays et Assembleés d'état* 17 (1959): 1–63.

Earl Rosenthal, "*Plus Ultra* and the Columnar Device of Emperor Charles V," *Journal of the Wartburg and Courtauld Institutes* 34 (1971): 204–228.

Cecil Roth, *The Last Florentine Republic* (London, 1925).

Alan Ryder, *The Kingdom of Naples under Alfonso the Magnanimous* (Oxford, 1976).

Juan Sanchez Montez, *1539. Agobios carolinos y ciudades castellanas* (Granada, 1975).

Armando Sapori, *Le crisi delle compagnie mercantili dei Bardi e dei Peruzzi* (Florence, 1926).

Rodolfo Savelli, *La repubblica oligarchica. Legislazione, istituzione, e ceti a Genova nel cinquecento* (Milan, 1981).

Heinz Schilling, "Veni, Vidi, Vixit Deus – Karl V zwischen Religionskrieg und Religions-frieden," *Archiv für Reformationsgeschichte* 89 (1998): 144–166

E. Scholliers, and Chr. Vandenbroecke, "Structuren en conjuncturen in de zuidelijke Nederlanden, 1400–1600," in D. P. Blok et al., *(Nieuwe) Algemene Geschiedenis der Nederlanden*, V, 252–310.

Kenneth Setton, *The Papacy and the Levant, 1204–1571* (4 vols., Philadelphia, 1976).

Luigi Simeoni, *Le Signorie* (2 vols, Milan, 1950).

Hugo Soly, "De aluinhandel in de Nederlanden in de 16e Eeuw," *Belgische Tijdschrift voor Filologie en geschiedenis/Revue Belge de Philologie et d'Histoire* 52 (1974): 800–857.

————, ed., *Charles V, 1500–1558, and His Time* (Antwerp, 1999).

Klaus Spading, *Holland und die Hanse im 15en Jahrhundert* (Weimar, 1973).

William Spencer, *Algiers in the Age of Corsairs* (Norman, Okla., 1976).

J. N. Stephens, *The Fall of The Florentine Republic* (Oxford, 1983).

J. E. A. L. Struick, *Gelre en Habsburg, 1492–1528* (Arnhem, 1960).

Sanjay Subrahmanyam, "Du Tage au Gange au XVIe siécle: Une conjuncture millénariste à l'échelle Eurasiatique," *Annales* 56 (2001): 51–84.

Elias de Tejada, *Napoles hispanico* (4 vols., Madrid, 1958).

I. A. A. Thompson, *War and Government in Habsburg Spain, 1560–1620* (London, 1976).

————, "Castile: Absolutism, Constitutionalism, and Liberty," and "Castile: Polity, Fiscality, and Fiscal Crises," in Philip Hoffman and Kathryn Norberg, *Fiscal Crises*, 181–225, 140–180.

Pilar Toboso Sanchez, *La deuda pública castellana durante el Antiguo Régimen (Juros) y su liquidacion en el siglo XIX* (Madrid, 1987).

James D. Tracy, *The Politics of Erasmus: A Pacifist Intellectual and His Political Milieu* (Toronto, 1978).

———, "The Taxation System of the County of Holland during the Reigns of Charles I and Philip II, 1519–1566," *Economisch- en Sociaal-Historisch Jaarboek* 48 (1984): 72–117.

———, *A Financial Revolution in the Habsburg Netherlands: "Renten" and "Renteniers" in the County of Holland, 1515–1565* (Berkeley and Los Angeles, 1985).

———, "Herring Wars: Efforts by the Government of the Habsburg Netherlands to Achieve Strategic Control of the North Sea ca. 1520–1560," *Sixteenth Century Journal* 24 (1993): 249–272.

———, *Holland under Habsburg Rule, 1506–1566: The Formation of a Body Politic* (Berkeley and Los Angeles, 1990).

———, ed., *The Rise of Merchant Empires, 1350–1750: Long-Distance Trade in the Early Modern World* (Cambridge, 1990).

———, ed., *The Political Economy of Merchant Empires: State Power and World Trade, 1350–1750* (Cambridge, 1991).

———, "Taxation and State Debt," in Brady, Oberman, and Tracy, *Handbook of European History*, I, 563–588.

———, *Erasmus of the Low Countries* (Berkeley and Los Angeles, 1996).

———, ed., *City Walls: The Urban Enceinte in Global Perspective* (Cambridge, 2000).

———, "Keeping the Wheels of War Turning: Revenues of the Province of Holland, 1572–1609," in Graham Darby, ed., *Origins and Development of the Dutch Revolt* (London, 2001), 133–150.

David Trim, "The Context of War and Violence in Sixteenth-Century English Society," *Journal of Early Modern History* 3 (1999): 233–255.

Modesto Ulloa, *La hacienda real de Castilla en el reinado de Felipe II* (Madrid, 1977).

Richard Vaughan, *Charles the Bold* (London, 1973).

Vito Vitale, *Breviario di storia de Genova* (2 vols., Genoa, 1955).

Andreas von Walther, *Die Anfänge Karls V* (Leipzig, 1911).

Herman van der Wee, *The Growth of the Antwerp Market and the European Economy, 14th to 16th Centuries* (3 vols., The Hague, 1963).

Hermann Wiesflecker, *Kaiser Maximilian I* (5 vols., Munich, 1971–1986).

Zygmunt Wojciechowski, *Zygmunt Stary (1506–1548)* (Warsaw, 1979).

Martin Wolfe, *The Fiscal System of Renaissance France* (New Haven, Conn., 1972).

James B. Wood, *The King's Army: Warfare, Soldiers, and Society during the Wars of Religion in France, 1562–1576* (Cambridge, 1996).

Gaston Zeller, *La réunion de Metz à France, 1552–1648. Ière Partie, L'occupation* (Paris, 1926).

T. C. Price Zimmerman, *Paolo Giovio: The Historian and the Crisis of Sixteenth Century Italy* (Princeton, 1995).

Index

Augsburg Interim, 217–20, 230, 315; Lutheran opposition to, 233; proclaimed by Charles V (1548), 219–20

Avalos, Costanza d', 160 n9

Avalos, Hernando de, 289

aventuriers, 32 n43, 41, 42, 47

Avignon, military camp at, 161

Ávila, and a Holy Union (Santa Junta), to oppose the crown, 89

Ávila y Zuñiga, Luis de, 13, 220; and a collection of maps of Germany, 213

Aytta, Viglius van, 205

ayuntamientos (town councils), 83, 84, 85, 86

Baba Oruç, 134

Baeca, Alonso de, 107

baking ovens, prohibition of, 55

Bamberg, prince-bishop of, 238, 239

bankers: of Antwerp, 225; of Augsburg, 129; and effect on economics, 309; Florentine, 95 n15, 96; interest paid to, 284; Italian, 95 n15; and *juros*, 246–7; of Lyons, 229; New Christian, 96, 97; and parliamentary bodies, 253; prefered having loans assigned to Castile, 108; and rates for short-term loans, 256; role of in European wars, 18; Spanish, 96 n22; Venetian, 95; *see also* Fugger firm; Gentile firm; Grimaldi firm; Herwart firm; Schetz firm; Spinola firm; Strozzi firm; Welser firm

Barbarossa Khair-ad-Din (c. 1466–1546), 117, 158; biography by López de Gómara, 14, 154, 155, 157; and blockade of Castilnuovo, 165; and Christian slaves, 133, 144; and Corfu, 164; death of, 232; fleet of, 37, 134–5, 137, 144, 171; and Fondi, 145; and funds on board, 308; and Gulf of Prevesa, 164, 165, 282; as *kapudan pasha* (admiral of the sea) of Suleyman, 144, 313; and Naples, 7, 145, 146; and Peñon, 148 n35; sails from Istanbul (1534), 280; and Sicily and Calabria, 191; and Tunis, 7, 145, 148–9, 157

Barbary Coast, 7, 134; extent of, 133 n2; slave raids along, 312

Barbary corsairs, 14, 29, 117, 133, 302

Barcelona, Treaty of (1529), 117, 121, 230

Bari, grain prices at, 284 n26

Barlandus, Adrianus, *Deeds of the Dukes of Brabant* (1526), 74

barons (of Naples) authority of, 54–5; confiscation of property of, 60; corruption of, 61; and marriages within comparable rank, 278; and privilege of appearing covered, 279; and trading outside the barony, 56; and unauthorized taxes, 57

"bastion trace," 188

Bazán, Álvaro de, 137, 146, 153, 154, 158

Bazan Pasha, 165, 313

beden, 252 n8

Béjar, duchess of, 107

Béjar, Francisco de Zuñiga, duke of, 297

Belgium: linguistic frontier in, 2 n4; urban population of (1550), 68

Belgrade, Ottoman conquest of (1521), 311

Bergen-op-Zoom, lord of, 262

Bernuy, Hernando, 10 n22

Bérot, Jean, *see* Etrobius, Johannes

Binche, 8

biremes, 135 n10

Black Band, 74, 75

Bohemia, Hussite armies of, 205

Bologna: and coronation of Charles V as emperor, 119–20; Palazzo Pubblico, 121; reconvening of Council of Trent, 217

bombardment (*batería*), 147

Bomelberg, Conrad von, 241

Bomy, armistice signed at, 163

Bona (Anaba), 173, 179

Bonnivet, Guillaume de Gouffier, lord of, 43

Boulogne, 194, 207

Bourbon, Charles, duke of, 44, 47, 160, 291 n7; army of, 125; death of, 48 n29; and a false truce, 46 n23; joins imperialists, 29, 43; and march to Marseilles, 124–5; and Sack of Rome, 34; and trouble with Spanish troops in Milan, 45–6

Brabant, 2, 4, 72; archives of, 249 n2; representative assemblies in, 68; revenues (1535), 50 n1; and subsidy for war, 73, 76; subsidy *renten* in (1520–30), 258

Brandenburg, Joachim, elector of, 217, 219

Brandenburg, Johann von, 222

Brandenburg-Küstrin, Hans von, margrave of, 230, 233, 241

Brandi, Karl, 165, 188, 197, 205

Bremen, 209, 220; unsuccessful siege of (1547), 223

Brenner Pass, 210, 224, 233

Bresse, Jean de, bishop of Bayonne, 233, 235

Briarde, Lambert de, 143 n25

bridge-boats, seizure of, 216

bronze arm bands (*manilhas*), 100

Bruges, 72, 195; as a financial center, 99; as one of the Four Members of Flanders, 68, 69, 167 n21

Brunswick, Henry, duke of, 34, 116, 183

Brussels, 5, 68, 72; archives in, 9

Bucer, Martin, 168–9 n24

Buda, 34, 170, 206

Buren, Floris van IJsselstein, count of, 74, 262

Buren, Maximilaan van Egmont, count of, 176 n42, 195, 210, 211, 213, 220, 221, 222, 225–6

Burgos, 96, 298

Burgundy, Adolph of, 256

Burgundy, Charles the Bold, duke of, 31, 35, 70, 183 n1